How to Work with the EU Institutions

A Practical Guide
to Successful
Public Affairs in the EU

Edited by
Alan Hardacre

How to Work with the EU Institutions
A Practical Guide to Successful Public Affairs in the EU

Published by John Harper Publishing
27 Palace Gates Road
London N22 7BW, United Kingdom
www.johnharperpublishing.co.uk

ISBN: 978-1-8380898-1-8

© John Harper Publishing Ltd 2020. All rights reserved. Reproduction or quotation of short extracts is permitted, provided the source is fully acknowledged.

The publisher has no responsibility for the persistence or accuracy of the addresses of any external or third party websites referenced in this book, and does not guarantee that the content on these websites is, or will remain, accurate or appropriate.

Typeset and design by Simone Meesters
www.simonemeesters.com

Printed and bound at the Short Run Press, Exeter.

Table of contents

Foreword XI
About the authors... XV
Acknowledgements XIX

Introduction 1

Part 1: How to Build a Successful Public Affairs Strategy   9

1. **The Art of Influence** 11
   1. Empathy 12
   2. Credibility 15
   3. Discipline 17
   4. Tactics 18
   5. Persuasiveness 20
      5.1 Ethos or 'Character' 21
      5.2 Logos or 'Reason' 21
      5.3 Pathos or 'Emotion' 21
      5.4 Metaphor 22
      5.5 Brevity 23
   6. Summary 24

2. **An EU Public Affairs Methodology** 31
   Introduction 31
   PHASE 1: PREPARATION 34
      1.1 Objective setting 35
      1.2 Monitoring and intelligence gathering 39
      1.3 Stakeholder mapping 45
      1.4 Data 50
   PHASE 2: ENGAGEMENT AND ACTION 52
      2.1 Direct engagement 53
      2.2 Indirect engagement 56
      2.3 Messaging and channels 59
   PHASE 3: FEEDBACK AND EVALUATION 64
      3.1 Audit of the preparation phase 65
      3.2 Evaluation of the engagement & action phase 66
      3.3 Successful public affairs strategies 68

3. Digital Information Management in EU Public Affairs 69
1. Objective setting (KPIs) 72
2. Intelligence gathering (monitoring) 75
3. Stakeholder mapping 79
4. Managing data for an ongoing strategy/campaign 82
5. Keeping track – managing through the engagement phase 83
    - 5.1 Engagement: Data and contact management 84
    - 5.2 Messaging and activity management 85
6. Evaluation 86

4. Working with the Media and Social Media in the EU 89
1. Lobbying and legislative work 90
2. Communicating with each of the institutions 90
    - 2.1 European Commission 90
    - 2.2 European Parliament 92
    - 2.3 Council of the European Union 93
    - 2.4 Other non-legislative actors 93
3. Understanding policymakers' communication consumption 93
    - 3.1 Brussels Bubble media 95
    - 3.2 International media 96
    - 3.3 National media 97
    - 3.4 Specialised media 97
    - 3.5 Media checklist 98
4. Social media 98
5. The hub and spoke model of web communication 98
6. Organisational, professional or personal communication 102
7. Agenda-following or agenda-setting, and broadcasting or interacting 103
    - 7.1 Senior people – is it really them? 104
8. A wider public in lobbying campaigns 105
    - 8.1 Earned versus paid media 106
    - 8.2 Wider organisation-building and reputation management 107
9. Conclusions 107

5. Third Country Lobbying in Brussels 109
1. Third country representations: the Brussels landscape 110
2. The diplomatic context for engagement 111
3. Advantages and challenges for third countries working in Brussels 112
4. Advantages for third country lobbying in Brussels 113
    - 4.1 Leverage relations with the EU – from the start 113
    - 4.2 Diplomatic status = excellent access 113
    - 4.3 European Commission DGs and the EEAS – Source of information/sherpas 114
    - 4.4 European Parliament Delegations 115
    - 4.5 Council contacts 116

  4.6 International memberships/alliances/networks/dialogue forums 116
  4.7 EU network of Embassies – Member State Embassies in your country 117
5. Challenges for third country lobbying in Brussels 118
6. Resources 118
  6.1 Staff, expertise and human resources 118
  6.2 How do you get more support from back home? 120
  6.3 Financial resources 121
7. Focus of the Mission/Embassy 122
  7.1 Connections/contacts in Brussels 122
  7.2 Understanding Brussels… and lobbying 123
  7.3 Generating leverage for engagement from the outside 124
8. Third country lobbying in the EU: Recommendations & Guidance 124
  8.1 Objective and priority setting 124
  8.2 Intelligence gathering 126
  8.3 Stakeholder mapping 127
  8.4 Data 127
  8.5 Direct or indirect engagement 128
  8.6 Messaging and channels 129
  8.7 Evaluation 130

Part 2: How to Work with the EU Institutions & Decision Making   131

6. Working with the European Commission 133
1. The policy cycle 134
2. The Political Guidelines 135
  2.1 Can you influence the Political Guidelines? 135
  2.2 The European Council 135
  2.3 The European Parliament 136
  2.4 The Commission President 137
3. When and how to step in 138
4. The European Commission's Work Programme and State of the Union 139
5. How can you influence the Work Programme? 139
  5.1 The long play 139
  5.2 The short play 141
  5.3 What does 'political discontinuity' mean? 143
6. Impact Assessment 143
  6.1 When should you step in? 144
  6.2 Why you need to start early 144
  6.3 How to make your case 144
  6.4 What to do when an Impact Assessment is not automatically prepared 145
7. External consultation 146
  7.1 Why does the Commission consult? 146
  7.2 What is the timing for consultations? 147

	7.3	How does consultation work in practice?	148
	7.4	What's the best way to contribute?	149
	7.5	Some points too often forgotten	149
	7.6	Practical recommendations	150
8.	Inter-Service Consultation (ISC)		151
	8.1	Timetable for Inter-Service Consultation	152
	8.2	Why you need a copy of the draft proposal	152
9.	How can you influence the political scrutiny step: the Cabinet and the College?		152
	9.1	Practical guidance for engaging Cabinet and College	153
	9.2	How to get your issue/concern in front of the College	153
	9.3	When are the files looked at?	154
10.	Summary of working with ISC and political scrutiny		155
11.	Working with the Cabinets		156
	11.1	What's the role of the Cabinets in reaching decisions?	156
	11.2	How can you work with the Cabinet?	157
12.	Working with the Commissioners		158
	12.1	How can you work with the Commissioners?	158
13.	The Regulatory Scrutiny Board (RSB)		159
	13.1	How can you influence the RSB?	159
14.	Conclusion		159

7. Working with the European Parliament 161

1.	Introduction		161
	1.1	Importance of national links	164
	1.2	Importance of constituency links	165
2.	How to engage in the two stage process: Committee to Plenary		165
	2.1	Choice of Political Group and Rapporteur	166
	2.2	Working with Committee stage	166
	2.3	Working with the Plenary stage	172
	2.4	Working with MEPs to set the agenda	172
3.	How to engage the key people		173
	3.1	MEPs	174
	3.2	MEPs' Assistants	175
	3.3	Committee Secretariat	175
	3.4	Political Group staff	176
	3.5	General engagement with the Parliament	176
4.	Key ways to achieve success		177
	4.1	See if you can obtain the following intelligence	177
	4.2	How can you find out who the kingmakers are?	178
5.	Overview		184

8. Working with the Council(s) 185
1. Introduction 185
2. Decision-making in the Council of the EU 187
3. How a Presidency will approach legislative files: what to look out for 188
4. How a Presidency will approach non-legislative files: what to look out for ... 189
5. Working Groups (Working Parties) 190
6. How the Presidency runs a Working Group (on legislative or non-legislative files) 192
7. The Working Group process for legislative files 193
8. The Working Group process for non-legislative files 195
9. Understanding how an attaché approaches negotiations in the Working Group 195
10. Coreper 197
11. Council meetings 199
12. Key people 201
    12.1 Officials and politicians in national capitals 202
    12.2 The Presidency 203
    12.3 General Secretariat of the Council (GSC) 204
    12.4 Permanent Representations 204
13. Concluding guidance for engaging with the Council 206
14. Engaging the European Council 207

9. How to Work with the Ordinary Legislative Procedure 211
1. Introduction 211
2. Should you focus on the Council or the EP? 212
3. The dynamics of a qualified majority negotiation in the Council 212
4. A word on the Commission 213
5. Working successfully with OLP 213
6. The three stages of working with OLP 217
7. Working with OLP: first reading 217
    7.2 Council's four-column document 218
    7.3 The trilogue process 219
    7.4 Actors: first reading 221
    7.5 Engagement guidance: first reading 222
8. Working with OLP: second reading 225
    8.1 European Parliament second reading 227
    8.2 Commission second reading 227
    8.3 Council second reading 227
    8.4 Second reading agreement 228
    8.5 Actors: second reading 228
    8.6 Engagement guidance: second reading 228
9. Working with OLP: third reading 230
    9.1 Actors: third reading 231
    9.2 Engagement guidance: third reading 232

10. Working with Delegated & Implementing Acts 233
1. Introduction 233
2. Identifying Delegated and Implementing Acts 237
3. Working with Implementing Acts 240
4. Working with Delegated Acts: introductory remarks 247
5. Working with Delegated Acts: the Commission 247
6. Working with Delegated Acts: Parliament 249
   6.1 Parliamentary scrutiny during an election year 254
7. Working with Delegated Acts: Council 255
8. Some legal considerations 257
9. Summary 258

Part 3: Summary   261

11. Recommendations for Best Practice in EU Public Affairs 263

Foreword

By Doug Pinkham
President, Public Affairs Council

The public affairs function has two major roles in business: to manage political risk and to create market opportunities. As governments further regulate commerce and as technology and globalisation transform how and where goods are produced and consumed, each of these roles has been elevated.

First, let's look at risk. While a firm's competitive and technological threats have always caused anxiety in board rooms, political threats to capital and earnings have become a third major risk component.

Management theory has identified at least three major forms of political risk: transfer risks, which affect the exchange of money, production, people and technology (e.g. tariffs); operational risks, which restrict the way firms are managed (e.g. local sourcing requirements); and ownership-control risks, which inhibit who owns and controls a company (e.g. foreign-ownership rules) (Fred Luthans & Jonathan P. Doh, *International Management: Culture, Strategy, and Behavior* (New York: McGraw Hill, 2012), 344-345).

Add to these the challenges posed by marketplace access risks (e.g. codes and standards favoring one product over another or outright product bans) and uncertainty risks (e.g. changes in government or waffling by politicians), and there's no wonder that public affairs is now considered an essential business function. This is especially true in Europe because of the complexity of its institutions, the differences in language and culture, and the nature of its politics. In the EU, as in the U.S., the only thing certain is a high level of uncertainty.

While these threats get the attention of corporate chief risk officers, it's the ability of the public affairs function to create market opportunities that is making true believers out of many CEOs. Enterprising firms in sectors such as technology and pharmaceuticals often begin the process of building a favorable constituency for products while they are still in development. Many firms across sectors find common cause with political leaders and movements to develop products and services that address societal problems – such as climate change – in a way that creates shared value for companies.

The complexion of lobbying and other forms of advocacy is also changing. While critics often demean lobbying as 'influence peddling', the fact is that network lobbying (using personal relationships to influence policy) is giving way to *knowledge lobbying* (using technical and political process expertise to influence policy).

In both the U.S. and Europe, this expertise includes a keen understanding of digital advocacy, in which software is used to prioritise stakeholders, recruit supporters, document public benefits, scale up political movements and affect policymaking outcomes. The field of digital advocacy is developing quickly, and anyone looking to engage effectively in Europe or the U.S. needs to learn new approaches or risk being left behind.

In fact, the COVID-19 crisis has accelerated these changes because face-to-face meetings have been largely replaced by video conferencing. A recent Public Affairs Council survey of 245 government affairs executives showed that 83% believe this trend will continue even after the pandemic has ended. And 61% say the COVID-19 crisis will bring about a decline in traditional lobbying and an increase in the use of digital advocacy strategies (Public Affairs Council, *Government Affairs Executive Survey*, Washington, D.C., 2020)

This is not to say that relationships no longer matter in public affairs. The difference is that advocates are focusing less on becoming close friends with political leaders and more on cultivating a 'community of allies' – a term coined by author James Moore to mean interrelated groups of companies that are sometimes friends and sometimes foes. Like business ecosystems, today's political ecosystems bring together people and groups that have common interests, be they in clean air, medical innovation, copyright protection or job creation.

Each of these disciplines and strategies – political risk management, market opportunity creation, knowledge lobbying, digital advocacy and ally development – are changing how public policy is formulated in advanced democracies. And, as a group, they are also redefining what it takes to be a successful public affairs professional.

A major global telecom company I know evaluates how well its public affairs employees display each of 10 core competencies:

1. Coaching and managing
2. Persuasive communication
3. Creativity and innovation
4. Collaboration and teamwork
5. Continuous learning
6. Political courage
7. Social sensitivity
8. Campaigns and strategies
9. Achievement orientation
10. Complexity orientation

It's ironic that while the public assumes most lobbyists are aggressive and single-minded, today's advocates are being evaluated by their supervisors for being collaborative, creative, courageous and socially sensitive.

In the pages that follow, the reader will gain practical knowledge of how winning public affairs strategies or campaigns are developed and how one can work effectively with EU institutions in policy development. Part 1, which takes a comprehensive approach to public affairs management, reviews innovative methods for building influence, setting issue priorities, employing IT tools, communicating with the news media, attracting a social media following, and advancing issues through third-country advocacy.

Part 2 helps the reader apply these strategies to dealings with EU institutions. It covers the roles of the European Commission, Parliament and EU Councils, following Ordinary Legislative Procedure, and working with Delegated and Implementing Acts.

In the concluding chapter, Dr. Alan Hardacre, who edited this comprehensive book, sums up the various insights from contributors and provides guidance for successful EU advocacy.

In Europe and the rest of the world, there is a growing appreciation for the strategic value of public affairs. This book shows how that value is created and how public affairs professionals using the right techniques can build support and find common ground with political leaders and the general public. In an increasingly complex world beset by crises and distrustful of institutions, that is certainly a useful approach.

The Public Affairs Council is the leading international association for public affairs professionals. It is headquartered in Washington D.C.

About the authors

Alan Hardacre
Alan Hardacre is both the editor of and a contributor to this book. He previously edited and co-wrote successive (2011 and 2015) editions of *How the EU Institutions Work and… How to Work with the EU Institutions*, and this new book builds on and greatly expands what had been the 'back end' of the old book. Alan's engagement with this major reworking to create the new volume is testimony to the continued passion that he holds for both public affairs and trying to share and disseminate best practice.

Alan has worked in varying capacities with the EU institutions and EU decision making for over 15 years. He currently works in the private sector as a lobbyist having previously worked for the European Institute of Public Administration (EIPA) in Maastricht and as a lobbyist for the Confederation of British Industry in Brussels. Alan has also consulted for Brazilian, Thai and African business groups, and UN bodies, on advocacy and communication strategies in the EU. Alan teaches and runs simulations on lobbying at the Institut des Hautes Études des Communications Sociales in Brussels and the University of Chulalongkorn in Bangkok. He also gives several speeches and presentations every year to different audiences. Alan holds a BA (Hons) in Modern European Studies from Loughborough University in the UK and a DEA de Science Politique from the Institut d'Études Politiques de Lyon in France. In 2008 he was awarded his PhD in International Economic and Political Relations from Loughborough University.

Doru Frantescu
Doru Frantescu is co-founder and CEO of VoteWatch Europe, a Brussels-based leading digital intelligence source on EU decision-making. A political scientist by training, Doru's data-driven research into the behaviour of Parliamentarians and Governments is used regularly by reputed public and private institutions, academia and the media across the EU and internationally (including Financial Times, Bloomberg, Euronews, CNN, France24, BBC, etc). A social entrepreneur and passionate futurist, Doru is also a member of the European Alliance for Artificial Intelligence.

Aaron McLoughlin

Aaron McLoughlin is a Senior Advisor at FleishmanHillard in Brussels. His works focuses on substance regulation, environmental policy, regulatory decision-making, and fisheries. A lobbyist and campaigner in Brussels for over twenty years, he has served as the Head of Public Affairs at the European Chemical Industry Council (CEFIC) as well as Head of WWF's European Marine Programme. He has worked in DG Environment on waste and air pollution legislation and for two British Labour MEPs on passing legislation on fisheries and air pollution. He teaches and blogs on EU decision-making, lobbying and fisheries.

Roland Moore

Roland joined Burson Cohn and Wolfe (formerly Burson-Marsteller) following fifteen years in the UK Civil Service, where he worked on a wide range of environmental policy issues both domestically and internationally. As part of his government career, Roland worked within DG Environment, within the UK's European team in the Cabinet Office, as Private Secretary for a Defra Minister and as environment attaché for the UK Permanent Representation to the EU. He also held a number of policy specialist roles on chemicals, waste, water and sustainable development. Roland has a Master's degree (MSc) in Environment and Sustainable Development from University College London and a Bachelor's degree (BA) in European Studies with French and Italian from the University of Portsmouth. He has reasonable fluency in French, Italian and Spanish.

Leyla Sertel

Leyla Sertel is Quorum's Director of European Markets. In this role she led Quorum's first international expansion and established the European market for the company. Before her move to Brussels she worked at Quorum's headquarters in Washington D.C. and helped build the Customer Success team, which ensures clients get the most out of Quorum. Leyla guest lectures at Maastricht University and the Institut des Hautes Études des Communications Sociales (IHECS) on the digitalisation of public affairs. Prior to her time at Quorum, Leyla worked at the Atlantic Council, focusing on Eurasia and Latin America.

Laura Shields

Laura Shields is the founder and Managing Director of Red Thread, a communications agency specialising in media and presentation training and message and narrative development. A former journalist who graduated from Cambridge University in 2000, Laura started her career at CNN, CNBC and the BBC in London, specialising in European business news and US politics. Based in Brussels since 2008, Laura now works as a communications consultant and panel moderator across Europe, Central Asia and the Middle East. Her clients include European government Ministers, EU Commissioners, EU and US Ambassadors, MEPs, Fortune 500 and FTSE 100 companies, trade associations, NGOs, thinktanks, scientists and philanthropic organisations. Laura is a visiting lecturer at Maastricht University and the IHECS Academy in Brussels. She has written for The Huffington Post, Politics.co.uk and Communication Director Magazine and has appeared on Euronews and ZDF TV.

Jon Worth

Jon Worth is a freelance communications trainer and consultant based in Berlin. He has run training courses for EU institutions and agencies, NGOs, businesses and trade associations. He teaches EU politics and communication at the College of Europe in Bruges, the Italian School of Public Administration, and the University of Maastricht. He has been blogging about the EU for 15 years - jonworth.eu is one of the best known blogs about European Union politics. He is also one of the most active commentators about the EU on Twitter (@jonworth – 62,000 followers). He regularly appears on TV and radio talking about Brexit.

The views expressed in this publication are those of the authors and are not in any way intended to reflect those of their respective employers, nor any of the institutions they describe, analyse and comment on.

Acknowledgements

After two successful editions of *How the EU Institutions Work and... How to Work with the EU Institutions*, the second of which I co-edited with Erik Akse, I was delighted that John Harper, the publisher, wanted to do a third edition. The twist was that John wanted to split the book in two – paving the way for Erik to take on the *How the EU Institutions Work* part and for me to take on *How to Work with the EU Institutions*. The idea was to let me deliver much fuller coverage of both the underpinning methodology and the practical realities of effective EU public affairs.

For this reason this new book is far more than an update of the back part of the second edition. Indeed, while the basic topic is the same, this book is essentially a new one with a huge amount of brand new material from a great new team of authors.

This is a book dedicated to what lobbying is and how you do it in the EU. In that sense the exercise of conceptualising, building a winning team of authors and then writing and editing a new book has been just as challenging and exciting as working on the first book a decade ago. To do this I have been lucky to have a group of experienced and dedicated authors to support me: Laura Shields, Aaron McLoughlin, Doru Frantescu, Roland Moore, Leyla Sertel and Jon Worth. All of them have contributed excellent chapters – going through the usual pains of writing alongside professional and personal challenges and also through the strange times of COVID-19. It has been a pleasure to build a new book together with all of you. I would in particular like to thank Aaron and Leyla, with whom I have had many discussions about content, structure and the future of lobbying in the EU – these have been inspiring sessions that I hope will continue.

I always recall that in the first edition I thanked the many people who gave me the idea and inspiration to write that book – the officials, students and professionals who were looking for a book they could use to find out 'how the EU institutions really work'. Well this third version is still for you. I can only hope that this book will help people understand, engage and succeed in ways that they otherwise might not have been able to. After all, that is what this book looks to do – share the combined experience (over 100 years of it!) of seasoned EU professionals to help others learn and improve. I think that all of us authors engaged in writing this book have learnt and improved as we have written and read the work of others – and we hope this is your experience too.

For a third time I would like to extend my appreciation to John Harper, the Publisher, for his continued support on this book series and for his suggestion to expand it for the third edition. Always a source of ideas, contacts and suggestions it continues to be a real pleasure to work with John. I also come to see that, more so with this third edition, writing a book requires both the indulgence and support of your family so I would like to thank my wife, Johanna, and my daughter, Juliette, for both.

Finally I can only hope that this book answers your questions and helps you navigate through the maze of engaging with the EU institutions and decision-making procedures. I wish you every success.

Alan Hardacre

Introduction

By Alan Hardacre

This book is dedicated to the subject of how *in practical terms* stakeholders can work effectively with the EU institutions. It deals with the ever-evolving profession of lobbying in Brussels – and how to succeed at it – in a way and to a depth that no other book does. It does so based on the combined experience of veteran Brussels professionals who share their insights, tips and strategies for success.

Let us start at the beginning when it comes to the European Union (EU) and lobbying. The EU is a multinational organisation of policy-making and law which has 27 Member States and close to 450 million inhabitants. It is a complex system of governance that supersedes the national level, operating in 24 official languages with institutions and bodies based in a number of European cities, but centered in Brussels. The EU is the largest political and economic entity in Europe, boasting a single market, a customs union, a common currency and its own diplomatic service amongst other achievements. Put simply, any stakeholder trying to engage on any form of public policy objectives in, or across, the EU (or that involve the EU) is obliged to engage with the EU in some way, shape or form. If you take the fact that the EU is responsible for a significant percentage of the legislation its Member States implement and also that EU legislation not only impacts Member States but also the rest of the world, you start to understand why there is so much at stake in lobbying the EU.

What this book will do for you

This book provides a practical step-by-step guide for anyone wanting to understand, study, or work with the EU institutions and decision-making. It looks at how to design the right strategies both in general and also for specific institutions and decision-making procedures.

Whilst there is no secret formula for working with the institutions and decision-making there are a number of fundamentals that any successful work must be built on. This book will detail them and show you how to integrate them into your work.

There is now virtually no policy area that is not directly or indirectly impacted by decisions taken by the EU. A direct consequence of this is that there is effectively no civil society stakeholder (social, environmental, consumer or business) or third country that can choose not to work with the EU institutions and decision-making in some capacity. It really does not matter where you are based in the world, or what your specific issue is: you will very likely have to engage with the EU.

This might be a one-off piece of engagement or part of a longer-term requirement to work with the EU institutions. Either way it is essential to have the best possible guidance to hand on how to do this.

All of these factors have been a potent recipe for the growth of a vibrant and diverse lobbying industry in Brussels. The industry is constantly evolving both because of changes in the way the EU institutions work together and because of changes in what the lobbying industry itself considers best practice. This constant evolution is one of the great learning curve challenges for anyone looking to work with the EU – you always have to change and adapt what you do. The EU is also importing more and more public affairs practice and tools from the US – notably with regard to the use of technology in public affairs, which is much more state of the art in the US. As ever, everything gets an 'EU twist' to make it relevant and adapted. Finally, it's the case that as lobbying has evolved in the EU, from a largely informal activity to an increasingly professional one, it has become more regulated and subject to scrutiny. This book aims to make sure that lobbying in the EU arena is possible for all stakeholders and not just a select few.

Two of the reasons why there is such a dynamic, and increasingly professional, lobbying industry are worth briefly exploring because of their importance to engagement in the EU.

Firstly the EU, like all democratic systems of government, is built on the principle of political legitimacy that itself is based on **accountability and open participation** in the political process. Lobbying is invaluable for generating dialogue and exchange to provide evidence and facts to EU officials to enhance the quality of legislation and decisions taken at the EU level – and to improve implementation and compliance later down the line. More than at the national level, **EU institutions need information and evidence from different stakeholders** across the 27 Member States, and from other countries and companies around the world who are also impacted. The EU needs this information to be able to legislate better and lobbying is the key mechanism to deliver this. In this sense the input of various stakeholders to officials across the institutions is an important means of creating democratic decision-making in the EU and is vital to giving legitimacy to the institutions' legislative output.

Secondly, the reason why so many stakeholders engage in lobbying is that **the costs and benefits of EU legislation are rarely shared equally**, and they can have very important localised consequences. This situation generates intense activity as stakeholders try to defend their positions and create new opportunities by working with the institutions. As we will see in the coming chapters the EU decision-making process is one of consecutive negotiations within, and then between, the EU institutions – which requires all stakeholders to stay vigilant and engaged at all times as they look to manage their interests. Engagement is rarely ever one-shot or done in a week – it is all about managing an ongoing, uncertain process. Furthermore, issues are never one-sided, so whatever you are working towards it is almost certain that someone else is working against it – either on the basis of principle or competition. As we have seen in the past some subjects can motivate a huge spectrum of stakeholders to engage, such as the well-known example of discussions on the Transatlantic Trade and Investment Partnership (TTIP) in recent years.

Fundamental to any attempt to work with the EU is a solid understanding of its idiosyncratic institutional and decision-making architecture. Erik Akse's companion volume to this book, *How the EU Institutions Work* provides a solid foundation. It details the workings of the EU institutions and their decision-making procedures in a practical and systematic way. Success in lobbying in the EU is premised on understanding the institutions and how they individually and collectively take decisions. This is foundation number one – and without it you will be building a house of cards.

This book therefore builds up from the base of *How the EU Institutions Work* and offers a

> **How the EU Institutions Work**
> **Edited by Erik Akse**
>
> This book lays the foundations for successful engagement with the EU. It provides a systematic and detailed guide to the EU institutions and their decision-making procedures. It identifies all the key people, key processes and key moments that are crucial to engagement.
>
> Make sure you fully understand how decision-making takes place in the EU institutions – it will be the basis for all successful work.

guide, for all stakeholders, on how in practice to engage effectively and consistently with the EU institutions and decision-making. It fills a gap by offering practical guidance and recommendations to those coming to Brussels, those currently working in, or with, Brussels and for students and other interested stakeholders on how things really work. The book offers the insights of seasoned professionals and it explains how they approach all aspects of EU lobbying – and always concludes with their guidance and recommendations. While knowing what constitutes best practice is, by itself, no guarantee of success it is an essential prerequisite for any successful engagement. In contrast, a failure to understand the process, the timelines, who takes decisions, what your interlocutor needs, or how to best engage your target audience, will almost certainly lead to failure. Enabling all stakeholders to get the right message to the right person at the right time is an objective that will at the same time enable officials across the institutions to get the best available information to make their choices and take their decisions.

It is worth highlighting from the outset that this book has a clear **focus on legislative files** as this is the main area of activity and lobbying in Brussels. It is obviously not the only area and we recognise that we do not explicitly cover more specialised areas such as budgetary decision-making, Common Foreign and Security Policy (CFSP) and international agreements and negotiations. But while these are not explicitly covered, many of the horizontal recommendations and guidance will be valid for how to engage in these areas as well.

Understanding the process

With the enlarged remit provided for this new edition comes a new ambition: to present, explain and demonstrate how lobbying is **a multi-stage end-to-end process**, starting from objectives and key performance indicators (KPIs) and running all the way through to how we evaluate our lobbying/campaigning success so we can learn for the future.

Viewing lobbying as a *process* in this way allows us to isolate and perfect our understanding, and practice, of each individual component – and also, crucially, to understand the hand-offs from one part of the process to another. This approach is so important in a profession that is ever evolving and allows us to better harness and understand how we can benefit from improvements.

> The ambition of this book is to present lobbying as a multi-stage end-to-end process. Breaking it down like this will allow you to understand, and perfect, each individual component of lobbying and better understand the hand-offs between them. It will then show you how to apply lobbying best practice both horizontally and to each individual institution or decision-making procedure.

This approach gives you three key benefits:

1. **It makes a lobbying strategy more complete**: because to be successful we need to deliver across a whole range of activities and not just one or two.
2. **It makes a lobbying strategy more robust**: because it is based on strength across the process and not in just one or two areas.
3. **It makes a lobbying strategy more adaptable**: because as internal and external events change it will be easier to understand what aspects of the lobbying strategy need to change – and the impacts that one change will have on other areas of the strategy.

Once you start to view, and work with, lobbying in this way it makes it easier to understand how you apply it to your issues and to the different institutions and decision-making procedures. Let us start therefore with a broad look at lobbying as it will help give us necessary context. There are three key dimensions to lobbying that can be seen in Figure 0.1.

Figure 0.1: The three key dimensions of lobbying

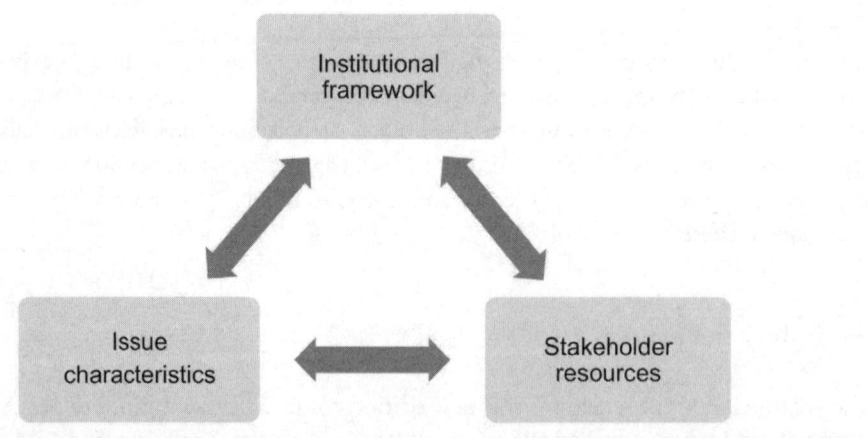

Source: Mahoney, C. (2008) Brussels versus the Beltway: Advocacy in the United States and the European Union, Georgetown University Press, Georgetown (adapted)

The three key dimensions of lobbying are:

1. **Institutional framework**: This refers to democratic accountability, the decision-making processes and the institutions that are involved in these decisions, as well as media coverage. Put together, this all frames the specific context in which lobbying will take place. These are all horizontal, i.e. they are applicable for all stakeholders and all issues. This book will be focused on this dimension because it underpins any attempt to work with the EU institutions and decision-making and is specific to the EU.

2. **Issue characteristics**: This refers to the key characteristics of any particular issue such as its scope, salience, level of stakeholder conflict, its history and whether there has been an event that focused public awareness. This dimension frames the lobbying context of a specific issue and is thus not horizontal: it is case by case. For this reason this dimension will not be dealt with in this book, although examples will be used to highlight important points. It goes without saying though, that to be successful, you will need to fully understand all the dimensions of the issue you are working on.

3. **Stakeholder resources**: The financial and human resources of a stakeholder are vitally important for lobbying. This is linked to things like membership, number of staff and the roles they play, organisational structures, ability to run campaigns and activities. Whilst this topic will not be directly discussed in this book, it is of course implicit in the discussion in Chapter 2 of an EU public affairs methodology, because how you build your strategy and actions will depend in part on what resources you have to hand.

It is the interplay of a specific system, a specific issue and the resources of a stakeholder that fundamentally shape how lobbying can and will take place. These will be the systemic issue and organisational constraints that you have to work with. It is from here that successful strategies can be built – so knowing and understanding these constraints is important as a first step. This book, as we have said, will focus on the first key dimension because the need to understand the institutional framework is fundamental to any attempt to situate an issue or deploy stakeholder resources. If you know your issue inside-out and have extremely good resources, but do not grasp the institutional framework, then you risk wasting your knowledge and resources. This book will show you how to lobby in the EU system to best deploy what resources you have (or help you understand what resources you will need) for your issue.

Objectives and structure of the book

The chapters in this book all have the double objective of presenting the most relevant information and of rendering it usable: that is, equipping you with the knowledge, tools and confidence to use it. The book is practical and aims to give solid recommendations and guidance every step of the way all the way to the final recommendations in Chapter 11. This approach is intended to equip you to integrate the knowledge into your day to day, or occasional, work with the EU institutions with more confidence and insight.

The book is structured to deliver **five key objectives**, as listed in the box below.

1. Understanding what influence is (and is not) and how to improve your ability to harness it.
2. Equipping you with the right thinking process (or methodology) to build, step by step, a practical strategy to engage in the EU and how to manage your data to do this efficiently.
3. Empowering you to engage with the EU media and social media space.
4. Giving you detailed guidance on how to work with the three main EU Institutions and decision-making procedures.
5. Offering a one-stop-shop of the most important EU lobbying guidelines that will help you succeed.

Figure 0.2: Overview of what the book covers

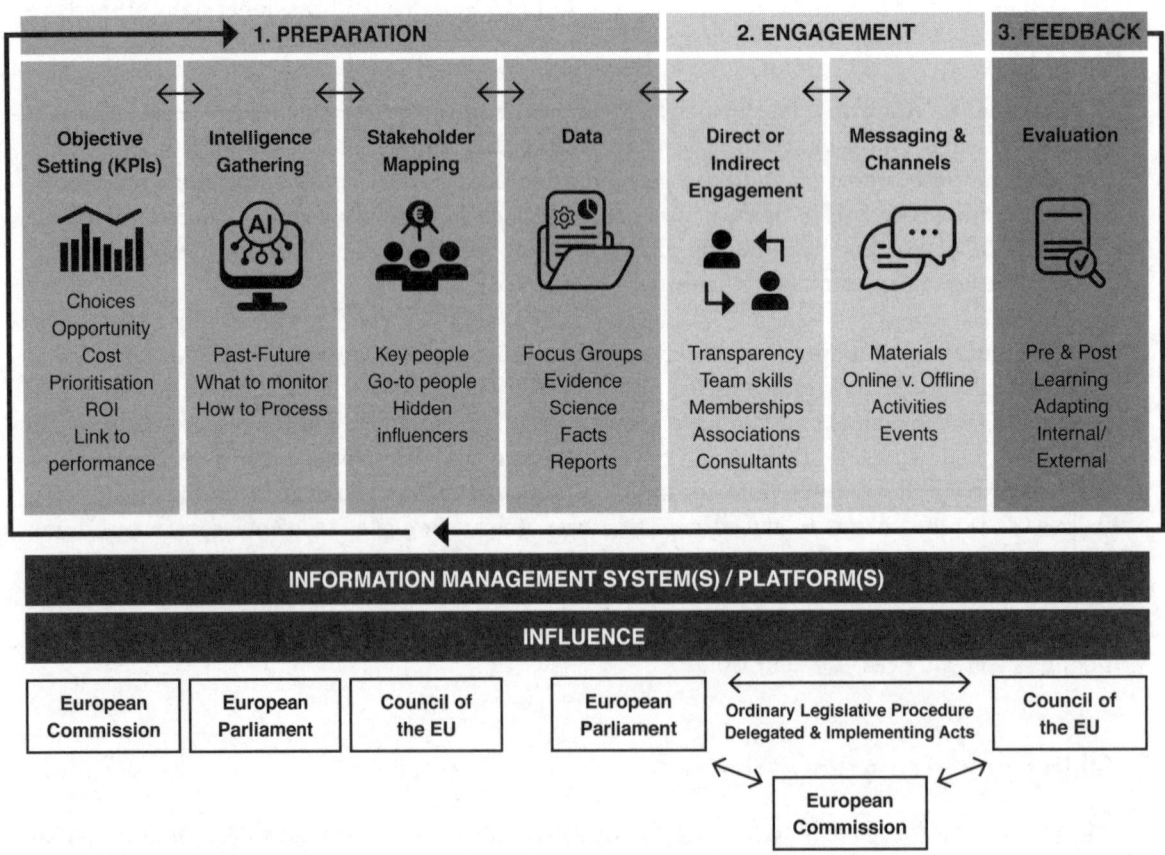

Source: Alan Hardacre

Figure 0.2 shows everything the book will cover. Let's look in a little more detail at how the book will deal with these topics in its three distinct sections:

1. **Section one** of the book starts with a look at the **art of influence**. What is influence and how do you get better at it? This is an essential starting place given that lobbying involves exactly this – the effort to influence. From this, Chapter 2 sets out a new **process driven methodology** for how to structure and think about lobbying. It outlines three stages and seven key steps to building a robust EU lobbying strategy. The third chapter is very closely linked as it outlines the **role of technology** in supporting and delivering your EU lobbying work. How do you best manage all the data and information in such a way as to leverage it as and when you need it? From there the book moves on in Chapter 4 to look at **working with the media and social media** in the EU – as a key part of the methodology and as a core activity in itself. Finally the section ends in Chapter 5 with a special look at how **third countries**, countries that are not EU Member States, can engage and work in Brussels – offering practical guidance to make their work more successful.

2. The **second section** of the book moves beyond the horizontal and strategic considerations into how to work with the three key EU institutions and the two main decision-making procedures. These chapters all build from the parallel chapters in Erik Akse's book, *How the EU Institutions Work*, or your own existing knowledge of how the institutions and their decision-making procedures work. They detail in successive chapters how to work with the **European Commission** (Chapter 6), **European Parliament** (Chapter 7) and **Council of the EU** (Chapter 8, also with reference to the European Council) and all end with clear guidance and recommendations to succeed. The final two chapters of this section are on the **Ordinary Legislative Procedure** (Chapter 9) and **Implementing and Delegated Acts** (Chapter 10). These two chapters put the work of the individual institutions into the context that you will need to work with – that of active decision-making in and between the institutions. This section as a whole demonstrates how lobbying in the EU is built on working with a series of negotiations within and then between the EU institutions – and gives you guidance on how to succeed.

3. The **third section** (Chapter 11) takes the **most important guidance and recommendations** from the book and distils them into a one-stop-shop list of EU engagement fundamentals upon which successful work can be built. As mentioned before, working with the EU is an ever-evolving process, because the institutions and the people in them change, the mix of stakeholders working on issues changes, the public affairs industry becomes ever more sophisticated and professional, and because lobbying can change due to business and political demands. But while taking all of this into account, this final chapter aims to make essential recommendations that will increase your chances of success.

While all of the experienced authors involved in this book recognise that there is no magic formula for successfully working with the EU institutions, what they set out is intended to help Brussels newcomers and old-hands from all policy sectors, third country officials, Member State officials, civil society stakeholders, regional representatives and students of public affairs and decision-making in their understanding of how to succeed in engaging with the EU.

Working with the EU is an intriguing professional challenge that can be equally frustrating and satisfying and part of the challenge is that there is single route to success. That said, we hope it will become clear from reading this book that:

1. You need to constantly adapt and change. Viewing lobbying as a process will allow you to do this much better.
2. You need to manage your data and interactions professionally to give yourself the best chances of (long-term) success.
3. There are fundamental things that you should always try to do.
4. There are fundamental things that you should always avoid doing.
5. There are myriad ways to be more efficient, effective and ultimately successful.

Finally it is worth noting that you can read the book sequentially or on a needs basis, i.e. delving into individual chapters as and when you need them. We want the book to serve as a reference for you in your work in the EU. All of the team hope that this books makes a difference to your EU lobbying!

Part 1

How to Build a Successful Public Affairs Strategy

1. The Art of Influence

By Laura Shields

If you work in policy and public affairs in Brussels, your main objective is to influence EU legislation to suit your own organisational objectives. This means that ideally you want to be able to manipulate a process in order to get a desired outcome. Most people who work in Brussels will not put it that bluntly as such descriptions can seem distasteful. They may talk loftily about 'contributing to the policy process' or 'achieving their advocacy goals'. But what they really mean is skilfully handling a process to achieve their end goals. After all, skilled craftsmen manipulate metals in order to make a high value end product. Why shouldn't it be the same in EU policymaking?

But what does this mean in practice? In fact, what does *influence* even mean?

This book will explore the myriad ways to engage and interact with the EU institutions and decision-making procedures – proposing best in class methodologies, technological solutions and communications support. Underpinning all of this is the intention and ambition to influence. All of the individual chapters outline best practice in *how* you *influence*, but before diving into that detail it is useful to spend some time looking at *what influence is* and therefore how you might best achieve it (and also what it is not).

So, in simple terms what is it?

> **Two definitions of *influence* from the Oxford English Dictionary**
>
> 1. 'The capacity to influence the character, development, or behaviour of someone or something, or the effect itself.'
> 2. 'The power to shape policy or ensure favourable treatment from someone, especially through status, contacts, or wealth.'

As you can see from the definitions above, having an influence is not about wielding power. If it were there would, heaven forbid, be no public affairs consultants or in-house lobbyists. It is also not purely about persuasion, although the latter is an important part of being influential. Nor is it necessarily about success. You might get the result you want without doing anything at all or, in some cases, not by actually doing the right things but simply by benefitting from other people's good work.

Real influence is about steering a process not a single decisive moment. In a crowded environment where lots of players are competing for policymakers' attention, it requires intelligence, both intellectual and emotional as well as persistence, flexibility and a degree of persuasive ability. It is about knowing when to work individually or with partners to get the results you want. It is about the judicious use of messaging and other forms of communication. Perhaps most importantly, it is also about knowing when to do nothing and simply observe and listen. As you will see across the rest of this book EU decision-making, within and between the EU institutions, is a process of *accumulated negotiated compromise*. This is the process that needs to be steered – in its entirety – to be influential.

In this chapter you will read about the five key traits required to practise the art of influence as well as practical skills you can work on to help develop and improve each and every one of them. They are:
1. Empathy
2. Credibility
3. Discipline
4. Tactics
5. Persuasiveness

These traits and skills are neutral, meaning they can be put either to malign or beneficial use. The tools can be used and abused which is one of the reasons Machiavelli gets such a bad press when in fact the stratagems he outlines in *The Prince* were simply his observations about how power operated in 16th Century Italy and what princes needed to do to hold on to it.

Mastery of these traits is not a guaranteed recipe for success. This is because there are so many other variables and interest groups at work in Brussels, meaning that you can do everything by the book and still not get the outcome you want. But what you can do is control your own behaviour and actions in order to maximise your chances of steering policymaking in the direction you want. The following pages are a toolkit to help you build and leverage influence.

1. Empathy

People who work in policy are often cerebral. And rightly so. The legislative process is complicated and requires technical expertise and persistence to understand and analyse the impact of different developments. But a good intellect is not enough; it needs to be accompanied by emotional intelligence and an ability to understand and work with other people's (often different) viewpoints.

> 'I have learned that answers even to difficult questions can be found if we always see the world through the eyes of the other person; if we respect the history, tradition, religion, and identity of others; if we firmly stand by our inalienable values and act accordingly; and if we do not always follow our initial impulses, even with all the pressure to make snap decisions, but instead stop for a moment, remain silent, reflect, take a break.'
>
> **Angela Merkel**
> ***Commencement Address at Harvard University, May 2019***

In other words, you can have all the evidence, facts and arguments at your fingertips and still be ineffective in achieving your goals if you do not have good people skills to go with them.

The people you want to influence are invariably busy, have fragmented attention spans and, in many cases, less knowledge of the subject than you. But no one is a blank slate. They will almost certainly have their own preconceptions, feelings and positions – both professional and moral - on an issue. The culture of the country they come from as well as the education system they were trained in may also influence how they think and approach an issue, even if (in theory) they leave that conditioning at the door when they start working for an EU institution. So even if you have never met them before they will meet you with their own agenda.

Influential people do not try and win arguments outright by bombarding their target audience with killer facts. These methods invariably do not work if you are dealing with someone who has strong ideas on a subject and they happen to disagree with you. In fact, presenting someone with evidence contrary to their view can reinforce the very idea you are trying to dislodge. And the same goes for neutral audiences. They may be more receptive to your arguments than critics, but they are not there to be lectured to.

This means you need to develop empathy. It is something of a buzzword these days but it's often misunderstood. Contrary to many perceptions it is not limited to feeling other people's emotions. It is also the ability to *understand* what others think and feel. Hostage negotiators say tactical empathy is a vital component of resolving kidnap situations successfully. And neuro-imaging shows that even psychopaths can flick the 'empathy switch' in their brains if it helps them to manipulate their target victims more easily.

Are you listening properly?

Most people aren't good at listening, even if they think they are. What they actually do is stay quiet while others are talking and then say what they planned to say anyway. Unsurprisingly, the scope for misunderstanding or even offence is large. And this is even in supposedly benign day to day interactions with friends, colleagues or family.

When you're dealing with audiences you are trying to influence or who are actively hostile the stakes are even higher. In 'Never Split the Difference' former FBI hostage negotiator Chris Voss argues that listening is the first step to resolving stand offs because it allows the negotiator to form tactical empathy with the perpetrator. This often leads to a rapport which can then lead to influence and behaviour change.

And if the FBI isn't your thing, then consider the other end of the spectrum: in Buddhism, the enlightened being, or Bodhisattva, is described as 'the one who observes the sounds of the world'.

If listening, observing and reflection can work for Buddhists and hostage negotiators, surely, they can work for us mortal lobbyists and communications professionals?

Framed like this empathy is far from being an easy skill. So, how can you develop it or refine your ability to use it? A first step is to keep quiet and listen to where your audience is on an issue and not where you would like them to be.

Influence begins with extracting and understanding someone else's position so that it can help you compare and, if necessary, adapt your own. The best way to do this is not to charge in and tell them everything you know, or your key message/policy ask. Ask lots of questions, be curious and do not draw conclusions about their views too early on. This also applies to written communication where you cannot read body language, and it is particularly important if dealing with challenging audiences. People need to feel validated and a huge part of that is allowing them to express their viewpoint without being judged for it.

A second way to be better at understanding your audience is to do your homework on them. If you are engaging with public officials and stakeholders, you should look to understand more about them before you meet them. There is nearly always a wealth of public information online (including LinkedIn profiles and online CVs) to get you started – and this can be invaluable in helping you have an idea about who it is you will be trying to influence. Information on positions, thinking or even hobbies can help you break the ice, build rapport and see things from their perspective.

An ability to form a rapport, even with people with whom you disagree, is essential particularly if you end up needing to leverage relationships to help you achieve your goals. It can also help you to understand if your own argument is so far removed from their own position that you have no common ground between you. In other words, whether you need to adapt your own goals and messages to locate a common buffer zone where you are more likely to get a warmer reception.

How to network

Depending on your personality, you may view networking as one of your job's perks or something that you have to put up with even though the idea fills you with horror. Fortunately, Brussels offers all sorts of opportunities – whether events, drinks or no-strings coffees – to meet people, make connections and build up your network of influence.

Very few people love walking into a room where they don't know anyone and introducing themselves. If you do, make sure you practise listening and not just talking. Ask questions but give people enough information about yourself too. If you hate this kind of thing, treat it as an exercise in getting out of your comfort zone. Introverts often make the best listeners so, if you are one, you may be pleasantly surprised at what you learn.

Setting up casual coffees with peers or other stakeholders in your field is a good thing to do as it helps you to understand what makes people tick and means the pressure is off for you to have to 'sell' them on your position. Plus, it's harder to get angry with people you understand and/or get on with.

Tips for becoming more empathetic:
1. Build stakeholder relationships face to face as much as possible, even if your primary form of communicating will be in writing.
2. Build the relationships before you need to use them.
3. Do your homework on the people you need to meet and influence. A little background information can go a long way in understanding who they are and what they want – and thus how to build a rapport with them.
4. Spend more time listening than talking and ask questions that encourage people to explain their thinking on a position.
5. Never get angry if people disagree with you. It is toxic and has the opposite effect to changing their mind.
6. Test your position against theirs. If they are poles apart you may need to re-think what you are doing in order to make your positions meet.

2. Credibility

Credibility is about being taken seriously as a source of authority on an issue. This does not mean you have to be an expert in the conventional sense (although it sometimes helps if you are) but rather that you are worth listening to on the substance. Or to put it another way, there is little point in being an expert if no one thinks it is worth paying attention to what you say.

Credibility makers	**Credibility breakers**
Consistency (but not stubbornness)	Inconsistency
Reliability	Unreliability
Accuracy	Sensationalism
Relevance	Irrelevance
Constructiveness	Dogma
Transparency	Obfuscation

In the digital age how societies construct, and perceive, authority is very much in flux. This is particularly the case as we struggle with the daily churn of opinion, misinformation and disinformation that can muddy the waters at best and strip facts of their meaning at worst. But there is still strong evidence that being knowledgeable on an issue matters, particularly in times of crisis. What matters is that the key people see and believe you to be credible.

When it comes to public affairs, expertise should be practical not just academic. A deep knowledge of your subject is clearly helpful but if you cannot package it clearly or use it to offer constructive policy solutions to the right people at the right time then you will not be effective. One crucial area that you can control relates to the quality of information that you and your organisation inject into the public debate. Even though we now understand far more about how impulsive and emotional much of human decision-making is, research and a strong evidence base are still key aspects of decision-making.

> **Don't overburden your audience**
>
> As is the case with many professions, in public affairs the people you are looking to influence have limited time and bandwidth for absorbing information. This leads them to make short cuts when making decisions. Known as 'bounded rationality', it can lead to less than ideal outcomes for both sides. For example, studies have shown that when presented with too many options, decision-makers often resolve the problem of making the best choice by making no choice at all, and walking away.
>
> You can reduce the risk of such outcomes by not overloading your target audience.
>
> Credible organisations don't produce huge quantities of research for public affairs purposes because they know it will overwhelm their audience. Former Apple CEO Steve Jobs was such a fan of the expression *'Simplicity is the ultimate sophistication'* (often but very doubtfully attributed to Leonardo da Vinci) that he picked it up and used it relentlessly when talking about his company's ethos. And what is true for designing iPads and MacBooks is just as true for policy products. It takes (more) hard work to make complex issues accessible and clear for a target audience, but it is essential. It is not dumbing down; it is wising up.

It is important therefore to make sure that what you do produce is of high quality and is clear and accessible to read. It does not matter how brilliant the thinking behind a report or position paper is if the intended reader has to machete their way through it. Badly structured or opaque communications will have a negative impact on your reputation and your ability to be taken seriously – and hence on your credibility. Put another way, there are no prizes for being clever if the way you package your message gives people a migraine.

However, as highlighted previously, facts and evidence alone are not a magic bullet. They matter hugely in public affairs but they are a means to an end, not an end in themselves. Getting into ping pong battles with critics over whose study is correct can often end up as pointless navel gazing. And other factors such as politics or public opinion will often carry more weight than evidence.

But, as psychologist Robert Cialdini argues in his 1984 classic *Influence: The Psychology of Persuasion*, consistency is important. If you are perceived as being a flip flopper on an issue it's hard to know what you stand for, so don't change an unpopular position if you think it's the right one and have the evidence to support it. It will damage your credibility and could also have long term consequences. However, at the same time it is important to keep watch on emerging evidence and be willing to change your mind if it shows your original position is no longer tenable.

Credibility is built on consistency over time. The longer you operate professionally in Brussels in a certain field the more likely you are to build credibility, stakeholder by stakeholder. It takes time – there is no short cut to building credibility. That said, you can lose credibility in a second. Unprofessional, not transparent or badly timed/worded or communicated behaviour can undermine years of credibility building. Brussels, like other centres of influence, is full of examples of individuals and organisations who have lost credibility on the back of an event, report or discovery of some unprofessional behaviour. So, as you build it you need to protect and preserve it.

Tips for becoming (and staying) more credible:
1. Focus on quality not quantity of output.
2. Produce high quality evidence but do not expect it to be the decisive factor in decision-making.
3. Write clearly: there are no prizes for being clever if no one understands you.
4. Do not sensationalise your case – the people you are trying to influence will not be impressed.
5. Be honest about addressing counter-arguments up front but do not make critiquing them a replacement for proactive communications.
6. Inject your industry, NGO or sector's practical experience into the discussion.
7. Be consistent and make sure you do this across stakeholders and over time.
8. View your credibility for what it is – hard fought and fragile – and treat it with care.

3. Discipline

If you want to steer events you need to be persistent otherwise there is a good chance your efforts will peter out and be ineffective. As noted, the EU policy process is one of consecutive negotiations within and between the institutions – so discipline over time is essential. The average piece of legislation in Brussels takes roughly two years from beginning to end, so influencing it is a long-haul process that requires grit and perseverance.

Furthermore, with so many variables and other players in the mix, the idea that you can intervene in the process sporadically and expect to help shape the outcome is fanciful. Persistence is hugely important because it demonstrates an ability and commitment to pursue a goal until you achieve the outcome you want (or as close to as possible depending on the other variables in the mix).

Discipline takes many forms and is closely related, but not identical, to strategy. A strategic approach is about having a goal-focused plan. Discipline is about developing the muscle to *actually follow through on it* while also recognising that events change, and you will need to be flexible in order to adapt and take advantage of them. Or to paraphrase the 19th Century Prussian military commander, Helmuth von Moltke: *'No plan survives contact with the enemy'*.

Disciplined people take this into account when deciding where to focus their energies. At some levels devising and sticking to a plan can be tedious, which is why discipline is so important. At the same time, it can be liberating because it gives you a better idea of when and what to act on, which is invaluable if resources are limited or internal politics is putting pressure on you to do things outside its scope. In Chapter 2, on building a best in class public affairs methodology, you will read more about the importance of objective setting and prioritisation – tools to support discipline in your work. Without clear objectives and strong prioritisation, your focus and efforts will end up being distributed and wasted on irrelevant tasks (both internal and external).

Keeping the end goal in sight will allow you to focus on the quality rather than the quantity of actions, enabling you to produce the best possible work to influence the process in the direction you want.

Tips for being disciplined:
1. Stick to the strategic plan you have developed (while building in scope for flexibility).
2. Focus on quality not quantity of activities. If they do not advance your end goals, ditch them.
3. Be relentless: if something is a good idea do not allow inertia to limit its ability to succeed.
4. Do not change what you do every six months just because you are bored. No one is paying a fraction of the attention to what you do and say as you are.

4. Tactics

Strategy and tactics are often confused but they are not the same thing. Whereas a strategy refers to an overall plan the tactics are the short-term actions that can help to achieve it. It is important to emphasise that tactics are not a replacement for a plan and should support it, even if in the short term it may not always be apparent that they do. You can read more in Chapter 2 on how to build the right public affairs strategy.

Tactical people cultivate the skills to work in the landscape they are in, not the one they would prefer it to be. Of course, their overall intention is to shift the policy direction in their favour, but they do it based on real, not ideal world conditions. This means that they understand what kinds of planned activities achieve the best possible outcomes. For example, if you are trying to introduce a new topic into the lobbying arena and knowledge levels are low it may be better to hold off on publishing a big report (which few will read) and hold an introductory big picture event that frames people's understanding and helps them become informed gradually.

In contrast **influential people** also know how to turn spontaneous events to their advantage and are capable of being unpredictable on an issue, provided it does not dilute their credibility or undermine their overall strategy. This can be as simple as being outspoken on a particular issue in the media and helping to build your organisation's credibility as a source of expertise. Or, it can be about adapting and creating new messages or evidence that shapes short term developments while also supporting longer term goals.

Tactical people can often judge which policy contexts and issues require different approaches. For example, they will know when it is best to exert pressure from outside (e.g. through the traditional media or social media) or to do private lobbying in small meetings. They are also often able to see when it is appropriate to work alone and when to work as part of a broader coalition. Building diverse coalitions can be hugely influential because groups that have little in common otherwise, but who are nonetheless able to align on specific issues, often carry more weight with decision-makers because these networks give the impression of broad cross-societal support.

Within these networks the levers of influence may not always be apparent to the outside world. For example, you can be the most influential person in a coalition because you are the person who links all the other actors and plays a vital connecting role. But your role may not be understood or seen more widely because other, potentially higher profile people, have more visibility in the public debate.

Clearly tactics, and tactical acumen, are key to success in Brussels (or any influencing environment) because they are what can ultimately make a difference and lead to changes in opinion. There is no magic recipe here that will tell you what to do in every situation. Faced with the same situation ten experienced lobbyists would likely propose fifteen different solutions. You cannot be sure in advance which of them would work – although you may already be able to identify those which will certainly fail. And the fact that something worked last time is no guarantee that it will work this time or next time. Just because you hold a very successful networking event or seminar does not mean you will be able to do it again – and perhaps it will no longer be the best use of resources. Things evolve quickly, so tactics also need to evolve. Tactical acumen is often built through experience – through trial and error, evaluation and adaptation. It can also be 'bought in' through consultants with more experience. It is incredibly valuable and can make a disproportionate difference to your chances of success.

Tips for becoming more tactical:
1. Make sure you know the difference between strategy and tactics before embarking on a planned course of action.
2. Pick activities that focus on real world conditions but also steer the debate in the direction of your long-term goals.
3. Be flexible: sudden events may present short-term opportunities to advance your strategic goals even if they are not part of the formal plan.
4. Decide which issues you want to lobby on individually or as part of a group – different circumstances require different responses.
5. Differentiate between being influential and being visible: getting attention is not always the best way to achieve your goals.
6. Make sure you take the time to evaluate what happened with your past tactical choices. Look for learnings and think about how you could improve next time.
7. If in doubt about a tactic trial it on smaller audiences first – test and learn. See what works and scale it.
8. Look at others and learn as much as you can. What did they do – or are they doing – and what seems to be working?
9. Build your own tactical playbook – which, whether you are conscious of it or not, you will be doing in your head anyway.

5. Persuasiveness

Persuasiveness is a key pillar of influence but is not identical to it. Its role in lobbying is often overstated, largely because of the weight it is given in popular culture and the news media. Based on TV programmes and films, we often associate influence with unscrupulous behaviour involving an ability to weave magic spells with words that make audiences swoon in a matter of seconds.

And you can really work at developing this type of persuasive ability if you want to. Advances in neuroscience and behavioural psychology have resulted in a proliferation of self-help and business books with tips and tricks on how best to engage and seduce your audience with powerful language, use of voice, the arrangement of your information or even visual and physical cues such as dress or room layout. A lot of these books are fascinating, and some are useful and worth reading for your broader self-development.

But, sadly for some, the reality of public affairs in Brussels is that it does not afford many opportunities to manipulate people's subconscious minds on a daily basis. The policy input process mostly takes the form of written communications that afford limited opportunities for lobbyists to hone their rhetorical skills and go in for that killer word or phrase that will tip the balance in an instant. Nonetheless, whether you are producing a technical study, advocacy report or position paper, you are still presenting an argument that you hope will convince your audience of the merits of your case and to act on your ideas. So, you had better make it persuasive.

But how do you do that? A good place to start is in classical Athens.

Nearly 2,400 years ago, the philosopher Aristotle laid out a toolkit on how to master the art of persuasion in his written text, 'Rhetoric'. The toolkit is composed of five principles some, or all of which may be already be familiar to you – which, appropriately enough, shows you how influential they have been.

Aristotle's 5 Principles of Persuasion

When 'Rhetoric' first appeared, it was considered a subversive text by the Athenian elites because they didn't want ordinary people learning these skills. Aristotle disagreed because he thought persuasive abilities – which can be taught – were a route to happiness and success in life and should be available to everyone.

The five essential traits he identified still work today:
1. **Ethos or 'Character'**
2. **Logos or 'Reason'**
3. **Pathos or 'Emotion'**
4. **Metaphor**
5. **Brevity**

The good news is that what worked in Ancient Greece still works today. This is partly because in addition to being a philosopher, Aristotle also had a pretty sophisticated understanding of what motivates and influences human behaviour and demonstrated considerable skill as an amateur psychologist and pre-scientific neuroscientist.

5.1 Ethos or 'Character'

Persuasive people use their own experience to build the case for why they are worth listening to. They do not demand respect by reading out their CV. Rather, they show what they have worked on, the knowledge they have gained as a way of connecting and building trust with their audience. It is closely related to credibility which, as identified previously, is another key pillar of influence.

5.2 Logos or 'Reason'

This is essentially the rational argument you construct to convince your audience. It is often supported by statistics, evidence and facts: the hard proof that you use to appeal to your audience's 'heads'. It is an indispensable part of persuasion (and credibility) but, as highlighted previously, it does not win the argument on its own. Skilful opponents, like courtroom lawyers, can be adept at finding ways to raise doubts about even the most fact-based and rock-solid case by chipping away at any small areas of uncertainty or ambiguity.

5.3 Pathos or 'Emotion'

Aristotle recognised that you also need to appeal to people's hearts as well as their heads in order to be persuasive. The best way to get people to care is through concrete examples and stories. In cerebral Brussels there are mixed views about whether to do this in order to influence policy. But developments in neuroscience show that the human brain is hard-wired for storytelling and that we are more likely to be receptive to tough arguments if primed with a good story first. Furthermore, stories are memorable, spice up dull technical writing and can also show the impact of policies that are made far away from where they are felt.

In short, influential people tell the right story on the right occasion. They know how to pick ones which are audience appropriate and reinforce a key message. They know that their target audiences are human beings too. At the very least you need to have a compelling public narrative on the issues you are trying to lobby on. If you do not, it will be very hard for your audience to know what you stand for and for you to influence their thinking.

5.4 Metaphor

Metaphors get short shrift in Brussels which is a shame because they can be powerful vectors for framing arguments as well as getting people to conceptualise, remember and share them. Aristotle thought metaphors created 'verbal beauty' – which may partly explain their limited use in a city where people are often working in a second or even third language and there is a pressing need to avoid confusion.

For the purposes of clarity, a metaphor is not the same thing as a media or social media soundbite. It can become both of those things of course, but it is primarily a way of organising your arguments and the frame through which you want your audience to see them. In that sense its potential usage in public affairs is much greater.

Metaphors are closely bound up with the language and culture of a particular country and are often idiomatic, meaning they are ripe for being misunderstood which, depending on the context, can result in amusement or offence. However, this should not put you off developing and testing them as part of a messaging strategy, even if you are working in Brussels which often tries to downplay these national differences.

> **Metaphors in Action**
>
> 'Brexit has been a vaccine against anti-EU propaganda and fake news'
> **Donald Tusk,** *former President of the European Council*
>
> 'It's a tectonic change. It's like going from horses to steam and from steam to petrol ... it's going to affect every human being on earth.'
> **Frans Timmermans,** *Vice President, European Commission on the challenge of decarbonising to fight climate change*
>
> 'If you know this story about the antique creature, when you chopped out one head, two or seven came up, so there is a risk that you do not solve the problem, you just have many more problems. And you don't have a way to try and control it.'
> **Margrethe Vestager,** *EU Competition Commissioner warning about the unintended consequences of over-regulating the tech industry*

As Joseph Campbell the mythologist once noted: *'If you want to change the world, you have to change the metaphor'*. Or, in other words, if you want to shape and frame people's understanding of an issue then you need to use word pictures.

There are plenty of universal metaphors (weather, health, the body are just a few) that can jump language barriers, attract media coverage and make your argument stand out from other people's. The main thing is to not fear trying them out and using ones that work. When you see the fruits of your efforts you may even start to find that making metaphors is fun. In short, influential people put their metaphor where their mouth is.

5.5 Brevity

Aristotle was ahead of his time when he identified (against the prevailing wisdom) that human beings cannot tolerate lengthy speeches and too much detail. This is true of adults, not just primary school children and people who spend their days on Twitter.

Influential people get to the point and do not waste words. They say or write just what they need to, and do not waste their audience's time by padding it with unnecessary fluff. Remember, you will be competing with other calls on your audience's attention. Keeping it concise and to the point will ensure you have a much better chance of succeeding.

Many people find it helpful to use the inverted pyramid of journalism (see Figure 1.1) to help keep their readers engaged and interested in what they are reading while not overburdening them.

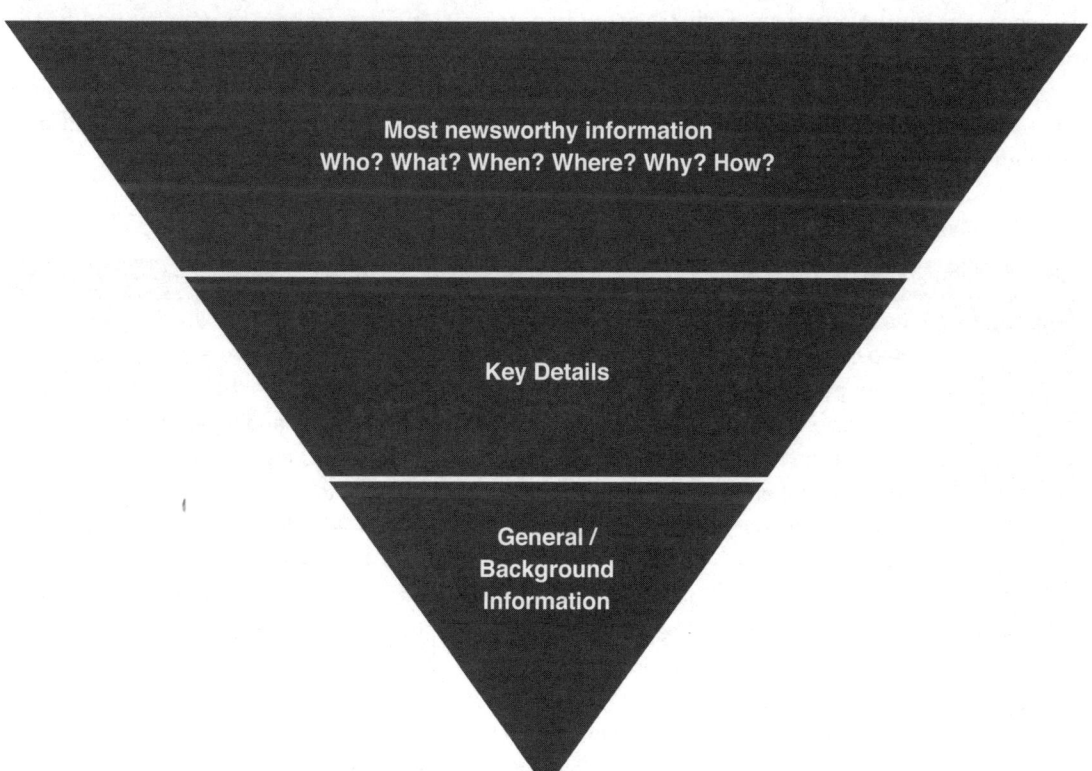

Figure 1.1: Inverted Pyramid of Journalism

Most newsworthy information
Who? What? When? Where? Why? How?

Key Details

General / Background Information

Tips for becoming more persuasive:
1. Sort out your narrative before going public. If you do not have a clear storyline people will project their own (possibly less favourable) one onto yours instead.
2. Do not waste your audience's time: keep messages succinct and concise and get to the point.
3. Experiment with the inverted pyramid of journalism when structuring and writing your work for external (and even internal) audiences.
4. Make sure you have the right balance of the rational (facts) and the emotional (examples or stories) to back up your arguments.
5. Set up a story pipeline within your network. It is the hardest bit of doing advocacy in Brussels because so much of the impact is felt back in the Member States not Brussels itself.
6. Design and test universal metaphors to frame the conversation in the direction you want.

6. Summary

This chapter has walked you through the main traits that define and contribute to influence. It is through understanding, working on and deploying effectively these elements that you will increase your chances of being influential while implementing the strategies described in the coming chapters. As you will have seen, there are many things that contribute to being influential so we will conclude the chapter with a table to help you see the full picture. In this table you will find the key drivers of influence, a reminder overview of why they are important, some tips on how to improve and finally some examples to bring them to life.

The rest of this book will focus on how to influence and to build strategies to influence – all of it based on the premise of this chapter and a clear understanding of the art of influence.

Table 1.1: Overview of the Art of Influence

Key traits	Overview	Tips	Examples
Empathy	Empathy is the ability to see things from another person's perspective. It does not mean you have to agree with them, but rather that you understand their position and what drives it. Without empathy you will not get far in public affairs, even if you got the top mark in EU politics in your MA programme.	Build stakeholder relationships face to face as much as possible, even if your primary form of communicating with them will be in writing. Build the relationships before you need to use them. Spend more time listening than talking and ask questions that	Brussels is full of networking events, some of which have a hard policy angle and others that are simply about mood setting and relationship building. Sign up and attend the ones that are relevant to you. If you are an extrovert, you will love building connections this way. If you are an introvert, it is a good chance to get out of your comfort zone by talking to new people. Brussels is the town of the 'no strings coffee'. Setting some up with peers or other stakeholders in your field is a good thing to do as it helps you to

		encourage people to explain their thinking on a position.	understand what makes people tick and means the pressure is off for you to have to 'sell' them on your position.
		Never get angry if people disagree with you. It is toxic and has the opposite effect to changing their mind.	Practise defusing phrases and use them if situations are getting heated. This may sound unbelievably cynical (as well as a bit tacky) but you can go far to calm a disagreement by telling someone you understand their position and/or you can see why they are concerned about yours.
		Test your position against theirs. If they are poles apart you may need to re-think what you are doing in order to make them meet.	Work on messages that create common ground with your target audience. Put simply, this is because you need to create a zone of acceptance for your audience to feel comfortable in. If your message and their goals are too far apart then it will be hard to match them up.

Key traits	Overview	Tips	Examples
Credibility	Credibility is about being taken seriously as a source of authority on an issue. This does not always mean being an expert in the conventional sense but rather that you are worth listening to on the substance. Or to put it another way, you cannot even think about being influential if no one else thinks it is worth paying attention to what you say.	Focus on quality not quantity of output.

Produce high quality evidence but do not expect it to be the decisive factor in decision making.

Write clearly: there are no prizes for being clever if no one understands you.

Do not sensationalise your case – the people you are trying to influence have high functioning bullshit detectors. | Work on how your organisation defines quality when it comes to producing materials that will contribute to the policy cycle. To be credible it should include a reliable evidence base and clear writing.

Make sure you have an in-house style guide. If nothing formal exists, build some minimum criteria so that you can be sure you are meeting those for any written materials that you are expected to produce for external audiences.

Avoid brinkmanship and inflammatory language unless you have a valid reason for using it. You can be interesting without being provocative and most policymakers in Brussels will stop taking you seriously if you consistently resort to scaremongering or wild exaggeration without anything to back it up. |

Key traits	Overview	Tips	Examples
		Inject your industry, NGO or sector's practical experience into the discussion.	Illustrate your position papers, reports, media op-eds and press releases with real examples. If you work in a trade association or network of NGOs, they are often the hardest to supply because the stories are distributed across Europe with your members, many of whom can be reluctant to share them. But it is worth persisting because real-world experience is like gold dust in Brussels and policymakers want to hear about it.
Discipline	If you want to influence policy in your favour you need to be disciplined, as it is a long- haul process that requires grit and perseverance. With so many variables and other players in the mix, the idea that you can intervene in the process sporadically and expect to help shape the outcome is fanciful.	Stick to the strategic plan you have developed (while building in scope for flexibility).

Focus on the quality not the quantity of your activities. If they do not advance your end goals, ditch them.

Be relentless: if something is a good idea do not allow inertia to kill it.

Do not change what you do every six months just because you are bored. No one is paying a fraction of the attention to what you do and say as you are. | Set up regular progress meetings where you check activities and completed work against the original plan. This is particularly important if you are managing other people's workloads as well as your own time.

Ask yourself if what you are doing is actually advancing your policy goals. If it is not, try to limit how much you get diverted into doing something that may end up being a vanity project for some of your members or clients. (NB – this is not always easy so it is a good exercise in diplomacy).

Find all the formal opportunities for pursuing your goals and seek out informal channels as well. Other people with competing ideas will be doing the same so it is not enough to submit a report or position paper and think that that is your job done.

If you have a clear message and a solid position, stick with it. The legislation may be moving so slowly that you may not get that many written input opportunities, meetings, speaking events or media interviews – so it is important to be consistent about your asks and recommendations. |

Key traits	Overview	Tips	Examples
Tactics	Strategy and tactics are often confused but they are not the same thing. Whereas strategy refers to an overall plan, tactics are the short-term actions that can help to achieve it. Tactical people cultivate the skills to work in the landscape they are in, not the one they want it to be. Of course, their overall intention is to shift the direction of policy in their favour, but they do it based on real-world, not ideal-world, conditions.	Make sure you know the difference between strategy and tactics before embarking on a planned course of action.

Pick activities that focus on real-world conditions but also steer the debate in the direction of your long-term goals.

Be flexible: sudden events may present short-term opportunities to advance your strategic goals even if they are not part of the formal plan.

Decide which issues you want to lobby on individually or as part of a group – different circumstances require different responses.

Differentiate between being influential and being visible: getting attention is not always the best way to achieve your goals. | Develop an action plan for your strategy with a detailed breakdown of activities, their objectives and the division of responsibility and tasks. Check it regularly for progress, not just in terms of tasks completed but impact made.

To the extent you can, pick activities that you can measure the impact of. Change your tactics if your metrics are not showing progress (but do not expect results straight away either).

Look for ways for your organisation or client to participate constructively in conversations (digital, policy, or media) that arise if events change and you have something relevant to say. Tweeting (constructively) or offering short media statements from your CEO can be effective ways to do this at short notice.

Some issues – particularly ones where the media are broadly friendly – are better campaigned on publicly and in coalitions. Others benefit from a more low-key approach. So, decide which issues fall into which categories and plan your activities accordingly. |

Key traits	Overview	Tips	Examples
Persuasion	Persuasiveness is a key pillar of influence but is not identical to it. Its role in lobbying is often overstated, largely because of the excessive attention given to silver tongued snake oil merchants in popular culture and the news media. While most policymaking input takes the form of written communication whether you are producing a technical study, advocacy report or position paper, you are still presenting an argument that you hope will convince your audience of the merits of your case and to act on your ideas. So, it needs to be persuasive	Read some books on persuasion – there's an army of psychologists, neuroscientists and communications professionals who have researched this topic and, while you may not be able to apply everything you learn, they will certainly be useful.	You can't go wrong by reading Book II of Aristotle's Rhetoric (you can read the whole thing if you want to, but it's hard work and Book II gives you what you need if you are pushed for time). In it Aristotle lays out five timeless principles, which have been influential throughout history and still form the basis of many of the most persuasive speeches and other written texts today. They are: 1. **Ethos or 'Character'** 2. **Logos or 'Reason'** 3. **Pathos or 'Emotion'** 4. **Metaphor** 5. **Brevity**
Ethos/ Character	Persuasive people use their own experience to build the case for why they are worth listening to and deserving of their audience's trust.	Do not flaunt your qualifications or boast about the size of your company. No one is impressed by arrogance for long.	Package your/your organisation's track record as a way of showing that you speak/write from a position of deep authority. This is a fine art as it is very easy to sound as though you are boasting if you are not careful.
Logos/ Reason	Logos is the rational argument you construct to convince your audience. It is often supported by statistics, evidence and facts: the hard proof that you use to appeal to your audience's 'heads'.	Make sure you have the right balance of the rational (facts) and the emotional (examples or stories) to back up your arguments.	Go through reports (both in-house and credible third-party ones) and mine them for useful facts and figures to strengthen your written work. Do not go for overkill – it is easy to overwhelm people with too much information. Focus on a few key bits of data and, where possible, put them in context or show how they illustrate a trend.

Pathos/ Emotion	Aristotle recognised that you also need to appeal to people's hearts as well as their heads in order to be persuasive. The best way to get people to care is through concrete examples and stories. But they must serve a purpose, i.e. to reinforce the argument you are trying to make.	Sort out your narrative before going public. If you do not have a clear storyline people will project their own (possibly less favourable) one onto yours instead.	Set up a story pipeline within your network. It is the hardest bit of doing advocacy in Brussels because all the impact is felt in Member States not Brussels itself. Case studies, anecdotes and hypothetical examples are good ways to illustrate your arguments and encourage your audience to engage with you in a way that is concrete, emotional and real.
Metaphor	Metaphors are under-used in Brussels but can be effective ways to communicate and illustrate an argument. Just remember that in a multinational environment like Brussels you have to be careful not to use culturally-specific metaphors that work well for some but may be meaningless (or worse) to others.	Design and test universal (not idiomatic) metaphors to frame the policy conversation in the way you want others to see it.	Seek inspiration from poetry, speeches and plays. It may be better do this in your mother tongue AND in English as we experience metaphor differently depending on our linguistic proficiency. Make sure you get feedback on what you have tried. Remember, you are trying to lead not follow a conversation, so it is important to make sure you are on the right lines.
Brevity	Humans have short attention spans. Influential people get to the point and do not waste words. They say or write just what they need to say.	Do not waste your audience's time: keep messages succinct and concise and get to the point.	Experiment with the inverted pyramid of journalism when structuring and writing your work for external (and even internal) audiences. Avoid pointless information and context when writing. Do not start writing until you know what your angle/messages are. You will quickly get lost otherwise. Stick to your word count or aim to undershoot it.

Source: Laura Shields

2. An EU Public Affairs Methodology

By Alan Hardacre & Aaron McLoughlin

Introduction

The objective of this chapter is to provide a **complete practical methodological framework to build and execute a successful public affairs strategy**. The chapter will separate out all the key elements required to pull together a public affairs strategy and explain them in detail. This structural basis will then provide the backdrop for the chapters on how to work with the EU institutions and decision-making coming later in the book. Setting out a clear and practical public affairs methodology is an essential first step to success. Only when one is able to sit back and assess every aspect of what one needs to do can improvements and additions be made. The chapter will provide practical guidance, examples and lobbying tools to bolster the methodology – ensuring that you can immediately make use of the guidance in your work.

> Whatever issue you are working on, no matter the context, there is always a need to prepare and structure your public affairs work. This is a critical thinking process that will help you build the right strategy for you. It will be based on:
>
> 1. Trying to find the best, most suitable and (cost) effective ways of achieving your objectives.
>
> 2. Making choices. Choices around what to do, how to do it and how much resource to allocate to what.

A fundamental starting point should be that **a successful public affairs strategy needs to be able to clearly demonstrate its value-added and return on investment (ROI)** to the organisation – allowing it to compete for resources and get the allocation required to be more successful in the future. This is the case whether for a trade association, company, or an NGO. It is our firm belief that a robust methodology helps demonstrate, and deliver, greater ROI.

There are many challenges to setting up a best-in-class public affairs strategy that is right for you. To start with, what is right for you at a given time and place may well be different to what is right for others, and also potentially for you at a later date or in a different situation. There is no one-size-fits-all strategy and no strategy is ever static – it needs to evolve with time and circumstances. Also no two lobbying campaigns are the same (in time or context); each time you seek to engage on something you will need to do so differently. You will therefore always need to adapt, based on a robust methodology.

In the EU context, you need to consider:
- the complexity of the European multi-level decision-making process and what your focus will be.
- the intense flow of information that has to be managed in order to capture meaningful insights and opportunities.
- the time constraints dictated both by your internal organisation and by the EU decision-making procedure - into which you will have to fit your actions.
- the need to conduct a large number of actions at the same time.
- and finally having to do all of this with, very often, limited resources (both human and financial).

These challenges make the setting up of your public affairs strategy complex. Our ambition is to present, explain and demonstrate how public affairs can usefully be viewed as **an end-to-end process**, starting from objectives and **key performance indicators (KPIs)**, running all the way through to how we evaluate our lobbying/campaigning success, enabling future learning and growth. Viewing lobbying as such a process allows us to isolate and perfect our understanding, and practice, of each individual component – and also, crucially, to understand the hand-offs from one part of the process to another.

This approach is vitally important in a profession that is ever evolving, creating a capacity to harness and understand how we can benefit from improvements. This approach:
- **Makes a lobbying strategy more complete**: because to be successful we need to deliver across a whole range of activities and not just one or two (often at the same time).
- **Makes a lobbying strategy more robust**: because it is based on strength across the process and not in just one or two areas.
- **Makes a lobbying strategy more adaptable**: because as internal and external events change it will be easier to understand what aspects of the lobbying strategy need to change – and the impacts that one change will have on other areas of the strategy.

The key phases in a public affairs strategy are outlined in Figure 2.1.

In a real life public affairs strategy, the phases and areas identified in Figure 2.1 are in practice rarely in the exact sequence presented here. Often many tasks are – indeed have to be – undertaken in parallel under severe time pressure and with limited resources, making the task even more challenging than it already is. Nonetheless, looking at a public affairs strategy as an end-to-end process allows us to identify best-in-class for each individual element and, crucially, to understand the hand-offs between them.

One example of this is that it is common to hear that developing a strategy is an art and not a science, and that there is no single solution and likely many differing ideas. This is true for some of the areas above but not all of them. Yes, there will be discussion about how to engage – but when it comes to preparation there are some things that you simply need to do and where you can be state of the art. We will explore this more.

An EU Public Affairs Methodology

Figure 2.1: Public affairs strategy: Three methodological phases & seven key areas

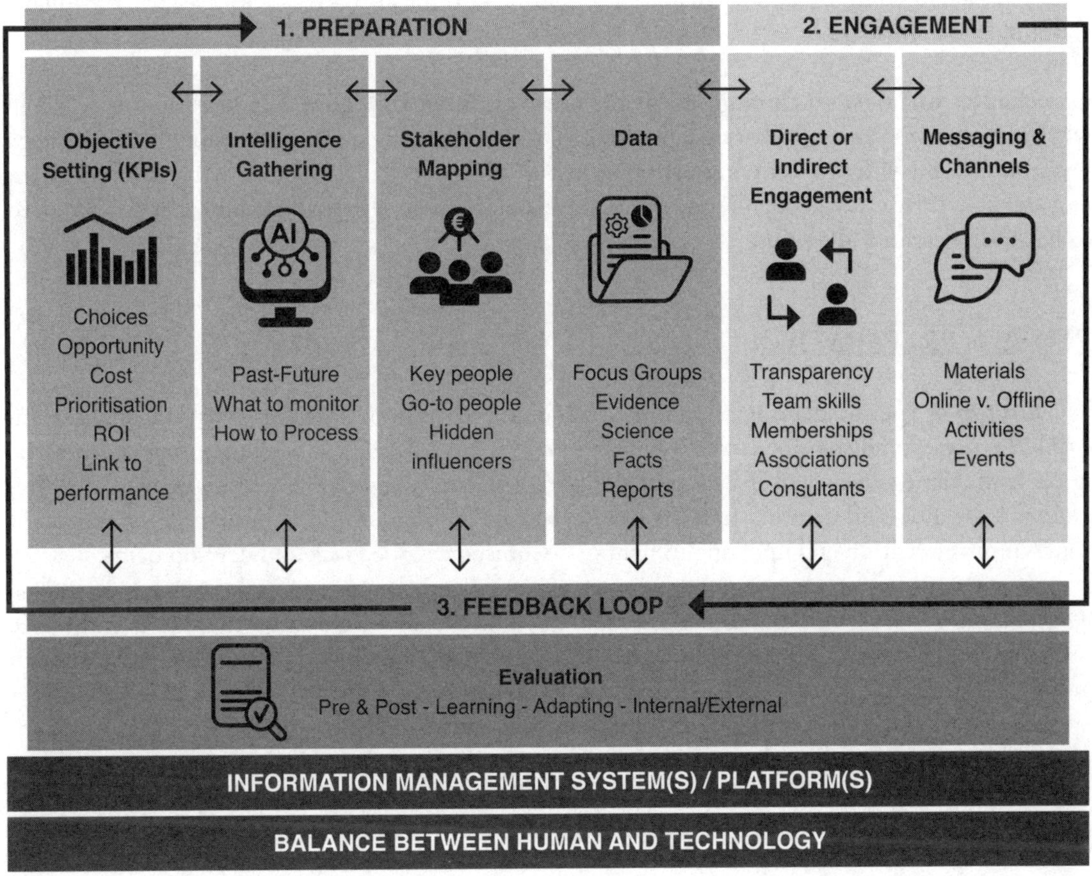

1. PREPARATION				2. ENGAGEMENT	
Objective Setting (KPIs)	**Intelligence Gathering**	**Stakeholder Mapping**	**Data**	**Direct or Indirect Engagement**	**Messaging & Channels**
Choices Opportunity Cost Prioritisation ROI Link to performance	Past-Future What to monitor How to Process	Key people Go-to people Hidden influencers	Focus Groups Evidence Science Facts Reports	Transparency Team skills Memberships Associations Consultants	Materials Online v. Offline Activities Events

3. FEEDBACK LOOP

Evaluation
Pre & Post - Learning - Adapting - Internal/External

INFORMATION MANAGEMENT SYSTEM(S) / PLATFORM(S)

BALANCE BETWEEN HUMAN AND TECHNOLOGY

Source: Martine Aunaas

As it starts to become clear from Figure 2.1, building a public affairs strategy will require a series of choices and will be dependent on resources. In essence this is at the heart of a public affairs strategy – the notion of opportunity cost. You can't do everything so you need to choose. Between providers of a service. Between target audiences. Between different types of event. It is always about how to best deploy resources to achieve what you want at any given moment bearing in mind the opportunity cost. Being able to effectively conduct a robust audit of each aspect of your lobbying methodology will help to drive change and the professionalisation of how you operate in the EU.

To be successful in EU public affairs it takes more than just money to drive an effective campaign. A stakeholder with ample resource, but a badly designed and executed strategy, can do more damage than good. In the same way a stakeholder with little resource but a well-tailored and designed strategy can achieve meaningful outcomes. Clearly, as will be highlighted time and again in later chapters, the earlier you engage with EU decision-making the better. Getting a robust strategy in place will equip you to engage at the right time – because the later you enter the game, the less your chances of success, no matter how good your strategy is.

Finally, another element for shaping your EU strategy is that EU decision-making is very much designed around compromise and shaping legislation. This means there is a long game, with many stakeholders, to be played.

The chapter will now go through all of the areas outlined in Figure 2.1, one by one, to detail why they are important and what best-in-class looks like. As the figure shows, a public affairs strategy begins internally with preparation, starting from objectives and KPIs, before moving to engagement and action to drive change. Finally, one needs to evaluate how things are going and what one achieved to be able to learn for the future.

PHASE 1: PREPARATION

The first part of a public affairs methodology is all about preparation. In an ideal world the preparation would be done in advance of engagement and action, but in reality everything often needs to be done at the same time – and in fact much of the preparation is ongoing and constantly evolving, and far from a one-off exercise. Indeed, every aspect of the framework is fluid and needs constant supervision, evaluation and updating in light of circumstances, feedback and developments.

This section will delve deeper into the setting of good public affairs objectives and key performance indicators as the bedrock for determining what success should look like. From there it will deal with getting the right monitoring and information gathering tools in place to ensure that you always have the right information at the right time to inform your choices. It will also look at the need to undertake, and constantly update, a stakeholder map so that you always know your target audiences and how to connect with them. Finally it will look at the need to have the right data and information, packaged in the right ways, to support your engagement and help you achieve your objectives.

These broad elements are required to build a robust platform for any engagement activities. Unlike engagement actions that we discuss later in the chapter, these preparatory elements are very much in your power to get right. You can control each of them and deliver best-in-class. And like any foundations, if you do not get them right you will be running risks ever after. Setting clear and realistic objectives gives you a platform, internally and externally, to deliver exactly what is needed. Putting into place the right monitoring and information gathering systems is essential and eminently possible no matter what your level of resourcing, so that you have no surprises in understanding everything related to your issues, as and when you need to. Stakeholder mapping and data development are also within your power to excel – again no matter your level of resource. Keeping track of your key audiences and continuing to develop better and more effective data allows you to ensure you have the right tools to do the job.

Every aspect of the preparation phase can be achieved by all stakeholders to a best-in-class level. Let us show you how.

1.1 Objective setting

For objective setting you will ideally have your strategy already in place and been able to evaluate previous, or ongoing work, to help you set your forward-looking objectives. This is not always the case. The more information, evaluation and context you have available the better. The reason we take it as a starting point is that the objectives and KPIs will be the foundation for the work needing to be done in the coming year – and, as such, act as the guiding light for your focus and thus how to act appropriately. Setting the right objectives that are realistic, attainable and clear and that will deliver for your organisation is not an easy task. Even more challenging can be how you then elaborate the objectives into KPIs to make progress tangible.

The **process of setting objectives** is the opportunity to establish criteria for the choice of priority issues and for robust dialogue within the organisation on what those priorities should be. This is a very important process to get right for several reasons – most notably because it will set targets and expectations that will then need to be delivered.

An EU public affairs office, function or even consultancy acts like an embassy for their organisation and the objective setting phase is a crucial moment of alignment and buy-in with the wider organisation. To build successful EU public affairs objectives you need to clearly understand the objectives of your organisation more broadly and in the EU. It is an opportunity that should be seized – and many of the tools below will help you do this with confidence. Investing time at this stage of the methodology is rarely time wasted.

Before getting into the details of both objectives and KPIs it is worth briefly returning to a broader point – that of the **return on investment (ROI)** that you are delivering for your organisation. This is a very good starting point in terms of two key aspects of what you want to achieve:
- Do you want to show to your organisation that you are delivering value for money?
- Do you want to be able to demonstrate your value in monetary terms? Reputational?
- How do you want to demonstrate your ROI? What does your organisation expect?

It is important from the outset to understand how you want to demonstrate your value to your organisation, both in terms of what the organisation expects and also in terms of what you yourself want. It is increasingly common for public affairs teams to want to show they generate bottom line success for their organisation – so they develop metrics to demonstrate their financial return. From this it is not a great extension to be able to show your ROI to the organisation by looking at what you deliver against what you cost. This exercise also tends to help your internal resource deliberations as you talk a language that is more familiar to your organisation – no matter whether it is a corporate or an NGO. Now trying to calculate the monetary value of your public affairs work is not an exact

> **ROI**
>
> The total people and non-people cost of your public affairs work must be financially exceeded (by whatever multiple you determine realistic) by your monetised achievements during the year / or over the course of a few years.

science and can be rather subjective, but it can prove to be a very valuable indicator of your success and value to an organisation. You just need to understand the impact that it will have on, or for, your organisation – which is something that should have come out when determining your priority objectives. There are both simple and complex ways to rank order your priorities:
1. You can attach a **financial value** to each priority and allocate your efforts based on the order they land in.
2. You can attach an **'importance ranking'** (of say 1-100) and get key stakeholders in your organisation to give ratings, allowing you to determine some order.

Both of these methods can be done by MonkeySurvey or in an Excel spreadsheet for feedback. The metrics, process and outcome will be key to engaging your organisation in a professional process to order priorities.

Once you have determined your approach to ROI and the priorities for your organisation you can move into setting objectives. Experience shows that having a limited number of objectives is ultimately likely to lead to greater success, because it provides greater focus. Pursuing too many objectives spreads your resource too wide and decreases your ability to deliver. From there mission creep is a constant threat. It infects many campaigns and leads to their failure because objectives get dropped, altered and expanded on a whim or due to developments.

You need to focus on what you agreed to do and on what is important. The more robust your prioritisation process the easier it will be to realign. With no real process in place you will simply move from one emergency to the next. So if you look to change or expand your objectives, you need to do it purposefully and make sure to set up formal roadblocks to stop mission creep.

Aiming for three to five objectives should be the target. Part of the initial conversation around objectives needs to be on how many can realistically be delivered given the resource available. Determining focus (what issues, how many) has important consequences for any resource discussions.

Any lobbying strategy must have clear objectives directly linked to, or cascaded from, the objectives of the organisation. The process of alignment and prioritisation needs to flush out what is important to the organisation. This obviously requires a good dialogue on what is happening and what is likely to happen (which is why you need good intelligence to be able to anticipate future developments). The elaboration of objectives is often then an iterative process, to be refined throughout the lobbying campaign.

The most obvious place to start with objectives is to make sure they are **'SMART'**. That is:

> **S**pecific (precise and concrete)
> **M**easurable (with solid KPIs – more on that later)
> **A**ccepted (by key internal stakeholders)
> **R**ealistic (something you can achieve)
> **T**ime-constrained (not just open-ended – linked to your reporting period)

Following these guidelines will go a long way to getting some solid objectives. Making sure you know the priorities will help you understand where to put your energy and resources when things get busy.

> **Good Public Affairs Objectives**
> - Focus on outcomes (not outputs)
> - Focus on impact (not quantity)
> - Tie in explicitly to organisational objectives
> - Have clear line of sight to financial implications if achieved (or not)
> - Build into ROI delivery

Failing to have clear and SMART objectives is one of the main explanatory factors behind many lobbying failures (too many objectives, lack of prioritisation, lack of clarity, misaligned expectations). The acid test needs to be: can your organisation understand the objective? If it cannot (and easily) then you will have problems down the line. Everything flows from these objectives – the choices you will make on every aspect of the lobbying process will be geared to deliver them. Aligned and universally understood and accepted objectives are the basic premise for any success. There are some key elements to consider when setting public affairs objectives. These are considerations that will need to be carefully taken into account and managed. They are:

1. **Realism**. It is important to understand from the start that you will likely not obtain 100% of what you (or your organisation) want. It is therefore important to rank your priorities in order to be able to adapt your lobbying strategy as you carry it out. Realism in your priorities is important to set expectations and allow for a fair evaluation of the actions taken later on. If your objectives are too extreme, inflexible or unrealistic you risk setting yourself up for failure before you even begin. For example, an objective in EU public affairs to 'stop legislation XX' is highly (statistically) unlikely to have any chance of success.

2. **Short-term v. longer-term**. The very nature of public affairs work is that the timelines are rarely well-defined and often well in excess of a 12-month planning and objectives cycle. Taking this into account is very important in ensuring that long burn issues get the right level of resource allocation through solid objectives. Here it is useful to develop objectives that are accompanied by clear milestones, i.e. key moments (internal and external) that you will use to gauge your progress towards your overall objective. It allows you to keep a multi-annual objective alive and relevant – and demonstrate your progress towards your objectives. If your goal is to change current policy, have the change incorporated into EU law, and effectively implemented on the ground you are looking at around a 7-10 year project horizon.

3. **Type of objective**. Public affairs work looks to achieve different goals for organisations at different times. Some are purely commercial. Some are reputational. Others can be about business development. Clearly the objectives need to differentiate and be clear on what is expected from the EU team/function and the objectives be set accordingly.

4. **Link to commercial priorities**. Exactly how you link to commercial priorities is not always immediately evident and can often take some time to understand. Investing the time to really think and articulate how the public affairs work in Brussels supports the commercial aspirations of the business will be time well spent.

5. **Resources**. This issue has already been alluded to. The objectives set have to take into account the resources at your disposal. Both the number of objectives and the nature of the objectives themselves are factors. Narrow and specific objectives are very different to wide-sweeping objectives to change legislation. Objective-setting is the time to have resource discussions in order to, once again, set expectations.

For all of these considerations, it is important to think how you incorporate the best information and data into the process of objective setting. The better your basis for discussions, the better your outputs will be.

So let's take some examples of **bad objectives**:
- Secure a favourable outcome to XX EU legislation
- Improve our reputation
- Stop XX Delegated Act

These objectives are either too vague, or lacking in clarity, or not linked to organisational priorities, or simply too ambitious. They also, between them, lack focus. It will be difficult to deliver against such objectives.

Good public affairs objectives should be more like:
- Achieve the following three (in priority order) outcomes in XX EU legislation
- Set up a robust monitoring and intelligence platform to ensure we capture everything of interest on XX issues at the right time – ensuring no surprises

Both of these objectives can be measured much more directly. They have focus. They can eventually be monetised to determine whether or not they are successful.

From the objectives you need to determine some key performance indicators. This basically means translating the objectives into deliverable actions – focused on outcomes and impact that you can follow throughout the year to understand where you are against your objectives. The KPIs should be much more tangible and action-oriented.

Bad KPIs would look like the following:
- Have at least 25 key stakeholder meetings
- Hold 3 events
- Column inches in a Tier 1 newspaper

These are easily remedied. You simply need to focus on *outcomes* to drive effective KPIs. So examples of **good KPIs** would be:

- Meet with top 15 identified key stakeholders (from continually updated stakeholder mapping). Be able to show tangible uptake of positions from these meetings in either written/oral questions, statements, public events, policy document etc.

- Hold an event that has at least 5 of our key identified stakeholders in attendance and from which we subsequently secure either better access, more shared information or uptake of our positions.
- Key decision maker publicly voices support for our position after reading Tier 1 newspaper.

These KPIs are more robust and produce a greater focus on effective outcomes. Too much of what happens in Brussels can seem to be box-ticking exercises against bad objectives and KPIs.

Finally we need to come back to something mentioned earlier in this section. Objectives and KPIs need to be reviewed on a quarterly basis or if some major event happens in order to keep them relevant, aligned and in keeping with the EU context. This is an exercise that should be conducted with your organisation and helps maintain the right alignment, understanding and expectations for your work in the EU.

Once you have your objectives and KPIs, and a robust process to keep them relevant, you can move into the next area of the public affairs methodology – monitoring and intelligence gathering.

1.2 Monitoring and intelligence gathering

Having laid out your objectives and KPIs, it is imperative to get the foundations of your public affairs strategy in place and on solid ground, and not on sand. An absolute keystone that you need to get right is the quality of the information and intelligence you gather and use. If your information and intelligence is not accurate or timely, or ignores political reality then it is unlikely that you will be able to build strong foundations that will survive the test of time and political scrutiny.

Fortunately, it is possible to build robust monitoring and intelligence gathering foundations without too much cost or hassle. There is no actual shortage of information. Sometimes, indeed, it feels like you are drowning in it. To avoid this, you need to set up a system to monitor the flow of intelligence and information. You need a system that deciphers the signals from the noise.

The goal is to read what is important and discard the rest. You can do this yourself, delegate it to a colleague, get a consultancy, or use management software to do it for you. A mix of options is the smart choice that will nail the sweet spot of a system that presents you with the right (verified) information ahead of time. This opens up the door to do something with it.

You don't have all day to review memos and information. Your colleagues and leadership certainly don't. So, the system can help you and your colleagues avoid cognitive overload. Swamping colleagues with 'stuff' and information is unpleasant and resented. It is too common and leads to all your advice being ignored.

At the start you need to set up filters to determine what goes in and what stays out. Your watchword should be for your system to inform on the key issues only – the priorities and objectives you have clearly determined before. If it does not do that, cut it. This falls on you. Don't delegate this task to an intern or junior. They don't know what you need to know.

Any system needs regular, say six-monthly, iterative updates. Check in with your colleagues getting the information. Is it what that they need? Is it too much or too little? Is it clear and well-presented? The monitoring and intelligence reports will constantly improve.

90% and more of the information you get that is in the public domain is reportage. It gives you background and the building blocks to go further. It tells you what happened or is going to happen. It helps you keep up to date on events and decisions made by others. But the real goal is to play a constructive role and influence decisions. That means a change of gear, from being an observer to becoming a participant. To play at this level, you need good political intelligence.

What to monitor

You will monitor the flow of information from a number of key public sources. Below is a practical list of the sources tracked. How much you check in with developments is up to you. Ideally, it is a mix of daily, weekly and monthly review. So the *basics* of what you need to monitor are the following:

News
Financial Times
POLITICO
EurActiv
Newspapers of record for your areas:
e.g. Chemical Watch, ENDS Europe
Key national press in your area

Services
VoteWatch Europe

Institutional
(a) European Commission
College meeting
College Agenda
College Minutes
College future items
Register of Delegated Acts
Register of Implementing Acts
Commission Press Releases
Commission Daily News
Commission Work Programmes
Better Regulation – Roadmaps etc.
Current Public Consultations
Feedback on Proposals
Feedback on draft delegated acts/ implementing acts
Submit ideas for REFIT
Directorates-General press releases and Twitter feed
Commissioner Twitter feeds

Institutional
(b) European Council/Council of the EU
Council Press Releases
European Council Agenda
Council – Working Party Agenda
Council – Coreper
Council – Agenda
Council – voting results
Council – the Council configuration you follow, e.g. Environment Council
Council – Voting calculator
Key Council stakeholder Twitter feeds

Institutional
(c) European Parliament
EP Legislative Observatory
Plenary agenda
EP Watch live
Parliamentary Questions and Answers
Twitter feed for key MEPs
Committees: For example,
the Environment Committee (ENV):
EP ENV Committee, EP ENV Newsletter,
EP ENV Meeting Agenda, EP ENV Meeting Minutes, EP ENV Voting Records, EP ENV Video record of meetings;
EP Political Groups News,
EP Political Group Twitter feed

Institutional
(d) Agencies
The work of the European Agencies is important in many areas. You will need to monitor their work. As an example we take the European Chemicals Agency (ECHA). In this case you could follow: ECHA News, ECHA RAC, ECHA RAC Meetings, ECHA MS Committee, ECHA MS Meeting, ECHA SEA, ECHA SEA Meetings, ECHA Twitter feed

Institutional
(e) European Court of Justice
European Court of Justice Press Release

As a rule of thumb, the best newspapers to follow are the same ones as the key officials and politicians in your area read. See more on this in Chapter 4 on working with the media and social media.

How to keep on top of the information

Keeping on top of this information is not a small undertaking. You can do this yourself, delegate it to a colleague, or contract a service provider – agency, issue monitoring service – to do this for you.

Table 2.1: Example annual monitoring costs

EU Monitoring Costs (Annual)	
Dods	€22.500
Media monitoring software	€33,000
Politico	€40,000
Agency	€30,000
Issue management subscription	€9,000 - €50,000
In-house monitoring	€24,000
Trade association membership	€20,000 - €150,000
Think Tank membership	€2,000 - €50,000
Politico event	€40,000 - €80,000

You need a flow of information to make informed choices. It is going to come largely from public domain monitoring, media updates (mainstream media, political press, trade and regulatory media, social media), raw political intelligence and analysis from outside counsel. As you see from Table 2.1, the core costs for memberships, subscriptions, and services are going to take an important chunk of any public affairs budget.

The shift from monitoring to political intelligence

The real goal is to play a constructive role and influence decisions. That means a change of gear, from being an observer to becoming a participant. To play at this level, you need good political intelligence. This is the key 10% but it is not a commodity and it is not easy to find.

Best Sources for Political Intelligence

Face to face meetings/ calls with MEPs, political staff, Commission, Perm Reps
Attend EP Committee meetings
Attend think tank policy briefings
Attend trade association working groups
Politico briefings
Outsource to agency (who have the contacts to get information for you)
Attend receptions

There is a direct cost and opportunity cost to getting this intelligence. Again, you can choose to do it yourself, delegate to colleagues, or outsource this. **The most valuable route is establishing your own network of key influencers and decision-makers.** This takes work to grow and maintain, however, and is going to take up a large chunk of your time. You are also going to have to provide useful information to secure useful information in return. This can be as simple as flagging to an MEP that one of their key issues is being worked on inside the Commission, or providing objective research to an official who follows that issue.

The real challenge of effective monitoring and intelligence gathering is that you need to fit this into your day-to-day work. You need to find the time to place calls, meet people, and summarise and read the flow of political intelligence in-between your internal meetings and calls and team management.

To get good political intelligence you first of all need to *listen to people*. This was underlined in Chapter 1 when looking at the value of active listening – its importance cannot be overstated. The challenge you will face is that many people have preconceived views about what is driving events. Confirmation bias afflicts many lobbyists, but you need to try and avoid it. Take the time to speak to the people making or influencing decisions and really listen to them. It is a good technique to get to understand what is driving events.

Secondly, *meet people*. The surest way to get good political intelligence is 'old school'. It is meeting and listening to the people making and influencing the decisions. You want to understand what is driving events, and the best way to understand is to meet people and listen to what they have to say. You will spend a lot of your time meeting officials, MEPs, their advisers, face-to-face. This can be done over coffee or lunch, but usually over the phone, getting their impressions of issues and events.

Thirdly, *become trusted*. The best political intelligence will flow to you if people trust you, and that requires a great deal of anoynmisation of your sources. The upside is that this does not involve too many people – as an initiative first develops, you are looking at around ten to twenty people. Once a file goes into the legislative machinery this goes up to 200-250 people, but to be honest the effective core is always around 25 key people. These are numbers anyone in sales would think on the low side. Having a working relationship with as many of the offices and individuals in your identified key 25 people will make monitoring and gathering intelligence much easier. Reaching out to them regularly and providing useful and timely information will make your work easier. As a rule of thumb, it makes sense to provide the key policy networks with ten useful pieces of information or insights for every question you put to them. There is a clear divide between getting political intelligence and lobbying for a position. It is useful to keep them for two separate conversations.

Acting on the information
You need to find the best way to sit down, read, understand and act on the information. Having the knowledge, but not having the time to act on it must be resisted. If you have important information early enough, it can change decisions. Understanding what is driving a decision or process is vital. After all, if the public affairs work is based on a series of false assumptions, ideas that could easily have been resolved at the start with good intelligence, it is unlikely that you will achieve your public affairs goals.

As an example you can see from the basic flow of decision-making in the Commission below a new policy idea goes through a period of germination before it ever becomes public.

Figure 2.2 : Policy ideation

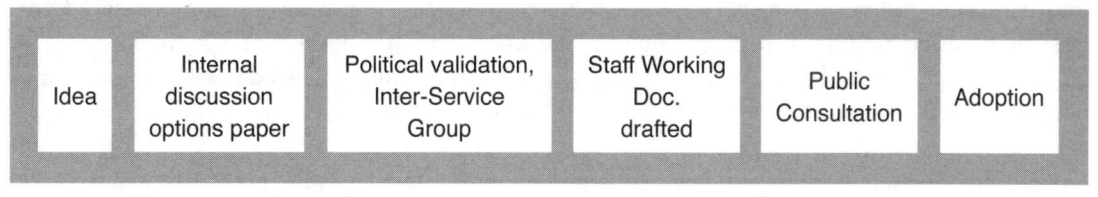

| Idea | Internal discussion options paper | Political validation, Inter-Service Group | Staff Working Doc. drafted | Public Consultation | Adoption |

Source: lucidchart.com (adapted)

The earlier you get political intelligence or monitoring about the issue, the more useful it is in helping to influence policy development. The opportunity to influence an idea decreases once it is firmed up inside the Commission and made public.

When is the best time to start monitoring and gathering intelligence?
You need to use a mix of good monitoring and political intelligence. Having one at the expense of the other is not going to help you in the short, medium or long term. Skimping on either will harm you. Good monitoring will show you the tell-tale signs that policy or political action is coming. There are veritable canaries in the mine that indicate that change is coming. For some areas, the tell-tale signs come as long as seven years out, but for most issues the direction of travel is clear at two years out. Good political intelligence will tell you an issue or story is about to be taken up by politicians and regulators, and when you need to act.

Despite a huge amount of flagging by the Commission or the Regulatory Agencies, many people only engage when a proposal is about to be tabled. When you step in late, your chance of changing the outcome in a significant way is limited. Having a good intelligence system that tracks political developments, policy and scientific journals of record can provide a good canary in the mine.

Some governments, companies, consultancies, trade organisations and NGOs have developed their own bespoke systems. They flag relevant developments that enable them to take action before the Rubicon is crossed. Despite this, most governments, EU and non-EU, industry and NGOs are frequently caught out by EU developments. When you look behind the shock and surprise you will normally find an inadequate monitoring system. Many organisations and governments have scarce resources and consider this policy wonkery an extra they can live without – when in fact it is the foundation the house is built on.

Making it readable and useful
Your monitoring reports and intelligence need to be clear, concise and actionable. You need to find a way to get actionable intelligence to your team and those paying for your work. Hoping that the information will flow by osmosis to the right people is a delusion. Indeed, just forwarding the raw information to colleagues is counter-productive – you need to re-package it. For example, Euro-English needs translating into plain English. Just forwarding a Commission Communication of 20 pages without providing a few lines saying why it is important to the reader, and what action to take next, is too common and often (if not always) leads to the message being deleted.

Outside the Brussels bubble, very few people are interested in EU public policy for its own sake. Even in Brussels, few people are focused on serious public policy. Remember that your colleagues outside Brussels do not care about political gossip and they don't want to receive long documents with no explanation clogging up their email. If the information is not clear, concise and relevant, do not send it.

Furthermore, the information needs to be easily accessible. Any information system needs to pass the Sunday afternoon test. An ideal is to get hold of the state of play on an issue in around two minutes. Most traditional issue management is done by a mix of the monthly report (Word or Excel), daily email, and bi-annual trend analysis. It fails the Sunday evening test.

Quorum and FisacalNote allow all colleagues to get access to the information, feed in updates, and understand what's happening in near real-time. Politico are entering this market too because they see the value in providing this service.

The sweet spot gives you a mix of timely, credible high-quality information that has a predictive quality. It tells you what is going to happen, and why it is happening, and gives you a window of opportunity to change events.

1.3 Stakeholder mapping

Decisions are taken by people and not by institutions. This means that if you want to influence public policy and political decisions, you need to know at all times who the most important people making and influencing those decisions are. Understanding the confluence of connections at work is key to influence the decisions.

Chris Rose, in the NGO campaign bible, *How to Win Campaigns*, details the core reason for preparing a genuine stakeholder map:
'A campaign might come down to wanting to influence one individual, or even to influence one individual to influence another' (p.116, 2nd Ed).

As highlighted in the last section, the number of key people involved in any particular file is actually relatively low. We noted that as a rule of thumb around 250 people will work on, and influence, an ordinary legislative proposal, but only around 25 of them will be key. It is not hard to meet with (the offices of) most of this reduced list of key people. All successful legislative and policy campaigns come down to knowing the right people making and influencing a decision, then stepping in at the right time, and with the right information, to get support. It does not happen by chance – and the key foundation that is **stakeholder mapping** is crucial. As with intelligence gathering, it is eminently possible to do this well no matter what your resources. This is another preparatory phase so that you can be best-in-class. Let us explain how.

What is the best system to prepare your stakeholder mapping?
Your stakeholder mapping is going to include a list of decision-makers and influencers, including: key officials, politicians, advisers, journalists, academics, think tanks, experts, and important business and not-for-profit players.

The mapping can take many forms. At its heart, it is a list of people making and influencing a decision along with their publicly available contact details. How long it takes to do depends on how deep you want or need to dive. If you go Europe-wide, it can take around 5-8 hours to prepare. If it is just Brussels, then it will be shorter (25 or so people) so 1-3 hours would be enough. It will be time well-invested.

EU GDPR and Stakeholder Mapping

All of your EU Public Affairs activities need to be EU GDPR compliant – that is with EU data protection laws. Nowhere so is that more the case than with stakeholder mapping – which whilst a standard practice in public affairs, as you gather information about stakeholders, is also one that can stray across the line.

In simple terms, for your stakeholder map to be compliant you need to use only information obtained from public sources such as social media, websites, the media or public hearings.

Today, many still use Excel or Word, which works fine. Then you can also use Customer Relations Management (CRM) software to log people and interactions. And finally you can use dedicated IT platforms for Public Affairs such as Quorum and FiscalNote, who provide stakeholder engagement systems that allow you to prepare insightful stakeholder mapping. You will find more detail on this in the next chapter on Information Management for Public Affairs.

A promising tool is **Social Network Analysis**. This looks to uncover the patterns and connections between people's interactions. It provides a clear way of identifying political connections and networks. Good examples of social network analysis can be found on the website of Vienna-based strategy consultancy FAS (www.fas-research.com) and on the Politico site: www.politico.eu/interactive/lobbyists-brussels-social-network-meetings-commission-strategy

Key officials and politicians
You can identify the key decision-makers and influencers in many ways and then map the key individuals as required. From this list you can then identify those who influence them in a form of concentric circles. Your resources will determine how far out you want to reach in these circles – because you are mapping ready for action not as a creative exercise. So for example your mapping could start with a Minister or Commissioner and then move out through political advisers, cabinet members, key civil servant(s) (director, policy adviser, desk officer). The good thing is that most of this information is online and freely available – all you need is an understanding of the central key players and some time.

The organisation chart will not tell you who all the key players are. In practice, officials and politicians tend to defer to the advice of a desk officer or group adviser. Likely these names are not on an organisation chart. These are the officials and political aides that the key decision-makers go to for advice, the so-called hidden persuaders.

> **The Hidden Persuaders**
>
> Hidden persuaders often hide in plain sight as you will see them in public meetings and in records of meetings. They are people that politicians and senior officials go over to for a quiet exchange of words. They ask their advice and usually follow it; their influence does not depend on their title. They are the players sought out for their expertise and they are trusted by many. The machinery of political and policy-making depends on them so if you do not know who they are in your area, ask around.

Journalists, academics, and think tanks

Journalists, academics, and think tanks also play an important role in the EU. Some journalists and think tanks in your area of interest will have a significant following, reach and ultimately influence. This influence is often at a national level, although some like George Monbiot have their message taken up in other countries.

Academics and think tanks often have a symbiotic relationship with government and policymakers. Mapping them is therefore a good (and often required) option. You need to find the key academics who are already, or could become, engaged on your subject.

> **A Hidden Persuader**
>
> George Monbiot is a Guardian newspaper columnist and author. His columns are widely read throughout Europe.

The best way to get hold of this political decision-maker and influence map is to ask the issue lead in the Commission's Cabinet. They'll know the key officials at the Brussels and national level working on a file. Often this will be down in an Excel file itself or within an email chain. It is also likely to contain the key influencers – journalists, academics and think tanks. The easiest way to get hold of it is if you support the Commission's position and are helping them.

Key players on an issue will often communicate with each other via WhatsApp groups. If you come across such a group on your issue, you'll know most of the key stakeholders.

> **Farley File**
>
> It is useful to keep a Farley file. This is named after James Farley, who served as Franklin D. Roosevelt's campaign manager. He kept a file on everyone the President ever met – something many politicians do today. You should have a file on all your key stakeholders: for example, their public statements and voting record on your issues, when you last met, and their stated position.

You can connect with key decision-makers and influencers by harnessing your existing network. It is likely that even if you do not know some of the key players, you know someone who does. This is the value of the Social Network Analysis highlighted earlier in the chapter. The technique is used to look at key figures who influence votes in the US Senate and it is useful for identifying likely political allies and opponents.

NGO campaigners often deploy this tool. Practically, if you need to get a position to one person and know someone they trust, send it to that person. They can pass it on. Overall you can work out your political connections both on paper and by AI. A mix of both is good.

Using your network
You need to harness the connections that your organisation, colleagues and network have. This network is often the most useful, so you should make use of it. Maybe a colleague's father is going to spend a weekend with an old friend who happens to be the prime minister of a government whose position you want to change. Maybe a short briefing note for the father to assist any conversation is a better use of your time than a letter direct to the prime minister. Perhaps a colleague's sister is the new foreign minister of a government whose support you need. If the sister meets with government officials they may be more receptive to listening than if you met them. Perhaps an MEP whose support you need is on the advisory board of a think tank you are closely aligned to. Maybe you are a regular at the same church? Your connections are broader than you think.

Using technology and data to find the real picture
Technology like AI provides added objectivity. For example, VoteWatch Europe can help identify 'politically connected' MEPs and governments. These are politicians and governments who act as catalysts and bring along others to vote in the same way. Data analysis often reveals undercover political correlations that are not obvious on the surface – but more of this in the data section later in the chapter. Seasoned political players can provide much of this information because they instinctively know the non-public political alliances. Many may claim to have this insight yet only a few do. Data, on the other hand, tends to reveal the existence of, if not the reason for, alliances.

Some practical advice on using stakeholder maps:
1. With your stakeholder map you need to have a good idea of who is going to oppose you, who will support you, and who is undecided. Focus on the 'undecided'. Many lobbyists like to spend time with their allies, but this is a waste of scarce time and resources. This group of MEPs and governments are backing you come what may. Work with them to get political intelligence and win over the undecided.
2. Many lobbyists like to try and convert opponents. This can be a thankless task. Professional courtesy dictates that you should send them your position paper, but no more. Don't spend your time trying to convert them to your position because the chances of it happening are limited.
3. Your stakeholder map should also be useful to help you identify people to carry your message. Often it is better for a 'trusted expert' to speak up for your interest, rather than yourself. Trust is a rare commodity in politics and public policy, so if a respected expert supports you, and wants to speak up for your cause, let them.
4. You need to use social network analysis. You need to know not only your target audience, but also the connections they have to each other.

5. The best way of building your stakeholder map is a combination of AI – a system such as Quorum or FiscalNote – and human interaction.

One final element of stakeholder mapping that we need to mention is the visual element of mapping and how useful this can be to both understanding your situation and also to presenting the information as and when required. Most detailed stakeholder mapping is done in Excel simply because this can hold all of the data you need – it is functional. But when it comes to *presenting* the data, then you can look at different ways. For example in the graphic below you can see the key people presented in concentric cicles – a good idea to help you focus on your core targets.

Figure 2.3 Graphic stakeholder mapping

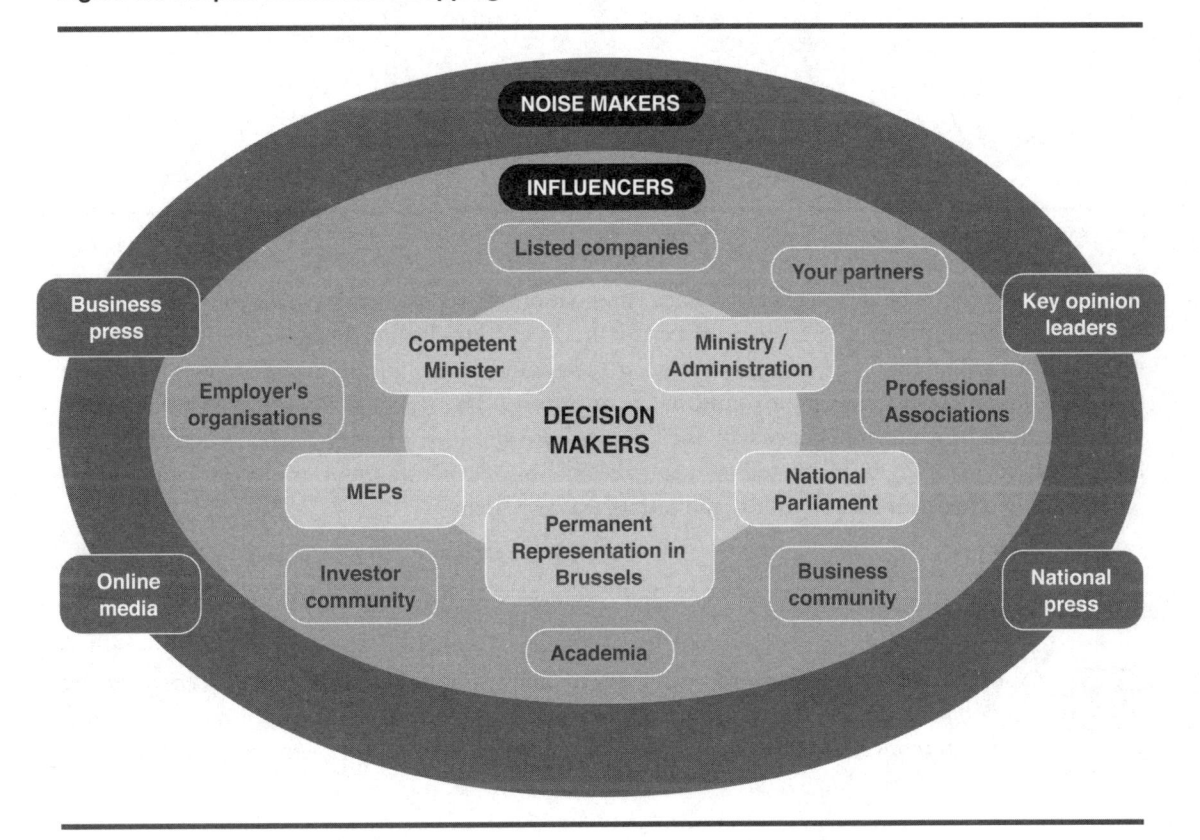

![Graphic stakeholder mapping diagram showing concentric circles with DECISION MAKERS at the center (Competent Minister, Ministry/Administration, Permanent Representation in Brussels), surrounded by INFLUENCERS (Listed companies, Your partners, Professional Associations, National Parliament, Business community, Academia, Investor community, MEPs, Employer's organisations), and outer ring of NOISE MAKERS (Business press, Online media, National press, Key opinion leaders)]

Source: Hill & Knowlton (adapted)

Another common way of presenting stakeholder mapping is by using a twin axis of influence and interest as in Figure 2.4.

Figure 2.4: Mapping by influence and interest

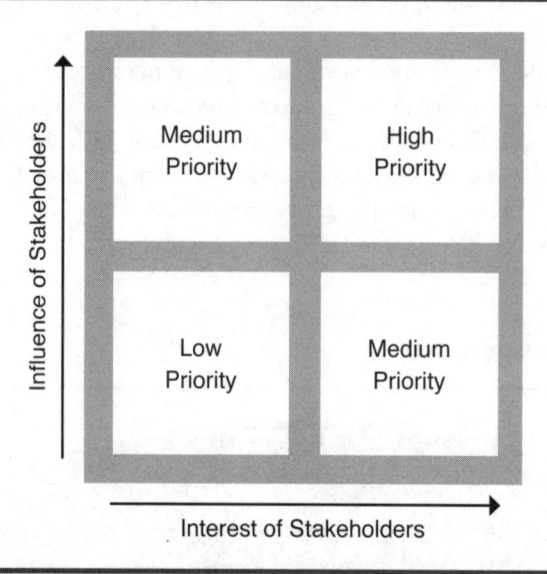

```
         ↑
         │  ┌──────────┐  ┌──────────┐
  Influence│  │  Medium  │  │   High   │
    of    │  │ Priority │  │ Priority │
Stakeholders│ └──────────┘  └──────────┘
         │  ┌──────────┐  ┌──────────┐
         │  │   Low    │  │  Medium  │
         │  │ Priority │  │ Priority │
         │  └──────────┘  └──────────┘
         └─────────────────────────────→
              Interest of Stakeholders
```

Source: Alan Hardacre & Aaron McLoughlin (adapted)

In this instance you would chart the influence you believe a stakeholder to have on your issue against the interest they hold in it. As you can see this leads to four distinct boxes into which you can place your stakeholders. The bottom boxes cover stakeholders you consider to be of low to medium influence which is why they are low and medium priority. The upper boxes are stakeholders who you estimate to be influential hence why they are medium and high priority. Such a visualisation can bring an Excel mapping to life and allow you to see the bigger picture for your engagement – and it will certainly bring it to life for your organisation/team or client.

1.4 Data

'Use tools to collect data and process it into conclusions and actions. Foster an environment of confidence and fairness by having clearly-stated principles that are implemented in tools and protocols so that the conclusions reached can be assessed by tracking the logic and data behind them.' Ray Dallio

The data-driven approach of Bridgewater Associates is not yet mainstream in EU public affairs. These tools are more common in law firms and the financial services industry, but they are now rapidly gaining an important foothold in public affairs in the USA.

Statistical tools and data mining are being employed by organisations like VoteWatch Europe to provide insightful analysis on how the Member States and MEPs vote. Looking at previous similar voting records is an underused but powerful predictive tool. So far VoteWatch Europe only monitors the votes in the European Parliament Plenary and in Council. However, not all votes in Plenary are roll call votes, so you do not know how each MEP voted on every issue. In the Council decision-making is by consensus, so this is also limited. When it comes to, for example, voting in secondary legislation committees it is even more difficult to get an immediate read out. Clearly there are some limitations to data here.

It is best to supplement the sober power of numbers with raw political intelligence – as discussed in the previous section. The best source is speaking to the people behind the vote or in the room when the vote happened. Politico and the FT tend to have a privileged insight into the votes in Council and Committees.

Despite any impression that 'your issue' is unique, it is likely to be similar, if not near-identical, to a previous vote. Checking previous votes gives you a good indication of how any new vote may go. If you want to dive deeper and look at all governments' positions in detail, use the EU's freedom of information rules. Just ask for all the documents for a given piece of legislation after the file is concluded. Be clear that you want the documents 'in their full and unredacted form'. For one Directive, this is likely to give you around 70 documents from a one to two-year period. This way, you'll be able to identify the positions of the Members States, the European Parliament and the Commission. The positions are clear from the negotiating documents and the files give both the reasons and reasoning. These reasons and reasoning do not tend to change that much over time, so this sort of intelligence is invaluable and freely available to anyone with the diligence to ask for it and the time to process it.

Keeping a record of votes on your key issues is also useful. A mix of watching the Committee votes, first-hand intelligence, and tracking roll call votes, will give you an unerring ability to predict future similar votes.

An emerging trend, though not yet generally observed in Brussels, is to deploy AI to provide predictions on regulatory decisions and votes. VoteWatch is the major player today. This has much promise. Using VoteWatch for a customised analysis at the very start provides an accurate estimate of the political feasibility, likely alliances, and winning arguments.

The main advantages of such data are:
- It helps **identify in advance if your issue is winnable or unwinnable**. This makes it a good resource and expectation management tool. It is true you may want to fight on principle and ignore political reality, but this rarely tends to change the outcome. The main beneficiaries are the consultancies who you will employ to do a lot of the work.
- The data allows you to **micro-target swing votes** (the undecideds you identified in your stakeholder mapping for example). You do not need to focus your time on getting support from those MEPs and Member States who are going to back you, no matter what, or vote against you, no matter what. Data enables you to identify the undecided and they are the votes you absolutely need.

These two advantages alone should be the reason to invest and use data heavily. They are available to everyone and they can make a huge difference to your chances of success. It is important to clarify that *what you are looking to win is a numbers game*. The ultimate goal is not looking to win the debate or convert opponents into allies, but actually about getting the majority you need. In this direct sense, data helps you identify, often far in advance, whether you have the votes or whether you are living a pipedream.

Over time, predictive software and data will become more accurate, and make the vital role in public affairs of understanding the 'likely outcome' more objective and accurate. This is already available in Washington DC and soon will be in Brussels and national capitals. A large part of the mystery, or snake oil sales pitch, will be overtaken by cold hard data.

PHASE 2: ENGAGEMENT AND ACTION

The previous section of this chapter has focused extensively on the first three areas of a public affairs methodology, all of them part of phase 1, your preparations. Getting each of those elements right is an essential platform for then moving on to the second phase, that of engagement and action – although we do again need to stress that this rarely happens sequentially; often every element of the public affairs process is live all the way through. It is more a case of ensuring that when you come to planning an external engagement and action that you are prepared – that you have some basis for your decisions.

We said that the preparation phase is something that is intrinsically under your control and that anyone can excel at, no matter their level of resources. There is process and structure involved in the preparation phase, which means it lends itself to a public affairs preparation audit that should be able to highlight deficiencies and gaps. But when it comes to *engagement and action*, it is a very different story. In the realm of HOW you achieve your objectives things become very subjective and it is very difficult to determine whether one idea has more merit than another. Ask three experienced public affairs practitioners how they would deal with a certain situation and you would likely get three (all very good) different ideas. So here the elements of experience and choice comes to the fore.

Finding the most (cost) effective ways to connect with your key audience is very difficult. In theory it is quite simple. You need to convince 25 key stakeholders of your position and see it advanced into legislation. In practice, this situation likely plays out over 12 to 36 months, your voice is one of hundreds and you may only get to meet directly with (say) three of your key stakeholders.

How, in this maelstrom, do you achieve your objectives? Well, there are many ways and this section will outline the series of choices you face in going about this. Much more than in the preparation phase you will face conflicting choices and always need to consider the opportunity cost of one action against another. It is also here that budgets can escalate quickly – as you will see when referencing the costs attached to many of these choices. Engagement and action in a direct simple sense can be very cost effective, but as this is so difficult it often needs to be supplemented to increase the chances of success.

Finally, with regard to the engagement and action phase of the public affairs process, it is important to highlight the importance of **timing**. Quite simply, the earlier the better. Once the EU institutions have defined a position and are in full flow, it is very difficult to get your voice into the debate and propose alternative solutions and compromises. Even a well-developed, sequenced, and planned public affairs campaign will only bear fruit if it starts on time. Last minute panic (reactive) public affairs is rarely ever successful.

In an ideal world you would always be engaged in **proactive lobbying**, i.e. working for future actions and changes. This is actually quite rare because the resource required to focus on structuring the future debate around your own priorities is large and an investment that many organisations are not willing to make. You need solid thought leadership to bring new ideas and directions to the EU institutions – and you need patience as it is a process that can take years – hence the investment required.

This is a broader issue of how an organisation views public affairs (as a cost centre or as an investment arm), but suffice it to say that most organisations tend to (under) use their public affairs function to manage more current and immediate initiatives and circumstances. This is what we would consider to be more **reactive lobbying**. All of the choices in this section can be deployed in the service of either proactive or reactive public affairs, the only difference being the point at which they are deployed and the objectives they are designed to serve and deliver.

We will now discuss the different benefits and challenges of **direct versus indirect engagement**, starting with direct engagement.

2.1 Direct engagement

The first place to start when it comes to engagement is that if you want to be listened to, you need to be in the Commission's **Transparency Register**. If you are not, officials and politicians won't meet you. Despite this being obvious, some interests are not registered. The main requirement to register is to declare how much you spend on lobbying. The other requirements are not onerous and reflect common sense. Simply put, if you want to move to engagement in the EU, you need to be in the Register.

The most obvious, and effective, way to promote your case is by meeting the key officials, politicians and political aides who are drafting the policy and law you are working on. It is often possible to get meetings with them or their offices and it's easy to try. Phone them up or email and ask for a meeting. There is no better way to get your position co-opted than meeting the people who have the power of the pen.

A good lobbyist will spend around half of their time in external meetings with officials, politicians, political aides and influencers. This is the easiest and most effective way to have your position and text appear in the final policy or legislative text. There is something almost primal in seeing if your position has the legs to stand by getting face-to-face feedback. Stakeholders will give you live and direct feedback, ask for proof points, that will help you seal their support or not. If they look up at the ceiling, cross their arms, or spend the meeting working on their phone and not looking at you, you know your message is not getting through.

Face-to-face meetings
A face-to-face meeting is simply the best test of the strength of your case. If it's weak you can go back and reflect and adapt your case. You can bolster proof points, remove weak points that do not resonate, and through an iterative process improve your chances of winning. This is what we alluded to earlier in the chapter: no strategy is ever static, it needs to evolve based on the feedback you receive. This feedback can also lead to you tweaking your stakeholder map and your intelligence gathering so as to be better prepared in the future.

The use of the one-on-one meeting is perhaps seen by many as 'old school' – a relic of a bygone era of lobbyists. Many seem to think that you can influence policymakers, legislators and influencers by modern-day telepathy. Today, too much time is spent in internal meetings agonising over tactics, strategy and approach, with the obvious consequence that all this takes the place of face-to-face meetings and calls with key decision-makers. Internal meetings are of course required to hammer out internal positions that achieve a consensus, but these positions may fall flat outside the organisation if they do not have enough real-life input from the key stakeholders. One-to-one meetings have innumerable values in engagement and should be used for all the benefits they provide, as listed in the box below.

Benefits of face-to-face meetings

1. You'll get a direct answer to the question you raise.
2. Writing is an imperfect medium of communication.
3. It is claimed that 7% of communication is verbal, and 93% non-verbal. This helps you pick up most of what is being communicated.
4. You can provide a clear answer to any questions raised.
5. They can tell you the real reason driving decisions.
6. If you listen, you can have a dialogue.
7. You can understand better if your objectives are realistic.
8. Meetings are one of the key steps in building trust between people.
9. Often, in the last minutes of the meeting, or when you are leaving, you'll be told something important.
10. You will get more high quality and actionable information and intelligence during a face-to-face meeting than anywhere else.

How lobbyists are viewed
Europe does not have the tradition of the US Political Action Committees. There is no financial link between politicians' votes and donations to their election war-chests. Financial donations to political parties are heavily regulated in the EU and actually, in most countries, banned. Raising the prospect of a political donation will, at the very least, tarnish your case.

It is useful to look at how officials, MEPs and political aides view lobbyists. They are likely to have mixed feelings about dealing with you. Either you will be seen as a mercenary for narrow interests or as the bringer of welcome and needed facts and data.

You are, at root, asking officials and politicians to use their good offices to advance your objectives. If you are exceptionally well-informed, pleasant, and seen as representing important constituency interests – and if you provide useful data and perspectives that spare them the need to research – you will have influence. After all, you argue on behalf of real people, entities and interests who are going to be affected by legislative action. Your aim is to be seen as an expert, as someone who is informed about the process, the issue, and the politics. You want to be someone who can clearly present their case, is listened to and called upon. You need to be trusted by your audience. Trust is won by civility, expertise and following up, when you have promised it, with additional information. Trust also extends to keeping confidences and never revealing sources. It is easily lost.

Skills you need for direct engagement
In terms of skills, it is key to be pleasant and enjoy working with officials and politicians. If you don't, you should consider another role in the public affairs world. Officials and politicians often switch sides from support to opposition because of real or imagined slights from rude representatives. There are also some traits that representatives can't have. Speaking ill of others is taboo. Brussels is too small a place and you are likely to be accidentally speaking to someone about one of their friends.

If you sense a meeting is going wrong, close it down quickly, give your apologies and leave. Never get baited into an argument, and if an argument gets out of hand, stop. Raised voices in meetings harms political interests. It is smart to put a colleague new to lobbying through a simulated meeting and see how they perform. If they are a gibbering wreck of banality and rudeness, take them off the front line. It's good to record the training so they can then see their Jekyll and Hyde personality.

Letting people out of the door to represent you unchecked or uncoached is high risk. Just because somebody worked as an official or a political aide doesn't mean they are a good lobbyist. You should accompany them a few times to meetings with Commission and Perm Rep officials, MEPs and their staff to see how they perform in prime time. Check how your colleague gets the case across and deals with questions. The only real measure is, are they persuasive? Persuasiveness comes down to whether your audience supports you, or at least, choose to moves from voting against you to abstaining – a topic covered in Chapter 1.

If your lobbyist doesn't meet your self-imposed quality bar, pull them back. If you receive negative feedback from both friends and opponents about the behaviour of your lobbyist, have a serious think about whether you need to redeploy them. An organisation represented by a discredited lobbyist carries a political millstone around its neck.

Often organisations divide the roles of lobbying the European Commission, Perm Reps, and European Parliament. The real benefit of this guild-like demarcation is unclear. A good lobbyist should be equally at home dealing with a politician, political aide, Commission official or Perm Rep official.

Who to bring to the meeting
There may be a need to bring along a technical expert to meetings. They will be there more to answer questions than to speak at length. They'll add weight to a solution and provide authority to support the case. You should coach experts beforehand – notably on being concise and not so technical that they lose their audience. In many ways, experts need to see themselves as translators – turning difficult subjects into easy (and quick) to understand issues for policy makers.

CEOs often delight in providing advice to officials and MEPs. It is often too general to translate into concrete legislation. Their travel schedule often dictates that they come in too late in the process, often after the draft law is drafted, and key policy asks locked in. Their powers of persuasion tend to be weaker with politicians and officials who don't directly report to them. Unless they have a direct and substantial constituency interest, their intervention may raise more questions than it answers. There are some 'rock star' CEOs who people will change their schedule to meet, but they are a rare breed. If your CEO is one, use them.

2.2 Indirect engagement

Direct engagement is rarely enough in the EU, for a variety of reasons that differ between stakeholders. One thing that is common for all stakeholders though is that memberships can help support, bolster and add value to your engagement. It is for this reason that they are so important. It might even be said that in some cases memberships actually replace an organisation's own engagement. So you have a number of choices when it comes to memberships. We will look at the most important ones here.

Trade associations can provide you with a valuable source of intelligence and a vehicle to promote your message. They offer dedicated issue coverage and a place to gather intelligence from other stakeholders. They are also often the first port of call for policy-makers who want a quick overarching 'industry' position that is easiest to get from an association. At the same time trade associations offer organisations a sense of anonymity (as they offer a way of acting indirectly) as well as a sense of strength in numbers. Simply put, for many, trade associations are an essential public affairs vehicle in Brussels.

Trade associations can offer a significant number of advantages. One obvious advantage is that some trade associations are going to be able to open doors that an individual stakeholder will find closed, so their staff can take your message forward. Also, many provide members with excellent political intelligence and monitoring, so they can become an integral part of your preparation phase. They also often have experts on their staff who focus on specialised areas, making this expertise available to you at a fraction of the price you would have to pay elsewhere.

On the other hand, to be harnessed properly, you need to invest substantial sweat equity in a trade association. This involves drafting positions, attending committee meetings, and promoting your point of view. You need to decide how much time you are going to spend in your association because it can amount to a full-time job and possibly even cost as much as one. There is almost always a membership fee and this ranges from perhaps a thousand euros to hundreds of thousands. If you are a member of several trade associations, the bill can become significant and your workload unmanageable.

After trade associations, Brussels houses many excellent **think tanks**. Bruegel, EPC, Friends of Europe, CEPS are amongst some of the leading ones. They impart an intellectual rigour to the public policy debate in Brussels. As such, when your interests align, they are excellent vehicles to promote policy debate. They are useful in keeping your finger on the pulse of the policy and political debate on your files, and many people use them to develop their network and to meet key decision-makers and influencers. Active participation comes at a surprisingly reasonable fee – although bespoke research and reports obviously cost more (into the tens of thousands).

Some Commission departments, the European Political Strategy Centre, and even Commissioners seem to align themselves to certain think tanks. These think tanks often trial policy options and undertake the research that is taken up in Commission proposals. Identifying these linkages is easy to do. You just need to speak to the key officials and politicians working on your files and ask them who they read, listen to and respect. You will come to understand that think tanks are often the drivers of new legislative ideas: i.e. their influence shows in shaping upcoming policy in a very proactive sense.

Think tanks are rarely knee-deep in the end of a legislative file when the debate has closed down – they are active early, when the debate is open and rigorous. This is an important distinction in considering how you spend your resource in Brussels. If you want to influence policy early (agenda-setting and proactive lobbying) then a think tank is a very good choice. If you need ongoing policy intelligence and extra lobbying support then a trade association is a better option.

No matter what your level of resource or experience you will usually, at some point, have recourse to **consultancy support**. Sometimes the amount of work you are doing is too much and you need to bring in expertise and assistance, and quickly. Sometimes you just need access to certain stakeholders or you need a second opinion on a high-investment strategy you want to undertake. Fortunately, Brussels has a small army of consultancy lobbyists, estimated at around 25,000, to help you. They range from the powerhouse consultancies to the one-man/woman offices. They can be generalists or they can specialise. For these reasons their fees vary enormously. Logically the cost of consultancy support – for monitoring, strategy, preparation of slides, meeting schedules, engagement, hosting events – has a large scale.

Retaining a consultant has the advantage that as soon as the issue is resolved, you can stop the work. If you hire staff, you have less flexibility in hiring and firing. A public affairs consultant will often have a greater political network that allows you to identify stakeholders in your field objectively, or a specialised skill that you don't have. The best use of a consultant is as a trusted advisor to test your strategy and ideas. If you hire a political consultant who is an expert in your given field and has a track record of winning for their clients on the issue, you can then tap into their experience and network. You don't have to start from the beginning.

A political consultant may also provide you with insights and access you or your team do not have. You are then bringing on board a specialist to help diagnose your problem(s) and recommend a course of treatment. You are free to take their advice or not, and if you are not qualified to do what is necessary, you can use their assistance. Few people have successfully, alone, taken their issues from Ordinary Legislative Procedure all the way through to Delegated and Implementing Acts. If you face that challenge, are you prepared to go it alone? In fact, can you do it alone? After all, the sentiment that 'a man who is his own lawyer, has a fool for a client' crosses over to lobbying.

In our view therefore, you will need a consultancy at some stage. The challenge will be finding the right one at the right price. It is impossible here to point you towards the right public affairs consultancy for you but a few guidelines will hopefully help:
1. **Know exactly what you want/need.** The clearer your brief, the better the service. Spend time talking to your network on how to get your brief right. This is absolutely key.
2. **Take the time** to look and ask around to find the right partner – this will be time well-invested.
3. **Ask around for references from your network** – personal recommendations and connections are usually better than cold calls.
4. **Try to see at least three potential consultancies** as this will give you more ideas and a sense of what is possible (and at what cost).
5. **Negotiate the price** – to get the tailored service you need.
6. **Understand who will deliver your service** – often the people who pitch will not deliver your service, so be sure to understand this.
7. **The consultant is more important than the consultancy** – the key is not the renown of the consultancy but the ability of the consultant.
8. **Take a look at** www.bestinbrussels.eu for some guidance on the best consultancies in Brussels. It has a very useful section called 'choosing the right partner'.

Consultancies, in sum, can be incredibly useful as a source of experience and expertise. You would be remiss to overlook thinking about how they could support your work in Brussels.

Coalitions are a good way to show that an issue is of greater importance than people might first have thought. There is a strength in numbers that helps to demonstrate credibility. A broad coalition helps you tap into a wider political alliance, but the challenge is that getting coalitions to agree on an issue is not easy. The best number of issues to campaign together on is one and the maximum should be three. Keeping the coalition focused and aligned is taxing and you will have to staff up this work. Do not under-estimate the work, and time, required and involved in pulling a coalition together – it can be a full-time job.

Finally, from a resource allocation perspective, public affairs presents strange and often **unpredictable opportunities**. As a rule of thumb, it is actually useful to set aside 30% of your budget to pay for these unexpected and unplanned opportunities. These can range from requests to bring a speaker to Brussels, run issue ads in the FT, sponsor Politico Playbook, commission a targeted study, or bring in a Hollywood celebrity to front a debate in the European Parliament. If you fix on a plan at the expense of any creativity and flexibility, you harm your chances of success.

2.3 Messaging and channels

Political communication is about persuading enough key decision-makers and influencers to back you. You are going to need to prepare your message, and get your message out.

This section looks at how to prepare your message, and then the ways and channels to get it taken up.

Messaging
You need to integrate your lobbying and communications work from Day 1 because you will discover that they are one and the same. Your messages need to follow this basic principle: 'legal, honest, and truthful'. Much hard work is destroyed by messages that are flexible with the truth, or irrelevant, or disingenuous. Organisations that retain high trust with key decision-makers and influencers stick to the basic principles, as Chapter 1 made clear.

You need real evidence to support your messages. In a non-partisan and technocratic Brussels, the quality of the evidence you need to bring to the table is high and you can't skip the evidence gathering stage. If you do, you will be caught out, so your evidence needs to be objective, credible and on-point. While getting the evidence from within your own organisation can be a challenge, it is not one we will take up here. It is what you do with the evidence that is important for your EU work and in that there are five core elements for a good message:

1. Credible
2. Authentic
3. Interesting/original
4. Speaks to the target audience
5. Uses language that resonates and is clear to target audience

Once the message is agreed on, anyone speaking on your behalf has to keep on message. This cannot be stressed enough: **you need to stay on message**. This demonstrates your consistency, which is important in getting your message across in the busy EU communications space (as discussed further in Chapter 4 on working with the media and social media). It is best to follow the advice of one US Republican political strategist: *'There's a simple rule: You say it again, and you say it again, and you say it again, and you say it again, and about the time that you're absolutely sick of saying it is about the time that your target audience has heard it for the first time.'*

If you can, test your message before you go live with it. A useful technique is to trial the key messages with a key decision-maker and influencer – someone you trust. See how they react. The gaps in your intellectual reasoning will be exposed quickly so take the chance to refine and improve. At the other end of the spectrum you can hold a **focus group** to test your messaging. This will likely involve a consultancy organising a group of your target stakeholders to come together to discuss your messaging. This can be done quickly and can bring real value to understanding how your message will land. This can, however, cost you from €5,000 to €20,000.

One of the key reasons you need to test your messaging is that it is quite likely that very few people are intrinsically interested in your issue (or as interested as you are). You need to make sure your messages speak to them. You need to use arguments not because you like them, but because it furthers your case. As Chapter 1 identified, as a premise of influence, you need to put yourself in the mind of your audience and make sure the messages speak to them.

You should always look to frame your message to create images and mental shortcuts so that your audience can see the issue through your lenses. If you do not, and instead follow the framing set by your opponents, the chances of persuading your target audiences diminish. And one thing to make very clear about your messaging: you need to be careful to avoid sounding negative. Being negative rarely works in Brussels and can, in fact, damage your case and your reputation. Remember that Brussels is about accumulated compromises – so everyone wants solutions.

Channels

Once you have your message, and you are comfortable and ready to work with it, there are many channels that exist to get it out. It will simply be a question of understanding which channels are the best to reach your target audience – and how much you can pay, as they often come with a price tag. These channels, as they relate to media and social media, are covered in detail in Chapter 4.

Marketer or Political Communicator?

'A perfect marketer would be a: relationship builder, storyteller, researcher, reader A/B tester, content writer, artist psychologist, strategic planner, copywriter, thought leader, influencer, budgeter, artist, listener, brand ambassador, data scientist, analyst, teacher and communicator.'

Source: Marketing and Communications, by PR Smith and Ze Zook, 7th edition, figure 1.4

There are a variety of channels through which you can indirectly get your message to your target audience and be co-opted by them. In fact there is today a proliferation of channels, meaning you have some important choices to make as you will not be able to make use of all of them. The key is to understand the channels that they will reach, because they are used by your target audience.

The following is a list (not necessariy exhaustive, but fairly comprehensive) of channels you can use. The list is constantly evolving; many of the channels available today did not exist five or ten years ago. These key channels include:

1. **Advertising**: Interactive ads, banner ads, newspaper ads, trade press ads
2. **Public relations**: discussion groups, newsletters, viral campaigns, work with the media, promoted stories, infographics, published reports, ads in airline inflight magazine
3. **Sponsorship**: talks, events, receptions, online events, site visits
4. **Exhibitions, events and conferences**: webinars, parliamentary events, stalls at Commission events
5. **Direct mail**: newsletters, direct mail, outreach to MEPs, leaflets to MEPs
6. **Press releases**: to mainstream or trade press
7. **Social media campaigns**: Twitter, LinkedIn, Facebook, Instagram…
8. **Video production**: for use across social media (talking heads, animations)
9. **Policy briefings**: for journalists, decision makers, and influencers
10. **Infographics**: to be used on social media and position papers
11. **Position papers**: to be shared publicly
12. **Poster campaign/billboards**: in, for example, the Schuman area of Brussels

As noted earlier most of these channels cost money so let's take an overview of this.

Table 2.2: Example costs for Public Affairs Messaging Channel Activities

Public Affairs Channels - Estimated Costs	
Infographics	€4,000 - €6,000
Micro social campaigns	€1,000 - €1,500 for 15 second video
Talking head videos	€1,500 - €2,000 for one video
Video telling a story	€20,000 - €35,000
Movie trailer video	€10,000 - €15,000
Schuman Area Poster ads	€4,000 a month
Politico Playbook ad	€20,000 a week
FT advertisement	€30,000 a day
Exhibition with installation in the European Parliament	€70,000 - €120,000 for a week long exhibition
Twitter ad pay per click	50c to €1 (you can set the limits)
Twitter account management	€30,000 - €60,000 a year

As Chapter 4 discusses in more detail, perceived free resources, such as Twitter, are not free if you are to use them effectively. Twitter requires you to set aside the time and resources for someone in your team to manage the account, post and respond to the conversation before you even look at using ads to generate greater traffic and visibility.

Making your case through a position paper
The strength of your case will often stand and fall on the robustness of your **position paper**. It should be clear, concise and no more than two pages. The smart deployment of visuals, like charts and infographics, make the case more effectively than spoken words can. You need to leave a copy of the position paper behind. Your position paper needs to offer a solution and the evidence to back it and ideally you will provide the necessary legislative language and explanatory text.

Officials, MEPs and political aides face a whirlwind of meetings during the day and it is unfair (and unrealistic) to think they'll have perfect recall of all the intricate details of their meeting with you. A good position paper will assist their recall and provide them with solutions that can be co-opted. After meeting with an official, MEP or political aide, follow up with a copy of the position paper you gave them. You will have sent it to them in advance of the meeting to help focus the discussion. You will provide them with any extra information that they asked for. If you said you would send them information, like a new report or findings, by a given date, do so without fail. If you do not follow up within the agreed conventions, you will find your case is discounted, and the door closed on you. A lobbyist who is not trusted is a liability.

A lot of messaging in Brussels is still done through the position paper, so it is important to get this right. To be clear, a position paper by itself does not persuade – it is mostly used as a tool for internal alignment, to put your position on the record and as a professional leave-behind from a meeting. If you are going to draft a position paper here are some golden rules you should follow, taken also partially from Richard Haas, Professor of Public Policy at Harvard:

1. **Concise**: 1 page is the right length. Supporting information, if needed, can be in an annex. An ideal is 1 page, A4, font 12 point. 11 is too hard to read.
2. **Public**: Whatever you put in must be for public consumption, i.e. you must be comfortable with anyone being able to read it
3. **Visual**: Good visuals work better than paragraphs of words
4. **Clarity**: Be clear in your position. If you have priorities state them. If you have a solution spell it out. If you have questions ask them.
5. **Identity**: Make sure you put your logo/name and details on the paper in an easy to find way.
6. **Creative**: Yours will be one of many papers…try to be creative and catch the eye.
7. **Anticipate**: What issues are of concern to the reader? Address something that is of importance or interest to them. And there is no point raising an issue that is not on the agenda.
8. **Objective**: Understand what work a position paper needs to accomplish. Is your memo a door opener to a meeting, or is it the only chance you have to get a decision? The amount of time you put into drafting the memo will vary depending on what you are looking for.

9. **Solid Analysis**: Use sound analysis, and not fake facts, so that even those who don't agree with your recommendations can accept your analysis. If you do this, your briefing will be read and acted on.
10. **Costs and Benefits** of each option/recommendation should be assessed over a period of time that is relevant. Be honest about the baseline scenarios.
11. **Acknowledge opposition**: This shows integrity. Policymakers will want this information and it is best coming from you rather than them finding out in their next meeting. Because they certainly will find out.
12. **Divorce politics and partisanship from the analysis**: It's best to keep your political views out of the memo because it can shroud the analysis. If there are political points you'd like to raise, whether within your organisation or directly with the politician, do that face-to-face. Being silent about your political preferences in your analysis will serve you well because Brussels officials are faintly apolitical. While officials may be party members, the best officials keep their work and politics very much apart, so be aware of this.
13. **History**: If there is some history to your issue, mention it. It helps if what you are trying to get has worked somewhere else. If what you are asking for has been tried but failed previously, then say what will be necessary to implement your recommendation successfully this time.
14. **Include any weaknesses/risks/open question in your own case**: You are better served pointing out the weak points in your position paper than having them exposed by others.
15. **Preempt** opposing arguments or perspectives by including them. It's best to address any opposing points upfront especially if you can do this in a fair and analytical way. If you don't do so, you'll have lost a good opportunity.
16. **Recommendation**: Do not provide analysis without offering judgement about what is the best option. You have to propose a better way to go forward.
17. **Facts**: In an age when too many 'facts' are fake, there is no surer way to discredit your own case than by stating as facts things which are nothing of the sort. Make sure the facts you use are accurate.
18. **Appearance**: You need a professional position paper that is visually compelling. A sloppy position paper gives the impression of sloppy thinking and that will detract from what you say.

When you have your position, make sure it is easy for people to access. It is hard to influence people if you hide your thinking. A dedicated policy website, or section of a website, is useful as it allows officials and politicians to read your case in advance. It makes sense to promote your case through social media, though the returns on Twitter, Facebook and LinkedIn, are hard to measure. Chapter 4 will look at this in more detail.

Finally, do not forget that you are looking to persuade human beings. You need to be interesting and to tap into emotions and feelings – many position papers are too dry. NGOs have long learned the persuasive power of emotions and storytelling as discussed in Chapter 1. The imagery used to promote an issue is more effective than any words.

PHASE 3: FEEDBACK AND EVALUATION

The final phase of the public affairs methodology, the one that is without a doubt the most often neglected and certainly one of the most difficult, is that of **feedback and evaluation**. The essence of this is quite straightforward – you need to evaluate what you did, how you did it, what happened, what impact you had and how successful you were. You then need to use all of this to make improvements in your objectives and KPIs, internal processes, preparations and finally in your engagement and actions. Many systems in theory have effective feedback loops to ensure continual improvements. In practice, however, many public affairs strategies develop and change iteratively without ever formally really being subjected to auditing and evaluating. It is worth briefly expanding on this.

Formal full public affairs audits or evaluations are quite rare. They do not have to last weeks and cost significant amounts of money. At its most simple, it is about taking a day with some key internal stakeholders and taking stock of all internal processes and communications, all public affairs preparations, engagements and actions to critically evaluate and seek improvements. As we have highlighted before, there is a difference here between preparations, engagements and actions.

The preparations stage of the public affairs methodology lends itself to being audited. You can really step back and look at each step in the process and evaluate what is in place, what exists, what has been created and used, and determine what is working and what can be improved. Everyone should always be striving for incremental improvements in their preparations because it is something they can control. For example: improving the objective setting process; tendering for monitoring and intelligence gathering to get better coverage or better value; or assessing the stock of data, identifying gaps and filling them one by one. When it comes to engagement and actions, this is more outside the realm of evaluation because not everything is in your control and so much is subjective.

As discussed in the section on objective setting, public affairs is an activity whose results are often difficult to quantify. This is why setting solid objectives and KPIs is so valuable – you put the effort in upfront and make an evaluation of success and impact much easier. At the same time, perhaps the ultimate evaluation will be the ROI of the team/person/function.

Finally, to be clear, the goal of evaluation is not to apportion blame or highlight inadequacies for the sake of it. It is all about trying to learn, improve and deliver more effectively in the future. This is particularly important in public affairs because this is a profession that has so many internal and external variables and where the recipe for success is rarely the same twice. The focus will be just as much internal to the organisation (inadequate processes, acting too late or slowly, unclear priorities, inadequate data, lack of senior management engagement or buy-in) as external (political environment, ability to access key stakeholders, social media trends and reactions). The continuous improvement of your public affairs work is essential for your own personal development as much as it is for the success of your organisation.

We will now look in detail at how you can audit your preparations and evaluate your engagement and actions.

There are three types of evaluation that should happen in a robust public affairs process. The first type of evaluation should take place in the objective setting phase: a **pre-mortem**. This is where the objectives are stress-tested and scenarios discussed to get the best and most appropriate objectives in place. Effective contingency planning will allow you to plan and adapt better. After this, as mentioned previously, the objectives and KPIs need to have **continuous evaluation** through regular check-ins through the year to ensure they are still valid (either because the organisation has changed priorities/resources, for example, or because the external environment has changed in some way that was unforeseen). This constant evaluation is necessary to ensure that resources are always allocated in the best possible way, thus allowing for agile decision-making and ensuring that the public affairs support for the organisation is always on point. Finally we come to the **post evaluation**.

The first place any evaluation should start is by looking at the objectives and KPIs. Were they achieved? If so, how? If not, why not? The strength of this evaluation will be based entirely on how good the objectives and KPIs were. Here is also where the nuances start – and why we will consider preparations and engagement/action separately in this section. It is entirely possible to achieve all your KPIs but not your objective in public affairs. Perhaps your objective was to secure one amendment for your organisation in a legislative text. Your KPIs detailed how you would go about this. You could conceivably achieve all of your KPIs (meeting key stakeholders, uptake of your position, positive media etc.) but find that in the end, for reasons outside of your control, your amendment did not get into the final text. Such is the challenge of public affairs. In this situation you need to understand what you can influence and also what you cannot influence, i.e. what is out of your control. In this case you did everything right but it did not lead to the outcome you wanted. Nonetheless you can still evaluate and learn.

Now we will look at the two separate areas of auditing the preparations and evaluating the engagement and action phases of the public affairs process.

3.1 Audit of the preparation phase

The preparation phase of the public affairs process lends itself to being audited because each stage of the process is distinct and can be subjected to effective check-listing of what needs to be in place and what happened to be effective. This is much more objective than the engagement and action stage of the process. Let's look at each of the stages in turn.

Monitoring and intelligence gathering
An audit here is about ensuring that you have tools in place to have the right information at the right time to inform your strategy and deliver your objectives. So did you, for example:
- Know all the deadlines in your process (to be able to respond)?
- Know what all the key stakeholders were saying and doing (in order to know who to target and what to say)?
- Not miss any key moment, information, deadline, opportunity, conference or event?

In auditing you need to focus on what you are monitoring and gathering information on. Is it correct and accurate? Does it give you what you need? You then need to look at how you are getting that information – are those sources providing what you need, when you need it and packaged how you need it? You can even assess whether you are getting value for money from the resources you have put into this exercise.

Stakeholder mapping
When you audit this part of the process you will be focused on ensuring you have the right key stakeholder overviews in place to know who your key audiences are.

Data
For this part of the audit you need to take stock of everything you have and look at what you have used, how you used it and what the feedback has been.

3.2 Evaluation of the engagement & action phase

In contrast to the preparation phase of the public affairs process, the engagement and action phase is very subjective when it comes to determining whether things worked or not. As you operate in the external space things are somewhat out of your control. But you can assess several things:

Impact
This is a very direct measure and usually the most common one used. At its most obvious, did I get my proposed text into the final legislative text? Was my opinion reflected in the official position? You are looking to establish direct cause and effect. You wanted A, and A was in the final outcome. Here you can do a direct text comparison to see whether ultimately you had an impact. In many cases you cannot, and should not, attribute this solely to yourself, as you have no way to verify that you alone managed to achieve this outcome. In some rare and very specific cases you can show this – and if you can, you definitely should.

If you do not have a direct impact in this way it does not mean your evaluation should stop or draw a negative inference. As discussed before, there could be some very good reasons why the outcome landed as it did, despite your best efforts. There are other measures you need to look at as well.

Perception
First of all, there is the question of how political decision-makers perceive your organisation and your objectives. Questions to ask here revolve around the following: Did we clearly identify ourselves? Do key stakeholders know who we are? Who did we mobilise for an amendment? Were we better

known (for the right reasons) at the end of the period than at the beginning of the period? This can be based on your observations and any supporting documents (attendance at events, access to key people, statements etc.) or, budget allowing, you may wish to conduct a survey among key stakeholders whom you have identified in order to learn how well your organisation and your ideas were received.

There are more measures relating to perception that you can look at. For example, how many calls did you receive from key stakeholders? How many invitations did you receive to participate in events or panels or meetings? How many meeting requests were accepted by your key stakeholders?

Relevance
A further element of evaluation is to assess the relevance of your arguments and positions in the debate. So you could be asking: Were my arguments credible? Did I have the right data? Were my arguments understood by my contacts? Which ones were taken up and why? Did aspects of my position find their way into the public debate or public view? Such an assessment allows you to verify if you managed to be relevant, in a meaningful way, to the debate.

Impact, perception and relevance are three general areas to evaluate. Beyond that you need to evaluate the individual elements of your engagement and actions, thus:
- Direct engagement (access/uptake of positions)
- Media and social media campaigns (coverage/uptake and spread of positions)
- Events (key audience attendees/follow up actions)
- Trade Associations (objectives and KPIs met)
- Reports commissioned (coverage/uptake/contacts made)

Every individual engagement and action you took was an opportunity-cost moment and therefore you need to evaluate how it worked and how you could have improved it – or replaced it with another activity.

Linked to this notion of opportunity cost and evaluation is the question of when do you walk away from an activity or campaign, and how do you do it? This is the realm of tough choices. If you feel a membership is not giving you what you need (i.e. directly contributing, in some way, to you achieving your objectives) you need to address that. You should start by making it absolutely clear what it is you need – and if you cannot get that, you should step away. Every membership you hold and every event you run should add value, in a coordinated and non-duplicating way, to what you are doing and what you want to achieve. If it doesn't then you are wasting resource – something that is likely precious to you.

Another area of learning is from other organisations working in your space. You will be close enough to observe what others are doing and also to see what is working and what is not working. This can be a great opportunity to shamelessly steal other people's ideas and incorporate them into your own work. You can also learn from your peers through horizontal platforms such as the Public Affairs

Council, who do specific issue and horizontal public affairs webinars, discussions, conferences and roundtables. You can learn so much from sitting back for a short period.

One aspect of the evaluation is that it will inevitably lead to considerations about resource. Did we not achieve what we wanted due to resource restrictions? In reality only a thorough audit and evaluation will answer this question – and extra resource is often not the solution to the issue. Being more structured and having greater focus is often a good first step to address perceived failures, which again comes back to objectives and expectations.

Finally, to close this section on feedback, it is important to highlight that much of what is needed to be effective in auditing and evaluating is good data. Look at the data to learn should be the mantra, but people often squander data because they are not capturing it correctly or adequately. The next chapter shows you what state of the art information management in public affairs looks like. If you have such a system in place you will have a clear record of what you did and what happened. If you don't keep track you won't have the data to evaluate and learn effectively.

3.3 Successful public affairs strategies

This chapter has outlined an EU public affairs methodology for how to plan, structure and execute your work for maximum effectiveness. To do this is has shown public affairs as a process composed of three main phases: **Preparation, Engagement & Action and Feedback**.

One of the most important aspects of a public affairs strategy is that you must never hesitate to revisit your plans, preparations, data, stakeholder mapping – in short, every aspect of what you do and how you do it. You should be constantly making small, and large, changes and modifications as they become necessary. The lobbying environment can be very fluid, with change being driven by your own organisation or the external environment. As a public affairs professional you need to make sure you are prepared to be flexible and adaptable enough to steer your efforts in different directions at different times. It is important to always be alert to new elements that might impact your work. Breaking down a public affairs methodology into seven key areas helps you to do this – by giving you a focus on what you do in each area and how to (a) do it better and (b) make sure it links better to other areas in the methodology.

All three of the phases, and all seven areas, of the public affairs methodology are critical individually but they only come to life together. Excelling in one area is not enough. Average in all areas is also not enough. You should always be striving to be best-in-class across every single element of the public affairs process. You should always be considering how to adapt this process to you organisation and your needs. You should be considering how to smooth the hand-offs from one part of the process to another so that it works seamlessly, saving you time and resource. And finally, you should build in robust feedback loops to ensure you are always learning and growing in your work.

3. Digital Information Management in EU Public Affairs

By Leyla Sertel and Alan Hardacre

In the last 50 years there have been significant technological developments in almost every field and public affairs is no exception. While the rate of progress has been slower than in some other industries, there are a number of digital solutions on offer today that can aid in all aspects of public affairs work.

This is not to say that technology should, or can, replace the importance of human relationships in engaging with key stakeholders and undertaking public affairs work. It can, however, serve as a powerful complement to traditional human-driven coalition building, analogue information management, monitoring and the like.

When people think of digital tools for public affairs they often think first (or only) of monitoring because that was the first way that digital tools helped public affairs professionals do so much more. Monitoring remains a mainstay of the digital offering but it is now far from being the only one. Technology can help all aspects of your public affairs work, all of the phases and areas outlined in Chapter 2 on the public affairs methodology. In essence technology is no longer an option in your public affairs work but something you need to integrate. This chapter will show you how to go about doing this by looking at where technology exists and how to benefit from, and integrate, it in your work.

Chapter 2 described the seven key areas for building a robust public affairs strategy, complete with best practices for how to excel in, and across, all of them. This chapter will mirror the methodology chapter to demonstrate how digital tools can help you set, manage, deliver, and evaluate your public affairs strategy.

Following the sequence shown in Figure 3.1 on the next page, we will look at the role of digital across the full spectrum of the EU public affairs methodology. We have tried to evaluate the role of human and digital in excelling in each aspect of the strategy, from which you will note that as of today there is a fine balance between the two. We will explain this balance in more detail as we go through the methodology stage by stage.

Digital Information Management in EU Public Affairs

Figure 3.1: Interface between human and digital in public affairs

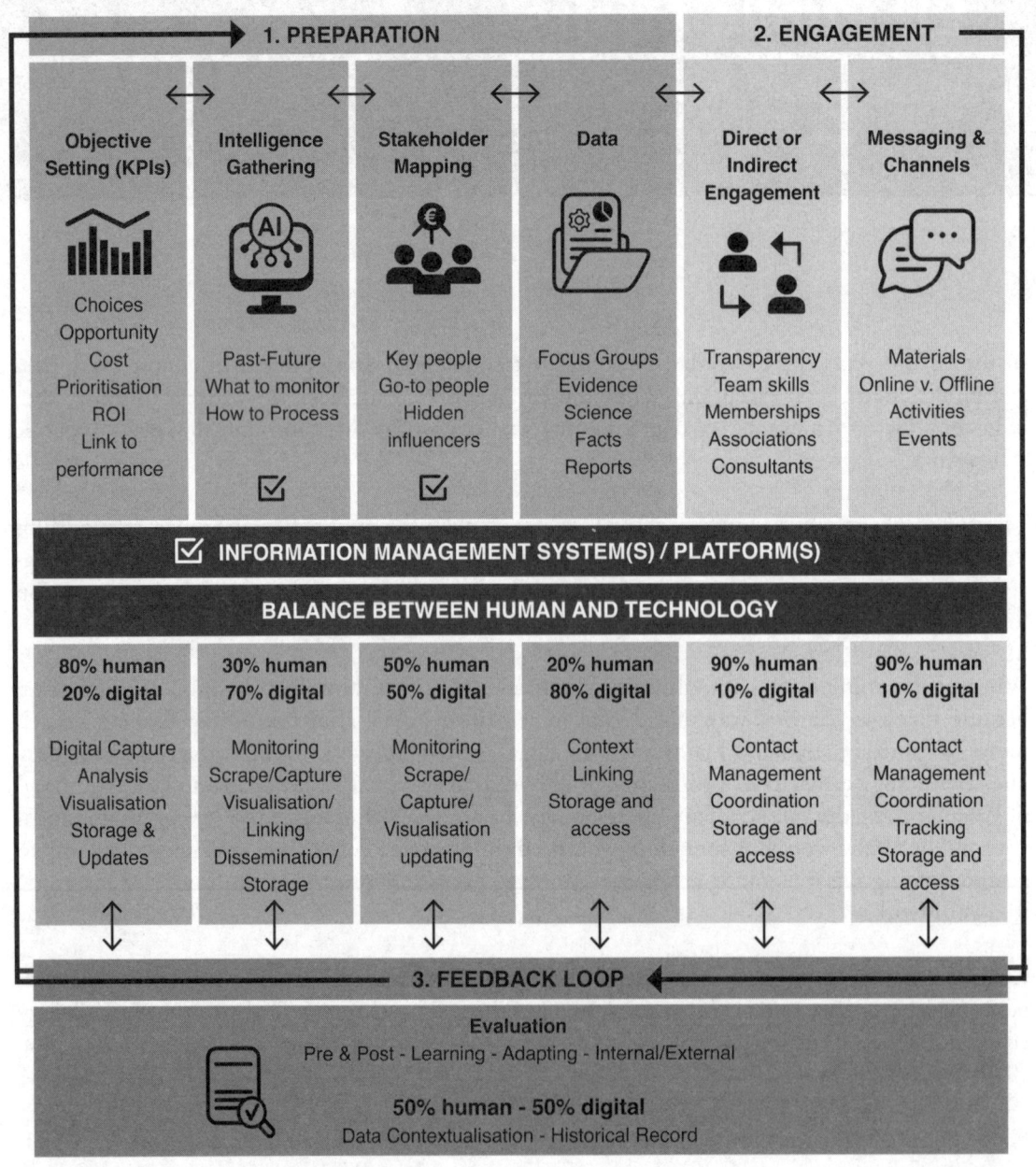

1. PREPARATION | 2. ENGAGEMENT

Objective Setting (KPIs)	Intelligence Gathering	Stakeholder Mapping	Data	Direct or Indirect Engagement	Messaging & Channels
Choices Opportunity Cost Prioritisation ROI Link to performance	Past-Future What to monitor How to Process	Key people Go-to people Hidden influencers	Focus Groups Evidence Science Facts Reports	Transparency Team skills Memberships Associations Consultants	Materials Online v. Offline Activities Events

INFORMATION MANAGEMENT SYSTEM(S) / PLATFORM(S)

BALANCE BETWEEN HUMAN AND TECHNOLOGY

80% human 20% digital	30% human 70% digital	50% human 50% digital	20% human 80% digital	90% human 10% digital	90% human 10% digital
Digital Capture Analysis Visualisation Storage & Updates	Monitoring Scrape/Capture Visualisation/ Linking Dissemination/ Storage	Monitoring Scrape/ Capture/ Visualisation updating	Context Linking Storage and access	Contact Management Coordination Storage and access	Contact Management Coordination Tracking Storage and access

3. FEEDBACK LOOP

Evaluation
Pre & Post - Learning - Adapting - Internal/External

50% human - 50% digital
Data Contextualisation - Historical Record

Source: Leyla Sertel & Alan Hardacre with design support from Martine Aunaas

It is first worth noting some horizontal aspects of the use of digital tools in public affairs:

1. Many aspects of a public affairs strategy can be done manually by people. This was always the case and will remain so. Some aspects can now only be done digitally. What is important is that many aspects that can be done manually can now be done much better, faster and more efficiently by digital tools. It is not that a digital tool necessarily replaces human work but it just does it **more efficiently (and often more cost-effectively)**. So if nothing else you need to think of a cost-time pay-off. Often you will save time on repetitive tasks allowing you to focus on higher value public affairs work.
2. What you can see in Figure 3.1 is that **the benefit of using one single digital system** throughout the public affairs process to capture, store and allow the sharing of all information is **a potential game changer for you**. It is also very much best practice in public affairs today. Getting a whole team on the same system will allow you to reap significant benefits. Single system public affairs digital tools are the future of public affairs.
3. Whilst some aspects of having one single digital information management system for public affairs are horizontal, others can be tailored and local. **You can build a system that is bespoke for you**. For example you may need a monitoring tool that is local to a country so you simply need to 'plug this in' – the benefit being that you can then manage your information in the same horizontal system, which is the absolute key.
4. The adoption and use of such a digital system is a **real culture change** and a change in the way of working. For example, ensuring that everyone logs meetings with stakeholders involves a real mentality shift that can be difficult to overcome, but there is such value in ensuring everyone uses the system that it is worth the effort to get there. This human/cultural aspect of moving from human/established ways of working to more digital ones should not be underestimated.

Finally, as a caveat, we will use many **Quorum-specific** examples in this chapter as this is the system that we know best. There are other quality horizontal and specific digital systems out there (many of which have been referenced in other chapters) and we will refer to some of the main ones through this chapter. The services, principles and benefits that we discuss can be delivered by a variety of competing systems in the market today. This is testimony to the vibrant digital public affairs profession that is building up – which means you will need to follow carefully to take advantage of any first mover benefits.

European Union General Data Protection (EUGDPR)
One crucial area that this chapter needs to address upfront is that of **European Union General Data Protection (EUGDPR)**. Much of what this chapter will discuss relates to how you collate information and data in one place, with the many obvious benefits that we will outline. The EUGDPR represents a hard line on both what and how you can/should do this. EUGDPR is quite a complex process but the main area of concern for digital information management comes when you are putting information about third parties/people into your system – essentially **your stakeholder mapping work**. Ideally before doing this you should have clear and demonstrable policies in place as well as being prepared to give access to the data upon request. This in itself should already point

towards what type of data you should hold (only things you would be happy being made public, for example). In addition to the financial risks (from a fine) you also run reputational risks if found to be infringing EUGDPR, so it is an area that needs to be taken very seriously. You may have to invest in advice to get yourself to a solid level of EUGDPR compliance but for here let us outline some good practice for EUGDPR and stakeholder mapping:

1. It is likely that the majority of the data you will be collecting will be **publicly available data** which it is perfectly fine to collect and collate.
2. If you are collecting data you need to have **EUGDPR policies** in place – make sure you do.
3. As you will be in possession of the data you need to ensure **data protection** – which is something you might want to discuss in more detail with your digital system providers.
4. You should **only collect, log and use personal information that is strictly required** for your exercise of stakeholder mapping in order to ensure you remain within the confines of the EUGDPR.
5. You need to ensure the data you have collected is **adequately protected** (check with your digital system provider on this).
6. Be **ready to grant access** to the data of any stakeholder who may request it.

So now let's move into looking at the use of digital tools across the EU public affairs methodology.

1. Objective setting (KPIs)

Coordination across teams starts immediately when prioritising issues. Many public affairs teams face the challenge of having too many issues and not enough resources, be it of time, budget, or manpower. While everything might feel like a top priority for those closest to the issue, it is important to have a unified set of prioritisation criteria across the organisation. This will help identify which are actually the most pressing issues for an organisation to devote their resources to.

The EU public affairs methodology chapter talked about the importance of setting criteria and then how to conduct the process of objective setting. This chapter will discuss how an information management tool can help gather inputs, weight different criteria, and ultimately display the criteria side by side to enable team members to prioritise. It can then capture and record progress through the year as well as visualising all of this for internal audiences.

In the last chapter you read about things to consider when selecting your prioritisation criteria. One of the things touched upon was relating public affairs metrics to other metrics within your organisation. For example, if you're a business, can you articulate benefit to the business and speak like other business units? If you're an association, can you talk about benefit and value-added to the industry so your members can determine impact to them based on market share? This is a challenging task, no matter who you are, but technology can help get you part of the way there. Ask internally, or ask your members, what modelling software they might be using or for examples of how they've done this in the past. What is important is to understand the different metrics of success they are looking at so you can do the same.

Once you've set your criteria it's time to turn to your public affairs information management system. Ideally, you've selected an information management system that the entire public affairs team will use, starting with the prioritisation process.

Before gathering input from the relevant stakeholders, take the time to set up the infrastructure in your information management tool. In fact, this is a best practice as you work through all different stages of the methodology process. Whenever there is a set of criteria to be decided (whether it is for prioritisation or information you want to capture about stakeholders) work with a few team members to establish the criteria. Then make sure to set up these criteria in your information management system before asking the wider team to adopt or modify the process. If team members go into the system and see familiar infrastructure that relates to their work, it will make the system easier to learn. Remember what we said about the challenge of making a shift in ways of working – you need to make this as easy as possible. In the case of prioritisation, plug in the criteria so they appear in the issue profile when heads of departments or regions are asked to fill it out. With technology you can also assign weights to different criteria that will automatically factor in as they are filled out.

Figure 3.2: Digital prioritisation

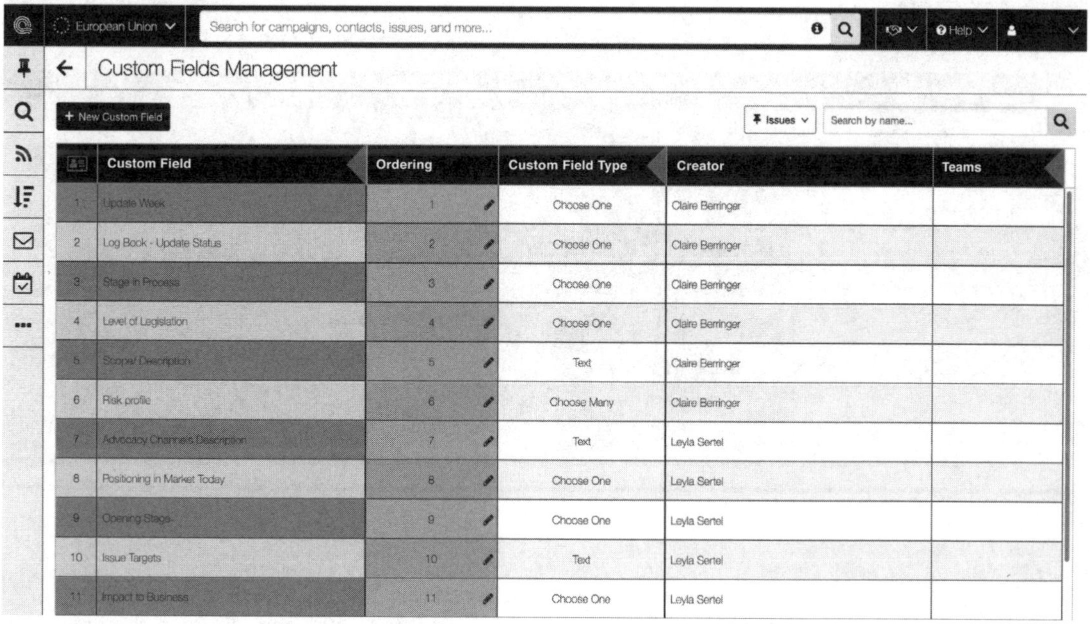

Source: Quorum

> **Pro-tip:** the more you can encourage team members to work in the information management platform the better adoption you'll see and the less of a burden it is on their workflow.

Now think about who needs to provide input before you can identify your organisation's key issues. Do you want to survey your direct reports to see what they think about how urgent an issue might be, or how open it is to influencing, or do you want to decide for yourself? Whichever approach you opt for, technology platforms can make it easier to gather, evaluate, present and ultimately recommend. Some public affairs platforms allow you to send a survey to your team to gather their inputs on factors like importance, urgency, and openness to influencing. From here the technology can average the answers for you and provide a separate column for the head of the function to do their own ultimate calibration. Some platforms allow you to set up an auto-updating and auto-populating sheet (similar to Excel) that will auto-populate the criteria for each issue as different heads of departments or heads of regions fill them out and will then automatically calculate the weighting you have set up. This will create a place where all decision-makers can have a side by side comparison of different issues on the table.

Figure 3.3: Issue evaluation sheet with some weighting

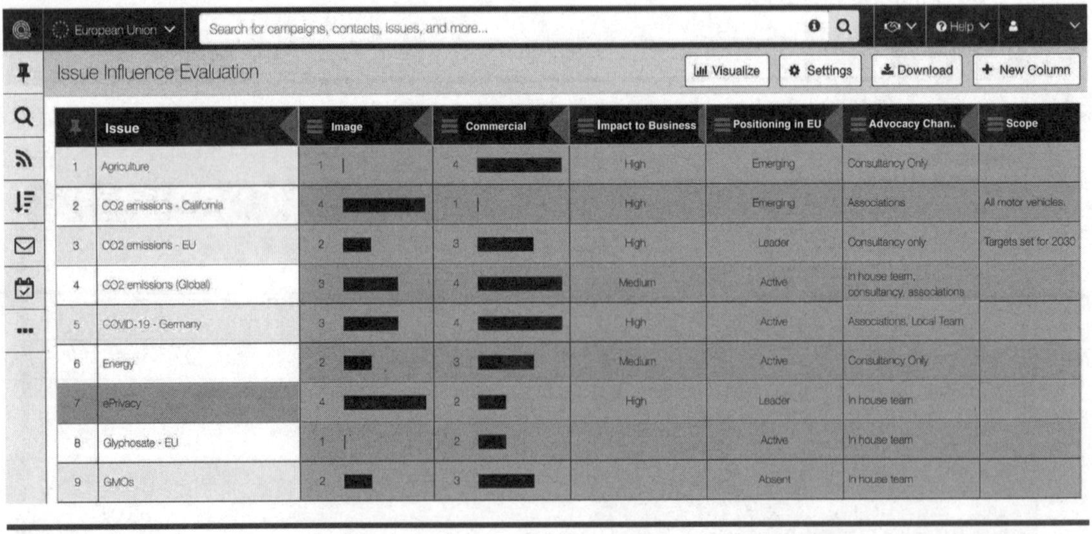
European Union
Search for campaigns, contacts, issues, and more...
Help
Issue Influence Evaluation
Visualize
Settings
Download
New Column
Issue
Image
Commercial
Impact to Business
Positioning in EU
Advocacy Chan..
Scope
1 Agriculture 1 4 High Emerging Consultancy Only
2 CO2 emissions - California 4 1 High Emerging Associations All motor vehicles
3 CO2 emissions - EU 2 3 High Leader Consultancy only Targets set for 2030
4 CO2 emissions (Global) 3 4 Medium Active In house team, consultancy, associations
5 COVID-19 - Germany 3 4 High Active Associations, Local Team
6 Energy 2 3 Medium Active Consultancy Only
7 ePrivacy 4 2 High Leader In house team
8 Glyphosate - EU 1 2 Active In house team
9 GMOs 2 3 Absent In house team

Source: Quorum

Having equal access to information and seeing things side by side will hopefully help the group see the global picture and make it clearer about which concessions to make and which issues to prioritise. This is a very professional, transparent and efficient way to determine priorities that are aligned to and built out of your organisation.

Once the priorities have been set it's time to build out KPIs or **Objectives and Key Results (OKRs)**. Make sure to create measurable goals so you can track incremental progress. Many OKRs and KPIs can relate to the rest of the methodology process such as identifying key stakeholders, monitoring, and meeting certain engagement goals. Public affairs platforms can help you quantify many of the previously qualitative goals, such as how many minds you changed, what percentage of your meetings were positive, or how much engagement you got on social media. They can also help you track your progress to date as well as expected progress in a quarter or other specified time period. For example, you can set up an algorithm that will calculate percentage completed and expected percentage completed over a certain period of time.

Clearly, a digital platform can track your success in undertaking your work in terms of the *process*. It is more difficult to track *success* (and your role in it) when it comes to the actual outcomes you are looking for in public affairs. This was discussed in the previous methodology chapter and the distinction is important to make here. The digital platform is better at tracking your internal success than your external outcomes – and being able to demonstrate success in the latter is of course extremely important.

What is clear is that there are dedicated digital tools available to help you build, track, manage and visualise your public affairs objectives and KPIs/OKRs. We assessed that currently the balance between human and digital is currently 80/20 given that the system requires human input to function (which will always be the case). But the 20% digital can make a huge difference to the foundations of your public affairs work.

So now that you've laid the groundwork of prioritising your issues and integrating an information management tool, the next step is intelligence gathering.

2. Intelligence gathering (monitoring)

It's now time to get a sense of the landscape around the issues you've prioritised.

There are multiple ways to gather intelligence. Traditional ways include using your team's own intelligence, hiring an agency, or using your organisation's association memberships. These methods remain an important part of the monitoring equation but digital tools are now an equally important part of the monitoring toolbox. There will be certain things you can't automate, such as on the ground intelligence from human relationships, but you should automate the things that you can both to save time and extract additional insights.

Monitoring tools are set up in different ways. Some are powered by a team of humans manually feeding data into the system and others are built on automated scrapers aggregating many different sources (and some are both). Some digital monitoring tools focus solely on the legislative process, or non-governmental stakeholders like the media, while others combine things like the legislative process and social media into one platform. Effective automated monitoring should reduce the noise, save your team time, and provide data-driven insights – all in a cost effective way.

With a vast amount of open government data in the EU and with social media mattering more and more, the amount of information one needs to process is constantly on the rise. Digital monitoring tools are almost all based on the premise of aggregating this vast amount of data and then applying their own method to filter the results based on specific search criteria. The goal of this is to reduce the noise and allow public affairs teams to focus on the content relevant to their issues as and when they happen. Not only should digital monitoring reduce the noise, it should also proactively alert each team member about relevant information on their issues so they never miss a mention. Look for a digital system which really allows you to tailor alerts by issue and by team member so that the whole team isn't receiving everyone's alerts and you can work with the system in a push and pull manner.

Figure 3.4: Monitoring email alert

Quorum	TEST
DSM	**3 New**

Tweet by MEP Assita Kanko (ECR - Belgium) | European Parliament **(Source Link) (Quorum Link)**

Region:	European Union
Document Type:	Tweet
Date:	Thursday, July 23, 2020
Matching Search Terms:	Digital Single Market OR DSM
Full Content:	I believe in fiscal responsibility, respecting the competences of member states, and putting money where it is most needed to create a future proof economy, protected external borders, supported research & innovation & strong **Digital Single Market**. What the next generation needs. https://t.co/FqMrXzYKlj

Source: Quorum

If you choose your digital monitoring system well and take the time to set up tailored search queries and alerts, it will save your team time in the long run. This additional time can then be spent on processing the raw content and turning it into meaningful intelligence or in looking for the meaningful human intelligence that an automated system can't give you.

While processing the information be sure to make use of the additional insights a digital monitoring tool can deliver. Because all of the raw content is aggregated into one place you can often layer different algorithms on top of your search results to generate high-level insights such as which stakeholders are most vocal on this issue or what the key social media hashtags are to engage around. We'll come back to many of these algorithms in the section on identifying stakeholders, but the key thing to retain at this stage is that having all of your data in one place allows artificial intelligence (AI) to provide you with additional insights, visuals and information that you would otherwise not have access to. This aspect of digital systems is improving all the time so you need to stay tuned to what the latest possibilities are; they can make a real difference to your public affairs work.

Figure 3.5: Monitoring search insights

Source: Quorum

Don't forget that in conjunction with digital monitoring you will also hopefully be doing manual intelligence gathering. You will recall from the EU public Affairs methodology chapter that you are looking for a sweet spot of the different forms of intelligence – crucially, though, to all be put into the digital system. This brings us back to the information management aspect of a digital public affairs tool as you think about how to manage, analyse, and disseminate all the different information you're gathering.

An information management tool gives you a place to combine and organise all the information you've gathered from your different monitoring sources. Look to organise your information according to the issues you have prioritised. You should be building the issue profile we first discussed in prioritisation so that step by step you have one central hub for all the different pieces of information associated with a public affairs methodology. If done consistently across members of your team and your different country colleagues and consultants this will allow for information flow at the local, regional, and global levels.

Figure 3.6: Building an issue profile

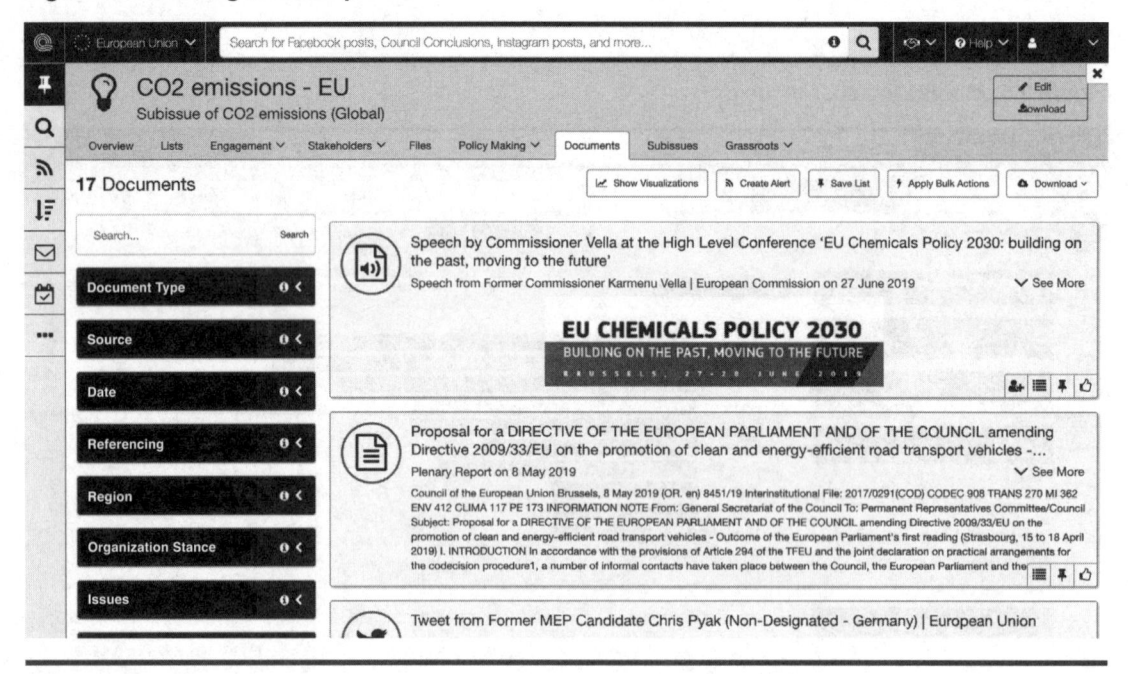

Source: Quorum

Now that you've brought all the intelligence into one place you can focus on processing the raw content. Parse through the data to derive insights and find connections between different pieces of intelligence. This is the foundation for the stakeholders you'll target, the materials you'll produce, and the advocacy channels you'll use to take action. It is fundamental to the preparation stage of your EU public affairs methodology.

Different team members often need different levels of information. Information management tools are great at providing this via customised dashboards and targeted reporting so that different members of your team can see varying levels of information. For example the issue expert might want to see all the information and different combinations to help process the information but the head of public affairs might only want the high level overview for each issue.

By holding all of your information in a tool that the entire team has access to you'll help keep everyone on the same page and allow for analysis at the local, regional, and global level. You can of course limit the permissions for sensitive information should you need to.

Our assessment of the human/digital state of play for intelligence gathering is 30/70. We believe that there will always be a need for human intelligence – especially for forward looking information – but that the bulk of monitoring is now better done digitally. The most important aspect of this is the increase in AI capabilities that allow you to analyse your gathered intelligence and package it quickly (and visually). Using state of the art digital monitoring in one digital system can offer significant advantages for the preparation of your public affairs strategy.

3. Stakeholder mapping

With a solid understanding of the general landscape surrounding your priority issues, it's now time to focus specifically on the people who are going to impact your issues. These will be the ultimate decision-makers, of course, but there will also be sub-groups of people who influence the decision-makers that are just as, if not more, important to engage. Stakeholder mapping is much like monitoring in that it's most comprehensive when using an array of sources, ranging from your own intelligence on hidden decision-makers to analysing public activity levels on an issue. Again, the sweet spot is created by using human and digital capabilities.

Digital monitoring can help you identify stakeholders who have been publicly active on your issues. One of the benefits of using an integrated software platform is that you can continue to build on the digital monitoring you already started when creating your stakeholder mapping. You will have already run certain queries to look at mentions of your issues across different sources. Now identify the stakeholders behind the content. Use the pre-built algorithms in your information management tool to see which stakeholders talk about your issue the most, which EU political parties talk about your issue the most, and which country has the most vocal stakeholders.

These visualisations are a starting point. From here you can determine which stakeholders played a key role on similar legislation in the past, sit on relevant committees, and speak about your issues on social media to an engaged social media audience. Doing this will help you start to assign influence to publicly active stakeholders and also to know where they are active. A digital system will create a clear visualisation, such as Figure 3.7, that shows your results. This can then serve as a catalyst to think about someone's surrounding institutional structure and about other stakeholders within that institution who can influence the ultimate decision-maker.

The growing presence of public officials on social media has created another important space to evaluate in your stakeholder identification. However, it can be a challenging space to keep up with, and derive real insights from, because of the pace of posting and the informal manner that allows for the discussion of everything from a family weekend away to an opinion on a policy issue.

Often the real value in social media monitoring comes from analysing patterns and networks. Look for a monitoring software which includes social media of policy-makers in their offering to get you started. From here you can run the same searches you set up for your issue monitoring within the institutions and start to work with the social media algorithms.

Figure 3.7: Digital stakeholder identification

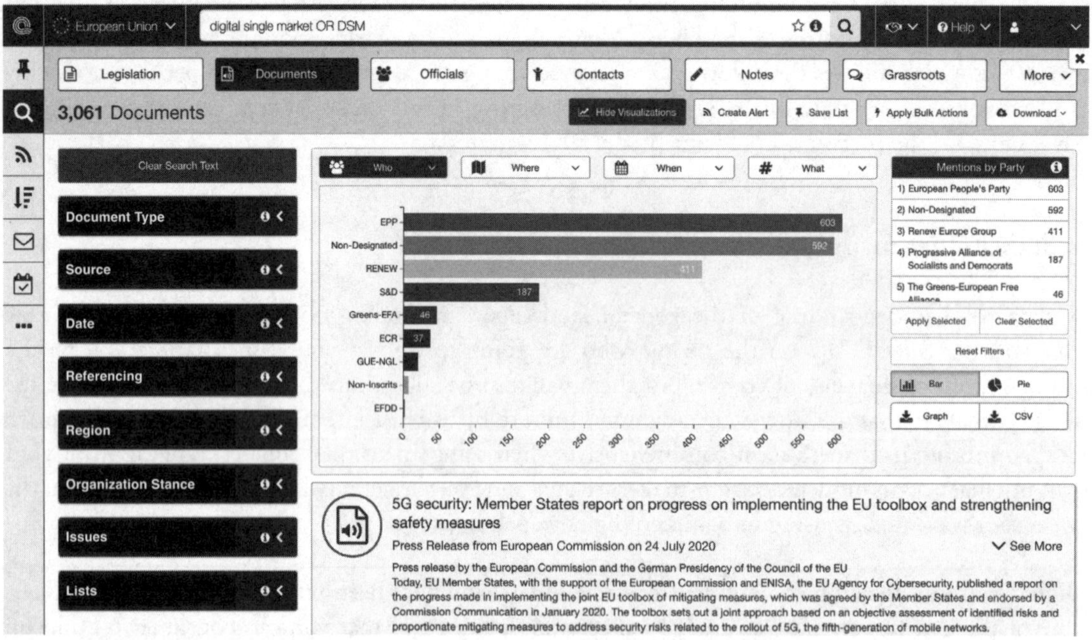

Source: Quorum

At the most basic level, a monitoring software which includes social media can help solve the problem of the pace of posting by alerting you only when your issues and key words are mentioned. This will allow you to cast a wider net of stakeholders you monitor but will only pull in relevant content for you to parse through. To take it to the next level, identify patterns and networks by running algorithms that will tell you who a policy-maker retweets or mentions the most in their content. This begins to shed light on that sub-level of who influences the policy-maker and who might be more accessible, or important, to engage with.

Similar to monitoring you now need a place to organise, compare, and categorise all of the different stakeholders. Tag all the stakeholders you've identified to their relevant issue profile and from here you can auto-generate a stakeholder mapping for each issue. Similar to the process for prioritising issues your information management tool should have a calibration feature which will allow you to gather stakeholders by issue and rank them on things like influence, importance, and interest. You are now able to merge your different sources of information into one clear view.

The next step is to group the stakeholders into lists in your issue profile. Think about the different ways you need to categorise your stakeholders. Maybe you want to keep track of champions or opponents? Or maybe you want to separate out stakeholders who are important at different parts of the process?

Figure 3.8: Social media mapping visualisation

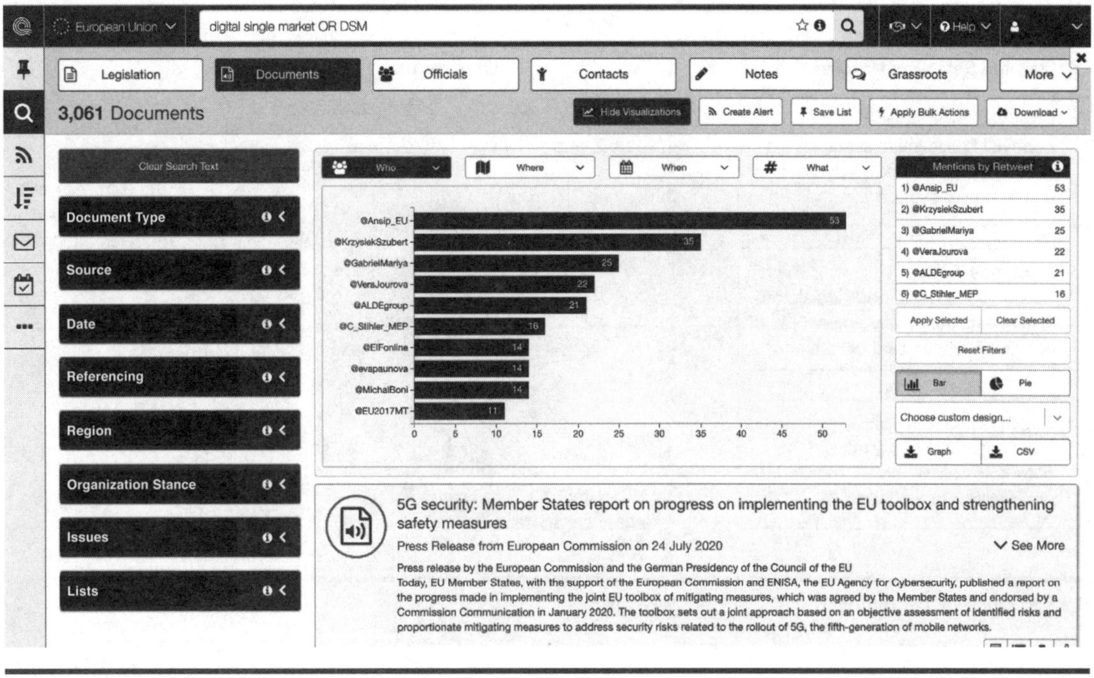

Source: Quorum

The benefit of doing this in an information management system is that the information builds on itself. For instance, once you've entered a stakeholder's importance it will populate in all different parts of the information management system. You can use this to run more specific searches or set up different tiers of alerts. For example, as you continue your monitoring you could now run a search looking at any mentions of your issue but only those coming from priority stakeholders. The information can also flow from EU to Member State level and vice versa.

At this point you will have done a significant amount of aggregating, analysing, and organising information. It is time to use the analysis and infrastructure you've set up in your digital tool to turn inwards and craft your engagement strategy.

We determine the human/digital balance in stakeholder mapping to be 50/50. Once again the sweet spot lies in a combination of both. Human data is required to build the picture but digital systems can give you very accurate pictures of who the key stakeholders are in short timeframes. And from there the AI can help you understand relationships and patterns and also identify the right channels to approach key stakeholders. The AI capabilities in this area suggest that the digital component can give more in the future – so be sure to keep an eye on this.

Figure 3.9: Effective stakeholder mapping visualisation

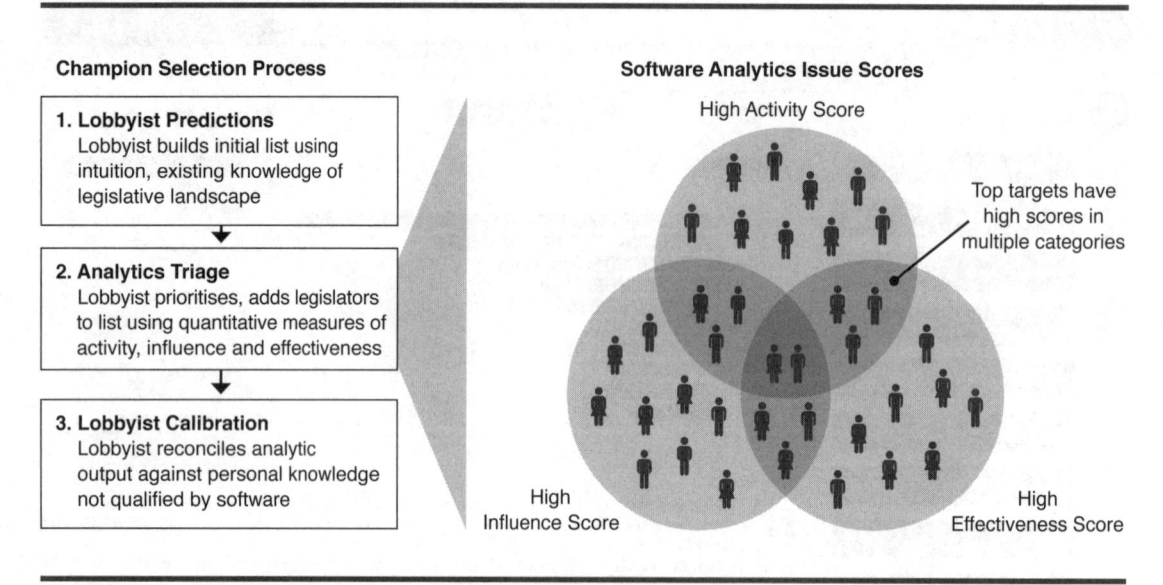

Champion Selection Process

1. **Lobbyist Predictions**
   Lobbyist builds initial list using intuition, existing knowledge of legislative landscape

2. **Analytics Triage**
   Lobbyist prioritises, adds legislators to list using quantitative measures of activity, influence and effectiveness

3. **Lobbyist Calibration**
   Lobbyist reconciles analytic output against personal knowledge not qualified by software

Software Analytics Issue Scores

High Activity Score

Top targets have high scores in multiple categories

High Influence Score

High Effectiveness Score

Source: Quorum (adapted)

4. Managing data for an ongoing strategy/campaign

All through the chapter to date we have highlighted the importance, and value-added, of managing your data in one system. This is the biggest current trend in the digitalisation of public affairs and one from which the industry will build in the future. Data contextualisation offers real value added to your work and this is achieved best by having one integrated system that you build and refine over time. At its most basic, however, there is still value in having your data managed in one place for a campaign or strategy:

- Having all your data in one place, managed effectively, can **save time and build efficiencies** in your ways of working.
- **Access to information is increased**. You make it easy to find as and when people need it (often over several platforms – more on this later).
- You build an **historical record** that survives changing people and circumstances so you will have an effective handover tool and institutional memory.
- You can **perform more AI on aggregated data** that you otherwise would not be able to do.

These are all key reasons to want to manage your data in one place for your public affairs work. As we will come to in the next section, there are also advantages with those technologies that allow you to use their systems from multiple platforms (mobile being the most useful one here).

The benefits listed above are relatively straightforward to understand but two of them require a little extra explanation. Firstly, holding data in one place allows you to have an **historical record** that can be useful for many reasons. It gives you a picture of how things have evolved, what your positions used to be, what stakeholders did and said in the past – in short it gives you access to ever more context that you can use. Another benefit relates to losing staff and on-boarding new staff. How many of us have taken on new jobs where there has been scant or no handover – and certainly no detail of the key stakeholders and what they said (and expected) in their last meetings? The ability to bring new colleagues up to speed in a short period of time, so as to maintain the same high level of professionalism and activity, is greatly boosted by having one system. This benefit should not be underestimated.

Secondly as you build more data your **digital system can perform more AI**. You will be better able to discover patterns, key word changes and developments and effectively mine the data that you have pulled together. Over time the value of this will increase and the outputs will only get better.

We assess the human/digital balance here as being 20/80. Once again the system needs human input and discipline with data – but it is then the system that manages the data and provides the benefits. We believe that the digital capabilities here are only getting better over time, so there will be additional benefits to deploying one digital system in the future. At the same time there will always be a requirement for sustained and disciplined data entry. This takes on to our next section, on the use of digital tools as you manage the engagement phase of the public affairs methodology.

5. Keeping track – managing through the engagement phase

You've prioritised issues and stakeholders, made a plan of action and used digital tools to help you complete your planning phase. The final planning will be done largely offline via team discussions and making final decisions based on calibrating all of the information your team has gathered. However, all final decisions should be plugged into the information management infrastructure you've been building before engagement starts.

If you've taken all of these preliminary steps before you start engaging you're in a better place than most to succeed in your engagement.

So from here in your public affairs work you need a plan to keep track of all the moving pieces that come with an advocacy campaign. Even if you've done detailed prioritisation and methodology setting-up to this point you still need a logistics plan to manage all the different people and flows of information that come with an ongoing campaign. It's important to create a plan and communicate it to all participants engaging on your organisation's behalf.

As we now move into the 'engagement phase' of the EU public affairs methodology, with engagement and messaging as the key stages, digital tools largely take a back seat, though with some very important caveats because the system should still be used to capture ongoing developments.

The most important roles of digital tools at this stage are therefore linked to the two key aspects of the engagement phase, which are (1) data and contact management and (2) messaging and activity management.

5.1 Engagement: Data and contact management

Now that you've laid out the plan and made information available to the team in a clear and accessible way, make it clear what you need from them in return. There are two parts to managing ongoing advocacy. One is making sure that the day-to-day logistics are happening, and the other is ongoing evaluation. We will address the first of these straight away and come on to ongoing evaluation in the next section.

One of the most important things to track on a day to day basis is the external engagement your team is having with stakeholders. This will help with team coordination and will also start to build the data foundations to do meaningful analysis later on. In addition to the benefits listed previously, and looking now from a team coordination perspective, tracking engagements allows you to:
- Avoid making too many asks of the same stakeholder
- Avoid ending up in a stakeholder meeting not knowing that a team member was also there recently
- Keep track of the different ways you are engaging with stakeholders
- Share information to enhance coordination across regions/areas

So what we see here is the continued need to plug information from your engagement back into the system. Logging all your meetings in the system, and flagging some metrics in the system (as you tailor it to your needs) can help you massively in understanding your direction of travel and your progress towards your objectives. So, for example, if you tag whether the meeting was a success or not it will start to give you an overall picture of whether your message is landing or if you need to change something. By flagging any questions, pushbacks or issues in live time it will help others prepare, flex and respond. You can respond in live time to the requests of your key stakeholders. A good digital system will allow you to do this on the go as Figure 3.10 shows.

This mobile capability allows you to work on the go, access information wherever you are and always remain alerted to developments – which can be very useful when you are in engagement action on a live issue. Gone are the days of walking into a meeting without having seen the latest tweet from the stakeholder you are going to meet, or without feedback from a colleague in another country who has vital information for your meeting. All of this increases your professionalism and ability to influence (which is the key outcome you are looking for).

Figure 3.10 Data and contact management on the go

Source: Quorum

5.2 Messaging and activity management

As we noted earlier, you need to focus on laying out as much information as possible to the whole team in advance. In each issue profile be clear about which advocacy channels you are using for that issue. Identify key stakeholders at different parts of the process and why each stakeholder matters.

From there be even more specific: which individual(s) are assigned to which key stakeholders. Make these assignments visible to the entire team working on this set of issues. If you are going to disseminate any type of position paper or other written material, have a folder of all pre-approved material that the team can draw from. If you are using social media channels you will need to track what you have done and what the responses have been – and a good digital system will do all of this for you – giving you more data and metrics to refine your efforts and achieve the greatest influencing outcomes. It is also very useful to have a record of your messaging and activities (not only the metrics of success and how things developed) so that others can borrow ideas and materials and learn from your successes and failures. Capturing everything gives you better data to work with for the future.

Our evaluation of the human/digital balance for managing engagement is 90/10 – which is explained by the fact that in this stage the digital platform is there to capture, store and learn for the future. The work, in this stage, is evidently undertaken by you and your teams.

6. Evaluation

The final piece of the EU public affairs methodology is that of evaluation. Not that it should just be considered at the end: evaluation should be ongoing and not just conducted in a one-time post mortem format. Counting meetings and keeping a log is not enough in itself to generate meaningful insights. When looking through your data you need to be asking, so what? Why does this matter? How can we shift our strategy to achieve more success? What worked? What did not work? The most effective public affairs professionals combine gut and data to answer these questions. Some things you will know intuitively (for example, if a meeting with a key stakeholder went well and ended up changing legislation) whereas other things you will more likely not be clear on (was our social media campaign a success?). You will need to build in data to your evaluation.

As you think about how to conduct meaningful ongoing evaluation consider the following. Who needs what information, how often do they need it, and what is the best format to deliver it? Once you've answered these questions you will be in a better position to set up the required reporting. You will need a certain foundation of data in the system before you can pull meaningful analytics, but if your team has been disciplined in inputting data through all the previous stages of the methodology then by the time you come to looking at evaluation you should have what is required to generate meaningful data to support your exercise.

Once you've entered enough foundational data you can combine that with all the mapping you've already done in your information management tool to pull analytics like:
- Total engagement per issue
- Total engagement with each EU party – are you meeting with the parties you need to engage with or are you just meeting with people that are easy to schedule with?
- Number of meetings with stakeholders that have influence over your issue
- Percentage of meetings per EU institution on a specific issue
- Number of positive vs negative meetings
- Analytics on key meeting feedbacks
- Analytics of any social media campaigns

If you've been good about keeping the information in your information management platform you can likely auto-generate a lot of the above reporting for evaluation purposes. For example, the next visual shows how, by having a complete issue profile, you can auto-generate a visual to see if you're meeting with the right stakeholders.

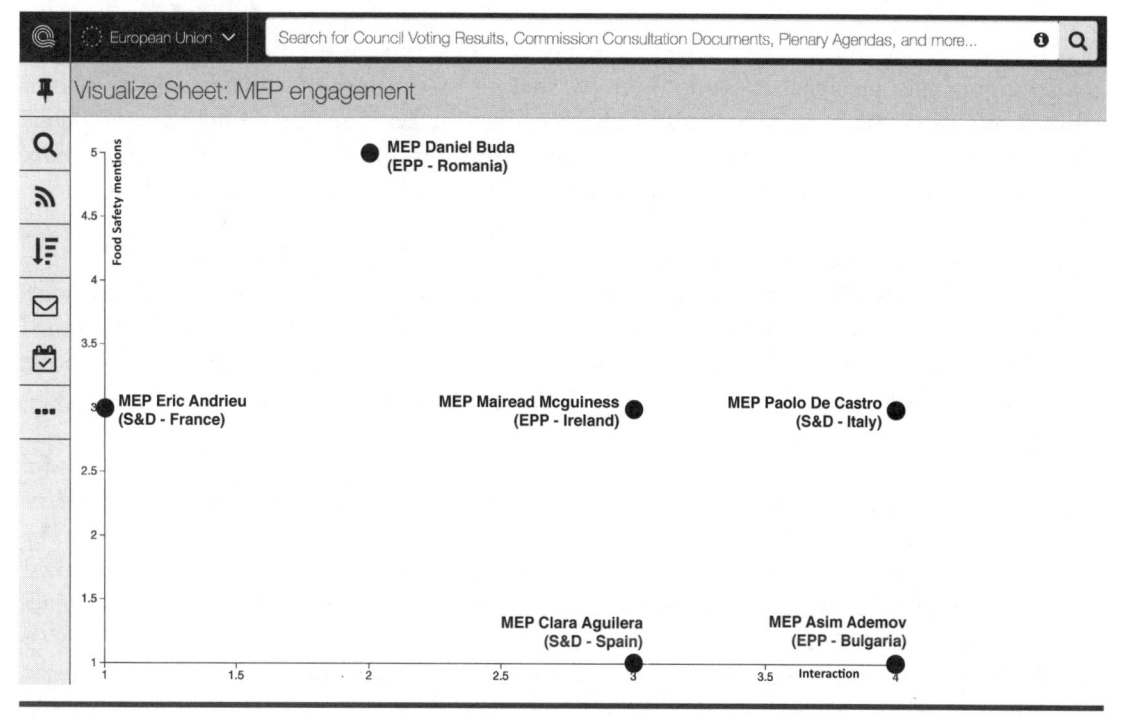

Figure 3.11 Visualisation of influence v. Interactions

Source: Quorum

The above illustrative visual looks at stakeholder influence (on your issue) on the x axis compared to how many times your team has met them on the y axis. This can give you an idea of whether you're focusing your engagements on the right group of stakeholders or if your team needs to shift their efforts. It is a solid metric for evaluation.

In essence serious evaluation is both ad hoc (ongoing) and also structured (periodic). You should be constantly looking at what you and your teams are doing to find better and more effective ways to achieve influence. Data from a robust digital platform makes it easier to do this on an ongoing basis as you have instant access to metrics that allow you to refine what you do and how you do it. In a second phase you should always schedule in periodic broader evaluations that look at all the stages of the EU public affairs methodology, and at the balance between human and digital as this is always evolving.

No single successful public affairs campaign is executed as planned on day one. Almost inevitably your monitoring, stakeholder identification, the channels you use and your message will change along the way.

For both ongoing and structure evaluation our assessment is that the balance of human/digital is currently 50/50 – the balancing point between intuition and data. The digital side of things here is about the fast and efficient presentation of data to help you evaluate, thereby adding to your own understanding and intuition.

7. Summary

Hopefully this chapter has conveyed the importance of looking to embed digital tools (beyond just monitoring) in your public affairs work. As you've seen, there is massive potential for digital tools to enhance your work. We hope to have also highlighted that the key digital trend right now in public affairs is the movement towards embedding one single system for the public affairs of an organisation. We hope this chapter has made it clear why more and more organisations are making this leap.

So why are there still many organisations not making the leap and using digital more?
1. **Culture/Mentality/Way of Working Shift** – A first reason to cite is that the use of digital tools involves a big change in ways of working. Many public affairs professionals are not accustomed to using such a system and some may actively resist it (which experience shows us is often the case). So the use of digital has to fit both with the agenda and drive of an organisation and also the leaders of the public affairs function.
2. **Data entry** – As an extension of the first point, one of the biggest hurdles to the successful leveraging of a digital platform is the discipline required (by everyone) to continually input data. Logging meetings. Actions. This requires a major change in the way of working and needs to be embraced by everyone because in many senses the platform can only be as strong as its weakest link. If key internal stakeholders are not using the system as they should then it undermines the whole intention.
3. **Discipline** – You may recall that this was a key attribute behind influence flagged in Chapter 1. It finds its relevance here in a slightly different context: the use of a digital system requires continued discipline to be effective. Everyone needs to adopt the system as an intrinsic work habit – which can often mean it needs to displace other internal systems to allow your people to focus in/on one place.
4. **Cost** – As always there is the potential for upfront and ongoing costs to frustrate an organisation's desire to take on technology. From a basic Microsoft Teams licence for your people to a subscription with a dedicated public affairs digital platform you have a big spectrum of costs. If you want a dedicated public affairs platform (depending on what options you want bolted into the system) you will be looking into the thousands of euros a month. Dedicated digital systems operate on a 'bolt-on' model such that you buy the basic system (usually on a user-fee basis) and then you look to see what you want to bolt on (for example monitoring of X number of issues in X country).

Every individual and organisation will need to weigh up these considerations when looking at their move into digital. It is worth noting that there are significant potential economies of scale from moving all of your activities into one platform – even if that means working with other service providers to feed into your one selected system.

Finally, it is important to finish by saying that one of the most exciting things about the use of digital tools in public affairs is that it is evolving every day. All of the human/digital percentages we have used in this chapter are evolving. Digital tools will never replace humans in public affairs work but they are finding ever more creative ways to help them succeed.

4. Working with the Media and Social Media in the EU

By Jon Worth

Communication is central to the business of public affairs in EU politics. Chapter 2, on the EU public affairs methodology, highlighted the key role that communications has in engagement success. Yet poor quality communication is all too common – from contorted press releases to impenetrable reports, from tedious tweets to incomprehensible blog posts. This chapter will explain how to not fall into those traps and to work with the media and social media in EU affairs in a manner that is practical, efficient and interesting.

Guides to the individual tools of the communication trade abound – how to do media relations, how to do online marketing, how to write tweets – but most of those are hard to apply to the very specific business of EU public affairs. This chapter will take a different approach. It looks at the public affairs environment in EU engagement – in the Brussels Bubble – as a complete and interlinked system, and explains how to do communication work within that.

The core public affairs business in EU engagement remains legislative work and lobbying, and that will form the main part of this chapter: essentially, how to use media and social media for lobbying purposes. This is a congested, competitive and busy communication environment, with a wide variety of political actors (both institutional and non-institutional) competing for attention. However unlike the public relations business the focus is on who you can reach, not necessarily the total number of people who will see your message. In other words this is about quality and relevance, not quantity.

This chapter will first take a look at the target institutions and stakeholders for the majority of communications activities. It will then look in more detail at the specific communication channels through which these targets consume, i.e. the channels through which you can reach them. It will end with some guidance on how to be as effective as possible.

1. Lobbying and legislative work

Communication in lobbying work is part private, part public. That is to say, some communication is sent directly to lobbying targets and some is done in public. The former is covered in other chapters of this book, and so the focus is specifically on the public component in this chapter. Here we concern ourselves with what an organisation or an individual is willing or able to say in public, and in most cases on the record, about their legislative interests, and to find ways to make sure those interests are met. It is about making sure that you are able to communicate your priorities effectively to help you succeed in your broader EU engagement. It is also about making sure you avoid making things worse for yourself – which is always a risk and one of the reasons so many individuals and organisations are nervous of communications.

> **Target Audience**
>
> The starting point for lobbying communication is to determine the target audience: *who* am I seeking to reach? *Why* am I looking to reach them and *what* do I want to achieve?

The starting point for lobbying communication is to determine the target audience: **Who** am I seeking to reach? From this follows a series of further questions: with **what message** am I seeking to reach them? And **when** in the legislative process is this going to be the case? And then, having answered those questions, **which channels** am I going to use to reach them.

These questions need to be answered in that order, and **this chapter is concerned with the first (who) and the fourth (which channels)**. The chapters later in the book on the Institutions and Decision-Making will cover specific messaging and legislative process points on **what messages** work best **when**.

2. Communicating with each of the institutions

The target audience in EU lobbying is nearly always policymakers in each of the main EU institutions: Commission, European Parliament and Council (and hence national administrations), and possibly other non-legislative actors that might be closer to power than you are. Each of these actors needs to be examined in turn, their communication consumption and incentives understood, and then an approach developed as to which channels can be used to target them.

2.1 European Commission

For communications purposes the Commission needs to be split in two – the Commissioners, and the Commission Services. The two parts are different. The Commissioners are political and can themselves determine what they choose to communicate, while the officials in the Commission Services are restricted in what they can say.

The 27 Commissioners themselves are among the hardest to reach policymakers in the Brussels EU Bubble. They are shielded by their Cabinets and each of them has a communications adviser. Their own media consumption is a combination of the Brussels Bubble and EU focused, together with one eye on the media 'back home', and their consumption of digital media depends on the individual. The extent to which they also communicate publicly depends on their character

> **Midday Briefing**
>
> Commission Spokespeople and, when it is important, Commissioners themselves providing a briefing followed by a Q&A to accredited journalists. It is always live streamed. It's important to find out what is top of the Commission's agenda today.

and background. At one end of the spectrum you have a natural communicator such as Margrethe Vestager who can drive major media coverage more or less whenever she wants to, and is in command of her social media channels too. At the other end there are Commissioners who started in office in late 2019 who are yet to find a voice, and indeed struggle for relevance and an audience in the noisy and busy Brussels communications environment. The **Spokesperson's Service** of the European Commission – officially under the political authority of the Commission President – is an extension of this political aspect of the Commission. Spokespeople are responsible for relations between the Commission and accredited journalists, with the spokespeople facing questions from journalists at the Midday Briefing. Most also have a presence on social media where even non-journalists may occasionally receive answers.

On the **Commission Services** side, each Directorate-General (DG) of the European Commission is responsible for its own digital communication (website, social media channels) and will maintain contact with more specialist journalists (for matters more detailed than at the Midday Briefing). Official DG channels are useful for keeping abreast of what is happening in a policy field, but are essentially of no value for lobbying. This is because any communication back to an official channel will simply land with the communication team (although that team might be able to tell you who the actual responsible official is).

The 25,000 or so officials working for the Commission are restricted in what they can say on the record, and are not normally in direct contact with journalists. Their social media use is also highly restricted, with those daring to say anything in public usually sticking to the official line, or to topics not central to their field of work. The more senior the official, the more they can trust themselves to communicate publicly.

The European Commission, then, poses a conundrum: those with the most freedom to communicate are busy, shielded, and hard to reach, and while the Midday Briefing can help you understand what is going on, it is not a tool if your aim is to influence the Commission. Conversely, those in the Commission who are specialists and might have more time on their hands – in the Commission Services – are the ones whose public communication is more restricted due to the independence required of Commission staff. This ultimately means that public communication might not always be the right route to influence the European Commission.

2.2 European Parliament

Here again the institution needs to be examined in two parts: the official communication of the European Parliament as an institution, and the communication of individual MEPs and the Political Groups in which they sit.

The European Parliament – in contrast to, say, the Bundestag or the House of Commons – feels it has to communicate as an institution, rather than simply allowing its members to do the primary communication work. The Parliament has a press and communication team, and a very well-resourced digital communication operation to maintain its web presence and high levels of activity across a wide range of social media channels. In the context of lobbying work, this communication effort by the European Parliament as an institution is largely irrelevant – by the time the Parliament, as a whole, has communicated something, the decision has long been taken. However the European Parliament's unerring need to look good in the eyes of European citizens can act as a strong driver of behaviour earlier in the legislative process.

Lobbying focus in the European Parliament must instead be on the Members of the European Parliament and their staff, and the communication from Political Groups.

How **Members of the European Parliament** choose to communicate varies enormously, but in essence depends on a small number of key factors. Does an MEP view their political future as becoming a big fish in the Brussels EU Bubble, or do they have political aspirations back home? Do they even have a political future, or is this their last term? Do they view hard legislative work – as a Rapporteur or Shadow Rapporteur or as a diligent member of a Committee – as their central task or not? And when it comes to communication, are they the sort of person who wants to shout about what they do, or are they happy for others to do that?

How MEPs relate to their own staff has a major impact on their communication as well; only some allow their staff to build their own profiles, trust the judgement of the people they employ, and trust their staff to communicate in their own right. The large turnover of MEPs at the 2019 election also means many MEPs are still finding their way in the Brussels Bubble communication environment.

Staff employed by Political Groups in the European Parliament can help give thematic work some policy and communication coherence, but there is always a tension between what a Group can do and communicate and what individual MEPs feel they themselves can do. Larger and more established Political Groups have generally mastered this task better than smaller, newer or more extreme Groups.

Overall the nature of the European Parliament means it is the EU institution most open to public communication. MEPs, because of their need for re-election, are receptive to public messages. Even MEPs' staff and those in Political Groups are not as cautious in their public statements as Commission staff can be. However, you are not going to be alone in being aware of this: while the openness of the European Parliament can be an advantage, it nevertheless means everyone is trying to get their messages through to its Members, so you are going to have to compete for attention.

2.3 Council of the European Union

Both institutional communication and transparency are considerably weaker in the Council of the European Union than in either the Commission or European Parliament. Meetings at Working Group and Coreper level are held behind closed doors, and public communication about what is agreed is scarce. Each Member State's Permanent Representation to the EU does some limited public communication, some of it digitally and some of it as press briefings, but the picture is a patchy one. The strong incentive for the Member States of the European Union is to present every European success as a national success, and to communicate it as such. Simply put, public communication for lobbying purposes is less likely to be effective towards the Council than towards either the European Commission or European Parliament.

The best means to reach the Member States of the European Union is at the national level, in national capitals, if you have the resources to do so. If not, and other lobbying techniques are not available to you, then messaging through intermediaries is the best bet – while you might not find many public statements from those working at Permanent Representations, they are going to be consuming the same media as the rest of the Brussels Bubble.

2.4 Other non-legislative actors

Lobbying does not happen in a void. What you do is part of a wider conversation involving many different actors, all of whom have different communication strengths and weaknesses. Corporates, associations, NGOs, think tanks, academics, and representatives in consultative bodies such as the Committee of the Regions and Economic and Social Committee all want to have their say in EU affairs, and sometimes they will have the ear of policymakers when you do not, and vice versa. Sometimes you will be the nimble, swift actor, while at other times you will be the slow and methodical actor.

To be an effective communicator in the Brussels Bubble you have to be dispassionate about who is doing the messaging (it does not have to be you), and focused on ensuring that the person or organisation doing it is the one that is most likely to be heard by the policymaker you are seeking to reach. Sometimes this might mean acting alone (as a single company or NGO), and sometimes this will mean working as a group (as some kind of association or confederation).

3. Understanding policymakers' communication consumption

Having identified the relevant policymakers who are to be the target for lobbying activity, and some of the challenges and issues when trying to communicate with them, the next step is to understand their communication consumption and to design communication with that in mind. Basically having understood some of the specific constraints linked with the three main target institutions you need to identify how best to approach them, i.e. which channels you can use to greatest effect.

And this is not a straightforward task. Here we need to break down the media consumption patterns of policymakers into five groups:

1. Brussels Bubble media
2. International media
3. National media
4. Specialised media
5. Social media

There are two important pieces of research that provide the basis for this: the 2018 Brussels Media Consumption Survey by ComRes for Burson-Marsteller, and the 2019 Euractiv and EPACA survey of communication trends in corporates and associations. Both not only explain how channels are used, but also give a comparative perspective on how consumption is changing. If you are wanting to be more effective in your EU communications you should take a look at both. The ComRes report lists 6 sources that a cross section of Brussels influencers judged to be net influential ('very' or 'fairly' influential) in their survey:

1. Politico (69%)
2. Financial Times (62%)
3. BBC (59%)
4. The Economist (57%)
5. Twitter (55%)
6. Euractiv (52%)

Of these two are Brussels Bubble media (Politico and Euractiv), three are international media (BBC, FT and The Economist), and one is social media (Twitter).

Digging deeper into the numbers – and cross referencing the Euractiv / EPACA survey – the picture becomes more complicated. Both corporates, with a Brussels presence, and trade associations see 'Industry media and newsletters' and 'National specialised media' (what I refer to as specialised media), and 'National general media' as being increasingly important, although Brussels Bubble media remains the most important overall.

The problem of course is that which national media are going to be consumed will depend on the nationality and language(s) of the policymaker in question, and the topic will determine the choice of specialist media they consume. And the challenge for public affairs professionals is not only to identify how media is to be consumed, but to find ways for their messages to be covered by those media.

The European Commission maintains a list of media staff accredited to the EU, and public statistics on the number of accreditations by category.

Table 4.1: Overview of accredited media staff to the EU (in 2020)

	Cameraman	Journalist	Media intern	Other	Photographer	Producer	Technician other	Totals
non-declared	5	13	-	-	9	1	2	**30**
Audiovisual Radio	5	65	-	-	1	3	-	**74**
Audiovisual TV	61	223	5	1	1	48	24	**363**
News Agency	9	199	2	-	34	2	-	**246**
Online press only	2	139	9	-	-	2	-	**152**
Production company (photo, video)	103	26	2	1	19	25	65	**241**
Written press	-	295	4	-	3	1	2	**305**
TOTALS	**185**	**960**	**22**	**2**	**67**	**82**	**93**	**1411**

The 2020 statistics show 960 accredited journalists, and 451 others (cameramen, photographers, technicians etc.). The number of accredited journalists is slightly higher than the last time this topic was researched in depth in 2015, while the number of others has risen sharply. Online and written press totals 434 journalists, TV 233 and radio 65. This makes the Brussels Press Corps one of the largest overseas press corps in the world, although the vast majority of these journalists are reporting for national media and do not directly concern us here.

3.1 Brussels Bubble media

By Brussels Bubble media I mean those with operations dedicated primarily to covering the everyday politics of the European Union and whose business model depends on a predominantly Brussels based and a completely EU politics focused readership. In this sphere there are two main players, Politico Europe and Euractiv; two minor players, EUObserver and New Europe; one institutionally more niche player, The Parliament Magazine; and a number of players that bridge the gap between journalism, analysis and monitoring such as Mlex and Agence Europe, but that produce close to no public content (examining these is beyond the scope of this chapter).

Politico Europe, the successor to the long standing EU newspaper European Voice, runs the biggest news operation of all in Brussels, with at least 36 journalists (based on my own research). The vast majority of its content is online only, with a small residual print edition. Its free morning *Playbook* newsletter has become a must-read for Brussels policymakers, although its long and dense format does not always make it an easy read. The crucial distinction at Politico is between the content produced for public consumption, for free, on its website and in its newsletters, and its pay-walled web and newsletter content – Politico Pro. While full pricing detail for Politico Pro is not public, the average price for public affairs professionals is between €7,000 and €11,000 a year. Additional revenue streams are sponsorship of Politico's newsletters, and an events series.

Euractiv, from the start always an online-only news operation, operates on a similar business model to Politico, with sections of its website supported by either corporate or public sector sponsors. It too also has daily newsletters – both generally about EU news, and more specifically for policy areas – and an events operation to assist with its revenue. However unlike Politico, which operates only in English, Euractiv also offers content in French and German, more targeted at audiences in Paris and Berlin.

EUObserver, ranking 8th in the Burson-Marsteller report for influence, is an online-only service, with some public news on its website and some pay-walled content. Originally considered to be somewhat EU-sceptic, it has in recent years become a solid EU news source, albeit not with the depth of coverage of its larger competitors.

New Europe still has a print edition, and an annual subscription model for that, and its online structure is similar to its rivals – a mixture of free content and its 'New Europe Insider' subscription system. Promotion of events acts as a revenue stream.

The Parliament Magazine focuses heavily on the European Parliament, and carries sections that profile MEPs and their work, as well as some news coverage of wider EU political topics. It is run by Dods Group, a London based wider parliamentary monitoring company that sells advertising in the fortnightly printed magazine and on the website of the publication.

You cannot hope that all of these media will cover all of your issues, all of the time, although due to their dedicated EU nature they will cover your topics more often than some of the other media listed below will. What each will cover will depend on the journalists they have covering a topic, whether what you have to say is relevant to them, and whether you have a way of reaching those journalists. The extra clout wielded by Politico Europe and Euractiv means you should not seek to over-use these two – keep those in reserve for when something is really important.

3.2 International media

Media with an international focus of course cover the European Union and its politics, but not to the same extent or with the depth the Brussels Bubble media can. The Financial Times (2nd), BBC (3rd), The Economist (4th), Euronews (7th) and Wall Street Journal (9th) all feature in the Burson-Marsteller Top 10 for influence, yet the extent of these publications' EU coverage varies widely. On matters relating to the future of the Eurozone, financial markets, and trade, the FT provides considerable coverage, but on many matters important in the EU – agriculture or climate policy for example – its coverage is inevitably thinner. Euronews and Wall Street Journal will cover EU matters when a story has genuine newsworthiness beyond the confines of the EU Bubble. The Economist is predominantly dedicated to broad analysis, not every day reporting. And while the BBC might be internationally known, its Brussels operation is so intrinsically connected to Brexit these days so as to mean its coverage of everything has to be seen through this prism.

Trying to pitch a story to one of these media is a very hard task as most of the time they are likely to go to their established sources. Contact with these media should be attempted on a case-by-case basis, and only when something is exceptionally important and you can imagine them covering the issue. Long-term trust-based contact with journalists will help – when you say to them that something is important once every 6 months, they need to be able to trust you that it is indeed the case.

3.3 National media

Most major national newspapers, TV and radio stations (especially public service ones), will maintain offices in Brussels to report on the EU. They will also fly in extra staff to cover major events, especially European Councils. What is, or is not, covered by national media is shaped by a number of factors: does the EU story have a national component to it, or are the politicians involved from the media's home country? Is the EU theme one that has resonance at the national level? Do the journalists doing the reporting have the freedom to report as they see fit, or are they more editorially constrained? The nature of EU politics as a combination of the national and the international means that policymakers will keep at least half an eye on the press 'back home' as well as the Brussels Bubble press.

Your approach here needs to be more on a case-by-case basis. Coverage of the EU will be more patchy and sporadic in national media, so you need to find a way to make sure your story will resonate with the audience of that media. Using a local connection or the local language in your communication will help. Also, many Brussels correspondents for national media struggle to persuade their editors back home to carry their stories: you can assist with that by underlining how what you say has national relevance.

3.4 Specialised media

The general nature of this chapter means a detailed examination of specialised media (the trade press, in other words) is not possible, and the extent to which specialised media will cover EU political matters depends on the sector in question and the extent to which EU politics is central to that sector. Specialised media in policy sectors with a heavy EU focus – agriculture for example – will maintain a small staff in Brussels. The total readership of specialised media will be considerably lower than the other media listed above, but the total amount of articles dedicated to relevant topics will be higher. The influence of specialised media will depend on how many policymakers in the sector in Brussels will regularly read it; knowing how much any particular publication is read requires very specific knowledge of a sector.

3.5 Media checklist

In summary, for Brussels Bubble media work you need to ask yourself the following questions:

1. Is this media going to be read, seen or heard by my target audience?
2. Is this media going to cover my topic as news?
3. If it is not news now, is there any way to make my issue newsworthy, either now or in the future?
4. Is there someone in my network who works for that media who I could approach to enquire as to how to proceed?
5. Will this media possibly carry some analysis or op-ed by someone from my organisation?
6. If not, is there any other way to get content there (advertising, sponsorship)?

If the answer to all those questions is no, then it is probably best to look for alternative ways to reach policymakers with your message – and potentially through social media.

4. Social media

Although this chapter is entitled media and social media, the two are increasingly inseparable from each other. A typical media – social media cycle is shown in the box opposite.

> **Typical media – social media cycle**
>
> A journalist may spot a story on Facebook, call the source to check it, write up the story for the website of their media organisation, tweet out a link to that story, and put up a video summary of it on YouTube.

The important distinction, then, is not the technology per se because everyone is using social media technologies. It is instead about the **platform, ownership of information, and control**. A public affairs professional, an NGO campaigner, a Commissioner, a Political Group, or an EU institution can determine *what* it communicates, *when* it communicates it, and to some extent *who* it communicates to through digital channels in a way that cannot be done when working through media organisations.

The problem of course is that messages might not be trusted, might not be seen, or might be lost among the cacophony of noise on social channels. This poses challenges, but also offers opportunities, for public affairs professionals.

5. The hub and spoke model of web communication

In digital communication and social media, the starting point is not to think about the channels, but to think about the message you wish to convey, and to whom you wish to convey it, and only then work out which channels to use to target those people.

Related to that there are **two hard rules of social media communication**:
1. It is better to use few channels well than many channels badly
2. Only use a channel if you have the right content to reach people there

In other words do not ask yourself (for example) *'Should we be using TikTok because it is popular?'* but instead ask *'Is the audience we need to reach on TikTok?'* and *'Do we actually have any quirky videos we could use on TikTok?'* Given that the answer to the latter two questions is probably no for most public affairs work, the answer is to not use it, however cool it might be.

It is also vital not to fall into the trap of looking at vanity metrics in digital communication. Almost anything can be measured – visitor numbers, time spent on a site, number of followers, number of likes, etc. But that only matters in public affairs terms if these are the *right* people engaging with what you are doing. In other words, digital communication for public affairs is about looking for quality of engagement with the right people, not simply the quantity of engagement – the latter is just a vanity metric. (The important element of having solid key performance indicators was addressed in Chapter 2 on the EU public affairs methodology; the focus should always be on outcomes and not processes).

As a point of departure it is important not to restrict your thinking about digital communication only to social media (Twitter, Facebook, Instagram etc.) but also to integrate websites and email services into a holistic and integrated strategy. To do this use the hub and spoke model shown in Figure 4.1.

Figure 4.1: Hub and spoke communications model

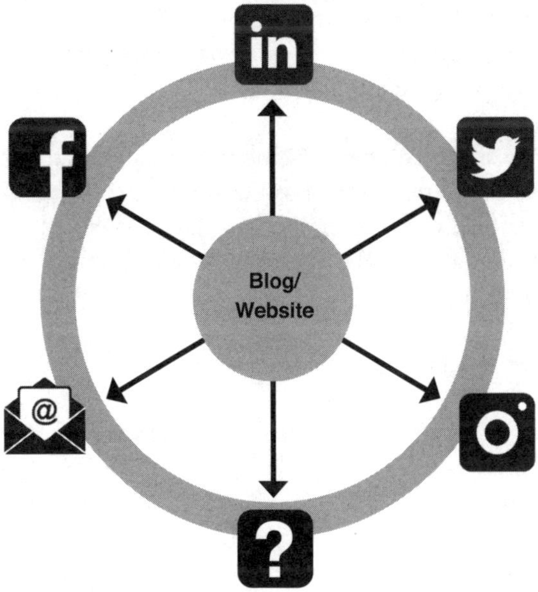

Source: Jon Worth (adapted)

A traditional website or blog is at the heart of this approach for two reasons. First, traditional web communication remains the best form of digital pull communication. Anyone with a question in their mind starts with a web search, and that search will find content on a website or blog, if that content is well structured. Second, a website or blog allows complete flexibility of design and structure of the information presented. Versions of the same message can be produced for direct reading on the web, for use by others (press releases), for detail (reports to download). The combination of text, images and video is completely at the behest of the site owner.

Social media and email notifications or newsletters can then be used to push the message out to key audiences – and the choice and combination of tools to use here depends once more on the sorts of audiences you are seeking to reach.

The balance between as-and-when communication (email notifications being one example), versus communication to a structured timetable (newsletters being an example) will be examined in more depth below. Here it suffices to say that news dissemination by email is the quintessential push communication: you need a person's email address to make it work, and the effectiveness of your email communication depends not only on who is on your list, but how many of them at least read what you send them.

The picture as to what digital channels are used, as opposed to what digital tools are most effective for advocacy in EU affairs is a complicated one, and needs some dissection.

The Burson-Marsteller report cited above puts Twitter 5th (influential for 55% of those asked), and Facebook 10th (32%). However, behind the numbers there are quite some differences. Twitter is more or less equally influential for MEPs, institution staff and opinion formers, while Facebook matters much more (44%) to MEPs than to any other group. This can be attributed to the role Facebook plays for politicians keeping in touch with their base back home – it is not the place where everyday Brussels Bubble politics is played out in public.

In 2018 a Brussels-based public affairs company, Cambre Associates, asked trade associations what social media platforms they used. Twitter (64% of associations using it) and LinkedIn (59%) came out well ahead of all other platforms. However Burson-Marsteller asked how often those in the Brussels Bubble used different digital tools and found 56% WhatsApp at least daily, 46% Twitter, 39% Facebook and just 18% LinkedIn.

So what is going on here and what should we take from this?

Firstly, there is a clear public affairs rationale for the use of **Twitter**. It has featured from Neelie Kroes's 2010–2014 term as European Commissioner for Digital Agenda, when she put Twitter at the centre of her digital communication, to Donald Tusk's account tweeting news of agreements at European Councils before he faced the press. Twitter has become the place to break news in the Brussels Bubble. In both the 2014–2019 European Commission and the current one (2019–2024) every Commissioner has a Twitter account and more than 75% of MEPs do so also.

The neutral vocabulary of Twitter (to Follow rather than to Like), the text based nature of the platform, the shortness of the messages, and the prevalence of Brussels-based journalists on the platform have helped cement its place as the single most important social media for EU affairs. Politico's tool, released immediately after the 2019 European Parliament elections, is a good starting point to understand the dynamics between MEPs, other politicians, and journalists in the Brussels Bubble. Politico researched the 2019 European Parliament on Twitter and built a tool to show how many MEPs follow you, For more, take a look at https://www.politico.eu/article/how-many-meps-follow-your-twitter-account

The picture for **LinkedIn** is a more complicated one. In comparison to other social networks, LinkedIn feels professional and safe. You can make a profile there as a public affairs professional and not expose yourself to the personal versus professional contradictions that make the use of other networks so hard. And then, as an organisation, if all of your staff are present on LinkedIn, this increases the internal pressure for an official organisational presence there too. As Cambre's report documents, trade associations like the European Federation of Pharmaceutical Industries and Associations (EFPIA), or Invest Europe, have built large follower numbers on LinkedIn, and the professional nature of the content associations post there no doubt does not come cheap. But engagement levels remain stubbornly low.

The nature of **Facebook** as a network poses major challenges for public affairs work. More personal and frivolous in nature than Twitter or LinkedIn, the Facebook algorithm that dominates the news feed when users log in prioritises long-term, fan-like, deep engagement over the more sober and dispassionate sort of communication more typical of public affairs work. There is also a social norm attached to liking things on Facebook – liking the page of an MEP from an extreme Political Group would be frowned upon by your friends, while following the same MEP on Twitter would be perfectly normal. All of this explains why Facebook works better for Members of the European Parliament than for other EU political actors – MEPs can use it for their communication with their base and especially with their activists, people who already have a strong bond with the politician.

Other public networks – **Instagram, Pinterest, YouTube, Vimeo, TikTok** – suffer a different fate. The nature of EU public affairs – people talking to each other at events, in conferences, in committees – does not lend itself to compelling images or video content that are vital for success on these networks. Taking your complicated political message, putting it on a sign and photographing it or filming it does not make for success either.

WhatsApp – and other messenger equivalents such as **Telegram, Signal and Wire** – serve a rather different purpose. I am only going to allow someone to even have my messenger contact details if I know and trust that person. Further, what is published in a WhatsApp or Telegram group is not generally for public consumption. These tools are hence more for the maintenance of networks and notification of what is happening elsewhere than for outright content production.

All of these social media channels are now well embedded into the Brussels Bubble communication environment. You gain rather little advantage by going running after the next shiny new thing, and instead need a level-headed assessment of what works, and a relentless focus on your target audience and whether they will be using a platform or not. In simplest terms, Twitter remains the main tool for public digital communication, with WhatsApp and other messengers of use for private communication. A case can be made to use other social networks such as LinkedIn or Facebook based on individual circumstances.

6. Organisational, professional or personal communication

An organisation does not communicate, its people do. Yet much of the communication we consume in EU affairs bears the name of an organisation, not the name of the person who actually produced that piece of content. An official position of an organisation lends that document more weight and more credibility. Yet social media, and even relations with media organisations and journalists, rely not only on the quality of what is said but on the personality of, and the connection one has with, the person communicating the message.

Anyone involved in politics is used to interpreting these sorts of organisational and personal signals in the offline world. The raising of an eyebrow before answering a question, a clever pause at the right moment in a phrase. Media and social media are no different – skilful digital communicators can work with this grey area, to be edgy enough to be interesting but not so edgy so as to be dangerous.

One of the central reasons why LinkedIn struggles as a network for policy advocacy is that it is so professional it makes the network too dry, leaving too little room for interpretation. Conversely Facebook is so personal, even frivolous, meaning it is not serious enough for public affairs. Twitter – with its 'anything goes' combination of organisational, personal and anonymous accounts – puts the responsibility for determining where the line is as to what is acceptable in the hands of its users, both in terms of the information they consume and the information they produce. 'Tweeting in a personal capacity', accompanied by a person's work affiliation in their biography, is the height of this ambiguity – essentially it says trust me because of the role I have, but do not think of suing my organisation if you dislike what I say.

Not every member of staff in your organisation will have a public communication role, but almost all of them will have social media profiles, even if most of these are for personal rather than professional use. To avoid accidental reputation damage, and to protect your staff, every organisation needs a social media policy – explaining what is and is not allowed, and outlining what to do when things go wrong.

Social Media Policy

Every organisation (no matter the size) needs to have a robust social media policy (or guidelines) to educate everyone as to what is possible, what is not allowed and also what to do if things go wrong.

7. Agenda-following or agenda-setting, and broadcasting or interacting

One of the most complicated aspects of modern media and social media communication is its always-on nature – how can anyone actually do any other work if they have their eye on the news or their social media feeds all of the time? A further major challenge is to fit this into the structure of an organisation that might operate according to a very different tempo or rules. If you or your organisation are struggling with this issue, you are not alone.

Further on we will explain individual aspects of running social media channels, but at the outset do not think all of this can be centralised into one staff unit. At least some of the responsibility for social media needs to be spread across the whole of an organisation, not least because the correctness and timeliness of responses are often more important than their style, and only the experts in a field can answer with the necessary credibility. The official channels of an organisation, and social media analysis and monitoring, are the two main areas that can be dealt with by a dedicated team.

Many organisations have complicated and cumbersome sign-off procedures for any piece of content. These must be at least streamlined for the social media environment, which also lessens the burden on staff. The best is simply the 'four eyes rule', meaning that any piece of content must be read by one other person before it gets sent, and that any staff member with communications responsibility can sign off any other staff member's content. Any system more hierarchical than this will prove to be too slow.

The problems social media pose for political organisations are summed up in Figure 4.2, a sort of typology of Brussels Bubble tweets, broken down in terms of agenda-setting or agenda-following, and broadcasting or interacting, although the essence of the problem is not channel specific.

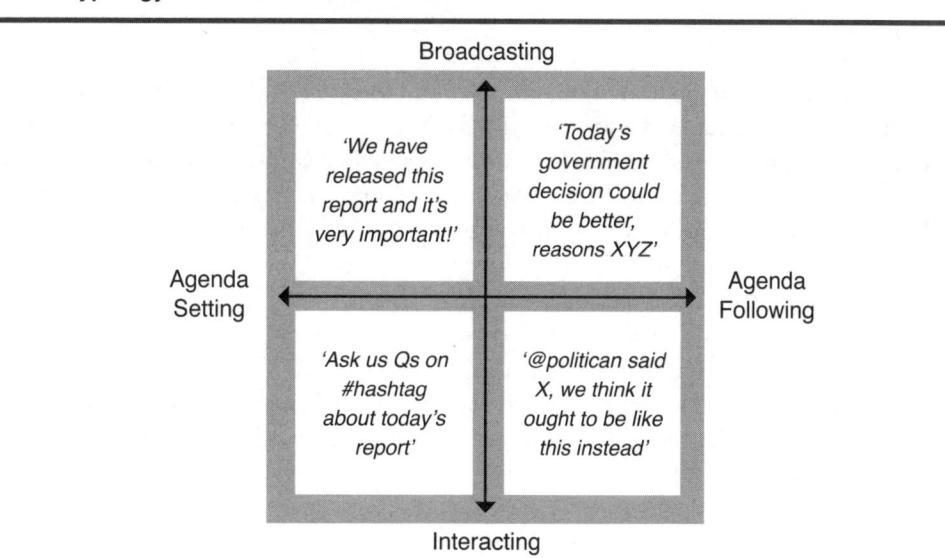

Figure 4.2: Typology of Brussels Bubble tweets

	Broadcasting	
Agenda Setting	'We have released this report and it's very important!'	'Today's government decision could be better, reasons XYZ'
	'Ask us Qs on #hashtag about today's report'	'@politican said X, we think it ought to be like this instead'
	Interacting	Agenda Following

Source: Jon Worth (adapted)

The easiest and quickest is (attempted) **agenda-setting and broadcasting**. The timetable according to which a report has been produced will be a function of an organisation's internal procedures and constraints, and then when it is released the communications team will be charged with getting eyeballs on this content to the greatest extent possible – either through media relations or on social media. Yet to try to set an agenda, to get your message heard against the background noise of everyone else trying to do the same, and the hubbub of other news that is breaking, is a hard task. A person is only going to be receptive to a message if it is not only relevant but also timely.

The opposite – **agenda-following and interacting** – is the most complicated and time consuming of all, for it first requires an understanding of what is going on, and the ability to engage with that topic in real time.

A solution, at least in part, is a division of labour. Monitoring what is currently hot on the news agenda, or will be hot in the coming days and weeks, can be allocated as a task to a dedicated team, or expertise on that issue bought in from a monitoring company. For example, Political Groups in the European Parliament provide this sort of support for their MEPs, informing them of what the hot topics on a given day will be, and even which Twitter hashtags to use, but not actually formulating the content for the politicians themselves. This then frees up time for more senior colleagues to focus on the message itself, not on the timeliness of the message.

While the quadrant in Figure 4.2 is designed for Twitter, the same dilemmas apply across all digital channels, and particularly to email. Most newsletter systems are designed to send to a fixed schedule – once a week or fortnight normally – but in today's swift news environment that might not be fast enough. Email notification systems that send once a piece has been published online can overcome this problem.

7.1 Senior people – is it really them?

One of the thorniest issues in modern public affairs communication is this: when we read something from a senior person on social media, do we really believe that it is them? The reputational danger of releasing something to media organisations in one's own name without having read it is too great a risk, so one can safely assume an op-ed, even if ghost written, has at least been OK'd by the senior person. Radio and TV are likewise clear – you can see or hear the person.

Yet in digital media it is much more complicated. If I see a tweet, blog post, or LinkedIn post from a Commissioner, MEP or senior business person or NGO representative, do I know if that is actually from that person – even if it is written in the first person? There is a reputational danger here too – for if that 'person' has interacted with me, and then I encounter that person in real life and ask them about it, and they do not know anything of the conversation it is clear the personalised communication on the digital channel was faked.

The essential aspect here is honesty. Audiences can well understand that a senior person might not have time for all their own communication work, so do not build up a false impression that communication is personal when it is not. Even if you can get away with it for a time, it can bite you in the future.

8. A wider public in lobbying campaigns

So far this chapter has been relentlessly inward looking – identifying the right actors in the Brussels Bubble and choosing the channels to reach them. Yet once in a while EU politics breaks out of these narrow confines, an issue captures the public's attention, and thousands or even millions of people seek to make their voice heard.

Brussels has of course seen its fair share of protests on the streets over the years, but digital communication allows citizens to express their views from their homes and campaigners have been able to use this to demonstrate to policymakers that an issue really matters to a wider public. The cost of mass campaigning has dropped in the digital era; gathering signatures digitally is quicker and cheaper than on paper, and mounting protests digitally is simpler than physically having to move people.

The European Parliament in particular cannot be immune to public pressure – its members want to be re-elected after all. Even the European Commission, fearful of the existential threat to the EU posed by the aftermath of the financial crisis, wants in some fuzzy way to show it is responding to the public mood. The introduction of the European Citizens' Initiative system a decade ago has provided a further mechanism for public participation.

Issues as diverse as wanting to stop the clocks changing each spring and autumn, banning neonicotinoid pesticides, stopping discards in the Common Fisheries Policy, and preventing the ratification of the Anti-Counterfeiting Trade Agreement (ACTA) have all been causes for successful online protests directed at the EU institutions over the past few years. Each case pitted NGOs and their supporters on one side against business interests lined up on the other side, and in each case the EU institutions, at least partially, sided with the protest movements.

The important issue to bear in mind here – whether as someone mounting such a campaign, someone on the other side of the argument, or indeed as a policymaker in the middle – is to separate the signal from the noise. A one-click signature from a random citizen is less of a signal than a hand-crafted email from a fisherman. A tweet about a topic took less time for a person to prepare than a phone call made to an MEP's office. The jobs or yields lost through a fishing or pesticides ban are going to be more powerfully told by a person from a policymaker's local area speaking about their livelihood than they are through statistics presented in a report by a lobbyist.

> **The power of human stories told in person cannot be replaced – but they can be relayed on social media.**

The most important issue to bear in mind here is the *signal* that you are able to send to policymakers, not the total number of signatures or the platform that you use to gather signatures. This is the case whether you choose to use the European Citizens' Initiative system (that also offers technical guidance on how to do so), a petition platform such as WeMove.eu or Change.org, or host your own tool. A petition platform can help speedily gather signatures, but the method of deluging policymakers deployed by those platforms can also annoy MEPs and Commissioners. In designing a campaign think about the messaging, campaign goals, and targeting first, and only then make your platform choices.

8.1 Earned versus paid media

The vast majority of media and social media work in EU affairs is earned. This means that the coverage that you gain from journalists, the readers of your online content, and the quality and breadth of your network on social channels is determined by the energy and commitment that you have invested in your communication work. In other words, you get a readership because you have something worthwhile to say, and have built a network receptive to that message. Building this network is a slow and grinding process, done systematically over a long period. Building a strong network online uses the same sort of combination of skill and relentless determination as it does offline. Trust is hard and slow to gain, but can be lost very quickly.

However it does not always work that way. It might be the case that a media organisation does not consider your issue to be newsworthy enough to merit coverage. Or on social channels you need to build an audience quickly; or the increasing prevalence of algorithms to filter news feeds means the network design is against you. Advertising or sponsorship might be the only solution in these cases.

The rules to bear in mind when it comes to paid media, advertising or sponsorship are not too dissimilar to those that apply when structuring the rest of your public affairs communication work. Where is your target audience, and are they going to see the message that you pay for? Do not simply fall for the availability heuristic *'Predecessor X sponsored Politico's Playbook, so we should too'*, or for vanity metrics on social channels. *'Why do we not advertise to get more people to like us on Facebook?'* is the wrong question – instead ask *'Can advertising on Facebook help us reach X number of policymakers we otherwise would not reach?'*

When it comes to advertising on social media, start small (with even just a few euro), test, iterate, improve, and repeat. Sponsorship or advertising in Brussels Bubble, international media or national media is going to need a much more considerable initial investment (at least a five-figure sum for a one page advertorial for example).

8.2 Wider organisation-building and reputation management

The focus of this chapter has been on media and social media for lobbying purposes, but Brussels-based organisations cannot completely ignore organisational development and stakeholder management functions. A trade association needs to remind its members why it exists, the Brussels office of a corporate needs to justify to headquarters why it is necessary, and the EU policy office of an NGO cannot neglect its supporters and funders. Media and social media work can of course play a part in these cases as well.

It is wrong to assume that members, a headquarters, donors or supporters will all be content with private communication about the Brussels operation, or with just a periodic newsletter informing them what is going on. Social media in particular, when engagement is sustained and long term, can be used as a tool to build a strong and authoritative network that can then be deployed at a later date for more specific lobbying purposes, or for reputation management in the case of a crisis. The problem is to quantify the cost of ongoing engagement when times are quiet and smooth – and here however, as in all aspects of media and social media work in EU affairs, the issue is the quality of the connections made, not necessarily their number.

9. Conclusions

Media and social media for public affairs in EU politics is a very particular environment. By definition the communication is public, but the topics at hand and the nature of public affairs work constrain the audience for any message. The emphasis has to be relentlessly on reaching the *right* people, not on the sum total of the people, with the partial exception of some campaigns that can deploy wider public support to good effect. It pays well to always remember to focus on the outcomes and not the process metrics – which are almost always related to how you manage to influence key decision-makers (as opposed to how many people follow your account). Personalisation and honesty about who is communicating are central to success, and paid media can in part act as a substitute for earned media. In today's modern communication environment, a clear separation between media and social media is no longer possible.

From this it is possible to give the following guidance for work in EU media and social media:
1. Media and social media are only any use for public communication – lobbying without using these tools is still possible.
2. The neat separation of media and social media is no longer possible – the two areas are increasingly overlapping. A good public communication strategy in the Brussels Bubble will need to cover both.
3. Be relentless in your focus on your target audience, and work out where that audience will be and what media it will consume.
4. Use media channels sparingly and only when you need to – even Brussels Bubble media will not cover everything you have to say.

5. Do not fall into the trap of using the shiny new tools on social media, or using vanity metrics. Social media is a stable and established part of the Brussels communication environment and will remain so.
6. Be human. Organisations don't communicate, people do. Think of that in all of your communication across all channels.

5. Third Country Lobbying in Brussels

By Alan Hardacre

The objective of this chapter is to provide some practical guidance on **how third countries (i.e. non-EU countries) can represent their interests in Brussels**. It looks into the challenges and opportunities that third country Missions and Embassies in Brussels face in their tasks of representing their home countries. It also develops, in more detail using the EU public affairs methodology which was the subject of Chapter 2, a series of specific recommendations and guidance, drawn from experience, to execute a successful third country lobbying strategy and campaign in Brussels.

For the most part the chapter will focus on third country Missions and Embassies as a proxy for the engagement from/by a specific country. That is to say, it will focus on the third country mission as the main, or central, vehicle for engagement on behalf of the interests of their country as opposed to other stakeholders such as business or NGOs. For many countries it is often the case that their Mission or Embassy is the sole national representative active in Brussels. Clearly there are some major exceptions to this – notably bigger countries with extensive business networks in Brussels such as the US, China and Japan to name but a few. Where appropriate, the chapter will also refer to the ways third country companies can find hooks and opportunities to engage in Brussels beyond their Embassy or Mission (which, to be successful for their specific issue, is often necessary). Finally, it is worth stating the obvious here – the UK, and UK companies, are now firmly in this third country category and will thus benefit from the guidance and suggestions in this chapter.

> Working with the EU institutions and EU decision-making can be complicated for EU Member States and European stakeholders. Third countries have specific advantages and challenges when it comes to engaging in Brussels. Often their remit is very large and their understanding of Brussels limited.
>
> On the other hand their special status opens doors others would usually find closed. Building a well-structured and effective lobbying strategy can be a challenge for many third countries in Brussels. Using the lobbying methodology outlined in Chapter 2 will assist you in planning exactly how you can do this.

1. Third country representations: the Brussels landscape

The 164 third country Missions and Embassies in Brussels are a very powerful group of stakeholders with a strong vested interest in EU decision-making. The very fact that so many countries have accredited representation to the EU itself, and the resources they then devote to these representations, is testimony to how seriously they are trying to engage with the EU institutions. It is, however, one thing to have representation and resource but something entirely different to be effective and successful. It is also worth mentioning that non-EU companies also have a significant presence both in Brussels and in the EU decision-making procedures. This fact is only natural given the potential (and actual) impacts of EU legislation on their business operations. We will look, later in the chapter, at why companies from some countries have no foothold in Brussels whereas companies from other countries are so well represented in Brussels.

As outlined in the introduction to this book, the more powers Brussels has gained the more lobbying has naturally followed, making Brussels the second largest centre of lobbying after Washington DC in the US. One aspect of this is the increase in powers that the EU has seen in its external relations with third countries, not only in trade and economic policy but also in the realm of politics and security through its Common Foreign and Security Policy (CFSP). The EU is a major global actor and also a major global market. Its vision and endeavour to be a global security actor, alongside the US and other global security players, was clearly stated in the 2016 EU Global Strategy (EUGS) – the strategic document setting out its interests, principles and priorities. It also focused on how the EU can deliver more coordinated foreign and security policy actions in a more connected, contested and complex world.

Third countries therefore need to deal with Brussels both in terms of traditional political diplomacy and also in terms of trade and commercial diplomacy to protect and advance their business interests. Whilst these might be two very separate domains, they also very much overlap when it comes to how third countries can work effectively in Brussels and this is something that this chapter will try to address. That said, the main focus of the chapter will be on the commercial diplomacy side of things given the almost identical nature of it to lobbying in the EU as outlined elsewhere in this book. Lobbying on CFSP and other 'high political' matters are different environments and, while there may be some parallels, they are sufficiently different to warrant omission from most of this chapter. We do, however, need to recognise that all Embassies and Missions to the EU will cover all of these elements in their work, which will impact both their focus and their resources. We will come to this later.

Before moving into an assessment of the advantages and challenges faced by third countries in Brussels we should first look at the specific context that Embassies and Missions find themselves in when looking at relations with, and how to engage, the EU.

2. The diplomatic context for engagement

The EU is both a major global actor and also a major global market. For now, we need to focus on the former and how it deals with third countries because this is important context for the question of how to work, and succeed, in Brussels. The EU manages its external relations based on its own values and interests and from there through a series of semi-formal and formal agreements, associations, alliances, summits and trade agreements. It is a complex web. Let us start with the EU's values and interests as they are a key cornerstone for any third country engagement.

The EU itself (European Parliament website) states that;

> **Know Your Agreements**
>
> An absolute priority is to know what agreements/declarations and other bilateral instruments your country has with the EU. Ensure you do a sweep of everything from the last 10 years. You will then have a basis for dialogue and the hook for engagement.

'The European Union's action on the international scene is guided by the principles that inspired its own creation, development and enlargement, and which are also embedded in the United Nations Charter and international law. The promotion of human rights and democracy is a key aspect. The Union also highlights its strategic interests and objectives through its international action.'

Shared values can be an important foundation for effective work with the EU. This is not to say that the EU will not work, and productively, with countries that do not share its values but it is an important premise on which to build relations. For any third country with difficulties in this respect it is often advisable to set up a dialogue or process to discuss shared values (which will be important for other agreements and discussions down the line).

The quote above also gives a nod to the international and multilateral role of the EU which it takes very seriously. In this it is always looking for alliances and support and this can provide third countries with opportunities to subsequently leverage. As the chapter will discuss further later, relations with the EU need to be seen in a global context to be leveraged effectively.

The EU has different types of relations with third countries depending on its own, and also mutual, interests. We can categorise the following:

1. **Strategic partners**. Some time back the EU focused on having strategic partners, something that had symbolic but not legal weight. The ten countries concerned were Brazil, Canada, China, India, Japan, Mexico, Russia, South Africa, South Korea and the US. These are clearly key partners for the EU across the spectrum of its interests – and as such will benefit from this status in their relations with, and ability to engage, the EU.

2. **Assistance and funding partners**. The basis for many countries' relations with the EU is premised on assistance and funding support from the EU, be that through development aid/assistance to Generalised System of Preferences (GSP) status.
3. **Alliance partners**. These are the many countries with which the EU has standing or ad hoc alliances in and across international organisations. These are partners that are important to supporting the furthering of EU values and interests in the world.
4. **Security partners**. Born out of the EU Global Strategy mentioned earlier, the EU is looking to build a new category of partnership based on responding to external conflicts and crises, building the capacities of partners, and protecting the Union and its citizens. This is currently a key focus for the EU: to get its security partnerships right. Quite a number of countries, for different reasons, have been granted this status – from Australia to Georgia and New Zealand.

These categories of EU external relations highlight evolving EU interests and how they look to work with the rest of the world to fulfill them. Each third country will need to look at how and where they fit into this EU scheme and from there what this means for them – and for their ability to engage in the EU. There is clearly a difference between these categories of relations and how different countries will get access, be received and listened to. Logically the more important you are to the EU the greater your potential influence in the EU. At the same time, outside of this somewhat official categorisation, all third countries have opportunities to successfully work with the EU.

Having outlined the diplomatic context for engagement in the EU, we will now move to look at a summary of the advantages and challenges that third countries face in their work in Brussels – before moving on to make some recommendations for third countries in how to leverage their advantages and address their challenges to get robust public affairs strategies in place for their commercial diplomacy.

3. Advantages and challenges for third countries working in Brussels

All stakeholders looking to engage with the EU institutions have advantages and challenges related to who they are, what they do, where they come from, who they know, and what they want to achieve. As the box to the right highlights, undertaking a SWOT analysis is a great place to start to understand the situation you (and you alone) are facing. It will help you understand what you can leverage, what you need to focus on and where you have issues that you need to deal with. In essence it will give you a reality check moment for the work you are looking to achieve. For third countries this should include any existing agreements and dialogues with the EU that could be leveraged/updated/renewed or any opportunities to build new and different types of

---

SWOT Analysis

A good starting point for anyone looking to build a lobbying strategy in Brussels is to do a SWOT of their situation.

Strengths
Weaknesses
Opportunities
Threats

Make sure this is based purely on lobbying considerations.

relations with the EU. The following two sections are in essence the strengths and weaknesses from a generic SWOT analysis of the lobbying situation of third countries in Brussels.

Let us start with the advantages (strengths).

4. Advantages for third country lobbying in Brussels

Third countries, when they look at their specific situation in Brussels, will discover that they have a set of advantages that are quite unique to them. They must understand what these are so that they are able to effectively leverage them, which will be very important in offsetting the challenges/ weaknesses that they also have. Perhaps the biggest weakness **many third countries** have is that they **don't fully know and understand their advantages and how to exploit them**. Let us take these in turn.

4.1 Leverage relations with the EU – from the start

Given the privileged nature of diplomatic relations (see next point for more on this) every third country has the opportunity to directly ask the European Commission for what they want. When new Ambassadors start in Brussels the European External Action Service (EEAS) usually sends them a proposed Roadmap for the coming years of their relationship. This need not be a one-way street. It is an opportunity to add key items to the agenda for relations (e.g. funding, alliances, taxation, Schengen waiver, modernisation of FTA/ GSP, etc.).

As mentioned earlier a key premise for this is to know exactly what type of relationship you already have with the EU. What is the existing web of relations? What needs updating? Renewing? Extending? What else could be done? This is constantly evolving and should be based on what you want as much as what the EU wants. The key question then becomes, what are your priorities for relations with the EU?

The point about sweeping your agreements and relations with the EU is also that it gives you history and context to your relations and requests, which can be important.

4.2 Diplomatic status = excellent access

A key, and hopefully one of the most obvious, advantages that an Embassy/Mission of a third country has in Brussels is the ability to use diplomatic status to gain access to decision-makers. The strategic use of diplomatic status, networks and privilege can be a huge opportunity for third countries. It is premised on knowing who to meet, when to meet them and what to say/give them. Brussels is a very active diplomatic city, awash with activities and events every day. Embassies and Missions in Brussels organise all sorts of things: formal meetings, receptions, cultural and family activities. These activities cover a wide range of their interests – from promotion of their country/culture to trade and commercial through to more political issues and geopolitical diplomacy.

As an accredited representation the third country will have privileged access to decision-makers. It is often easy, and without consequences, for decision-makers to refuse meetings with many sorts of stakeholders, but this is much less so with diplomatic ones. So whilst not a card to overplay or abuse, the fact that third countries can achieve excellent access gives them opportunities that many others do not have. The best access will obviously be reserved for the Ambassador, or key national officials coming to visit, and a fully engaged and Brussels-savvy Ambassador can alone be an immense asset to a third country – building networks and making timely interventions with the right people to put their country's interests into the spotlight as and when required. National representations can also make the most of national delegations visiting Brussels, especially Ministers and high-ranking officials. Done well this can be a very powerful means of influence.

This is an advantage that should not be underestimated in any way as access is one of the most difficult things to achieve in EU lobbying. Having the ability to use your status to open doors is incredibly valuable, but like many privileges it should not be abused. Used in the right way, it can be a strategic asset that will ensure the country has the opportunity to be heard by all the key people on the subjects of importance to it. Used in the wrong way, it will quickly lose its power and will have the opposite effect to that desired, tarnishing the country with a bad image and one which will mean its representatives are not taken seriously.

4.3 European Commission DGs and the EEAS – Source of information/sherpas

A third advantage (although many third countries might not necessarily see it as such) is that they have on hand an internal Sherpa to help them navigate the decision-making maze of the EU – the European External Action Service (EEAS). At the EEAS, every country has a desk officer (or officers) assigned to it. Although the primary focus from the EU side is to ensure alignment in interaction to protect EU interests and priorities, there is simultaneously an opportunity for the third country to understand more about the EU from inside the EU institutions. As well as the country (geographical) desk officer(s) at the EEAS, it is important to identify the thematic or dossier desk officer(s) matching your thematic interests in various European Commission DGs. This is a bit more difficult to navigate as you have to find the right person(s) under each DG and establish contacts with them. This level is more of a technical than diplomatic discussion and engagement. Your EEAS desk officer can always navigate you through the network of EU institutions.

Once again the third country finds itself with privileged access to people within the EU institutions and to their knowledge and networks. To some extent this role as a Sherpa will depend on the individual desk officers – but in a generic sense it is an opportunity that third countries should look to exploit. Trying to set up meetings, run events or find information is always easier with the help of someone from inside the institutions.

4.4 European Parliament Delegations

The European Parliament has Delegations of MEPs for literally every country, region and international organisation in the world. These present an opportunity although in some cases they can also be a threat to third countries' interests. The European Parliament outlines the role of its Delegations thus:

'As elected representatives, EP Members are committed to make the voice of EU citizens heard internationally, reflecting our values and strategic interests. And it is through the work of the delegations, that we pursue dialogue with our partners from third-countries, to seek shared prosperity and peace for our citizens, particularly through the reinforcement of Democracy and respect for Human Rights.'
Source: European Parliament website

At its most basic what this means is that within the European Parliament there will be a group of MEPs (possibly just a few) who will have a specific interest in your country. These Delegations are not the main role of an MEP, but it is one that is often taken very seriously. So again within an EU institution, you will have excellent access to decision-makers who are specifically interested in your country/region.

The Delegations meet at regular intervals and they interact not only with the Ambassadors of the countries and the EEAS (always the Sherpa) but also with think tanks working on and looking at the country as well as with NGOs and stakeholders from the country itself. In addition the Delegations often pay visits to the country in question – so-called inter-parliamentary meetings. The opportunity for access, information-sharing and influence through these Delegations is clear. At the same time, the risks should also be quite clear given the focus and drive of Delegations towards *'values and strategic interests'*, as quoted above. The Delegation is going to get involved in your affairs, whether you like it or not, with some specific angles of interest that may not be what you want to focus on or even have mentioned in Brussels as you try to work on something else.

Whichever way you look at Delegations they represent both an opportunity and also an engagement necessity. Here are some steps to help;

1. Firstly map out the members of the Delegation: there are usually from 6 or 7 up to 20 to 30 MEPs.
2. Understand who is most interested in your country by checking MEP questions on VoteWatch, or looking at minutes of past meetings, or media reports from past Delegation visits.
3. Through your research identify any potentially friendly MEP(s) and look to meet them.
4. When you meet the MEP get a firm understanding of the focus and interests of the Delegation.
5. You are now ready to support the Delegation from a position of knowing their focus and interests and you should provide all the support needed.

Beyond the work of the Delegation itself, the key MEPs you encounter this way can act as excellent conduits into the Parliament on files you are concerned with. They can help explain context and politics, open up doors in their Political Group, or even work as your internal advocate. Once again you have a privileged opportunity to leverage internal access to your benefit.

4.5 Council contacts

This one is slightly more problematic and to a considerable extent dependent on both history and current international relations. We have seen how every third country has privileged access and opportunity in the European Commission and European Parliament, but the Council is more difficult. In essence you are looking for relationships, such as those that your Ambassadors to EU Member States may have, that will allow you access to information and an ability to exert influence in the Council. The effectiveness of your lobbying will depend on your ability to work with the Council as well as the Commission and Parliament.

Historic ties are the first opportunity that could yield the relationships you need. Many third countries will have some historic link with an existing EU Member State that could, in some way, be leveraged. One only has to think of, say, Brazil's relationship with Portugal or many African countries' relationships with France. If not that, then perhaps economic ties with a particular Member State due either to investment by it in your country or investments you have in the Member State in question. These links need to be explored and understood before they can be leveraged. There will always be some solid trade, investment or aid links to Member States that can ultimately be leveraged. And, as we come to shortly, third countries have the resource through their Embassies (or through Member State Embassies in their country) to reach out and build the required relationships.

One thing that is very important in this regard is to have a clear view of your two-way trading relationship with the EU, broken down by Member State. You need to find leverage in this exercise as a basis for conversation and for potential action, with a focus on identifying mutual interests between the EU Member States and your own country.

4.6 International memberships/alliances/networks/dialogue forums

On a broader scale it is likely that your country will interact with the EU and individual EU Member States, as well as with a wide range of other European and non-European stakeholders, in other forums than just the EU. Be that within the Brussels networks, or in international organisations or regional bodies around the world, there could be great relationships or opportunities that can be leveraged. It is a case of looking at and mapping these stakeholder networks and alliances to understand any additional points of access, sources of information, and vectors of influence or opportunities. The next important step is to select which network, forum or contact it is useful to build an alliance with to achieve your objectives and also which ones are working against your positions.

Looking for common interests with the EU in the International Monetary Fund, World Trade Organisation or sectoral discussions on the environment could all lead to an enhanced ability to work in the EU itself. The Brussels Embassy or Mission needs to make the links to its other Embassies and Missions in these key places (New York, Geneva etc.) to make this point very clear. There are some real opportunities in this if coordinated correctly.

As will be becoming clear, there is a great deal of homework and coordination needed to be effective. The stakeholder mapping exercise, as discussed in Chapter 2, is a key starting point in identifying the relevant actors and contacts, but the more important task is to keep it updated and to engage with these actors strategically. The EU Mission/Embassy needs to have the capacity to coordinate all of this work required to leverage the opportunities. We will touch on this when we come to the challenges.

4.7 EU network of Embassies – Member State Embassies in your country

One of the biggest assets, if used and deployed effectively, is the network of Embassies that the country will have across the EU. Being able to interact across all EU Member States is something that most companies, NGOs and other stakeholders can only dream about given the resources required to do this. So the question is less one of having the network to get information and access for influence but rather of how to coordinate and manage this. Let us therefore look at some guiding questions/considerations for this to happen because this is too big an opportunity not to exploit in some way:

1. The Brussels-based Embassy/Mission needs to take on a **coordination role** because it has to direct other Embassies in the Member States as to what is needed and when on EU matters. The coordination role is the key to everything that comes next – without it the network will be a wasted opportunity.
2. Every Embassy across the EU needs to be **directly tasked** (through objectives ideally) with a clear picture of what they are expected to deliver to the Brussels-based Mission so it can plan and interact accordingly. What information is required? What are the priorities? What is expected and needed?
3. There needs to be **central guidance** and regular information updates/flows/calls so everyone knows what is happening and what is required. In essence it is like running a team or a project – and that is perhaps a good way of understanding how this can work.
4. The main aim of this coordination is to have **coherence in your positions and messages** on EU matters, meaning not only in Brussels but also in the EU Member States where the same messages and positions should be advocated through your Embassies. A very likely chance is that your messages and positions will be reported back to Brussels through the EU Member State Permanent Representations. This would help your lobbying at the Council.

When it works well, the ability of a Brussels-based Mission to operate a multi-Member State network – a network that transfers information on Member State positions and EU developments and simultaneously is able to go out and influence locally – is invaluable. It requires some investment in coordination, management and running but the payoff will be far greater than the investment.

Overall these are a significant set of advantages; indeed, advantages that most EU companies and stakeholders would welcome (or can only dream of) having. And the fact of the matter is that these advantages are all available to all third countries. The question is how well they understand this in order to make use of these advantages and whether they are able and prepared to invest in the effective coordination required to make it all happen. For third countries these advantages need to be exploited to maximum effect for them to have an impact in Brussels. All of them can be integrated into building effective EU lobbying strategies and campaigns – as we will see later in the chapter.

So now let us move on to some of the challenges that third countries face and need to find ways of offsetting.

5. Challenges for third country lobbying in Brussels

Having looked at the advantages that third countries enjoy in Brussels we must now turn our attention to the challenges (weaknesses in a SWOT). This section will identify the main horizontal challenges encountered and explain in more detail the nature of each one, building towards some potential work-arounds and solutions. The main challenges are essentially to do with resources (section 6 below) and focus (section 7).

6. Resources

One of the first things any stakeholder in Brussels will tell you is that they don't have sufficient resources, and third countries are no different. They are not geared up to be professional lobbying machines and therefore they are not resourced to do so either. The issues with resources, for third countries, come in a few different shapes and forms. Let us look at them in turn.

6.1 Staff, expertise and human resources

The first one is a human resource issue – both in terms of the number of people and also the skills and knowledge they have. Firstly, it is likely that the Mission/Embassy will be fulfilling many different roles, which means that people will be stretched thinly and unlikely to be 100% focused on EU lobbying activities. This makes it an internal question of priorities and focus. We will come to that next. Secondly, does the EU team have enough background and expertise on EU issues? The likely answer, in a diplomatic rotation service, is no. There is no easy (or quick) fix to this one – and sadly a one-week course in the College of Europe (as prestigious as it is) will not fix the problem. Getting to know the vagaries of the EU takes years and then only if you are knee-deep in it with a willingness to learn. Rotating staff in and out on a 4-5 year cycle means you are effectively getting people to hit their peak (after say 3 years) only to see them leave shortly thereafter. When you rotate staff you lose the retention of information, networks, contacts, skills and knowledge – especially if (as is seemingly often the case) you do not perform a full handover

Third Country Lobbying in Brussels 119

or have the required IT systems to act as an institutional memory (for example with stakeholder maps, contact log and all past activities and materials).

In simple terms here we come up against one of the biggest impediments to exploiting all of the advantages highlighted previously. If you do not have the staff equipped with the requisite knowledge then you will not exploit the opportunities at your disposal. So here are some ideas on how to circumvent this happening:

1. A developing trend in many EU-based Missions is to **hire local staff** to act as an institutional memory and source of EU expertise – people who can act as a bridge between departing and arriving staff and therefore deliver some consistency and alignment. Just one (even part-time) local staff member will be a massive boost to your ability to engage and exploit the opportunities. They will become your own internal Sherpa.
2. One step back from this is to form a **long-standing consultancy relationship**, although oddly this is likely to be more expensive than hiring in staff. It is seeking to fill the same gap, by providing EU expertise on tap and then some institutional memory and consistency in actions between staff changes.
3. If the previous two options are not available, there are a few things you can do to try and smooth both the passage and knowledge gaps of staff. Firstly you can ensure **robust handovers** so that while not everything will make sense from day 1, at least everything is there. There should be a required core of materials to be handed over (which means they must be created and updated in the first place) such as Stakeholder Maps, Contact logs of who spoke to whom (with notes from meetings), lists of actions undertaken, notes on any consultancy agreements. Another way to do this is through working with the **right technological solution**, i.e. one that actually already holds and stores all of this information. There are specialised providers of such platforms (which could also be used to work on EU projects across Embassies/Missions, for example). Such a system drastically reduces the need for a robust handover because there should be a full overview already available. It certainly makes it easier if there is no handover. See Chapter 3 for more information on this. Finally **training** and (more importantly) **coaching** needs to be part of the incoming staff requirements. Here a few pointers:
   a. Some **pre-reading** should be mandatory – but not treaties and (only) academic books. **Practical books** and articles on how things really work in Brussels.
   b. A **training course** is a good starter. And here the key word is starter. Like much in-depth training without follow-up it is often forgotten. The College of Europe is a good place, but it's expensive so maybe think of tailored training from specialist providers or Brussels consultancies.
   c. Irrespective of the training and reading already done, one of the most critical things is **follow-up**. This can be either by **coaching or consultancy** but it should be something that offers a safe learning space on a regular basis. As most people will be learning on the job (they don't have the luxury of doing otherwise) this coaching will be based on their job. This will allow them to learn and develop over time, which is essential to them becoming fully operational.

Linked to the human resources within an Embassy a further key element is the right investment in language skills – in the EU, this usually means English. An ability to communicate effectively is a prerequisite to successful engagement. If you have staff members who speak good English then make sure to send them to meetings with other colleagues as this will vastly improve communications.

6.2 How do you get more support from back home?

The second aspect of resource that is (or can be) an issue relates to how the Embassy or Mission is able to coordinate and get the right (timely) information from HQ back home. This brings the challenge of how to prepare and package information in the right way, and in the format and style the EU institutions will read and digest (and the requirements of the institutions will vary).

It is essential to name and identify documents correctly and of course not every piece of information sent from your national capital should be sent on to the EU institutions. This can be tricky, because requests from Brussels can often lack context and not be entirely specific about what is needed. It could also be the case that people at HQ in your national capital might not understand the EU context and procedures well enough to find and send you the information you want. Furthermore, information (often) needs to be made available promptly – which with time differences and different working routines and cultures can be a challenge. In simple terms the Embassy will depend on its ability to get the right information, packaged in the right form, in the right language at the right time – and this challenge should not be underestimated. In fact dealing with it should be an absolute cornerstone for a robust EU Mission/Embassy.

The issue of how a Mission/Embassy works with its HQ is vitally important as your HQ is an important mechanism to help you in establishing your country's interests and positions and also in linking you to national actors and stakeholders. It is a relationship that can, in itself, pre-determine success or failure. So, for example, how important is the EU (issues) for your HQ? How well do they understand the EU and how to get things done? Whatever the answer to these questions, there is likely to be an important educational role for the Ambassador and other staff in getting EU issues to land back home. Time spent back home educating your HQ colleagues on EU issues, processes and priorities will rarely be time wasted. From there, how do they react to EU issues – are they cooperative or are they ignorant of the impacts? Do they send your reports and information from Brussels to the right national stakeholders? Clearly, the answers to these questions will determine how seriously they will take your issues and how much support they will give you. So a lot of work is required at national level to ensure the support that is needed in Brussels.

There is a key role for the EU Mission in educating those back home. Part of this relates to how they share information, how they update and how they invite and receive delegations from back home. These are all major elements of how a Brussels outpost should work if it is to succeed at EU level.

Here are some suggestions on how to improve this:

1. **Educate, educate, educate**. There needs to be solid ongoing education of key national partners to keep them in the loop and updated. You can't escape this need.
2. **Context** is everything. Make sure you understand the request before you send it on and be as exact and precise as possible. The better the ask the better the return.
3. Give a **clear timeframe** allowing others to then make a choice of what is possible within that timeframe; and of course look to give as much time as possible.
4. **Speaking** can help immeasurably. One call can save hours.
5. Ensure that Ministries back home understand the **importance of providing information to you**. This might sound obvious but often these requests will arrive outside of people's usual routine and objectives, meaning they can be resistant or put the request to the back of the queue.
6. **Review and repackage** information from HQ to match the EU style and format for each EU institution.

Invest in a good press attaché. You need to understand and work with EU journalists to shape your messages.

6.3 Financial resources

No discussion of lobbying constraints would be complete without a word about financial resources. Does the Mission or Embassy have enough resources to train and coach its people to do their jobs effectively? Does it have the resources to engage consultants and think tanks, to work with NGOs and other stakeholders, and to run campaigns in the same way that other stakeholders are doing? As we have seen elsewhere in the book all of these things cost money – and in some cases a lot of money. So the likely answer to the question is: no, it doesn't. In this case the question becomes one of correctly prioritising the resource it has. I would suggest the following order of priority:

1. **Empowering staff** needs to be the first priority, so they can then undertake the various tasks required of them. Effectively exploiting the opportunities open to a third country will, alone, make a real difference for the country. In this respect the most important item is the continuous coaching of staff to help them learn while doing so in context and to evolve with the needs of their job. Investing in your own team should be the absolute priority because the ability to leverage a team will be a major boost to your chances of success. You can also look to have dedicated point people for institutions or key relationships to help them develop and ensure that you are covering all the engagement bases that are important for you – as opposed to just trying to have it all in the hands of one person.
2. **Local staff or consultants** should be the second priority as a means to ensure the necessary EU expertise and continuity required to be effective in Brussels. Ideally, as discussed, this would be a local staff member, but a consultant is a good back-up. They can train, coach, support, act as an institutional memory and provide strategic guidance as and when required.

3. Beyond these two priorities the most important thing would be to have an **effective campaign fund** for any other priority needs. So, as opposed to just randomly joining think tanks or allying with NGOs or other membership bodies, the emphasis should be on allocating resource to priority issues or relationships and on coming up with a clear budgeted strategy for these. It is more important to put your money behind focused priority initiatives than horizontal memberships.

7. Focus of the Mission/Embassy

As was discussed in Chapter 2 on the EU public affairs methodology, having clear objectives and key performance indicators (KPIs) can be a determining factor in lobbying success. It is if anything even more important for third country Missions and Embassies given the multi-faceted nature of their work. Without focus and priorities, Embassy staff can get pulled in every direction given that almost all EU legislation could have an impact on their country. They need to know very clearly what the priorities are and how this integrates into their overall workload.

Clarity and transparency sound simple but can be elusive. Here the guidance would be:

1. Develop a **clear EU priority plan** that lists out the main EU priorities for the Mission/Embassy. This should be developed with key stakeholders back home and the network for EU Embassies to ensure all stakeholders are on board.
2. Cascade elements of the plan into the **objectives and KPIs of individual staff** to show accountability and responsibility.
3. Translate the EU priority plan into the Mission/Embassy's concrete activities, annually, monthly, weekly, daily.
4. Have **regular check-ins** both with the wide stakeholder group on the priorities and with staff on progress against objectives.

7.1 Connections/contacts in Brussels

This point is a bit of an extension of the challenge of having rotating staff but is sufficiently important to be expanded on here. People take years to develop effective networks in Brussels – indeed people are hired on the basis of their networks alone. For a new member of staff in Brussels it will be vital to be building the right networks from day one. So where should they look?

1. The **European External Action Service** – the most obvious (and actually required) place to start is here. And the first question should be to ask for their views on who else is key for you to know.
2. The **European Commission DGs** – for more technical aspects and focused on dossiers that match your lobbying objectives.

3. The **European Parliament** – MEPs from your own country delegation or other MEPs who have shown an interest in your country (e.g. through MEPs' questions or other media work).
4. Any **diplomatic contacts** from current or previous lives who are now in (or have been in) Brussels. These can be a great potential source of helpful information, insights and further contacts.
5. The **network of EU Member State Missions/Embassies** – especially with any colleagues who have worked on EU files.
6. Any **regional body networks in Brussels**. Perhaps your country belongs to a regional grouping and maybe they organise themselves in Brussels to share information and to pursue common objectives? If they don't they are at least a good first port of call, maybe with a view to creating something.
7. Any **alliance of countries or networks outside of regional bodies**. These can be issue specific, linguistic, based on WTO alliances – you name it. The theme is that there is a common denominator pulling you together to work in the EU.
8. **National companies in Brussels**. Are there companies from your country working in Brussels? Are they organised together? You should find them and reach out – perhaps with a view to pooling together as and when required.

There are many places to go to build a network quickly and effectively – and always remember to ask every person you meet who they think you should meet. This can be a surprisingly quick way to build a stakeholder map and network.

7.2 Understanding Brussels… and lobbying

Again, this point is somewhat linked to the resource issue of staff knowledge of the EU. There is a further aspect that requires some elaboration. That issue is understanding lobbying, both in the EU and generally. The first comment to make here is that almost all diplomatic staff do not see themselves as related (in any way) to lobbying or lobbyists. In seeking to work effectively with the EU institutions they do not need to actually become lobbyists – they merely need to learn to adopt the right techniques to be effective.

For many third countries a lack of understanding of lobbying, or even a reluctance to engage in lobbying, can prove detrimental. This can manifest itself in the activities carried out. For example, trying to influence and engage only by using classical diplomatic channels and activities; or failing to understand the value and services of Brussels-based consultancies and other service providers.

A key item to be added to the educational list for incoming diplomatic staff should be something on lobbying in the EU. Even better would be to equip diplomats with training on lobbying back home as part of their core curriculum. Those skills would help them wherever they posted.

7.3 Generating leverage for engagement from the outside

So how do third countries go about generating leverage from outside of the EU itself? We have seen that they have potential for excellent access into the institutions (and thus decision-making) but once inside they need to be able to exert some leverage. Let us look at some items for this:

1. There needs to be a **link to a Member State or Commission or Parliament interest** to be effective. The more links (in the more Member States) the better your case will be.
2. You will need the **data and statistics** to demonstrate your case. It will allow your key decision-maker to take on your issue more easily.
3. As was identified earlier in the chapter you will need to **map your economic and political relationships** so as to be able to leverage them when required.

This section has discussed a number of potential challenges and weaknesses that all third country representations need to deal with, along with some recommendations for how to overcome them. Every third country is able to harness its opportunities and mitigate its weaknesses without too much investment although it may take some time to get thing right. We will now look at what this could mean for more effective engagement in the EU.

8. Third country lobbying in the EU: Recommendations & Guidance

In this final section we provide a series of recommendations and guidance, drawn from experience, to build and execute a successful third country lobbying strategy and campaign. This is a build out from the previous sections on opportunities and challenges, integrated into the EU engagement methodology described in Chapter 2. When you put them together you are able to create a dedicated set of recommendations, across all seven stages, for third county lobbying in Brussels. Figure 5.1 provides an overview.

In Figure 5.1 we recommend specific actions and guidance for third country lobbying across each stage of the general lobbying methodology. Let us now look at each stage in turn to give the most robust recommendations and guidance possible.

8.1 Objective and priority setting

As was mentioned earlier it is vital that clear EU public affairs objectives are set for, and from, the EU Mission/Embassy. Such clarity will help individual staff members and with handovers; and it will give focus to learning, knowledge acquisition, networking and any consultancy support. At the same time, and perhaps even more important, there has to be a process for creating, checking on and evaluating these objectives. Some suggestions would be:

Figure 5.1: EU lobbying methodology: Recommendations for third countries

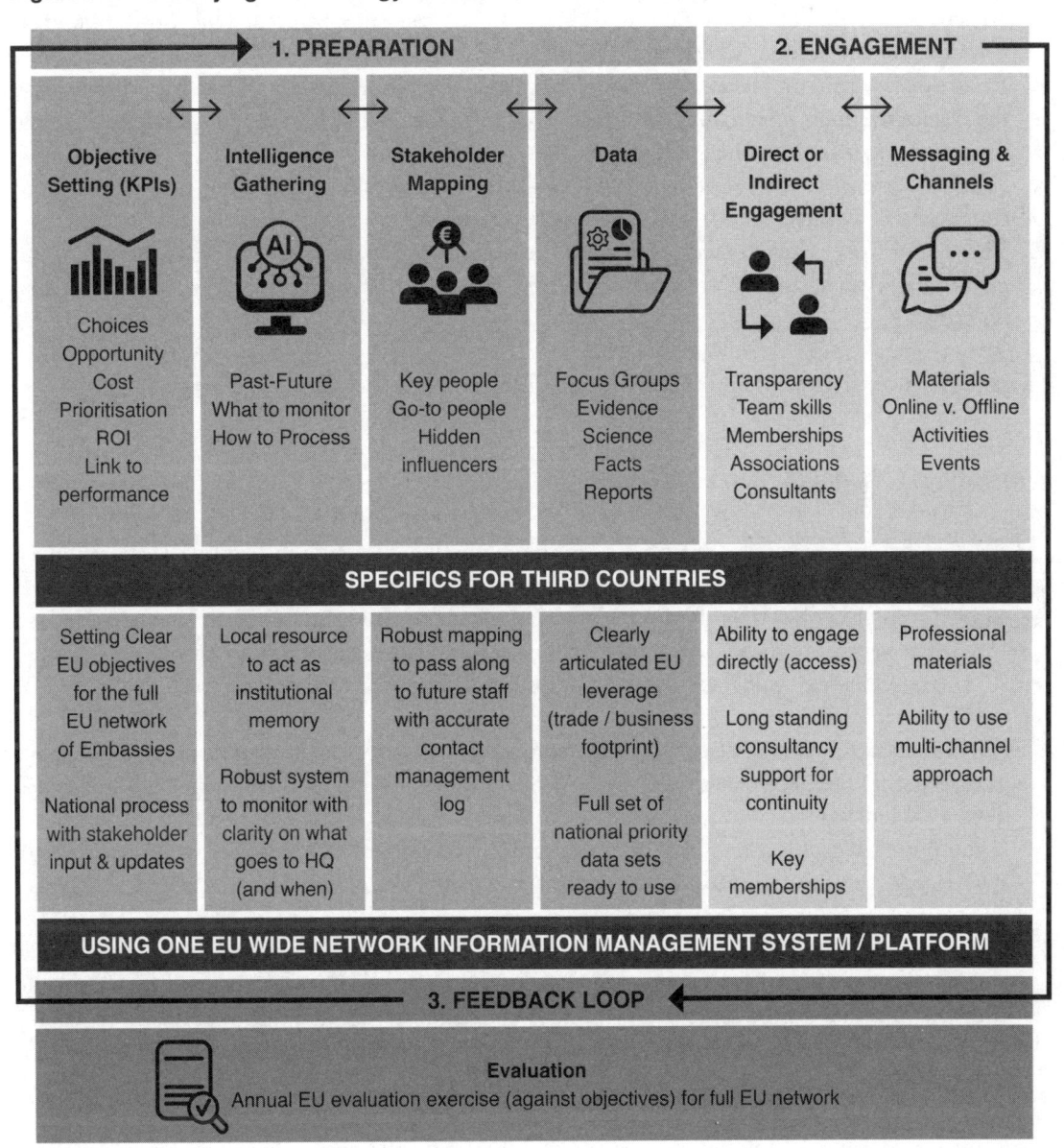

1. PREPARATION

Objective Setting (KPIs)	Intelligence Gathering	Stakeholder Mapping	Data
Choices Opportunity Cost Prioritisation ROI Link to performance	Past-Future What to monitor How to Process	Key people Go-to people Hidden influencers	Focus Groups Evidence Science Facts Reports

2. ENGAGEMENT

Direct or Indirect Engagement	Messaging & Channels
Transparency Team skills Memberships Associations Consultants	Materials Online v. Offline Activities Events

SPECIFICS FOR THIRD COUNTRIES

Setting Clear EU objectives for the full EU network of Embassies National process with stakeholder input & updates	Local resource to act as institutional memory Robust system to monitor with clarity on what goes to HQ (and when)	Robust mapping to pass along to future staff with accurate contact management log	Clearly articulated EU leverage (trade / business footprint) Full set of national priority data sets ready to use	Ability to engage directly (access) Long standing consultancy support for continuity Key memberships	Professional materials Ability to use multi-channel approach

USING ONE EU WIDE NETWORK INFORMATION MANAGEMENT SYSTEM / PLATFORM

3. FEEDBACK LOOP

Evaluation
Annual EU evaluation exercise (against objectives) for full EU network

Source: Alan Hardacre

1. Create some form of steering group back home amongst key stakeholders to ensure that EU objectives have the full buy-in (and understanding) of everyone required. This form of building from the bottom will pay dividends later.
2. Ensure that, within the stakeholder group consulted back home, business, NGOs and others have the chance to input, present and comment. This will allow you to both build a stronger platform for action and also flush out interested parties.
3. The EU Mission/Embassy needs to itself *own* these objectives, but it also needs to delegate and coordinate as required across its EU diplomatic footprint.
4. There need to be regular meetings of both the steering group and the EU network, in order to give updates on changing objectives and new objectives as well as updates against existing objectives.

These four simple steps will provide a robust platform for both back home and across the EU.

8.2 Intelligence gathering

This is where these seven stages of the methodology shown in Figure 5.1 can fall like a house of cards if not done properly. If you have not properly identified (and verified) your EU objectives then it becomes very hard to gather intelligence in a way that will serve your purpose. Too many EU Missions and Embassies employ consultants to gather intelligence against very open and obscure briefs. So for this:

1. Having a local resource will help you understand how to leverage all of your advantages to gather intelligence. Remember that already within your specific advantages there is a lot of intelligence to be gathered.
2. If you don't have a local resource (or consultant at this horizontal level) then you need to look at the opportunities outlined in this section as a first port of call for gathering intelligence. Use your assets before you look to pay for information.
3. If you have robust and clear priority issues you can take basic monitoring services (such as DeHavilland or Cicero) for very good annual prices (circa €10,000). This will be a valuable safety net for you. At the same time you need to recognise that this information is raw data – so you will need an in-house expert (diplomatic, local or consultant) to decode it and turn it into actionable intelligence.

These three recommendations will help to put the most cost-effective monitoring system in place. Something else that is important at this stage is understanding what information to send back to HQ and in what format. Clearly, the raw data you are receiving from your intelligence gathering will not be sufficient – it is raw data without real context or any intended actions/suggestions. You will need to establish a clear link between all of your intelligence gathering and what and how you report back to HQ. If you have clear objectives and good in-house EU expertise then you will easily be able to craft this.

8.3 Stakeholder mapping

There are two key elements in the recommendations here:

1. A robust and up-to-date **stakeholder map** is essential: there is no way around this and the rotation of staff in Embassies and Missions makes it even more important. Each office needs to develop (or buy in if really pushed) a clear stakeholder map for their issues. This can be done in-house by using all the opportunities the Mission/Embassy has at its disposal and the EU knowledge it has to hand. Or, if this is not possible, you can look to get one done by a consultancy; a basic mapping should not be too expensive. A best-in-class mapping would include all relevant EU network contacts and any international contacts relevant or useful for the EU.
2. You need an equally robust and up-to-date **contact log**: this is secondary to actually having a map but is an invaluable support for it. Whereas a stakeholder map can be created relatively quickly, or bought in for a small cost, there is no escaping that the contact log needs to be built in-house and over time. Essentially you will need to ask all staff working on EU matters to log and record all meetings. As we have seen in Chapter 3, this is technologically possible with providers offering dedicated state of the art services for use in public affairs. A cheaper (but less sophisticated or efficient) solution is of course to just record everything in a Word or Excel document – the essence being that a record is kept. Not so many organisations prove able to do this properly, but the discipline within the diplomatic world should allow it to be possible. It can become an invaluable resource for all public affairs work and especially (not to overplay this point) when there is staff rotation.

Knowing who your key stakeholders are, what their views and positions on your issues are and who met them last (and what was said) is a best-in-class aspiration. But it is one that is eminently achievable for any Brussels actor with the determination to do this.

8.4 Data

As with the last section there are two key components to the recommendations here and they are very much generic for all stakeholders in Brussels.

1. You need to develop a **full view of your EU leverage** and put this into a variety of engagement materials and formats. This is about telling your story and how you are relevant and linked into specific EU interests. You need to be able to explain why something that is important to you is also important to whoever you are talking to. So think economic, political or aid links. Think about the agenda and interests of the key stakeholders and how you can tie into this. From there you need to turn this into professional engagement material. An obvious starting point is creating some visual factsheets, ranging from general information about your country and your country's

relationship with the EU through to more specific issues. You should aim to develop a core library of these assets that you then keep updated on a periodic basis and add to as required. These will be valuable engagement tools when you come to it and to have them to hand like this will save you time and energy when you need to spend it elsewhere.
2. An extension of this is to make sure you develop a **full set of position papers** and other relevant materials in your library. Once again the one-off exercise of building this and the ongoing exercise of updating it will mean you always have what you need to hand when the time arises – allowing you to focus your energy on the engagement and not the content creation. Also as an 'inheritance' for new staff it can be a great boost to know they have materials to work with from day one.

Getting this right is going to be a combined job for the Mission/Embassy and the HQ but it should be done with the support and insight of an EU expert (in-house or consultant) to ensure that it always has the right EU tone and focus.

8.5 Direct or indirect engagement

When it comes to recommendations here we will need to separate them into a few different subsections because there are different areas that need attention. So each of the individual headings below will group relevant recommendations.

1. **Direct engagement**. As we saw in the section on opportunities, third countries have a rich array of engagement options at their disposal. Let's break these down a little as there are three key direct engagement opportunities:
   a. **Ambassador:** The EU Ambassador will have excellent access to senior stakeholders and should be used for these meetings as a priority. They should also be able to gain fast access to other stakeholders which on occasion could prove very useful or necessary. This is an important card to be able to play but it needs to be played in a strategic way.
   b. **First Secretary/Director level:** At this level there are many contacts to be coordinated and met with – partly to set up any meetings for the Ambassador but also to be cultivated in accordance with objectives.
   c. **National delegations:** If there is a major issue that the country wants to give air time, visibility or a push to, then it should organise a national delegation visit to Brussels. While time-consuming these can be impactful if used and timed right. Clearly the seniority of the national delegation will determine the appropriate level of meetings in Brussels.

2. **Indirect engagement: Consultants**. Most Embassies/Missions will use consultants in one shape or form. Using them for engagement is a possibility – but here the best value would be as Sherpas as opposed to actually directly representing your interests. As outlined previously, third countries have excellent access that they should not need consultants to help with. Consultants can help with EU knowledge, perhaps even personal knowledge of stakeholders and issues, and generally act as a Sherpa.

Making use of consultancy is very important to many stakeholders, including third countries. Some things are important to stress:
   a. You should look for a consultancy with prior experience of dealing with third countries. This means they will have a better idea of the sort of information required and also understand the world you work in and your needs (and therefore be able to tailor their service to you).
   b. You need to be very specific in what you ask. The better defined your objectives and focus, the better service you will get in return.
   c. In working with a Brussels consultancy a local hire, or a general consultant or coach, can add great value in sorting out the good from the bad in terms of proposals. Actually taking a consultant (you trust) to help you take pitches from consultancies will be money well spent.

3. **Indirect engagement: Memberships**. Memberships are always tempting and almost always offer a good sell. You should, however, be careful in selecting memberships to think tanks and the other plethora of organisations in Brussels by asking the following questions:
   a. Will this impact/support the objectives I have?
   b. Do I have the resource/time to follow the organisation to make sure I get the most out of it?
   c. What value-added does this offer my needs?
   d. Is this a general 'nice to have' or a specific 'need to have'?

Taking the time to understand what actual value the membership will bring is important. It will help you to use your budget with a focus on what matters for your country.

4. **Alliances**. From an engagement perspective there is one last important area to return to – that of alliances. So do you have, or can you create, any alliances with other third countries working in Brussels? Even a few countries cooperating on the same issue can bring economies of scale for monitoring, consultants and intelligence gathering (as this is competitively neutral). These do not need to be formal alliances – even just informally they can be very successful.

8.6 Messaging and channels

There are two key issues to highlight when it comes to how an Embassy communicates in the Brussels arena:

1. There is a need to play at the same level as other stakeholders in the EU so **professional materials** are necessary. The engagement space in Brussels is very competitive and to be seen and heard and impactful you need to ensure you are playing best-in-class. One important way to do this is to have professional engagement materials. You can do this in-house (if you have the right design skills and software), back home with agencies (as this is likely cheaper) or with a local Brussels agency (who will have the EU know-how). Your materials have to have the right content, format and style that match with the various channels you will use.

2. Secondly, you need to recognise the **multi-channel nature of EU engagement** and communication. This does not mean you need to be on all channels (as this is expensive and time-consuming) but you need to carefully understand where your key stakeholders are leaving information and being influenced. You will need to have more than one channel (meetings and calls) to be effective. (This topic is dealt with at length in Chapter 4.)

8.7 Evaluation

It was noted in Chapter 2 that evaluation is in practice probably the least developed and the least professional of the seven pillars in the EU public affairs methodology. It can too easily be seen as a luxury item (or expense) or as something that one never quite has the time to do properly. For third countries there would be two recommendations here:

1. Undertake **annual evaluations against objectives**. Every year you should be assessing what you have done and if it is working – are you achieving what you set out to achieve? At the same time you should re-evaluate all your consultancy and memberships and all of your communication channels, events and activities. Just spending one day on this can be incredibly valuable to understanding what you might want or need to change.
2. The rotational nature of the diplomatic service offers a second (natural) evaluation point when officials leave the post, a kind of **cyclical evaluation**. They could very usefully provide an evaluation (as part of their handover) of what is working, not working and what is on their horizon. Likewise, what were they thinking of doing next, or differently, or less of?

Both of these can be done in-house but ideally they would have some external element to them. This could be either a consultant (for the day) or an external stakeholder who is willing to help you stress-test your strategy and give input.

Part 2

How to Work with the EU Institutions & Decision Making

6. Working with the European Commission

By Aaron McLoughlin

The European Commission has a well-developed system for operating, developing and adopting proposals and decisions. If you understand this system and speak to the right people, at the right time and with targeted information, your chances of success increase. But before going into the specifics let us start with some general rules on how best to work with the Commission, as given in the box below.

> **Five core rules for engagement with the Commission**
>
> 1. If you turn up late in the decision-making process, without credible and objective evidence, you might as well not turn up at all. **You need to engage early.** You are going to have to rely on a keen political antenna and network to know precisely when meetings and decisions happen. If you step in late, your chance has gone.
> 2. The **points when decisions are going to happen are clear. These decision points are, however, not always publicly broadcast**. You have to identify these windows of opportunity in advance.
> 3. You need to **use a different tone when dealing with the Services and the political level** (Cabinets and Commissioners). You need to speak with (and listen to) your audience and not at them.
> 4. **You need to bring timely and high-quality evidence and data to the table.** This means you need to start work on preparing your case and the supporting evidence way ahead of time. Robust evidence is often independent or whose integrity stands up to the deepest scrutiny.
> 5. Don't forget that **the Commission acts as the Guardian of the European interest**. Ideally, start and end strongly on the European case. Officials often appear unmoved by national concerns, and nonchalant about the concerns of third countries.

These are important guiding rules that highlight both the opportunities and challenges in trying to work with the European Commission. What they demonstrate, though, is that with the Commission you have excellent opportunities to engage – in fact **the European Commission needs external input**. Stakeholders who respect the rules above and follow the policy cycle as outlined now in the chapter will have the greatest chances of success.

1. The policy cycle

The Commission has a clear journey map – known as a **roadmap** – for how it adopts policy, decisions and legislative proposals. It is a journey map that it usually follows strictly – so it is obviously essential to understand this internal decision-making process. Also, the roadmap is available to everyone as, like most Commission documents, it is openly available on the internet.

One of the first actions of each new Commission President is to publish their operating manual called the **Working Methods of the European Commission**. It spells out how the Commission will operate and reach decisions. It is not usually drastically different from the previous one but it will have several tweaks and differences that can be key for understanding how decisions get taken.

> Make sure you have, and know by heart, the **Working Methods of the European Commission** – it is a step by step guide to exactly how the European Commission will take decisions. It will tell you exactly who you need to speak to at what time.

This manual is prepared mainly for Commission officials. Along with the Political Guidelines, it is intended to show officials the differences in working methods to deliver the political agenda between the old and new Commission. Clearly, this document is as useful to outsiders as it is to insiders. This rule book is important for you because you can use it when dealing with officials as they prepare a policy.

Figure 6.1: Lifecycle of a legislative proposal in the EU

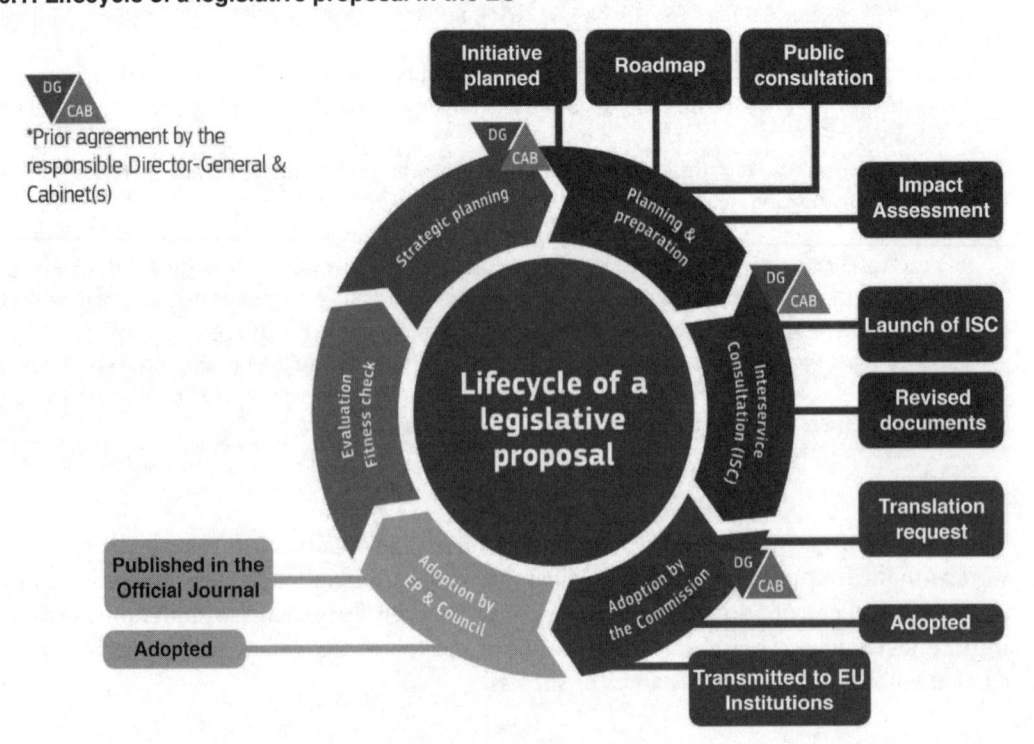

Source: The Working Methods of the European Commission, 1.12.2019, p.10 (adapted)

Figure 6.1 gives an overview of the internal decision-making process of the European Commission. (This is explained in comprehensive detail in Chapter 1 of our companion volume *How the EU Institutions Work: Your handbook and guide to EU decision-making* edited by Erik Akse.) It is essential to understand each step in this process so that you know who to engage, when and with what. It will, essentially, be the single most important roadmap for engaging with the Commission.

This chapter will now take you through these steps and identify how best to engage in each of them.

2. The Political Guidelines

We have already mentioned the Political Guidelines but they require more explanation. The European Commission's policy and legislative agenda does not emerge from nowhere. Each new Commission develops, and sets out, its own Political Guidelines. This document codifies the political agenda for the term of the Commission – and it is an essential context for anyone trying to work with the Commission. You need to know its agenda (not just your own).

For the five-year term of the Commission, new policies and proposals will emerge from this document. Any ideas that are at odds with the Political Guidelines face a high hurdle to get adopted. This means there is a constant evolution in the European political context because, with each transition from one Commission to the next, the political and policy agenda changes. If the new Political Guidelines opt for a different view on your issue, you will find officials quickly falling into line behind their new political instructions. Those who once supported you will follow new instructions and be against you.

2.1 Can you influence the Political Guidelines?

If you do not want to get caught out and flounder for the rest of the new Commission's term, you can play the long game and look to influence the Political Guidelines. There is no pre-set system for finalising the Political Guidelines. Commission Presidents, at least new ones, manage things their own way. President Juncker drew from the European Council's Strategic Agenda. President von der Leyen gave more weight to the ideas of some of the European Parliament's Political Groups. The three main sources that feed into the Political Guidelines, and hence your three avenues to influence them, are the European Council, the European Parliament, and the Commission President, whose input we shall now discuss, starting with the European Council.

2.2 The European Council

The broad EU agenda for the five years ahead is set by the Heads of State and Government. On 20 June 2019, the European Council adopted its **Strategic Agenda 2019-2024**. This is a five-year political roadmap for the EU, and it is drafted in broad brush strokes and lacks granularity. The European Council put great stress on this Strategic Agenda.

EU Sherpas prepare the Strategic Agenda for the EU leaders. Reaching out directly to this group of senior national officials is your best direct way of putting forward your agenda. It is important to note that drafting starts around a year before the document is published, so you will need to do a tour of national capitals to make your case. The significant challenge to meet these key officials is that they do not publicise their presence, nor is it a defined and/or fixed group. The best way to find out who they are, and approach them, is directly in the national capital through intermediaries who are trusted by the officials. Clearly, you can see that trying to influence the Political Guidelines through this route is a very proactive and time and resource-intensive method. It is therefore not surprising that so few organisations try to influence the Political Guidelines – it seems remote and unattainable.

> **EU Sherpas – Who are they?**
>
> The EU's leaders meet at regular formal and informal European Councils. The behind the scenes and advance work to reach agreements is performed by a set of top level advisers and technocrats known as EU Sherpas. The membership list is not public and most of the press seem unaware of their existence. Only a few people outside this closed group – who often communicate via WhatsApp – know the current membership. The membership is a rolling one as EU leaders come and go. Some are part of the government leader's political office and some are Ambassadors. For example Uwe Corsepius, the former Secretary-General of the Council of the European Union, is the chief adviser on European affairs to Chancellor Merkel.

The European Council's recommendations are subsequently taken up by the Commission President-designate who, supported by the Secretariat-General, develops and incorporates the European Council's ideas into the Political Guidelines for the Commission.

When the European Council's Strategic Agenda for the next five years is published a small team of officials in the Commission take the ideas and work them up into policy and legislative proposals – they start to add a level of detail to the broader more directional European Council recommendations. It is important to recognise the opportunity here because the European Council's broad-brush approach gives the Commission some level of discretion and hence you some level of opportunity.

2.3 The European Parliament

The Commission President-designate meets with European Parliament Political Group leaders to secure their backing for election as President of the Commission. The candidate will do this through a series of bilateral meetings – which may help explain why the Political Guidelines can look like a tapestry of European Political Group manifesto pledges. There is clearly backroom horse-trading to secure support for the election of the Commission President. So another opportunity to engage emerges.

The Commission President-elect's transition team leads the bilateral meetings. This time around, the Commission Services have little involvement except for preparing pre-meeting briefings. The transition team effectively draft the Political Guidelines in near isolation. They then call in the Commission Secretariat-General to fine-tune the text before the final vote in the European Parliament. Support for policy initiatives is often a precondition of support for some Political Groups.

2.4 The Commission President

The Commission President and their inner circle in the transition team and the key outside advisers are the main architects of the Political Guidelines. In effect, they need to be because this is going to be their political manifesto to deliver, and failing to deliver on promises is all too common in government. The Political Guidelines are a tool to mainstream the new political agenda throughout the machinery of the Commission and thus out into the other EU institutions.

Table 6.1: Example transition team: President von der Leyen

Name	Nationality	Previous position
Bjoern Seibert	German	Chief of Staff to von der Leyen
Stephanie Riso	French	European Commission
Jivka Petkova	Bulgarian	European Commission
Jens-Alexander Flosdorff	German	Spokesperson for von der Leyen
Maria-Luisa Cabral	Portuguese	European Commission
Pauline Rouch	French	European Commission
Olivier Smith	French	European Commission
Sonia Vila-Nunez	Spanish	European Commission
Kurt Vandenberghe	Belgian	European Commission
Anthony Whelan	Irish	European Commission
Dana Spinant	Romanian	European Commission

Source: European Commission website

Much of the heavy lifting on the Political Guidelines, once they have taken shape, sits with the Secretariat-General. This should not be a surprise. Civil servants are well versed in taking politicians' manifesto commitments and converting them into a joined-up policy and legislative agenda.

As you can see, at each stage of the elaboration of the Political Guidelines, there is some room for engagement. In this case, if you can show the officials in the Secretariat-General how your agenda and points mirror, and in fact bolster, the agenda of the new Commission then they may well co-opt them.

3. When and how to step in

The windows of opportunity to advance your interests are always narrow. In hindsight, those moments are apparent, but at the time, you can easily miss them. The astute policy entrepreneur knows when the windows of opportunity open and has pre-prepared solutions and evidence to back their case to present to the right person at the right time. The framing at the start of the Political Guidelines, the Mission Letters and the Work Programme are the absolute keys here. If you don't feed into them, you run the risk of seeing your agenda getting airbrushed away. Sitting on the political sidelines for the next five years is a lonely place.

> **Mission Letters**
>
> The President of the European Commission presents every Commissioner with a 'mission letter'. It is the same as a 'mandate letter' issued by government leaders to their Cabinets. They are guiding documents, marching orders, and instructions to Commissioners on how they will work and what they need to deliver.

> **Work Programme**
>
> The political priorities are turned into concrete political actions. The Work Programme details a 12-month work plan of initiatives. These include legislative proposals, non-legislative actions, and REFIT actions. There are proposals to repeal some legislation and to withdraw legislative proposals that stand no chance of adoption. The Work Programme provides a helpful planning tool. It gives you a schedule of when proposals are due. From that, you can plan your own work load for the year(s) ahead.

An inner circle of people drafts these key texts. Only a few outside the inner circle are asked for suggestions. If you want your points taken up, if asked, you need to have the pre-prepared text ready. You cannot wait for the lengthy sign-off procedures that plague many organisations, firms and NGOs. Your recommendations need to be clear, concise and backed up by high-quality evidence. The style needs to mirror the Commission's own, and there is no place for procrastination. In many cases, at this level of engagement, you will only have a few minutes to feed your views in. This is very fast and very top line – so if you get stuck in internal meetings and sign-off procedures you will see the opportunity evaporate. When you make recommendations, you should also ensure that they are not one-sided. You need to take into account the counter-arguments to give your submission some balance.

To succeed in this high-level lobbying activity, you likely need to be well-known to key decision-makers and influencers, i.e. this is going to be built on existing relationships and contacts and not speculative ones. When you are seen as a trusted source whose ideas and solutions are both practical and well-considered, you will have a chance of success in this most difficult engagement environment. Getting a hard-won reputation, such as is required here, takes years of issue leadership and explains why so few try, or have access, to engage in this crucial part of the process.

4. The European Commission's Work Programme and State of the Union

Next in the policy cycle come the **Work Programme** and the **State of the Union** address by the Commission President. The date the Work Programme is published is not fixed in stone. The first Work Programme of a new Commission comes around six to eight weeks after the new leadership takes up office. President von der Leyen's first Work Programme was adopted on 29 January 2020, after coming into office on 1 December 2019. President Juncker's first Work Programme was published on 16 December 2014, after taking up office on 1 November 2014.

This first Work Programme contains the likely timetable for the adoption of all forthcoming new initiatives (legislative and non-legislative), a list of priority pending initiatives, a list of repeals, REFIT initiatives and withdrawals or modifications of pending proposals.

Months of hard work go into preparing the Work Programme – which is in effect a proposed set of initiatives to take forward and items to drop. It is obviously a vitally important document in the elaboration of what the Commission will work on and yet most of this work takes place off the radar. It is possible to influence this package of measures but, like the previous stage of the process, few try to do so given how difficult it is.

5. How can you influence the Work Programme?

There are essentially two approaches to trying to influence the Work Programme: the long play and the short play.

5.1 The long play

The best approach is to start early on, which means around 12 to 18 months before the Work Programme is published. At this stage, you need to prepare the policy and political case for action. Once you have this, you will need to build a network of partners to echo your message to your target audiences; this means working with best-in-class national and European think tanks and experts on the issue. (See Chapter 2 for more on this.)

The key questions you need to answer: As to the questions you need to ask and answer it makes sense to mirror the seven that the European Commission asks itself:

1. What is the problem, and why is it a problem?
2. Why should the EU act?
3. What should be achieved?
4. What are the various options to achieve the objectives?
5. What are their economic, social and environmental impacts and who will be affected?
6. How do the different options compare in terms of their effectiveness and efficiency (benefits and costs)?
7. How will monitoring and subsequent retrospective evaluation be organised?

If you can establish robust answers to the seven questions above, then you have a case to make. First, you should take it to the key players in the Directorate-General (DG), The European Political Strategy Centre (EPSC, the Commission's in-house think tank), Cabinets and the Secretariat-General. If you can win the battle of ideas, it is far easier for the key players to co-opt your agenda. Most DGs have a planning/coordination unit that works directly with the Director-General. These units generally prepare the DG's inputs to Work Programme processes. Go and meet them.

All recommendations from the Director-General for the Work Programme have to go through the Cabinets and are discussed in the 'Jour Fixe'. The Jour fixe is when Executive Vice-Presidents and Commissioners hold weekly meetings with the senior management of their respective Services. There is also a monthly Strategic Jour Fixe meeting that brings together the relevant Executive Vice-President or Vice-President, and a Commissioner with his or her senior management.

Sometimes, back channels from the Services may look to bypass this political control, so you need to keep an eye on what is actually happening in practice as well as what is officially happening. If there is a divergence, you need to highlight the discrepancies to the Cabinet so it can step in.

As we have discussed before in this book, the key influencers you need to work with are not always identified as such on an organisational chart. You need to identify well in advance who they are. To do this, you will need to draw on your network to identify those key individuals who influence policy or to whom the leadership turns to for new ideas, solutions, and proposals. Once identified, you should deftly reach out to them in advance to start building your relationship(s). A good approach is to bring in key thought leaders, often on the back of new research, to promote your case. Key policy influencers are likely to want to meet with them, and persuasion is more effective than a hard sell.

5.2 The short play

Clearly, if you get it right, the long play will have been one of the best investments you can make. However, most people do not have the time and resources for the long play – it is a big investment to make against a difficult to achieve pay-off. This means that more people tend to play short, which in turn means that they go in with a lot less intellectual ballast to support their case and without the answers to the questions the Commission is going to ask. It is also already highly likely that the key influencers will have ideas in their mind taking shape – so you will often find yourselves adapting to what is already there as opposed to shaping it as you would want.

But even if you start late, you can still achieve a lot. In **June**, the Secretary-General informs Directors-General of the start of the process and all Services prepare an initial list of suggestions. It is useful if the Services work with their Commissioner otherwise you might see the undignified sight of a Commissioner calling up the Secretariat-General asking for their DG's suggestions to be withdrawn.

Around the **start of July**, the College of Commissioners holds its first exchange of what should be in the Commission's Work Programme, entitled 'Preparation of the Commission Work Programme for [date] and organisation of interinstitutional work'. It represents the last chance for any DG to get their new initiative considered in the Work Programme.

Again you need to work with key officials in the Directorate-General, the Secretariat-General, the European Political Strategy Centre, and the Cabinets because they will submit the ideas for proposals. If your issue/proposal is not on the first list sent in by the DGs you need to get them onto the list reviewed by the College. If your issue/proposal is not on the final list presented at the **end of July**, it is unlikely your proposal will go forward. If it is not adopted, you just have to wait another year for the opportunity.

August is then the critical month for key political decisions in Brussels. While most people are off on holiday, during the last two weeks of August, the Commission's Work Programme is agreed. There is a closed inner circle of officials close to the President, within the Cabinet and the Secretariat-General who are holed up preparing the final draft in **late August**. The challenge is that they are pretty much sealed off and it's difficult to lobby this drafting team because they are too busy. This is where you need to consider the most effective *indirect* methods of influence. For example, it is likely (as discussed in Chapter 4) that many of this group read the likes of the FT and Politico. Well placed mid-August adverts in Politico's Playbook have been known to focus their minds on new matters.

For this whole process, a great deal of influence, from start to finish, sits with the Secretariat-General. Possessing the power of the pen, and acting as the Guardian of the Commission, it ultimately recommends what is put forward. And it can certainly serve as an up-to-date source of information on what is in the latest proposals and where things stand.

You see the outcome of all this work in the State of the Union address in **early September**. The Commission President lays out, in detail, the political, legislative and policy agenda for the year ahead. At this stage only very specific feedback from key MEPs and Member States can help adjust what is put forward in the **mid-October** final Work Programme. If you come up short in your efforts you can work with the Political Group leaders in the European Parliament and with the Council, but this is really a last chance saloon and it is very difficult to drive meaningful change. They both enter into dialogue with the Commission to agree on these final priorities for the year ahead – which then leads to a final signed version in **mid-December** in the form of a Joint Declaration. To succeed at this stage you need someone (a key influencer) to champion your agenda and drive change. This is often best achieved by working at the national level where you are likely to get the best reception.

The window for engagement is therefore effectively open from June to late August. If you miss it, you will need to wait another 12 months. This means you need to get your sequencing just right; if you step in too early or too late, you won't get what you want. And remember that any proposal is going to be judged against the Political Guidelines. Those that fall outside are unlikely to be adopted – meaning you need to frame your agenda in line with the Political Guidelines.

Another consideration is that you have the first two to three years of a Commission mandate for a new initiative to be taken up. In the last two years of the Commission's term, they are reluctant to table anything substantially new that runs the risk of not being agreed to by the European Parliament and Council. This cycle is predictable and therefore gives you a clear, yet tight, window to work with.

The following is an illustrative timetable for the adoption of the 2017 Work Programme;

2017 Work Programme

10 July	Initial discussion in College on 'Preparation of the Commission Work Programme for 2019 and organisation of interinstitutional work'
End of July	Firm initial list of proposals
Mid-August	The State of the Union drafted
End of August	College Discussion at Commission retreat
13 September	President Juncker State of Union
24 October	Adoption of the Commission Work Programme
14 December	Joint Declaration on the Legislative Priorities between the European Parliament, the Council and Commission

The package of submitted proposals is decided at the highest level (Directors-General, Commissioners, Cabinets) and agreed to by first Vice-Presidents and the President and their Cabinets. Importantly, proposals that are tabled can if needed by-pass the detailed **Better Regulation** framework.

The machinery of checks and balances provided by Better Regulation can, when needed, go into hibernation. The proposals are fine-tuned into a coherent package by an inner circle of staff reporting to the Secretary-General.

5.3 What does 'political discontinuity' mean?

There is a clear reluctance to burden a new Commission with the political agenda of the old. This has three direct impacts.

1. At the start of a new Commission, old legislative proposals that are still being considered by the European Parliament and Council, but not yet agreed to, are reviewed. They can be withdrawn. This is especially the case when the political chances of adoption are low.
2. In the last year or so of a Commission's term in office, there is a reluctance to table a new legislative proposal. This is especially the case if there is little hope of getting the proposal adopted during the remainder of the mandate.
3. The best chance to get any proposal tabled and adopted into legislation is in the first two to three years. The chances of anything new being shelved increase towards the tail end of the Commission's mandate.

6. Impact Assessment

If you are serious about influencing a Commission legislative proposal then an excellent opportunity you have is to influence the **Impact Assessment**. In fact it is imperative that you try to do so because like so many processes, the further they go the more the debate has closed down. As discussed in the previous section, if you want to influence the final Impact Assessment, you will need to start early. A tactic that works very well is to prepare a 'shadow impact assessment' at the 'ideation' phase to feed in as early as possible and help frame the debate. You need to lobby the lead Directorate-General and the Secretariat-General. This is again where your echo chamber of partners – notably here, think tanks and policy experts/academics – will be of invaluable use.

In the 2019-2024 Commission, a Directorate-General has to put all initiatives into the Commission's planning tool, **Decide**. Decide is the IT tool for managing the Commission's decision-making process. This includes both initiatives that are politically sensitive and those which are not sensitive. The Secretariat-General will get the chance to object to the classification of non-sensitive. This means there is an opportunity for the Secretariat-General to insist on greater political scrutiny for initial validation/launch of **Inter-service Consultation** and the need for an impact assessment. So, it is also worthwhile lobbying the Secretariat-General early as well.

6.1 When should you step in?

The latest you should start is when political validation is given, and the **Inception Impact Assessment** published. It might sound clichéd to say that good public policymaking needs solid data, evidence and solutions – but it is the foundation of everything (especially at this stage and especially for the European Commission). You can engage with the lead Directorate-General, Secretariat-General, and the **Inter-Service Group** (formerly the Impact Assessment Steering Group) to see what information they need. If you opt to run a shadow impact assessment, you need to mirror the Commission's own assessment questions model. The Commission spells out what is needed in its Guidelines and Handbook. Don't skip this. Raising irrelevant considerations is an act of self-deception that will backfire on you.

6.2 Why you need to start early

You should not wait until the roadmaps or Inception Impact Assessments are published. You need to start early. Preparing credible and persuasive evidence is time-consuming, and your organisation, members, partners and others will often be reluctant or slow to provide the necessary information. You will need time to get a clear picture for yourself and this will take quite some effort and resource. As a general rule, preparing a high-quality submission or shadow impact assessment is going to take you at least six months. This exercise is not for the faint-hearted. Remember that it takes the Commission around 12 months. A good approach is to hire the very same technical consultants the Commission uses to prepare your shadow impact assessment or submission. They know better than anyone else what is needed and are skilled at delivering and messaging it. This could cost you in the order of €50,000 to €100,000.

One thing you need to remember is that anything that is public has been discussed at the political level and approved by the President's Cabinet. This means it is going to be difficult to change.

6.3 How to make your case

There is one important caveat if you decide to do a shadow impact assessment: you have to hand it over warts and all. If you go for selective editing and remove anything that is not good for you, you are going to get caught out, and your case (and credibility) destroyed. As discussed in Chapter 1, credibility is of critical importance in Brussels and it can be quickly lost. It is vital therefore that whatever you submit is data and evidence rich and the information must be credible and not resemble fairy tales that evaporate on closer review. Finally, it is essential to send in your input as early as possible, giving you the time to engage on it and the officials the time to absorb it. Too often people bring their contribution to the table too late in the day. If it is submitted early, you can help the Inter-Service Group before their thinking is firmed up. Remember: the constant golden rule for engagement with the Commission (and in general with the institutions) is that you need to always start as early as possible.

6.4 What to do when an Impact Assessment is not automatically prepared

Not all proposals automatically benefit from an Impact Assessment. There is simply not the time or resources to review all (1) secondary legislation or (2) Agency decisions.

1. **Secondary legislation**. The Commission adopts hundreds of Delegated and Implementing Acts each year. Some benefit from Impact Assessments, but not many. The Commission identifies cases when this should happen:

   '1. An impact assessment will be necessary where there are likely to be **significant impacts** and where the **Commission has discretion** about the measures which could be taken (including whether to act at all). For example, a scientific body may recommend a safe exposure level to a particular chemical but the Commission has the choice of how best to manage the risks of exposure to that chemical.
   2. Where the Commission is **likely to deviate from the recommendations of an Agency**, then an IA is also likely to be necessary.'
   Source: Better Regulation Tool Box #9, 'When is an Impact Assessment necessary', page 50

   Showing a 'significant impact' is not easy, and there are no hard and fast guidelines to determine this. So it tends to be case by case. From experience, we can say that the significance of the impact has to be self-evident, so in monetary terms this means 'billions of euros' and not 'millions of euros'. It also relates to issues that will have a wide impact and not just a narrow one, or that would 'derail a strategic European interest'. To establish any of these is not easy, but if you have a shadow impact assessment to present to the lead Directorate-General and Secretariat-General, your case is enhanced if it reveals such a potential impact. What is clear is that even if hundreds of third parties are calling on the Commission to launch an Impact Assessment and you have direct intervention from the highest political levels, it is not guaranteed to change the decision.

   Sometimes your best hope is that the lead Directorate-General is either selective in the evidence it presents or simply does not have all the evidence to hand. Such an oversight, deliberate or accidental, can be enough for the file to be called in for the rigorous scrutiny provided by an Impact Assessment.

2. **Agency decisions.** If you are dealing with an Agency decision, you need to flag up early on that what might appear to be an innocuous measure could need an Impact Assessment because of its complexity, the significance of the expected impacts, or because the Commission is expected to deviate from the advice of the relevant Agency, or where the Agency's work does not meet the Commission's usual standards. *Source: Better Regulation Tool Box #9, Box EU Agencies and IAs, page 51*

   You will need to explain clearly and early to the relevant DG and Secretariat-General that an important issue is at stake. Obviously, if you are claiming there is a significant impact then you need to have some evidence and data to back this up, potentially from your shadow impact assessment.

Securing an Impact Assessment for secondary legislation and Agency decisions is, however, very difficult. The threshold the Commission sets is very high, which results in few being able to bring a strong enough case for the lead DG and Secretariat-General to step in.

7. External consultation

The Commission consults a lot and provides visible flags when starting to work on an issue and when dealing with it. When it comes to consultation, there is no good reason for being caught unawares and no good reason not to get involved. It is actually an imperative if you want to be involved with the Commission and taken seriously. Do not think of consultations as options – they are mandatory.

Silence is not an option. If you choose to ignore this opportunity and sit it out, you are going to sideline yourself for the duration of the process. Stepping in only after the Commission has already adopted a decision means you are going to be working against the odds going forward. MEPs and Member State officials will naturally ask for your input during the Commission's consultation. They will tend to take a dim view of you and your case if you sat out the external consultation. It implies you are not serious.

The only justification for stepping in after the legislative train has left the station is if your issue was never part of the consultation. If you got added into the issue during the final moments and were not afforded the opportunity to make your case, you will be heard out by MEPs and Member State officials. Being added to a proposal out of the blue, with no previous indication, is rare, but it does occur.

7.1 Why does the Commission consult?

The Commission's own **Better Regulation Guidelines** provides the reasons the Commission consults. The operation of these guidelines is broken down in operational detail in the Better Regulation Toolbox.

Toolbox #56 provides three key reasons:

1. *'the collection of feedback offers an opportunity for stakeholders to express general views on a specific document (roadmap, inception impact assessment, draft secondary legislation, legislative proposals and accompanying impact assessments, established legislation), not based on specific questions or consultation background documents.'*

2. Consultation provides a chance for the Commission to get 'advice' on a specific issue. This makes a lot of sense. The Commission Services are under-staffed in many policy areas and officials in the Commission, like their counterparts in national administrations, do not have all the information required to make proposals and decisions. Asking broadly for advice is common sense.

3. As most initiatives are subjected to consultation three times any unintended consequences can be flagged up by the public far in advance, and on multiple occasions.

One should also not fail to mention that consultation is not optional for the Commission either; it is required by the **Regulatory Scrutiny Board**.

> **The Regulatory Scrutiny Board**
>
> The Regulatory Scrutiny Board (RSB) is an independent body in the Commission tasked with implementing Better Regulation. It reviews Impact Assessments, major policy evaluations and fitness checks. A negative opinion from the RSB leads to the draft being re-submitted. Getting two negative opinions usually, but not always, leads to an initiative being shelved. **You must not lobby the RSB.**

7.2 What is the timing for consultations?

The granularity of the operation of external consultation is in the Better Regulation Guidelines and Toolbox. The operational texts are clear, and you should consult them as and when needed. You can find the many opportunities to give your views on Commission initiatives at the 'Have Your Say' link on the Commission website.

Table 6.2 Time to give feedback on Commission initiatives

Initiative	Time to give feedback
Roadmaps	4 weeks
Inception Impact Assessments	4 weeks
Evaluations	4 weeks
Fitness Checks	4 weeks
Draft Implementing and Delegated Acts	4 weeks
Post-Commission legislative proposal	8 weeks
Public Consultations	12 weeks

Source: European Commission, Better Regulation, Have Your Say

This can be broken down into four openings for you to put forward your case:

1. **Fact finding**: Roadmaps, Inception Impact Assessment, evaluations and Fitness Checks. An Inception Impact Assessment rather than roadmap is used when an Impact Assessment is planned.

2. **Information gathering**: Public Consultations for new initiatives, or evaluations of existing policies and laws.
3. **Feedback on proposals**: Ordinary legislation. The eight-week period allowed for feedback post-legislative proposal is strange. It is not clear if the European Parliament or the Council take any notice of it.
4. **Feedback on technical rules or updates**: Draft Delegated and Implementing Acts, and Regulatory Procedure with Scrutiny (RPS) measures. The Commission's feedback on the submissions can be a helpful scrutiny step.

The only step that is not subject to public consultation is Inter-Service Consultation. Over time the number of initiatives subject to public consultation has grown.

Table 6.3: Summary of Consultations 2015–2018

Numbers	2015	2016	2017	2018
Roadmaps	76	57	77	51
Inception Impact Assessments	30	59	65	21
Evaluation Roadmaps	71	88	33	63
Commission Proposals	*	*	78	154
Delegated Acts		24	61	66
Implementing Acts		42	73	76
Acts following regulatory procedure with scrutiny		32	31	31
Average replies to public consultations	461	565	1838	2091

*Commission proposals were made available for feedback from 2017

Source: Commission Staff Working Document, Taking Stock of the Commission's Better Regulation Agenda

7.3 How does consultation work in practice?

It is not difficult to harness the opportunities provided by the consultation process, but it requires a re-alignment of expectations for stakeholders as to what can be got out of it. You need to be clear on what you can achieve and how to do that. So:

1. It is true that the feedback from public consultations may lead the Commission to change its thinking even at the very last hour. It is just unlikely to happen. There are cases when it has done so: for example, the draft Commission implementing measures on mobile phone roaming charges were withdrawn after the public consultation. Experience shows that by the time things are being consulted on they are a moving train – so you need to focus on modifying and not stopping things.

2. Some expectation management is needed. Don't confuse consultation with being handed the pen to draft. If you are going to send your thoughts on paper, there is every chance it won't change minds, policy or decision. This is especially so if the thinking is fuzzy and the evidence weak. Just because you are consulted, it does not mean that your suggestions are, or will be, co-opted.
3. You need to step in early, preferably at the ideation stage, to put your case forward. The longer a file develops the more firmed up ideas and policy options become. Stepping in at the very last moment, before the proposal is about to go through the door is a high-risk strategy. With each passing consultation, the window of opportunity is narrower – meaning you need to focus more and more on what is the priority for you.
4. There is some debate in Brussels on the number of responses and how this is taken into account. You will often see campaigns to drive huge response rates based on the assumption that if there is a majority view for something then it will likely pass. There is some credence to be given to this 'numbers game' approach but it comes with a caution. Copy-paste postcard style attempts to skew the numbers will not be well-received and will likely only damage your case. High numbers of differentiated responses (making the same point) from across the Member States are most effective. The organisation of such widespread activity is very difficult to achieve.

7.4 What's the best way to contribute?

1. If you want to change public policy thinking, you should bring forward a plausible public policy solution that helps remedy the problem raised by the Commission. You need to do this with evidence – preferably robust, respected and independent evidence.
2. If you are unable to do this, you are left with highlighting procedural errors or showing that the letter or the spirit of the legislation has been ignored.
3. You should always make sure that your submission and supporting evidence is public. Requesting confidentially raises questions as to the veracity of the submission.

7.5 Some points too often forgotten

1. The public consultation does not preclude you from making your case through the usual channels. Too many people have got it into their thinking that all hangs or falls on what is sent in during the public consultation. They overlook that this is an evidence gathering exercise and not a rule drafting exercise. Your submission is a good trigger to engage with all the key stakeholders on your position. A submission on its own is unlikely to drive change – but one backed by quality and targeted engagement has a good chance.
2. It is important to put your best case forward, but you should not have the preconceived belief that your thinking will be of such revelatory power that officials will immediately co-opt it. Consultation responses can often end up feeling like a lot of hard work (because they are) for nothing. Remember that, as said in the previous point, your consultation response is only as good as the evidence and quality it shows, and how you leverage and engage with it.

3. The Commission may organise targeted consultations. A targeted consultation does not replace a public consultation, and it is often used to reach out to specific groups and experts. These are obviously difficult to penetrate unless you are directly involved, but they do offer a privileged opportunity to give information. In fact, in many cases, just knowing what the questions are will give you an indication of what the Commission is looking for – which might be something you can engage on.
4. Sometimes the feedback period can be made shorter or longer than the standard guidelines. Don't forget also that public consultations can be launched on a Friday evening and run during vacation periods – and sadly many of them do.

7.6 Practical recommendations

Here are some practical recommendations on how to improve your chances of being heard through consultation:

1. The Commission provides a clear heads-up when it is going to start work. This gives you the opportunity to get your evidence together and prepare the case. Ideally, you would have your case and evidence filed away already. If you do, it means that when the policy window re-opens all you need to do is dust off and briefly update your position.
2. The questions raised by the Commission are standard public policy questions for which you should already have the evidence to hand. If you don't have the evidence to hand within a few months, it raises questions about your lack of preparedness or a lack of evidence to support your case.
3. The advantage of running a public consultation is that it provides an opportunity to raise any new points. One frustration of officials is that too often submissions bring little or nothing new to the table. Submissions read like bland mass mailings. Many submissions don't even pretend to hide this, but obviously, they carry far less weight.
4. The benefit of highlighting unintended consequences is powerful. To reach that requires a high threshold of credible evidence persuasively presented.
5. If the opportunity to make a particular point of concern to you is not provided by the questions, you can still make it; this is not forbidden. You are not bound by the questions in the questionnaire.
6. It is important to put your concerns on the record and on paper. After all, officials can't refer to problems or solutions out of the ether. They'll need to be able to point to a source, and the source will need to be on the record. The Regulatory Scrutiny Board will review the replies to the consultations, and if the Services act in reliance on a non-existing concern as the basis for a preferred policy option, it is likely to be dropped like a stone.

There are limited, but important, exemptions to the general requirement to consult. Here is a list:

1. Where there is limited margin for the Commission to act. This often happens for Delegated and Implementing Acts.

2. For procedures with set deadlines that preclude a four-week public consultation.
3. For Technical Barriers to Trade (TBT) notifications. *'The TBT notification does not replace the need for feedback. In practice, the two processes can happen in parallel, with the 4-week feedback running together with the 60 to 90 day TBT notification.'*
4. Risk Management measures. Some risk management measures can be exempted, such as individual authorisation decisions and general measures if they meet one of the following three grounds:
   a. *'(Based on a scientific opinion from an agency or scientific committee (not a consultant);*
   b. *On which a public consultation has already taken place on the scientific opinion, (not on the draft measure) and the recommendations concerning the risk management should have been clearly spelled out); and*
   c. *Where the Commission follows the agency findings (i.e. the recommendation is essentially translated in legal text and all that is added is the entry into force/applicability/transitional measures for products on the market, not if new elements are added).'*

Source: Better Regulation Tool Box #56, page 445

8. Inter-Service Consultation (ISC)

All decisions taken by the College of Commissioners are preceded by a formal internal consultation of all relevant Commission Departments. If Services issue a negative opinion, the file must be decided via the Oral Procedure where the issue is placed on the agenda of the weekly meeting of Commissioners. Non-contentious files can be adopted by the Written Procedure which is scrutinised by the different teams of Commissioners.

From an engagement perspective, you have two clear opportunities: consideration by the Services, and political scrutiny by the Cabinets and College. As is a common theme in this chapter, the longer the process goes on, the more limited the likelihood of success. Already by the time your file is in ISC, it is late in the Commission process so what you will be focused on here are not big-ticket ideas and items but just managing the detail of what is coming. This is because by this point nearly 99% of files will continue their legislative journey.

The ISC system stands and falls on the strenuous efforts of the Commission Services, Secretariat-General and Cabinet officials. They need to make a judgement based on a short description of the proposal. Often the title of a proposal hides its real importance. It is not uncommon for only a few officials – the desk officer and a few others – to understand the real substance and details of a proposal. Officials have few incentives to highlight if an initiative is sensitive; if that flag is raised in the Decide IT system, a considerable amount of work and extra scrutiny is going to happen.

The best way for the Services and Cabinets to know if the proposal is important is if you tell them. The earlier you do so, the better. Ideally, you will tell them far in advance of the ISC being launched.

Your first point of call is usually the group of officials, including the Secretariat-General, working on the preparation of any Impact Assessment in the Inter-service Group. They are likely to be involved in providing feedback for the ISC. If not, they will know who in the DGs are. The ISC at this stage is an issue for the Services, but sometimes they decide to already engage with the Cabinets about the issue – this obviously depends on the importance and political sensitivity of the issue.

The tricky bit is that you don't know exactly when the ISC is going to start because this is not public information. The only reliable way to find out is to be informed by good contacts in the Services, Secretariat-General and Cabinets. If you step in late, your chances of influencing the final text disappear.

8.1 Timetable for Inter-Service Consultation

The Inter-Service Consultation is launched by the Commission department preparing the file. It must seek permission from the relevant Commissioner/Vice-President, and the President's Cabinet. Once it starts, the process is over relatively quickly. If the package of documents is more than 20 pages, it will last 15 days (3 weeks). If under 20 pages, it lasts 10 days (2 weeks). For some urgent or politically sensitive matters, the lead DG can request the Secretary-General for fast track ISC which lasts 48 hours and culminates in a meeting where the various positions of the individual Commission departments are recorded.

8.2 Why you need a copy of the draft proposal

If you do not have a copy of the text being considered you are lost, so consider this your first and most important task. You are going to rely on your network to provide you with a copy of the proposal or at the very least, the text relevant for you. You should never make your text public if you get hold of a copy because the Commission now deploys software to reveal the source of the leak. Deliberate typos and strange punctuation are tell-tale signs.

Traditionally, Brussels is a leaky city. Draft proposals find themselves circulated to a close-knit circle of interested groups and journalists. The current Commission's leadership stress the importance of the confidentiality of internal deliberations in both the Working Guidelines and in practice.

Informing officials and Cabinets about the real-world implications of their proposals has never been more important. Significant changes to the draft text can occur during ISC. Getting those changes can be the difference between getting a proposal you like or one that you do not like.

9. How can you influence the political scrutiny step: the Cabinet and the College?

After Inter-Service Consultation, the draft proposal passes to the next step in the internal Commission decision-making procedure: political scrutiny by the Cabinets. During the oral decision-making procedure, the file is first discussed by the Cabinets (Special Chefs). The Special Chefs usually meet on a Thursday to agree on a deal ahead of the weekly meeting of the Heads of Cabinet, but the Special Chefs can meet on other days if needed. The Heads of Cabinet then meet Monday at 11 am, before the text is sent for adoption by the College of Commissioners where any outstanding issues will be discussed.

The Special Chefs and Heads of Cabinet will need convincing reasons to step in and make any changes. They set a high bar. At this stage, it is all about politics, so you need to highlight national political interests or anything that you feel goes against the Commissioner's political interests or the President's Political Guidelines. Your intervention at this stage, given how late it is in the process and also how senior your stakeholders now are, will naturally only be based on existing solid relationships; people who recognise your credibility and are willing to show you some political goodwill. If you don't have the right relationships or have little or no political goodwill, it is unlikely that anyone in this tight-knit group will step up for you.

9.1 Practical guidance for engaging Cabinet and College

You cannot intervene on every relevant file or on every aspect on one file. Interventions need to be focused on the files or issues that really count. In many ways, this is a time to be surgical and make priority choices of what matters for you. It also goes without saying that you will need to take year-round steps to build up your political network, goodwill and credibility. Shooting from the hip with broad brush interventions that are not supported by evidence and are given to contacts who don't really know you will only serve to wipe out your credibility, thereby making any future interventions all but impossible. You will then have to spend the next few years re-building relationships and credibility, which could be very costly for you and your organisation.

Like with other stages of the process, you will not always get what you want. You will find yourself meeting key officials, Cabinet members or Commissioners who straightforwardly pass on the news that they will not support you. Alternatively, you may find out that they did not actually support your position despite promising to do so. You need to be able to deal with such setbacks with a long-term mindset. Responding badly will lead to you being shut out for years to come. If you are in a meeting and you see it deteriorating, interrupt the meeting, politely thank people for their time, and leave.

9.2 How to get your issue/concern in front of the College

The College of Commissioners focuses only on the key political issues. Even then, it is open to question if the Commissioners actually genuinely discuss everything given the size of their agenda and the short length of their meetings (relative to agenda items). They may look at some specific matters, such as secondary legislation, only if it is of an *'exceptional nature or of particular political or strategic importance'* (Source: Working Guidelines, page 4, I(2) indent 2). Few issues pass that high threshold.

When it comes to the meetings of the College, most decisions are taken beforehand leaving the College to deal with only a few key files. The flow of decisions going up is thinned out by the Services and the Cabinets. Only a few decisions remain when you get to the very end of the internal decision-making machine. The College formally adopts measures by a simple majority (i.e. 14 out of 27), but a vote is very rare – decision-making is usually done by consensus. There are rare occasions when a Commissioner calls for a vote. Then French Commissioner Barnier, under President Barroso, called for a vote on support for bio-fuel. He lost the vote.

Before the College meets, there is a pre-meeting of political camps of Commissioners. They discuss the line to take for the College meeting. This has led to initiatives being adjusted or withdrawn in the past. Commissioners are often well-established politicians with their own political hinterland back in the Member States. Your network may be able to harness those local connections. Many Commissioners have a staff member keeping an ear to the ground back home.

9.3 When are the files looked at?

The schedule for the adoption of decisions is well laid out. Once the initiative is validated to start adoption via Inter-Service Consultation, it enters into a well-oiled pipeline.

Figure 6.2: When the College of Commissioners meets

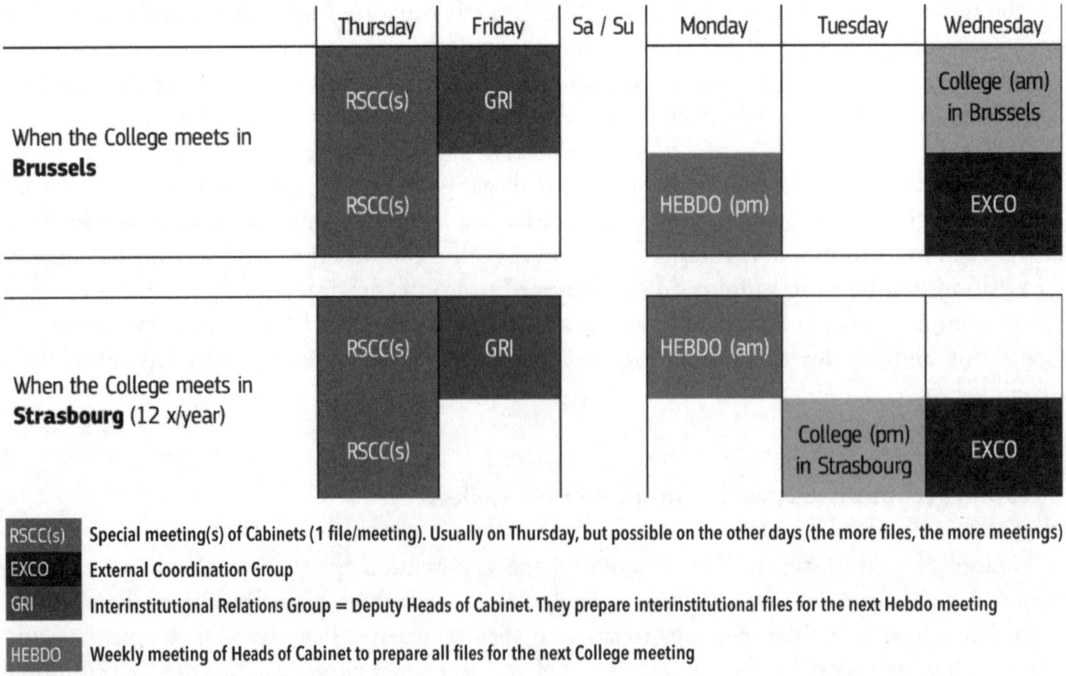

	Thursday	Friday	Sa / Su	Monday	Tuesday	Wednesday
When the College meets in **Brussels**	RSCC(s) / RSCC(s)	GRI		HEBDO (pm)		College (am) in Brussels / EXCO
When the College meets in **Strasbourg** (12 x/year)	RSCC(s) / RSCC(s)	GRI		HEBDO (am)	College (pm) in Strasbourg	EXCO

- **RSCC(s)**: Special meeting(s) of Cabinets (1 file/meeting). Usually on Thursday, but possible on the other days (the more files, the more meetings)
- **EXCO**: External Coordination Group
- **GRI**: Interinstitutional Relations Group = Deputy Heads of Cabinet. They prepare interinstitutional files for the next Hebdo meeting
- **HEBDO**: Weekly meeting of Heads of Cabinet to prepare all files for the next College meeting

Source: Working Methods of the European Commission, 1.12.2019, p.6. (adapted)

What is critical to understand is that once a matter is decided, it is closed. You can't hope the Commissioners will re-look at it. The College's remit is to focus on 'key political issues', and there are actually very few of those – so the machinery is designed to reach an agreement as early as possible to keep things moving. This has three direct consequences:

1. When dealing with the Cabinets and Commissioners, you are going to have **reframe your issue** and supporting material. It will have to be in plain English and be clear to a non-expert. Recycling what you used with the Services is not good enough.
2. As *'new issues are not raised at a later stage of the process, and issues that were closed at an earlier stage of the process, are not reopened'* (Working Methods, page 6, para 3), **you likely have only one shot** at raising your issue. If you step in late, your issue won't be re-opened.
3. **You need to engage early**. You are going to have to rely on a keen political antenna and network to know exactly when meetings and decisions are taken.

What this means is that you need to persuade both the Services and the Cabinets that your position(s) deserve to be taken onboard. If you step in at the eleventh hour, your chances of changing decisions are severely reduced.

10. Summary of working with ISC and political scrutiny

1. If you have not yet managed to persuade the Commission to support your position, lobbying the ISC is likely to be your last and best chance of making sure the proposal that goes through the door works for you. The importance of this can be seen from the fact that legislative proposals from the Commission are often ultimately adopted into law without significant alteration.
2. There is only a limited number of people deciding at this stage: officials from the Services, the Cabinets and maybe the Commissioners. That makes it a lot easier to meet with and put forward a persuasive case to them. It is crucial that you have allies within the Commission who can provide you with feedback on the take-up of your case at all stages of the process. It is likely you will need to map, and then try to meet with, around 25 key Commission officials at this stage.
3. You are going to have to adapt your arguments for the political scrutiny stage. Use clear examples, comprehensible charts, in no more than one page (annexes allowed). You are writing for politicians and not pure technocrats. Get to the point, detail the text you want to be changed, the reasons for the change and the proposed alternative.
4. If you want to close down any conversation, or at least close down the take-up of your message, a rambling briefing paper and intervention littered with algorithms and technical jargon is a sure-fire way of making sure officials shut down very quickly.
5. Many favour bringing in the CEO for meetings with officials, Cabinets or the Commissioner to make the case. While widely used it rarely succeeds. If you do, at least bring someone from the same country as the Commissioner. One or two Commissioners prefer to meet the CEOs directly.
6. It should be self-evident that as much of your case is made in writing, you need to persuade with your pen. This is not a surprise. After all, most Commission decisions are adopted by written procedure.

7. The most effective technique to master is a clear and compelling briefing if you want to win over officials who have no vested interest in supporting you. Your greatest challenge is to stimulate interest enough to raise an objection or reservation.
8. Officials do not like their draft proposals reaching the press before they are adopted. Coverage in Politico or the Financial Times alerts their political hierarchy that a sensitive issue is going through the political adoption machinery and that they may need to look at in far greater detail.
9. Well timed political news coverage can work but it is not easy to pull off. There are few things a Commissioner dislikes more than having to explain to fellow Commissioners that an innocent-sounding initiative is politically loaded and sensitive. If you go for this, you need to work back a week before the file is meant to be on the College's agenda. That gives time to get it changed or pulled.
10. Even if you secure a good proposal, it is not uncommon to find the same text you got removed re-tabled by a Member State or MEP. It may be that an official who did not get their way inside the Commission is hoping the European Parliament or Council will re-insert it. And remember the Commission will be the biggest lobbyist on its own proposals once they move into inter-institutional discussions.

11. Working with the Cabinets

Every Commissioner is supported by a private office of officials, and this team's official role is broad. Cabinets help Commissioners in carrying out their collegial and portfolio roles, which equates to providing political guidance to their Commissioner. All national Ministers have a similar support team of special advisers. The portfolio of issues the political staff follow is detailed in the 'my team' section on each Commissioner's website. The turnover in the Cabinets can be high because the workload can be challenging. So, before contacting Cabinet officials, it is useful to check they have not moved.

The Cabinets are the backbone for ensuring that the College of Commissioners meetings are well prepared. In advance, issues are filtered and what goes forward onto the College agenda is decided.

11.1 What's the role of the Cabinets in reaching decisions?

The Special meeting of the Cabinets (RSCC) meets on a **Thursday**, and they discuss one file at each meeting. If there are more files to consider they meet more often and on different days. The Cabinet member who is responsible for leading or oversight of the file attends, and they look to reach an agreement and conclude the file.

Then you also have the **Inter-Institutional Relations Group (GRI)** which brings together the Deputy Heads of Cabinet who manage inter-institutional affairs. The GRI exists to give mandates for trilogues and to oversee official responses and interactions with the other institutions. The GRI meets on a **Friday morning**. It deals mainly with legislative files being worked on by the Council and the European Parliament and it also looks to reach an agreement and prepare recommendations for the Heads of Cabinet meeting.

On **Monday** (PM during a non-Strasbourg session, AM when in session) the **Heads of Cabinet (Hedo)** meet. They prepare the agenda for the College of Commissioners and propose what should be discussed. Again, they look to reach agreement on outstanding issues. The Cabinets work closely with the Services and the Director-General. There is a weekly meeting of the Head of Cabinet and the Directorate-General. This political oversight helps ensure that Services have not gone astray from their mandate. The Cabinets of the President and the first Vice-Presidents appear to have greater weight on files than other Cabinets – and the influence of some Cabinet members is tremendous. You need to identify these people as soon as possible in your mapping.

It is possible to keep a file in limbo for some time if an agreement cannot be reached. If it goes on too long, and Cabinets do not lift their objections, the President's Cabinet intervenes. It aims to broker or impose a settlement. All of this said, in practice, most files go through with little to no discussion.

11.2 How can you work with the Cabinet?

You are going to have to work with the Cabinets of some Commissioners. If you deal with them in the same way you work with the Services, you are in for a surprise. Here are some practical considerations:

1. You are going to have just thirty to forty minutes when you meet. Their schedule is just too packed.
2. Realise that they don't control their own schedule. That's in the hands of their Commissioner so they may cancel their meeting with you at the last minute. It is not personal.
3. Tell them what you want and go in with a political message. You are going to have to put forward a solution. If you just put a problem on the table, you are wasting your time and (more importantly) theirs.
4. Make sure your briefing is just one page and have copies to leave behind.
5. The Commissioner's team is made up of a mix of technocrats elevated from the Services, and political players brought in by the Commissioner. Make sure your briefing is not too technical. At the same time, you have to be able to dive into the technical issues if they come up.
6. Their primary role is to guard their Commissioner and provide recommendations. As they speak for the Commissioner, their thinking will reflect the Commissioner's. Sometimes, officials may appear to deviate from their Commissioner's line. If fuzzy thinking appears you should ask for clarification or hope to meet the Head of Cabinet later in the day.
7. These political advisers finalise the lines to take and speaking points on issues prepared by the Services for their Commissioner. The Commissioner will often work through these on a Sunday afternoon and call the Cabinet staff for explanations.

8. If you want your case to be taken seriously, you are going to have to come forward with evidence and data. Slogans won't cut it at this stage. If you don't bring evidence, your case won't go forward. If you say the information is secret, then save your and their time and don't come.
9. There is usually a point person to communicate politically back home in the Commissioner's Member State. If you have an issue that in some way resonates 'back home' then reach out to that individual. Some countries have a tradition of fostering close links between their nationals in Cabinets. The alignment between certain capitals' positions and some officials is at times remarkable, so do not be surprised if some Cabinets ask you about the political positions of one or two countries.
10. Cabinets provide a political sanity check on the proposals from the Services. But they don't always align with the Services. They always consult the Services on files, and there is little freelancing on decisions.

12. Working with the Commissioners

You can track the meetings of the College of Commissioners. The agenda and minutes are online. The Commission flags in advance when they expect an item to be put on the College's agenda – something you can track the forward planning of online.

Many of the documents discussed at Cabinet level are published soon after their meeting or are available by way of request. You can search for and request documents from the Register of Commission Documents. If you can make your issue important enough, it may be considered by the Commissioner and the College of Commissioners. As we have noted, few issues are in reality resolved at the level of the College, so if you manage to get that high you are going to need to adapt your game. What got you to this point won't get you where you want to be next.

12.1 How can you work with the Commissioners?

1. You need to understand that you are now dealing with politicians and not with technocrats. If you don't act with this in mind, your chances of getting the support you need are going to flounder. Remember that Commissioners have a hinterland beyond Brussels and established political careers, so as such they have astute political antennae.
2. You are going to have to practise summarising your position down into three points and three lines. Bombarding a Commissioner with 'facts' beyond more than three clear points is likely to induce mental shutdown. Learn to do a pitch not tell a full story.
3. When you meet them, you need to walk in with a clear ask and a clear solution. If you waste their time, the doors will be shut for a long time.
4. Do not bad mouth their colleagues or the Services. If you do, you will find that your calls are never returned and the doors are closed to you for the rest of that Commission's mandate.
5. Do not be surprised if during the meeting they appear distracted. Their agenda and the decisions that they face are many. Commissioners are just people and they, like the rest of us, can have an off day.

6. During the meeting at least one member of the Cabinet will join. Sometimes the Services will join too and there will be a record of the meeting because all meetings with Commissioners and their Cabinets are listed in a register. Obviously, those meeting reports can be subject to a transparency request, so be sensible about what you say and assume that it will all end up in the public domain.
7. Bring a copy of the pre-prepared three key lines, including the solution, and leave that with the Cabinet member. If you leave it with the Commissioner, it may be lost.
8. There are certain times of the week that meeting them is not a good idea. Wednesdays are not good because they'll be in the College from 9:00 am (or Tuesday if a Strasbourg session). Afterwards, they'll often meet their team over lunch to de-brief on the College meeting. Tuesday evening is often set aside for a pre-College meeting of the Political Groups. On Fridays, many travel home and head back to Brussels on the Sunday evening or Monday morning. Sundays are spent reviewing the papers presented to them before they leave.
9. For each meeting, the Commissioner will be given speaking points and lines to take. These are prepared for them by their Services and then finalised by the Cabinet. Their recommendations are often followed.
10. The only real reason for a meeting is to get a decision. Letting off steam is a vanity project. You should send your one-page briefing two weeks in advance of the meeting to ensure it gets into the system and the attention required, i.e. for the Commissioner's team to prepare and respond. In your briefing, you need to ask what you want and come forward with a solution.

13. The Regulatory Scrutiny Board (RSB)

We have mentioned the RSB on a few occasions already so it is worth making it clear that you should never try to lobby it. The Board's own rules of procedure make clear that it should not be approached and its work is confidential.

13.1 How can you influence the RSB?

The best way to influence the RSB positively is by ensuring you submit lots of good data, evidence, facts and information to demonstrate your case. Therefore you must make excellent submissions. You should focus on proving your case by reference to the Commission's very own Guidelines and Tool Box.

14. Conclusion

If you want to advance your interests in the EU, you need to work with the European Commission at many different times and across all levels of the institution. There are plenty of opportunities to promote your agenda and some simple steps to take to give you greater chances of success.

This chapter has outlined both the stages and key groups of officials you need to work with – with guidance on how to do so.

There is a clear roadmap for how a proposal is adopted by the European Commission. Knowing this roadmap shows you when and where you need to intervene. The key checkpoints on this Commission journey are shown in the following box:

> ☐ Ideation phase
> ☐ Initiative planning
> ☐ Roadmaps
> ☐ Public Consultation
> ☐ Impact Assessment
> ☐ Launch of the Inter-service Consultation (ISC)
> ☐ Revision of the documents/proposals during ISC
> ☐ Adoption by the Commission

Finally, here is a reminder of some of the most important guidance for engaging with the European Commission:

1. You need to be on the **Transparency Register**. If you are not, the Commission is unlikely to meet you.
2. If you **start early**, you will be able to prepare the information, alliances and networks that you will need to advance your interests. If you start late in the day, your chances diminish.
3. The **best time to start is at the 'ideation' phase**. If you can get your agenda co-opted by the European Council in the Strategic Agenda, or by the Commission President in the Political Guidelines, Priorities, and Mission Letters, so much the better.
4. Getting your agenda taken up in, or dropped from, the **Annual Work Programme** is vital. If it is not there, it does not exist. Only if exceptional events happen will the Commission adjust the Work Programme.
5. Evidence-free lobbying does not work. You need to bring **best-in-class, reputable and up-to-date evidence** to the table.
6. You **need to participate in the consultation process**. Silence does not serve your interests. If the evidence on which to base a decision is not in the public domain, the Commission can't use it.
7. The Commission is a technocracy which acts in the **European interest**. You need to adjust your positioning to align with this mindset.
8. Don't lobby the Regulatory Scrutiny Board.
9. The job of the **Secretariat-General** is to enforce the President's agenda and the Commission's rulebook. Reach out to it early in the process if the President's agenda and the Commission's rulebook is being by-passed.
10. The Commission still works in silos. **Work with all relevant Commission departments** to advance your interests.

7. Working with the European Parliament

By Doru Peter Frantescu

1. Introduction

The European Parliament (EP) is often considered the most open, transparent and accessible of the EU institutions but this does not mean that it is easy to understand or work with. Openness, transparency and accessibility do not depend only on how much information is made available; they also depend on how much of it the public can actually grasp.

The Parliament is by definition a political body and things can move very quickly in a variety of unexpected directions, as a result of the multitude of interactions between its political factions and sub-factions. While the Parliament is, like the Commission, an EU institution, it is very different in that when it comes to making policy decisions there is no clear (or single) chain of command. Each parliamentarian can make their own choices.

For this reason, this is the institution that demands the highest level of vigilance and monitoring. Over the years, the powers of the EP have grown significantly, whereas the attention of stakeholders to this institution has not always kept up with this trend. This is why the EP has managed to 'surprise' stakeholders (including the Commission and the Council) with the outcome of some of its decisions, which should not be the case since so much information is available.

A week is of course a long time in politics and change is the only constant in the EP. The last few years have showed that the pace of political change is accelerating, and the balance of power can change fast. The outcome of the European elections in 2019, which have led to increased polarisation and fragmentation in the EP, adds an extra layer of unpredictability that we will address in this chapter.

For this reason, it becomes ever more critical not only to stay up-to-date with developments in the Parliament, but also to find the right tools to better understand the current directions/trends and the likely scenarios way in advance; the box on the next page lists a set of useful ways to try and keep on top of the files you are following.

Generally speaking, the Parliament lacks the human and technical resources to be on equal terms with the Council and Commission with regard to its information sources and expertise. As a result, the Members of the European Parliament (MEPs) need, and will appreciate, good quality, timely,

> **Follow the Parliament**
>
> 1. Use the Parliament website – it is a goldmine of information:
>   - live Committee meetings
>   - Committee websites (newsletters, etc.)
>   - live Plenary Sessions
>   - individual MEP information
>   - MEP questions and answers
> 2. Use Political Group websites and news feeds
> 3. Use national party MEP websites, and regional MEP websites
> 4. Use individual MEP websites
> 5. Follow MEPs on Facebook and Twitter
> 6. Use VoteWatch.eu
> 7. Try to be present in the Parliament during the key moments for your issues
> 8. Follow the committees and Plenary live on your computer
> 9. Follow www.EuroparlTV.europa.eu

and reliable information. Please note that while in this chapter we tend to refer to interactions with MEPs, you should not neglect the importance of their assistants as gatekeepers and negotiators (there are tips on how to engage with MEPs' assistants in section 3.2). Furthermore, while often overlooked, technical advisers of the Political Groups can be a formidable source of information, intelligence and expertise. They are also key influencers of MEPs.

It is important to address a number of strategic issues first:

1. Get an **annual pass** to facilitate access to the Parliament's buildings (otherwise, you will need to identify friendly MEPs or Parliament staff who are happy to have their assistants sign you in on a regular basis). This goes hand in hand with being part of the Transparency Register (as was discussed in Chapter 2).
2. The Parliament works according to a **strict calendar**. Plan your work and your interventions carefully and in accordance with this. Get yourself a pocket size Parliament Calendar – you never know when you might need it.
3. Your **window of opportunity can be very narrow** in the Parliament. While a file can be prepared over a number of months, decisions can be taken suddenly, so it is essential to monitor developments continuously. Make sure you maintain good relationships with the key MEPs working on the file, but also with those who can influence the institutional agenda. In this case, the influence that your insider connections have on the legislative outcome is less important compared to their access to information (they might not have a say on the outcome, but can still act as an effective source of intelligence).
4. **Brussels is very good for more substantive meetings** and for ongoing legislative files and issues.

5. **Strasbourg is very good for networking and short pre-vote meetings**. Note also that trilogues often take place in Strasbourg as do exceptional Committee meetings and Political Group meetings to organise Plenary positions.
6. **You need to understand who the MEPs you are working with are and what is important to them** – things such as their beliefs, professional, educational and cultural background, national ties, European Political Group affiliations, national political affiliations and positions. You can find much of this on digital tools such as VoteWatch.eu, their own websites and Facebook pages, press releases and by watching them in Committees and Plenary session. However, when researching information, make sure you stick within the boundaries of the MEP's public/professional life, as privacy of personal life is taken very seriously in Brussels.
7. **MEPs are usually not experts in the particular field that concerns you** and they will have numerous open files under consideration at any given time. They need understandable and easy to use information – and most of all real-life examples that spell out the implications for businesses, jobs, living standards, etc.
8. In the Parliament, like the Council, a **national approach to your issue is likely to be easier in terms of access but significantly limiting**. Approaching all national MEPs can be very useful for an important national issue but remember that MEPs from the same country that belong to different political families can have very different views, hence you need to work across Groups and nationalities for the most success in the Parliament. As you try to reach out to more national delegations, a common mistake is to focus only on MEPs belonging to your own cultural sphere. Reaching out to MEPs from outside your comfort zone may appear at first somewhat discouraging, due to the extra effort it takes to 'get in sync', but it can certainly be very rewarding to expand your channels. On occasions they can be more aligned to your position than some of those from your own country. For example, the MEPs coming from the newer Member States are sometimes overlooked, but they can be equally useful allies.
9. **You need to know the positions and structures of the Political Groups**. They are key actors in the Parliament decision-making process and their members tend to vote coherently on issues whose impact is spread roughly equally across the EU. Not surprisingly, however, when a decision impacts differently on the various Member States, regions, and even professions, some national party delegations or individual MEPs ignore the Political Group line and make their own decisions. On VoteWatch.eu you can check the extent to which each MEP tends to vote or not with their own Political Group on each subject.
10. **Secretariat staff and Political Group staff in the Parliament are extremely useful contacts**, sources of information and interlocutors on your dossiers. You can find their details on the Parliament and Political Group websites.
11. **When working with the Parliament you should ideally not be working with more than 25 key MEPs**. Focus your attention on the key influencers and drivers in the Parliament. These are usually rapporteurs, shadow rapporteurs, Group coordinators and key issue MEPs in committees. However, in the currently more fragmented Parliament, when resources allow, you should **always be on the lookout for new and possibly 'hidden influencers'** whom you may find among the more silent MEPs.

NB: in the EP term that started in 2019, about 62% of the MEPs are new. This means that they are in general likely to know less about the issues and be more reticent and less vocal than established MEPs (sometimes also due to language constraints). However, some may share your positions (which is what matters) and, especially if fed with quality information, they will likely become more assertive and gradually more influential. For example, they may become rapporteurs on files that come up for decision-making in one or two years' time that are key files to you.

12. **It is usually not necessary (except perhaps as a last resort), to contact all MEPs**. Most emails that start with 'Dear MEP' will end up in the spam folder.
13. **Working with the Parliament is always about the numbers game**, in Committee or in Plenary. You always need to monitor and work with the voting numbers. You should always keep track of all relevant information, including your meetings with MEPs (Chapter 3 discusses how to do this). Additionally, digital tools such as VoteWatch.eu allow you to save time and energy in tracking coalition trends in the EP and help you predict the likely outcome of parliamentary votes (more information on this in section 4).

To close this introductory part of the chapter there are two further issues that are frequently mentioned as being important when working with an MEP: **national links and constituency links**. When an MEP is working in the Parliament both of these will inevitably come into play, but they will vary in importance according to the role of the MEP and the circumstances. Let us look at each of them in turn.

1.1 Importance of national links

The power that nationality holds over MEPs is something that is a waning force in the Parliament in terms of voting patterns. MEPs often have stronger allegiance to their European Political Group, and Political Groups in the Parliament vote with high levels of coherence. MEPs also have much more in common (politically) with the MEPs in their own Group, irrespective of nationality, than they have with other same-nationality MEPs in other Political Groups. National MEPs can become united around a national issue, one of the rare occasions when nationality-based work in the Parliament can be successful, but otherwise nationality is more an issue for accessing an MEP than for influencing their position.

One aspect of nationality is important, however: the question of how an MEP gets onto (and stays on) a national party list for the next elections. Despite an MEP's adhesion to their European Political Group, they need to be on a national party list (and as high as possible on the list) to get re-elected. This fact is always important to bear in mind because it can have an influence on how an MEP interacts with their national party, especially in the run-up to elections. This is also relevant if you want to access a specific national government, in which case you need to know if an MEP's party plays a role in the government.

Data by VoteWatch.eu shows that, in cases where there is a divergence of views between a national party and its Political Group, the vast majority of MEPs tend to follow the instructions of their national parties, since they are the gatekeepers to their re-election. Some relevant exceptions include MEPs with significant leadership roles within European Parliament Groups, such as the Chairs, the Whips, etc. (who feel more pressure to stick to the course set by their European Group). Also, keep in mind that MEPs tend to act more independently from their Political Groups in the periods preceding and following the elections to the European Parliament.

1.2 Importance of constituency links

The second issue is that of constituency links. This is very much a spill-over from national politics because it is less important in Brussels than in a national capital. It is, nonetheless, not something to be ignored. For a start, most Member States do not have defined local constituencies for MEPs (as there are not that many MEPs per country); therefore most MEPs have to cover large areas – often the whole country. Only 5 countries had regional constituencies for the elections in 2019: Belgium, Ireland, Italy, Poland and the UK.

The fact that most MEPs are elected from country-wide lists, and also that MEPs have reduced visibility in the national and local media, tends to result

> **MEPs and their constituency**
>
> MEPs will have close links to their constituency and they will likely:
> - Visit their constituency
> - Monitor local press for stories of interest
> - Deal with constituency requests
>
> To work with a MEP, understanding their constituency will help you situate your arguments.

in MEPs being more distant from their voters than national-level politicians. But, while allowing for the fact that the constituency link is weaker than in national politics, it is still the case that most MEPs are receptive to good constituency evidence and links as they still must keep their eye on their core electorate. Many MEPs monitor the local press from their country and region to follow any European issues or developments that might help them in their work in Brussels. It also possible that an MEP may have their eye on a national role in the future which will make them even more attuned to good national arguments and opportunities.

2. How to engage in the two stage process: Committee to Plenary

The most important time to work with an MEP is usually at the Committee stage because this is where the Parliament does the bulk of its work. Here the key for stakeholders is to convey their arguments to a number of MEPs in a tailored way that respects the diversity of the MEPs they are trying to work with. Giving MEPs information that they can use in Committee to persuade their fellow MEPs is very important – the best being case studies and real-life examples that bring an issue to life in parliamentary discussions and debates.

Also important to note is that when you are working with the Parliament, the best people to know how things stand and how best to proceed are usually the MEPs themselves, so never hesitate to ask how they see things; this information can be very useful to help you develop your positions and refine your arguments and strategy. Additionally, you can ask MEPs whom you could work with or who could help you advance your position further. MEPs are quite open about this (as long as they are in line with your position). You will always need to advance your positions according to the changing context of the Committee discussions, both in terms of substance and politics.

2.1 Choice of Political Group and Rapporteur

1. **Try to anticipate who the key MEPs related to your file will be and get to know them (and about them) before the Commission proposal arrives** in the Parliament – the better your existing contacts, the easier your access once the issue is live and MEPs are being flooded with requests for meetings. MEPs who have been rapporteurs or shadow rapporteurs of files on similar topics in the past, including own-initiative reports, are the most likely to end up as rapporteurs. Also, senior MEPs are more likely to do so than more junior ones, especially at the beginning of a new EP term. However, this also depends on the level of political support an MEP has within their own party, so it would be useful to know which MEPs are more central and which are more peripheral within their parties.
2. Always **check to see if the rapporteur has been named in advance** of the file arriving in the Parliament, which can happen for major dossiers, rotation deals and if the Political Groups have reached some compromise in the past.
3. It is very useful to try to **keep informed**, through the Political Groups and/or Committee Secretariat, **of likely Group and rapporteur nominations**; this can give you a head start in your work.
4. At this stage it is also **important (at decisive times) to follow the nomination of shadow rapporteurs**. Shadows can play an extremely important role and trying to ensure a Political Group nominates a specific shadow, one with whom you can work, is something not to neglect.

2.2 Working with Committee stage

1. The **Committee is the key stage of work** to follow in the Parliament, because often positions found in Committee can pass through Political Groups to Plenary largely unchanged.
2. The key element in working with MEPs in Committee is to **provide them with the right information**: real life cases and evidence that they can use to convince their colleagues. MEPs need information that they can use, so bite-size information and sound bites work very well. Do not hesitate to ask MEPs what information or content they need.
3. **Follow the debates and stay informed of the state of play**: you can do this by following Committee meetings, hearings, etc. and through your contacts. You can follow Committee meetings live on the internet.

4. When following debates in the Committee, **be alert for Group co-coordinator positions, any opposition and for timetable information**; these are all key and will need to be acted upon.
5. **Identify all the key players in the Committee** you are working with and do your homework on their political backgrounds. Look through past MEP questions to identify the key issues that these MEPs are interested in.
6. **Suggest amendments to MEPs that you have identified as being favourable to your position.** Long-standing, well-respected MEPs, coordinators, shadows and rapporteurs with good cross-party contacts are more likely to add weight to your amendment, because the MEP will have to justify, explain and find support for it – and these MEPs will be better placed to do this.
7. Amendments can be tabled by any MEP, but **the status of the MEP in the Committee will be crucial to the amendment's chances of success**. Great care should be taken about which MEPs you work with to table your amendments because it could also impact your reputation in the Parliament. If you are presenting amendments, then follow the strict amendment guidelines presented below. Present your amendments in the right format at the right time.

Get your amendments right

There are three major types of amendment and if you intend to submit a suggestion to a MEP you will need to get it right:

1. **Deleting** a provision in the Commission's proposal
   Bold italic on the left, 'deleted' on the right

2. **Modifying** a provision in the Commission's proposal
   Bold italic on the right

3. **Adding** a provision in the Commission's proposal
   Bold italic on the right and 'new' in the title

You only need one amendment per modification – be aware of how this impacts the rest of the text. In addition to the amendment you wish to propose, you should add a **justification** (legislative only), which is also required. This should explain the rationale for the proposed change in a clear and concise manner (max. 500 characters). Look through a few Committee reports to understand these rules.

Amendment 49
Tsvetelina Penkova, Constanze Krehl

Proposal for a regulation
Article 1 – paragraph 1 – point 3
Regulation (EC) No 2012/2002
Article 3 a – paragraph 2

Text proposed by the Commission	Amendment
(2) The available appropriations for this goal shall be limited to **half** of the maximum available amount for the Fund intervention for the years 2019 and 2020.	(2) The available appropriations for this goal shall be limited to *30 %* of the maximum available amount for the Fund intervention for the years 2019 and 2020.

Justification

In order to allow the EUSF to operate efficiently in line with its original purpose, namely assistance for natural disaster situations, no more than 30 % of the maximum annual allocation of the EUSF should be available for Brexit assistance. Any additional assistance should come from the European Globalisation Adjustment Fund (EGAF), or other ad hoc financial instruments.

Amendment 47
Nicolae Ștefănuță

Proposal for a decision
Article 1 – paragraph 1 – point -1 f (new)
Decision No 1313/2013/EU
Article 13 – paragraph 1 – point f a (new)

Text proposed by the Commission	Amendment
	(-1f) In Article 13(1), point (fa) is added:
	"(fa) create capabilities of specific response expertise which can be used in the case of disasters affecting cultural heritage."

Or. en

Justification

More focus on the protection of cultural heritage during disasters. Cultural heritage sites and monuments require specialised treatment; otherwise, there is a risk to do more harm than good during an emergency intervention. The network should make sure that heritage specialists are included in the trainings and preparedness actions.

> **Amendment 372**
> Cornelia Ernst, Barbara Spinelli, Marie-Christine Vergiat
>
> **Proposal for a regulation**
> Article 3 – paragraph 2
>
> | Text proposed by the Commission | Amendment |
> |---|---|
> | 2. Hosting service providers shall include in their terms and conditions, and apply, provisions to prevent the dissemination of terrorist content. | deleted |

8. If you want to work effectively with an MEP at this stage of the process **you need to work within their constraints**. For explanatory statements and preparatory working documents the page restrictions are as follows: seven pages for a non-legislative report, six pages for a legislative report and three pages for legislative opinions. Motions for Resolutions should be no more than four pages and 'suggestions' in non-legislative opinions one page. When there is an amendment the justification should be no more than 500 characters (a page being 1,500 characters).

9. It also frequently happens that you get **co-signed amendments by different Groups and nationalities**, an initiative that brings broader support and weight.

10. **Work with assistants, Secretariat staff and Political Group staff** – all will be involved in the dossier at the Committee stage.

11. Through these contacts the aim is to **follow the politics; try to track the compromises** that are forming within and between the Political Groups and to indirectly influence the key MEPs around the dossier.

12. **A key document to get hold of is the voting list** (see the examples below). These lists can be obtained from the Committee Secretariat, and also from Political Group staff. Make sure you are aware of the links between the different amendments, i.e. which amendments fall automatically when other amendments are approved. Your amendment might fall if another one (with which it cannot coexist) passes beforehand, so keep an eye on the other proposals as well. Conversely, in the case that your amendment makes another amendment fall, see if you can convince the supporters of this other amendment to rally around your proposal (or at least not oppose it).

Budget item and title	Am. N° — Tabled by	Comments	Rapporteur position	Vote
enterprises				
02 02 02 Improving access to finance for small and medium-sized enterprises (SMEs) in the form of equity and debt	ITRE/5050 - Rapporteur	If adopted 5004 and 5164 fall	+	
	ITRE/5164 - Hayer, Toia	If adopted 5004 falls	(+)	
	ITRE/5004 - Rapporteur	Restore DB	(+)	
02 03 02 02 Support to organisations representing small and medium-sized enterprises (SMEs) and societal stakeholders in standardisation activities	ITRE/5167 - Ferreira, Pereira, Georgiou		-	
02 04 02 01 Leadership in space	ITRE/5165 - Grudler, Dlabajová	If adopted 5005, 5097 and 5051 fall	-	
	ITRE/5051 - Rapporteur	If adopted 5005 and 5097 fall	+	
	ITRE/5097 - Tošenovský, Salini, Tajani	Identical: Restore DB	(+)	
	ITRE/5005 - Rapporteur			

Concerned text	AM	Tabled by	Remarks	Vote
	47	Agnès Evren	*Falls if COMP C adopted.* *If AM 43 is adopted, vote only on "**especially for carbon absorption**" as an addition.*	
COMP N - Paragraph 18	COMP N	EPP, S&D, RE, Greens/EFA, ECR, GUE/NGL	*If COMP N is adopted, AM 49 and 129 - 133 fall.*	
Paragraph 3 a (new)	49	César Luena, Eric Andrieu, Simona Bonafè, Alessandra Moretti, Jytte Guteland, Manuel Pizarro, Mohammed Chahim, Monika Beňová, Delara Burkhardt, Cristina Maestre Martín De Almagro, Nicolás González Casares, Javi López, Sylwia Spurek	*Falls if COMP N adopted.*	
	50	Ulrike Müller		

13. **Check who tables which amendments.** This is useful information for the dossier as it develops and also for future work. On the EP website, it is also possible to go back to past Committee work and analyse the amendments tabled; this will give you a very good source of information on MEP and Group positions. Tools like VoteWatch.eu are also useful to identify the main trends and patterns.
14. **Do not over-rely on specific individuals**. It is not rare to see rapporteurs ending up on the losing side, especially if they come from Groups that are not particularly powerful/influential or when some of their views are not shared by a majority of their colleagues. There have been cases when the rapporteurs have lost so many votes on their own report that they requested their name to be removed from its cover. Hence rapporteurs always have to assess what is the majority view within their Committee (and the Plenary as a whole) before drafting the text, so that they avoid the embarrassment of having their dossier torn apart by their colleagues when amendments are voted. The lesson to learn is that, while the rapporteurs may be the visible people, they are a bit like the tip of the iceberg: you can see it moving in a certain direction, but you can't see the bigger mass below and the underwater currents that are pushing it in a particular direction (unless you do the work to find out). The opinions of the rapporteurs are shaped by the pressures coming from many directions, including those of their fellow MEPs, so always keep in mind that this is a numbers game.
15. **Follow the voting numbers in Committee** and try to support allied MEPs as much as you can in the numbers game. Make use of your network and resources (within the ethical boundaries) to help your allies build bigger coalitions; this will be appreciated.
16. Do not forget that **politicians are subject to multiple sources of influence**. While most MEPs who have promised their support will deliver on this, do not take their support for granted until everything is over. Their final decision will be, roughly, the weighted average of all the sources of influence that they have been exposed to. Try to get as big a majority in your favour as possible, and you will be able to afford some last-minute defections.
17. **Committee work is all about compromise between and within Political Groups** (much more than national blocs) so you need to show awareness of compromise solutions.
18. Remember that the **Committee could also be preparing for a trilogue negotiation with the Council**. Your position needs to be included in the Parliament negotiating position to have any chance of making it to the final compromise; and the Parliament's position is often established before the Committee vote.
19. A group of 'only' 71 MEPs (10% of component members) is needed in order to have the **possibility of blocking a Committee decision** to enter into negotiations with the Council by requesting that such decision is voted in the Plenary – so never lose track of the bigger institutional picture.
20. If a text voted by Committee has been agreed in trilogues for a first reading agreement, then the Groups and Plenary have **very limited room to change anything** (for fear of undoing the compromise. Therefore working with the Committee is vital.

2.3 Working with the Plenary stage

1. **Follow the agenda and your item very carefully**. Keep in contact with key people close to the dossier to see if it remains on the agenda: things change.
2. In preparation for the Plenary you need to **keep in contact with the Political Groups** to see what deals are being made or amendments prepared. This should be done during the Group week that precedes the Plenary week and then also during the Plenary week itself.
3. **The Plenary week is an active week for negotiations** between Groups, and things change very quickly – it is best to be physically present or in contact with someone close to the dossier to be kept updated.
4. **Proposing amendments in Plenary** is possible for Political Groups, a Committee, or a group of at least 38 MEPs
5. Similar to the Committee stage, try to **get hold of a voting list**.
6. **At the Plenary stage the rapporteur, Committee coordinators and shadows remain key figures** as they try to steer their Committee compromise deal through Plenary. They will try to keep their own Group in line with what they agreed, on the Group's behalf, in the Committee stage.
7. However, **the numbers game is important, and the Plenary can amend key parts of a report**, especially in a more fragmented and polarised Parliament as the one following the 2019 EU elections. This is also due to the fact that some nationalities tend to be overrepresented in specific committees (e.g. Nordics in ENVI, French in JURI, Germans in BUDG, and Italians in PECH) and underrepresented in others. In other words, the Committee is not always a mini-mirror of the Plenary and the contrast can sometimes be stark. You could find it useful to check on VoteWatch.eu the latest digital tools available to forecast the reactions of the majorities in the Plenary and, most importantly, which Political Groups – and, in some cases, which national party delegations within these Groups – will make the difference (i.e. who will be the kingmakers).

2.4 Working with MEPs to set the agenda

While this chapter mainly focuses on the EP's role in the legislative process, there are substantial opportunities to be seized for agenda-setting purposes. Namely, the European Parliament can help you bring certain issues higher on the policy agenda of other EU institutions, such as the European Commission. This is particularly useful if you find the members of the EP to be more sympathetic towards your cause compared to others (or perhaps you just happen to have better connections in the EP).

Among the tools that MEPs have at their disposal for agenda-setting, it is relevant to mention **parliamentary written questions and own-initiative reports**.

Parliamentary written questions: MEPs can ask the EU institutions for written answers to their questions. These written questions and their answers are useful for several reasons. Firstly, they bring an issue to the attention of decision-makers. Secondly, you can get additional information on how

EU institutions are planning to address such issues. These are official answers whose content can be further used in your future advocacy action. However, while written questions are a relatively easy option to pursue (you just need a friendly MEP's office to table it for you), their impact should not be overestimated, in particular as written responses are often vague and might add little to what you already know.

> **MEPs' written questions**
>
> 1. An MEP can submit at most 20 questions in 3 months.
> 2. The written question should not exceed 200 words and 3 sub-questions.
> 3. The written question can be addressed to the European Council, the Council of Ministers, the Commission or to the High Representative.
> 4. Generally, the addressee has 6 weeks to answer the written question. However, MEPs have the possibility of designating one written question per month as a 'priority question', in which case the addressee must answer in 3 weeks.
> 5. Written questions can also be jointly submitted by like-minded MEPs, or by committees and European Groups.

Parliamentary own-initiative reports: Own-initiative reports by the European Parliament are a more powerful agenda-setting tool. Importantly, legislative own-initiative reports (INL) allow MEPs to request the Commission to put forward new legislation on a specific topic. Furthermore, even though this request is not binding, the Commission is obliged to respond to such a request and justify its decision.

The importance of these reports was recently boosted by the bid of Commission President von der Leyen to strengthen the role of the European Parliament in initiating legislation. The Commission has committed to proposing a legislative act whenever the EP, acting by a majority of its members, adopts a resolution requesting the Commission to submit legislative proposals.

However, compared to other agenda-setting instruments, pursuing this path is relatively difficult due to the higher number of players involved in the process. Do not forget that, even if the rapporteur is on your side, other MEPs will table amendments at both the Committee and the Plenary stage. In order to make sure that the final outcome will be aligned with your preferences, you need to collect reliable intelligence and actively engage with decision-makers and stakeholders, in line with the suggestions mentioned in this chapter.

3. How to engage the key people

When it comes to the people in the Parliament it is important to make a series of specific comments and recommendations about the different actors involved. As with the Commission and the Council, it is very useful to map out all your potential contacts in the Parliament. To take things one step further, you need to have a solid picture of what each MEP actually stands for.

To do this keep an eye on **the speeches, the interviews and the social media** of the MEPs. This is always a good idea to try to understand their views and their plans in general. However, doing so requires a lot of time and resources and it is not enough to understand the nuances that will eventually drive their voting behaviour. For example, MEPs will readily line up to say they are in favour of certain widely popular policies, because that is how they maintain their public support. However, it is only when they have to make choices between conflicting priorities (e.g. budget discipline v. growth, social cohesion v. innovation) that you can spot what's more important to them. The way to do that is by following the exact phrasing of the amendments that they have drafted (in the case of those MEPs who are active on a topic) or/and tracking their voting record on specific (hard choice) amendments (which gives you the whole picture for all the MEPs in the Plenary). In this regard, you can complement the information from the already excellent websites of the European Parliament with digital tools such as VoteWatch.eu.

Now we can turn to guidance on how to work with specific groups in the Parliament.

3.1 MEPs

1. **Understand how MEPs work** – this will help you work with them.
2. **Develop long-term relationships** with MEPs to foster mutual trust. Things can change quickly in the Parliament and long-term trusted contacts are the only way to mitigate this and to be kept updated.
3. **National Delegations are important actors** and need to be engaged with and understood; this is especially the case for specific policy areas in which they can play a big role. They might not have the numbers to carry a vote, but they have influence in the Political Groups – and they also have inside information on all the deals being done there.
4. **Identify opinion leaders and builders of compromises** within and between the Political Groups.
5. **Meet the major players** before, when and after you need to work with them.
6. Be aware that there will likely be **turf wars** between various factions trying to influence and guide the rapporteur (and other key actors), as much from the outside world as from inside the Parliament itself.
7. **Check whether an MEP is from a national governing party or the opposition** as this could have an influence on their activity in the Parliament.
8. **Know what else is on the table** of the MEP at the moment you meet them; likewise know the political context of the moment.
9. Always remember that **an MEP will be interested in media stories** at the Plenary stage of the process (more so than at the Committee stage), so any opportunities you can develop will be warmly welcomed.

10. You will likely **only have a short time to convince an MEP**, so you need to be concise and to the point. Knowing what they need, and when they need it, is essential.
11. Try to **present suggested amendments to an MEP** as this could help them in their task – along with justifications to help them sell and support your suggestion.

3.2 MEPs' Assistants

1. **Develop long-term relationships with MEPs' assistants** as they are vital gatekeepers to the MEPs themselves. This also depends on the working methods and interests of the MEPs: in some cases the MEP wants to do everything himself/herself, while in other cases the MEP has other priorities and it is largely left to the assistants to collect the information and prepare the documents.
2. You need to **identify the exact role the assistant play**s within the MEP's office - are they keeping the agenda, providing policy expertise, etc.? This can be very important.
3. **Some assistants come from the party ranks**, often belonging to the same party factions as the MEPs they are working for. They may have helped them during the campaign and could become MEPs or MPs themselves in the future. These assistants are more sensitive to the national dimension/impact of proposals on constituents, etc.
4. **Other types of assistants are Brussels insiders**: they have been working in other EU institutions or European organisations before, they are not affiliated to a specific party and might have worked for other MEPs from different parties in the past. These assistants have deeper knowledge of the EU machinery and a stronger network in Brussels. However, their MEPs might trust them less when it comes to their policy agenda, since these assistants tend to be more invested in their EU career rather than seeing things from the party/national politics perspective.
5. **You can find MEPs' assistants on the Parliament website** – and you can search by assistant or by MEP. Or you can find the names of the assistants on VoteWatch.eu and on the profile page of each MEP.

3.3 Committee Secretariat

1. Developing a **long-term relationship** with Committee Secretariat staff is an excellent investment.
2. Committee Secretariat staff have a very good understanding of the state of a dossier, timetable information, voting lists, information on technical details and sticking points, and in some cases, they have a strong influence over the content and direction of a file.
3. Committee officials often have a good **institutional memory** of how things work in the Committee – they will be able to tell you about the dynamics, inter-personal relations and key drivers in the Committee as they follow it every day.

3.4 Political Group staff

1. Political Group staff are often **somewhat overlooked** in contacts with the Parliament, which is a lost opportunity to network and get information.
2. Political Group staff **work very closely with the MEPs in their Committee** – so they have a privileged position for information and influence.
3. Political Group staff have **detailed information** about the workings of the Committee and of the politics surrounding all files on the table.
4. Political Group staff have **privileged access** to voting lists and other internal information and documents.
5. **You should work with all Groups** – you never know when you will need them.
6. Political Group staff are **often senior experts** with competence in the subjects of their Committee.

3.5 General engagement with the Parliament

1. **The Parliament is very unwieldy from a news perspective**. There can be multiple press releases on the same day from the Parliament and MEPs on the same subject. It is important to know what to respond to, and how.
2. Your engagement will have to **strike a balance between the technical and political**, as well as between the European, national and local dimensions.
3. **Provide concise information** that has strong emotional/political/media content.
4. If possible, provide **real life cases and easy to use information** for MEPs in their Committee and Political Group work.
5. MEPs will need **different angles** to the information from the other institutions.
6. Facts and figures should have relevant **practical illustrations** of their meaning, with very clear explanations and an identification of what this means for the MEP.
7. Positions presented to MEPs need to be well-argued and be something that an MEP could use in their interactions with other MEPs and stakeholders.
8. **Do not use too much technical jargon**: the argument needs to be crystal clear. Remember that Parliament reports are not usually technical or jargon filled.
9. Try to link your information to the **institutional/constituency interests of the MEP**.
10. Generally, you will **not have much time to convince an MEP** as meetings can be very short. You need to get your message across in a clear and concise manner, while being able to elaborate if required.
11. **A relationship built on trust** is more important than what you are trying to sell. If you can consistently back up your information over a period of time you will be able to create a relationship of confidence in which you are a trusted source of information.
12. MEPs, like other officials identified in this book, are most susceptible to face-to-face meetings and good written material – but MEPs also engage in dinners and lunches (in Strasbourg and Brussels), so more events can be planned.

13. You can also raise awareness of your issues with MEPs through exhibitions (e.g. photographic), events (e.g. report launches) and informal lunches at the Parliament or in and around Brussels/Strasbourg.
14. **Do not mass mail MEPs** – this does not work very well. Rather, you should work with individual MEPs who can be your flag bearers on some issues and would email their colleagues, instead of you doing it.
15. **Share reports and interesting information** with them by email: much like the Commission, you never know what might be of use or of interest to them. MEPs and officials in the Parliament are the most open to informal meetings and coffees.
16. Written briefings should keep to the **one-page rule** to be most effective.
17. **Never try to impose your views/ideas** or positions on an MEP: you are there to provide information and justifications.

4. Key ways to achieve success

The European Parliament is a complex institution. In order not to waste your resources, it is essential to do your homework before deciding which MEPs, national parties or Political Groups will be the main target of your advocacy campaign. The importance of good intelligence is now bigger than it used to be, not least because of the increasing fragmentation in the European Parliament following the elections in 2019. The two biggest Political Groups (the EPP and S&D) do not have a combined majority of seats any longer, while the small Groups have become bigger. All of this means that the traditional political forces that have previously dominated the European Parliament are gradually losing their grip on the institution. Be aware of this: diversify and tailor your strategy, since talking to the traditional players only is unlikely to be particularly effective. Do not forget that this is a numbers game, so do not lose track of the overall picture.

4.1 See if you can obtain the following intelligence:

- How individual MEPs, national parties or Political Groups tend to vote on the issues that you are following;
- Which alliances between Political Groups are more common on the issues that you are following;
- Which Political Groups tend to be more united when voting on the issues that you are following and, conversely, which ones tend to be more divided;
- The names of potential kingmakers, namely those MEPs who belong to the middle-ground on specific policies and whose action can swing the outcome of key decisions.

While setting the strategy, you have to define which policymakers you need on your side. Gathering intelligence will help you to narrow down the targets of your advocacy action and be more efficient in investing your time and your resources. You might want to focus on those policymakers that can actually swing the outcome of the vote, rather than investing too many resources in preaching to the converted or reaching out to hostile forces. The kingmakers are often close to the middle of the policy spectrum and might vote in favour or against your cause, depending on the circumstances. In the case of these swing voters, the small details and the mood ahead of the vote will make the difference.

4.2 How can you find out who the kingmakers are?

Among the different options, you can consider hiring specialised organisations such as VoteWatch Europe to provide you with intelligence reports. Such analyses help you predict the likelihood of specific MEPs voting in favour or against a proposal. An MEP who is 50% likely to vote in your favour is a more appealing target than an MEP who is only 20% likely to vote in your favour (you have better chances to convince him or her). Since you can only reach out to a limited number of MEPs, you will also need to be able to assess the influence that MEPs have over their colleagues in order to maximise the impact of your advocacy action. If you are able to get an influential MEP on your side, more MEPs will follow suit.

Remember: **public visibility does not equal actual influence** over dossiers. One MEP can have a big crowd of followers and be very active on social media like Twitter, but have no power whatsoever to change the text of a proposal, while another can invest less in their social media and prefer to do the 'nerdy' work of drafting the laws. Keep in mind that the communication culture can be very different across Europe, e.g. in some countries Twitter is not used as a communication tool at all and inputting it as the main criterion may return an inaccurate picture of who is influential. You always have to ask yourself what you need an MEP for: is it making your point of view known to the public, or shaping a proposal? Depending on your needs of the moment, the right MEP to go to will be different.

You can get information on the influence of MEPs over legislation from specialised providers such as VoteWatch.eu, while other sources track their influence over social media.

> **How to identify key MEPs**
>
> 1. Identify where MEPs stand in the policy spectrum, as political cleavages change across different policy issues. For instance, an MEP might be part of the middle-ground on environmental regulation, but have more extreme views on budgetary policies. You should be able to identify 5 different groups of MEPs: 'allies', 'likely allies', 'middle-ground', 'likely opponents' and 'opponents'. 'Allies' and 'opponents' are the least likely to switch to the other side. In order to perform such mapping, data analysis of voting records is often needed.
>
> Dare to step outside of your regular (cultural) zone of comfort. Many stakeholders tend, out of (historical) reflex, to have on their radar only MEPs from the 'old Europe' (now the EU14) and they miss out on MEPs from the 'new Europe' (post-2004 enlargement countries). Let the objective data do the work for you and tell you where you can rally support. Once potential allies are identified, do the research on cultural differences and specific sensitivities before approaching them.

> 2. Identify whether MEPs are leaders or followers on your issue. Some MEPs are more likely to follow the lead of their Political Groups, especially if they have little interest or knowledge of the policy area. Narrow down the list of potential targets to the MEPs who are most influential on this specific issue. Be aware that some MEPs might be particularly influential in their own political faction, while others are better at building bridges between different political families.
>
> 3. Once you have identified the most relevant MEPs, collect further intelligence on them. For instance, if an MEP is a likely ally, find out the topics where he/she is more likely to disagree with you. For instance, if you are lobbying on energy, an MEP might agree with your proposals for higher targets, but disagree with you on other issues, such as energy subsidies. It will be easier to interact with MEPs once you know where they stand. In this case, data analysis is rather useful (and organisations such as VoteWatch can help you save time and trouble by performing the research for you).

If you decide to do the research in-house, you can start by gathering information from the official websites of the European Parliament. More advanced tools such as the VoteWatch website can help you gather more in-depth intelligence. An example of VoteWatch.eu data is given on the next page, a screenshot taken from the VoteWatch website – in this case, for an MEP from the Polish Delegation. This screenshot gives you an excellent indication of the wealth of information you can have at your fingertips when it comes to working with individual MEPs, National Delegations, Political Groups and, through all of this, with the Parliament as a whole.

A number of elements in the data are particularly useful if you are working with the Parliament. An MEP's loyalty to their Political Group and their national party is very important information. You can also break this data down into policy areas and individual Plenary voting patterns, providing solid empirical evidence to base your work on. The individual pages for each MEP provide a goldmine of information that you can use to really understand each and every MEP you seek to work with.

Check individual MEP voting records: https://www.votewatch.eu/search.php

Check voting records of Political Groups:
https://www.votewatch.eu/en/term9-political-groups-votes.html

---

In addition to what is available directly on its website, VoteWatch.eu is continuously upgrading its analytical tools and providing on-request services, so it is always a good idea to get in contact and find out how it can help you.

180   Working with the European Parliament

MEP » Adam JARUBAS	Poland

Start of mandate:	02.07.2019
Last name:	JARUBAS
First name:	Adam
Born:	17.12.1974, Busko-Zdroj
Group:	Group of the European People's Party (Christian Democrats)
Party:	Polskie Stronnictwo Ludowe
Committees:	Committee on the Environment, Public Health and Food Safety (Member)
	Committee on Budgets (Substitute)
	Committee on Industry, Research and Energy (Substitute)
Delegations:	Delegation for relations with Japan (Member)
	Delegation to the EU-Armenia Parliamentary Partnership Committee, the EU-Azerbaijan Parliamentary Cooperation Committee and the EU-Georgia Parliamentary Association Committee (Substitute)
	Delegation to the Euronest Parliamentary Assembly (Substitute)

Parliamentary activities — Disclaimer

Participation in roll-call votes:	1159 out of 1347 votes
86.04%	Ranking: 614th

Loyalty to political group:	1096 out of 1159 votes
94.56%	Ranking: 330th

Loyalty to national party:	1147 out of 1158 votes
99.05%	Ranking: 432nd

How this MEP influences EU policy (sample)

Voting behaviour reveals that, compared to the EPP group, this MEP is more supportive of maintaining EIB's funding of natural gas projects.

Additionally, we found that, compared to the EPP group, this MEP is less supportive of ensuring the full alignment of legislative and budgetary proposals with climate goals.

For more information on how MEPs work to shape EU policies, contact us at secretariat@votewatcheurope.eu.

DO YOU NEED TAILORED ANALYSIS OR TRAINING?

Contact us to save your time. Write us at: secretariat@votewatcheurope.eu

Latest Reports

- Latest Council data: EU clustering at new high post-Brexit
- Review: 'Parlement', the new series on the European Parliament
- New feature on VoteWatch.eu: key info on how individual MEPs influence EU policy
- Webinar: European Policy-Making Process in Practice
- How COVID-19 reshapes the EU budget battleground

ALL VOTES | KEY VOTES — All policy areas — Choose date

Found 1,347 entries

Date	Name of document	MEP's vote	Loyal / Rebel to political group
15.05.2020	Macro-financial assistance to enlargement and neighbourhood partners in the context of the Covid-19 pandemic crisis - Draft legislative resolution : *Article 1, paragraph 2*, amendment 1 - ordinary legislative procedure, first reading	👎	Loyal
15.05.2020	Macro-financial assistance to enlargement and neighbourhood partners in the context of the Covid-19 pandemic crisis - Draft legislative resolution : *Article 1, paragraph 3*, amendment 2 - ordinary legislative procedure, first reading	👎	Loyal

Source: www.VoteWatch.eu

Beyond the 'micro-picture' that concerns a particular MEP, VoteWatch also looks at the 'macro-picture', i.e. the interactions between parties, groups, nationalities etc. For example, you need to consider the issue of **voting cohesion within the Political Groups** (see Figure 7.1). The more cohesive Groups are, the more important it is to work with them (as opposed to individual MEPs) and the Delegations that compose them. According to VoteWatch, there is relatively high cohesion within the Political Group voting habits in the Parliament, although there are significant differences among the Groups. The Greens/EFA Group has a track record of being the most cohesive (which means that it is more difficult to get individual delegations or members to vote in a different way). Even big Political Groups such as EPP, Renew Europe and S&D tend to be quite cohesive, although the cohesion of the EPP has been decreasing substantially after the elections in 2019, showing rising tensions between different wings of the Group. Conversely, the cohesion of parties on the very right of the political spectrum (ECR and ID Groups) tends to be lower, and in those cases it makes more sense to target national parties rather than the Groups as a whole.

However, there are also significant differences within the Groups across **policy areas**. By way of example, when it comes to policies such as agriculture or fisheries, there is a stronger tendency to vote along national lines than with other policy areas. Additionally, some Groups tend to be particularly divided on specific policy areas. For instance, the S&D Group are less united when voting on international trade agreements (in these cases, it is a good idea to target individual national parties and even individual MEPs), whereas the Group is rather cohesive on matters concerning employment and social affairs.

On VoteWatch.eu you can also find the convergence/loyalty of each **national party** to the European Political Group it belongs to. The data can be broken down by Political Group, country, policy area and time interval, thus helping to easily identify the national parties who would be most or least likely to defect in a vote on a particular issue and, consequently, whom to approach.

Figure 7.1: European Political Group cohesion rates, all policy areas (01.07.2019 - 15.05.2020)

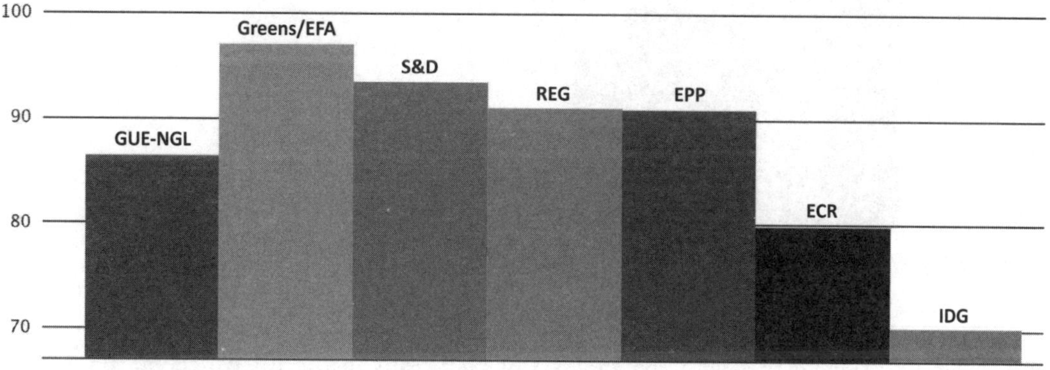

Source: www.VoteWatch.eu (adapted)

A further key aspect of this analysis of voting behaviour is the **relative strength of the Political Groups**, which tends to differ from the numerical strength of the Groups – something to be very aware of when trying to work with the different Political Groups. Also, in this case, tools like VoteWatch.eu can help. Figure 7.2 shows that the Renew Europe group, despite being only the third largest during the current term of the European Parliament (2019-2024), has thus far been on the 'winning' side more often than any other Group. This has led VoteWatch.eu to name it the 'Kingmaker' Group in the EP. For more detailed information, you should take a look at the VoteWatch website to find out the data by policy area. In this way, you can discover which Groups tend to be part of the winning coalitions that are formed when voting on the issues that you are following.

Figure 7.2: Percent of votes won by each Political Group, all policy areas (01.07.2019 - 15.05.2020)

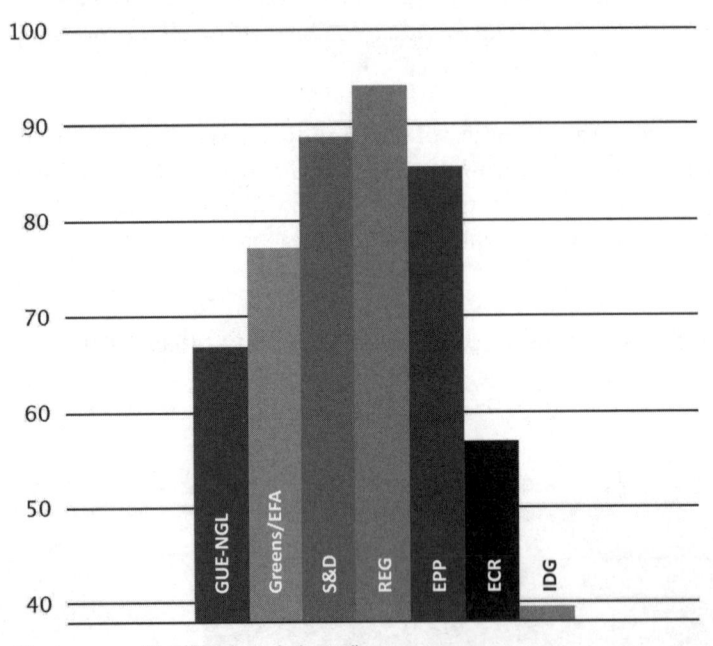

Source: www.VoteWatch.eu (adapted)

This is taken one step further with the **analysis of coalitions** in the EP, which can be seen in Figure 7.3. This shows that Renew Europe has thus far agreed more often with S&D than the EPP since the European Parliament elections in 2019, providing the centre-left forces with a slight advantage over the centre-right ones. The central position of the Renew Europe Group in the political spectrum provides it with a bigger advantage than its numerical strength alone might suggest.

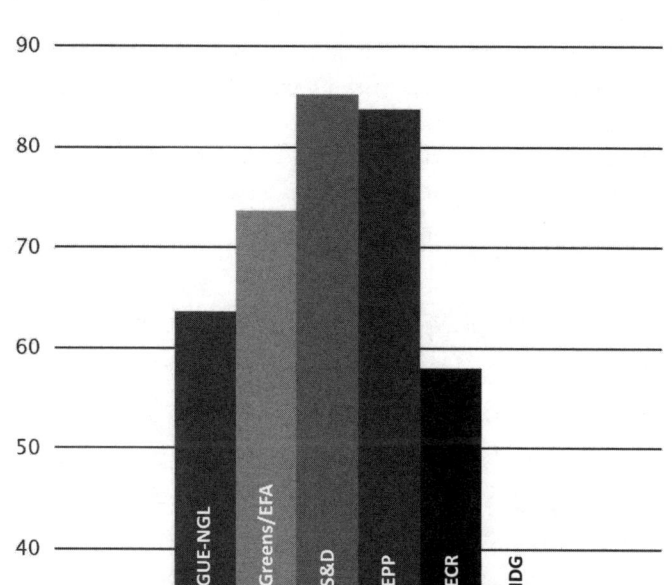

Figure 7.3: Frequency of Renew Europe (REG) voting with other Groups, all policy areas (01.07.2019 - 15.05.2020)

Source: www.VoteWatch.eu (adapted)

However, the data by policy area (which is also calculated by VoteWatch) shows that coalition arrangements in the European Parliament tend to change across policy areas. For instance, on some issues, such as home affairs and fisheries, centre-left coalitions tend to be more common (Renew Europe, S&D and Greens/EFA), whereas on other issues, such as international trade and internal market, centre-right coalitions tend to be more common (Renew Europe, EPP and ECR).

Such data is essential reading for any serious engagement with the Parliament as it provides a fundamental level of understanding of the likely politics that will occur on any given dossier. Knowledge of coalition dynamics makes it easier to predict whether a proposal will be approved or rejected in the European Parliament, as well as to identify the 'kingmakers' that can swing the outcome of Parliamentary votes. With this in mind, try to help the MEPs that support you to build broader coalitions and alliances – the support of one or two Political Groups is never enough to get a majority in Plenary.

5. Overview

Working with the European Parliament requires even more effort than with the other institutions, but this is a function of the greater opportunities and the more dynamic nature of decision-making in this EU institution. Something worth bearing in mind when working with the Parliament is that most MEPs are very heavily solicited by external stakeholders. This means that you need to be able to differentiate yourself by the quality of your information, knowledge and timing to make yourself a long-term contact whom an MEP values when they want or need information.

The key points to draw from this chapter are listed below.

Working with the Parliament: Key points

1. Know the MEPs you are working with – do your homework (use tools such as VoteWatch.eu).
2. Create a good network of contacts around your dossier, including the MEPs, assistants, Committee staff and Group staff.
3. Always remember the numbers game: this means you will have to work across Groups and nationalities. Step out of your comfort zone and get ready to talk to politicians with different cultural and political sensitivities.
4. You need to provide technical information, but package it for political use. You need to balance European, national and local arguments.
5. You should only try to work with the key MEPs on any given dossier – which should be around 20 to 30. Mass contacts and mailings are only actions of last resort.
6. You will always need to try and work with rapporteurs, Political Group coordinators and shadows, so try to build up long-term contacts in your key committees.
7. Work with the Parliament Calendar; get a copy to take around with you.
8. Never forget the media and how you can get them involved (national and European).
9. Understand the structures, dynamics and politics of the Groups in the Parliament (collect as much intelligence as you can).
10. Know the National Delegations within the Groups and within the Parliament as they are very influential players both in Brussels and in national capitals.
11. When you have a 'live' issue, be very attentive to any changes – things move quickly towards the trilogue negotiations and/or Plenary votes.
12. Be clear, accurate, concise and direct with MEPs – provide them with easy to use figures, examples, case studies and illustrations.
13. Always build for the long-term in all your contacts in the Parliament.

8. Working with the Council(s)

By Roland Moore & Alan Hardacre

1. Introduction

Working with both the European Council and the Council of the European Union (the Council of Ministers, or simply Council) is a challenge – but a challenge that is vital to meet (more particularly in respect of the Council) because of the pay-offs you can get from this angle of engagement. This chapter will build on Chapter 2 of our companion volume *How the EU Institutions Work* – which describes in full detail the functioning of both the European Council and the Council – to outline best practice in how to engage with each of these institutions.

In many ways the Council is the main driver of a significant number of decisions in Brussels and across all levels of policy-making. Whilst much is made of the European Commission holding the pen (and equally being present and active across all levels of policy-making), it is very often the Council dictating how the Commission should use that pen. It is here where the vast majority of EU rules are finalised before official publication. The Council will, however, often prove to be the most difficult of the institutions to work with, for four reasons:

1. Working with the Council in effect means working with national capitals.
2. The Council is the representative of national interests in Brussels so is more nationally focused.
3. Positions of Member States in the Council are informed by and brokered among their own national stakeholders.
4. Of all the EU institutions the Council is the least in need of technical information.

The first point is perhaps the most important to stress because **the national level is a key driver when it comes to working with the Council**. Whilst it is essential to work with the Permanent Representations in Brussels, the majority of the substantive decisions of the Council are taken back in the national capitals. National positions are represented by the experts and/or diplomats

Follow the Council

1. List of Permanent Representations available online
2. Council website including press room
3. Presidency websites: agendas/priorities
4. VoteWatch EU Council section

that they send to Working Group meetings. The key work, positions, mandates and decision-makers within the Council structure all originate in Member State capitals. This can present advantages if you are based in a national capital and represent a national interest as it will be easier to engage with the key national officials. On the other hand, understanding the different political systems and contexts of other Member States, and being able to find all the relevant national decision-makers can make successful engagement very complex.

This complexity increases when you start (as you will likely need) to engage across several Member States on an issue. For this reason, many stakeholders initiate their work with other Member States via the Permanent Representations who serve as the interface between the EU institutions and their capital. The responsible attachés will be in a position to advise on their Member States' positions, to relay concerns back to the capitals and provide you with other advice concerning your issue including the process and the position of other Member States. This is a pragmatic approach that can help you achieve good results.

For even greater success, you need also to contact the source of the information and influence those responsible for developing the Member State's position both at a technical and political level. We provide some advice for how to do this later in this section.

The second and third points listed above relate to the fact that there is a natural tendency, when working with the Council, to concentrate solely on one's own nationality, especially if you are based in a national capital. Successful work with the Council involves much wider efforts and engagement, while always bearing in mind that the Permanent Representatives and national officials of other Member States that you meet will all be assessing their own national interests. This will be discussed further below.

The fourth important point is that the Council's need for expert factual input is less than that of the Commission and European Parliament since national civil servants and politicians will more often have pre-formed positions based on the realities and their assessment of their own national situation. Member States implement law with all stakeholders which gives them a much greater technical understanding of the situation, the implications and what might be needed in the future. Simply put, they are often much better informed than their EU-level counterparts. You will recall from Chapter 6 that your work with Commission officials needs to take place within the framework of the Strategic Guidelines and Work Programme. Well the same is true in every national capital – your engagement needs to be sensitive to the national political and policy-making context. This is to say that Council members will rarely be starting from a blank piece of paper and your engagement should be mindful of this. It is the mix of different national interests, further complicated by linguistic and cultural factors, that makes working with different Member States very challenging.

The **key general strategic points to consider when working with the Council** are as follows:

1. **The Council is the least open and transparent** of the EU institutions, making it harder to find out what is happening, what is needed and who to speak to. The Council does not openly publish all its working documents and as such is generally the most difficult institution to access and work with. To work successfully with the Council you need a combination of good long-term contacts at the national level, including civil servants and key stakeholders as well as refreshing your engagement with attachés who usually move on every 2-4 years.
2. **The national factor**: the Council is generally more open to working with those who represent issues of relevance to their national interests. It is important to understand the national political agenda and priorities, and find the national connection, i.e. to identify and explain how a national sector is affected or how your issue supports a national cause. What is your national angle?
3. **Work in both Brussels and the national capitals**: it is essential to have a two-fold communication and engagement. While the decisions might be taken in the national capital, the Brussels antenna, the Permanent Representation, will always be involved in the process and will in most situations communicate and negotiate the outcome (with possible room for manoeuvre).
4. **Work with other Member States, not just your own country or where you have the most interest**: the national route is usually the first but should not be the only one. You need to find common ground with other Member States in the Council and work to build support for your issues. Understanding how your issue relates to other countries as well as the EU overall is key in this. The latter, the EU dimension, is particularly important to the Commission.
5. **Understand devolved powers**: meaning that working with regions (Länder in Germany, for example) can be as important, if not more important, on certain issues as working with national governments. Some Regional Ministers attend Council meetings, usually in an observer role. The regions will often have a representative office in Brussels, so working with both their home base and their representations in Brussels is important.

> **The Council on VoteWatch.eu**
>
> VoteWatch.eu has a very useful section on its website dedicated to the Council. In this section they have an easy-to-use database of all legislative votes, as well as explanatory statements made by the Member States with regard to their votes. You can search by individual Member State as well as by issue. You can also access information on coalitions and minority positions.

2. Decision-making in the Council of the EU

Chapter 2 of *How the EU Institutions Work* details the entire decision-making process of the Council step-by-step, and you need to follow this process as closely as you can. This can, however, be very challenging and will depend on having good long-term contacts within the Council structures.

You will also find a lot of important information on working with the Council in the next chapter below, on the Ordinary Legislative Procedure.

Before moving into more detail on working with the Council across its three decision-making phases we need to make three very important overarching points that will frame all of your engagement:

1. Firstly, the **scope for influence declines the later you leave your engagement**. Typically, by the time a file reaches the Coreper or Council level, the majority of issues have been resolved at the working level. This is not to say that issues cannot be re-opened or re-visited, but it will take a huge effort and often depend on new information being brought to light. Things can change very quickly particularly once the file reaches Coreper and you need to read the signs as soon as possible to be able to act appropriately.
2. Secondly across the entire Council, there are certain types of **ad hoc and standing coalitions**, which you should understand if you are working with the Council. This will help you know when there are coalitions at play and how majorities are moving in Council, for which you need to follow the political discussions very carefully. Coalitions are an intriguing part of Council dynamics and they need to be monitored carefully on a case-by-case basis. The coalitions can vary greatly between each sectoral Council, e.g. on climate ambition, liberalising the agricultural policy and/or the single market, social issues, etc. Some can endure over long periods, while other coalitions are very fluid and can form and disappear quickly in the Council on an issue-by-issue basis – and in many cases they can depend on who is in government in the respective Member States. In essence, there is huge diversity within the Council which is why effective engagement on your issue can make the difference. It is crucial to understand these dynamics – and often officials close to Council deliberations can give you a very good assessment of the state of play and the 'like-minded' groups of Member States and their constituents.
3. Thirdly, **the work of the Council, like most of the EU institutions is often extremely prosaic**. On legislative items or files, the Council works towards a single objective at any one time depending on the stage of the file. It is instructive to have an idea of what the Presidency wants to achieve by asking the key players what external pressures there are to achieve a deal (e.g. compliance with an international treaty, societal pressure, pre-agreed commitments in Council Conclusions or similar, the need to update existing EU laws in line with the pre-agreed review dates, etc). This will differ according to whether the decision in question relates to legislative or non-legislative files.

3. How a Presidency will approach legislative files: what to look out for

For legislative files (for more on which see Chapter 9 on how to work with OLP), a Presidency will initially be aiming, at most, to conduct an orientation debate or exchange of views in Council to provide a steer to the negotiations while kicking off discussions at the Working Group level.

The next major goal would be to enter negotiations with the Parliament. This will be achieved either informally (at the Coreper level in the form of a 'mandate') or formally (at the Council level in the form of a '**General Approach**'). The chosen route will depend on the culture in the Council configuration in question and/or the political nature of the file and whether the Council wants to send a strong signal to the Parliament ahead of negotiations.

Should a Presidency not be able to secure such an agreement, a fallback option would be to produce a progress report, which would usually be discussed at the Council towards the end of its Presidency (i.e. May/June or November/December). The progress report then informs how the next Presidency should take forward the negotiations. As part of the progress report, a Presidency can invite the Council to confirm a 'common understanding' reached at the trilogue as a means of solidifying its work in negotiations.

Once the file is in trilogue discussions with the Parliament, the Presidency will be singularly focused on securing a deal. At this stage, their focus is on having a clear understanding of the Council's red lines, where the Council has flexibility towards the Parliament, where the blocking minorities exist (and on which issues), and navigating a path through that seeks consensus as far as possible.

During this phase, attachés and Member State experts typically have a lighter comparative workload on the file in question as the principal work is with the Presidency and the Parliament. Instead, their main focus is on gathering intelligence on the trilogue discussions from the Presidency, the Parliament and other Member States (including the incoming Presidency who participate as observers in the trilogue) and preparing their Permanent/Deputy Permanent Representative, for the next Coreper discussion. This is where you can also help by providing or exchanging any information and intelligence you have picked up from other sources.

4. How a Presidency will approach non-legislative files: what to look out for

The main non-legislative item at Council's disposal is the **Council Conclusions** – a document where the Council may give a particular steer or instruction to the Commission or endorse an existing Commission position/Communication, which will help anticipate upcoming legislation. The Council Conclusions have the status of purely political commitments or positions with no legal effect. Nonetheless, they exert a significant influence on the other institutions, particularly the Commission. When the Council asks for a report, proposal or makes suggestions in its Conclusions, the Commission has to act. Although Council Conclusions are non-binding, Member States, the Commission and the Parliament may choose to quote Council Conclusions to seek to push Member States in a certain policy direction.

As they are proposed by the Presidency, Council Conclusions will reflect the Presidency's priorities. However, the Commission often plays a strong drafting role behind the scenes and the document may therefore also push its policy agenda; for example, where the Commission would like the EU to take a greater role.

The **journey of the Conclusions through Council** begins with the Presidency's draft and is then subject to a handful of Working Group meetings at which detailed and often substantive changes are proposed (there is more on this later in the chapter). Coreper will review any outstanding issues and in cases where Coreper cannot agree, the Council itself will deliberate and resolve the issues during its meeting. As a result, it is important to know when the Council meetings are taking place under a Presidency as they serve as the ultimate deadline for adoption.

The Council formally decides on Conclusions by consensus: they are not passed if any Member State opposes them. Consequently the Presidency seeks to find text which is acceptable to all countries. This is the key strength but also the weakness of the Conclusions. It is not current practice for any Member State to block Council Conclusions, which would be seen as a significant slight to the Presidency. It is extremely rare for a Presidency to hand over a set of Council Conclusions to the next Presidency and every effort is made to support the Presidency.

The focus is therefore on finding compromise text which is acceptable to all the countries around the table. This results in the situation that Conclusions are often hedged about with many caveats to clarify that what is proposed should only apply 'where appropriate' or 'voluntarily'. In those rare situations where Council cannot agree, the Presidency can adopt the Conclusions itself (so-called Presidency Conclusions), but these carry no official Council status.

At all stages of the EU policy cycle it is worth remembering that the Council, as a body, has a very strong power of persuasion vis-à-vis the Commission; this should be monitored and is also something that can be worked with. This point also holds true to some extent in relation to the Parliament, but in this case in regard to the relationship between the individual Member States and their national MEPs. Increasingly, many Permanent Representations have one or more officials to liaise with their country's MEPs and key MEPs in each Committee. In this sense the Council is very well-positioned with information and influence.

5. Working Groups (Working Parties)

Legislative and non-legislative files are prepared for Coreper and Council by the **Council Working Groups (also often referred to as Working Parties)**: there is at least one for every sectoral Council. Working Groups are usually attended by the relevant Brussels based attaché from each Member State's Permanent Representation to the EU, accompanied by the experts (i.e. the lead policy official from the relevant government department, who may or may not be an expert on the specific issue) from national capitals. Hence the importance of the dual approach of working both in Brussels and national capitals.

Nearly all Permanent Representations have clear and user-friendly websites that allow you to identify Brussels-based officials; alternatively the EU Whoiswho is very useful for this task.

> **The special case of Agriculture and Food**
>
> There are numerous Working Groups on agriculture to facilitate the work of the giant EU Common Agricultural Policy. These are almost uniquely attended by experts in the capital on their own, with oversight from the agriculture attaché(s) in the Permanent Representations. Their work feeds into the Special Committee of Agriculture (SCA) a preparatory body for the Agriculture and Fisheries Council established in 1960. It is composed of senior agriculture officials from the capital and the Agriculture Counsellor in each Permanent Representation. Coreper will rarely discuss agriculture-related files, leaving this almost uniquely to the SCA except on some highly political files – in these cases, it's also common for the attaché to be the lead in the Working Groups. Veterinary and files relating to the Common Fisheries Policy are prepared by Coreper with specific Working Groups and typically Brussels based attachés.

Other significant attendees include the Commission (the unit responsible for the file and occasionally other interested DGs), the Council Legal Service (a resource for all Member States to call upon at any given point), the Presidency (the attaché and support team from the Member State currently holding the rotating chair) and last but not least the Council Secretariat, which provides support to the Presidency. In short, a lot of people!

Some Working Groups have set days for their meetings, while others can meet on any day (or every day) of the week. In terms of advance notice, the Presidency will have a rough idea of the number and timing of all Working Groups during its Presidency, but to allow itself maximum flexibility only communicates its programme on a monthly basis (which it circulates towards the end of the preceding month). Occasionally, Working Group schedules and agendas are published on the Council website but typically with insufficient notice to enable you to prepare. To know when your issue is being discussed in the Working Group, it is important to talk to the key players.

> **A word on the interpreters**
>
> The unsung heroes in the room are, without doubt, the interpreters. They will usually be assigned to follow a specific Working Group and will get to know the speaking style of the group and the issues they cover. In accordance with their agreement with the Council, they must have a 90 minute break for lunch as well as work a maximum set of hours (usually around 7 hours). Working Group meetings can last longer but at some point the interpreters must leave whereupon the Presidency kindly requests the meeting to continue without interpretation and usually in English – much to the chagrin of the French delegation.

More often than not, a Working Group meeting will be convened on the basis of a single topic or file. Usually meetings run all day, with morning sessions running from 10am to 1.30pm and afternoon sessions running from 3.00pm to 6pm. For less substantive issues, a Working Group may convene only for a morning/afternoon and possibly even just one hour (e.g. to agree formally mandates for international meetings).

Ahead of each Working Group, the Presidency will communicate to Member States its plan and objective for the Working Group meeting, e.g. conducting a read-though with comments on a specific set of articles. It is an art to know when your particular issue will be discussed and this is again why it is important to have good engagement with the key players (and usually at least three sources to cross-check the intelligence – even if you receive directly the email from the Presidency via a source, it's always good to cross-check with others to confirm the approach and to unearth new information).

The old adage of 'get in early, and stay there' applies to all during negotiations. A well-organised Member State will have already seen the proposal or Conclusions coming, will have already held discussions with the Commission or the Presidency (perhaps even helping to draft it) and other Member States. They will come to the first Working Group well-prepared and with an initial position. Similarly, you should begin your engagement with Member States, the Presidency and the Commission as soon as possible to identify your interest, flag your expertise, explain your issues and engage with the consultation process of individual Member States.

Once the negotiation begins, you should work with attachés and their respective national experts in tandem and provide them with facts and evidence, formulated as arguments that can be used in negotiations. If you have expertise on a subject, you can be useful by helping them to decipher and understand a proposal from a particular Member State (which they may share with you) or likewise a Parliament amendment.

A significant percentage of the negotiation of the files and Council Conclusions are agreed at Working Group level, making it the key decision-making level to work with from the start. Statistically it is therefore likely that your issue will be agreed at this level. It is imperative for you to work with the national experts in the Working Group and to have a champion in the room for each of your main issues.

6. How the Presidency runs a Working Group (on legislative or non-legislative files)

Each Working Group is defined by a series of 'table-rounds'. A single table-round can last up to one hour and thirty minutes based on each Member State and the Commission intervening for an average of 2-3 minutes.

At the start of each table-round, the Presidency almost always invites the Commission to start proceedings. On legislative files, the Commission will usually set out its rationale for its proposal, the reason for the particular course of action based on consultation, Impact Assessment, etc. In cases where the main subject is a proposal from a Member State, or a group of Member States has proposed an alternative proposal, the Presidency would invite the lead Member State to start the discussion.

The Presidency would then open the floor to comments and reactions from Member States. The Member State attaché usually leads the negotiation on behalf of the Member State and will indicate their desire to speak by raising their country flag in front of them (this involves placing the country's name plate vertically).

As the flags go up, the Council Secretariat notes the order in which they were raised and relays this to the Presidency chair (who they will sit next to). The Presidency chair will go through the list in the order in which flags where raised. At the end of the round of comments, the Presidency will invite the Commission to react, followed by any further follow-ups from Member States before bringing the table-round to a close, possibly with some concluding remarks on how they will handle the situation and next steps.

In cases where there is a large table-round, the Presidency may choose to bring in the Commission earlier to respond to questions. In instances where a Member State asks for advice from the Council Legal Service (CLS), the Presidency would invite the CLS to intervene before handing back to the Commission

7. The Working Group process for legislative files

There are usually **five distinct phases** of a Working Group's negotiation of a legislative file:

1. **The Introduction** of the new proposal and appraisal of the Impact Assessment. The spotlight is entirely on the Commission to present, explain and defend its proposal in the face of questions and scrutiny from the Member States.

   In this phase, you should be providing the national expert and attaché with clear arguments on what you support and oppose with respect to the aims of the proposal and the projected cost and benefits. You should also be focusing on seeking maximum clarification from the Commission on its approach and what it considers to be its scope. This is an evolving area of scrutiny and it is fair to say that more attention and focus should be given to this area. What is often the case is that Member States are ill-prepared for this most vital discussion. Another reason for advance prior engagement.

2. **High-level article-by-article**: A Presidency will want to take the temperature of the Member States on the most and least contentious areas of the Commission's proposal. After each Working Group meeting, the Presidency will invite Member States to submit written comments on the text covered. This high-level read-through and Member States' written responses may be repeated one or two times. This gives time for Member States to organise themselves and reach a national position on the proposal. At this stage, every single Member State will enter comments under reservation (a so-called 'scrutiny reserve' i.e. indicating they do not yet have a national position).

   In this phase you should be asking national experts and attachés to seek clarity on any ambiguous definitions, meanings or interpretation. Again, Member States often have not had the time to conduct a detailed analysis, so the earlier you can communicate and get your issue known, the more likely it is to be given attention by others in the negotiations.

3. **Detailed article-by-article**: A more detailed read-through is then carried out and the Presidency may even decide to change the order in which articles are taken, grouping similar articles (and annexes) together. Based on the nature of the initial rounds of comments and on how ready Member States are, the Presidency would propose drafting changes for particular aspects of the text. An important consideration for a Presidency is how ready Member States are to negotiate. If the majority of Council does not have a formal position, a Presidency cannot make significant progress as there would be too much uncertainty in the room.

An attaché will likely be reluctant to share Council texts due to the rightful need to preserve the confidentiality of Council negotiations. Attachés from a single Working Group get to know each other very well by virtue of working together on a frequent basis. This means they often meet on an informal basis as well. This helps create a common bond and trust in the working of the Council. One work-around to this sensitivity can be to present your issue and ask them how the newly proposed text treats this. If you are aligned with the Member State and they see you as a partner, they may be more open with you on this and regard you as a partner.

> **Four-Column Document**
>
> The 'four-column document' is the basis for the negotiations. It is written by the Presidency with support from the Council Secretariat and the Secretariat of the lead Committee in the Parliament.
>
> Column 1: Commission proposal
> Column 2: Council text
> Column 3: Parliament text
> Column 4: The proposed way forward/compromise

Almost inevitably, however, the text does become available one way or another. More often than not this is through national experts sharing it with their key trade associations for input during the negotiation. It then doesn't take long for the text to circulate from the capitals back to Brussels via email. This is another reason why maintaining contacts in capitals is vital.

At this stage, it's important to provide specific drafting changes to the text that can be deployed to improve the text.

4. **Addressing the Parliament's comments**: The European Parliament usually reaches its draft first reading position before Council has solidified its position. A key part of the negotiation is for the Working Group to reach a position on all the amendments put forward by the Parliament. The Presidency will usually want to know if:
   a. the Council accepts the amendment and proposes to change the Council text immediately; or
   b. the Council accepts the amendment only with some changes to be clarified in negotiations; or
   c. the Council will accept the amendment in negotiations in exchange for Parliament accepting to drop one or more of its other proposals or accepting one of the Council's proposals. If agreed by Council, this will usually be kept in the 'back-pocket' by the Presidency and not recorded in the text for fear of undermining the negotiations when the text leaks; or
   d. the Council rejects the Amendment.

At this stage, you should provide input to the Member States on which Parliament amendments you support or oppose and why, and make the link back to previous correspondence, flagging all risks with examples.

5. **Trilogue preparation and reaction**: The Presidency will only want to take a file to Coreper which has broad support and where most of the minor issues are resolved. In this closing Working Group phase, the Presidency will constrain attachés only to raise issues that they know will be of vital importance for their Ambassador and Minister. This is a very effective way of filtering out the non-essential demands and helping the Presidency to identify the key sticking points to achieving support for its text. The Presidency will then be in a position to put forward a text to Coreper that represents a balanced negotiation in Council. It is important to keep in touch with the attachés and/or national experts to know when the file reaches Coreper and the status of your issue.

Once your issue is considered 'closed' it will take a huge effort for it to be re-opened and even harder for Coreper or Ministers to do so. The most successful approaches will highlight the political risks of not amending the text (perhaps drawing on new socio-economic or scientific information). Attachés will usually be completely overwhelmed at this stage of a negotiation and so more than ever, your communication has to be accurate, clear and brief. focusing on EU-level arguments, as well as specific impacts on Member States. This could be your last chance to influence.

8. The Working Group process for non-legislative files

For non-legislative files, the process for negotiating Council Conclusions is much more streamlined. Working Groups will usually be able to agree a typical set of Council Conclusions within just three day-long Working Group meetings over the course of one to two months. As such, the most effective time to secure any extensive changes to the Council Conclusions is prior to the first meeting.

Getting hold of the draft text via your network is key. It is most effective to be able to offer drafting suggestions to improve the Presidency's draft text in line with your interests and provide strong arguments for the position (in line with national and EU interests). By the third meeting, most Member States will have coalesced around a certain form of words and it will be much more difficult to achieve anything more than minor drafting changes, with some notable exceptions for highly politicised Conclusions.

9. Understanding how an attaché approaches negotiations in the Working Group

The more you understand about how an attaché approaches a negotiation in the Working Group meeting, the more effective you will be in your interactions with them throughout the negotiations. A Working Group is a long negotiation involving multiple parties, all with the purpose of creating a new law with a single EU aim. This should be reflected in the material you communicate.

Throughout the negotiation, a successful and well prepared attaché, supported by their national experts, can influence the outcome through a combination of means. They can do this via bilaterals with the Commission, the Presidency and other Member States. They can organise like-minded groups among Member States on a particular issue or the entire negotiation, ensuring they submit well-structured and well-argued written comments (where possible proposing drafting changes). They can also take what is called a 'whole of government' approach to negotiations: this is where different departments and Ministers bring pressure on their counterparts in other Member States to influence their positions in the Working Group. The intervention in the Working Group itself is therefore just the tip of the iceberg on the back of likely extensive engagement work from the attaché: it is effectively the culmination of all the hard work in the run-up.

> **Notes from a Working Group Attaché's Playbook**
>
> Attachés will consider the following approaches to advance their agenda. Ultimately different styles and approaches can work. No single method or approach wins the day in Working Group negotiations.
>
> - **The argument matters**: they will know if their ask holds water, is backed up by relevant stats and evidence, and is clearly articulated. Moreover, they will ensure their arguments are not locally or nationally centred but also have relevance at the EU level.
> - **Put it in writing**: the sooner you can share proposals in black and white, the sooner Member State experts can give their view on them. (Of course, sometimes you may want to catch them by surprise.) The most effective proposals show the Commission's proposal, the alternative proposal and a justification (in line with EU arguments and the aim of the Commission's proposal). While this sounds simple and obvious, it is often overlooked in the rush to prepare for a Working Group.
> - **The smaller the change, the better the chances**: some attachés know the power of this approach and use it very well. Keep it simple and better still with real-life practical examples.
> - **It's a linguistic/technical change**: if not over-used, this can be a useful ploy.
> - **Hostage taking**: this involves putting a major focus on something early in the negotiations which they then later give up. This tactic clearly cannot be over-used and for it to succeed it has to be in line with national policy and ring true. It is always useful for a Member State to have unexpected compromises such as these in their back-pocket.
> - **Splitting the difference**: where there are opposing views put forward by two groups of Member States, some attachés are very good at suggesting a third way, which at the same time addresses their issue. This can come across as being helpful to the negotiation, to Member States and to the Presidency.
> - **Look to help other Member States where possible**: this is where flexibility in negotiating positions is very useful. The smaller Member States tend to take a more pragmatic view on this.
> - **Always remember the Commission. Always**: if the Commission supports a particular proposal, this will give it an easier ride in the Working Group. The Commission's view carries huge weight whilst not having a formal vote. In extreme cases, the Commission can take advantage of Member State opposition 'to hold a file hostage' unless it gets what it wants. Furthermore, some smaller Member States look to the Commission to take their steer. The Commission is an experienced negotiator and as author of the proposal will often have a 'ready-made' plan B on certain proposals in the event of an impasse.

10. Coreper

The Permanent Representatives (PR) and Deputy Permanent Representatives (DPR) are the Brussels-based antennae of the Member States. The former meet as Coreper II and the latter as Coreper I. The PR and the DPR have an extremely good overview of everything on the table at any given moment, of the politics surrounding files and the likely coalitions and majorities that are forming. PRs and DPRs scan the horizon for the upcoming EU policy issues and ensure that national capitals prepare for negotiations in the best way with the maximum information. They can work with their counterparts in key EU capitals (typically the EU adviser to the national leader, known as the Sherpa – see page 136) to validate intelligence gathered in Brussels. Ahead of and during the closing stages of negotiations, they brief the national capital on the state of play and what is possible (or not) in Brussels.

Increasingly, **Coreper is responsible for agreeing the fate of the majority of files**. This is to say, they frequently agree the Council's position for entering negotiations with the Parliament as well as then agreeing on the final outcome. This is done on the basis of informal votes and the text must still formally go to the Council for vote and adoption. It is therefore vital to familiarise yourself with the Council voting matrix and all the permutations on your particular file.

Council Voting Calculator

A very useful tool to see how voting is shaping up in the Council and to familiarise yourself with the workings of the Council voting is the online Voting Calculator: http://www.consilium.europa.eu/en/council-eu/voting-system/voting-calculator/

The Presidency will never take a formal vote at Coreper, but the Council Secretariat will be keeping track of all those Member States in support and, crucially, those that have withheld support or look likely to abstain (e.g. because they have no formal national position). This is to establish whether this constitutes a blocking minority (for files conducted under the Ordinary Legislative Procedure) or if there is a lack of consensus (in the case of Council Conclusions).

When it comes to 'voting', **smaller Member States can often be overlooked**, which is a mistake. While the big countries have a larger voting weight, the Presidency will always try to work by consensus, so it usually attempts to accommodate all Member States in some way. According to VoteWatch, roughly 65% of legislative votes in the Council were unanimous between 2009 and 2019, even though in most cases unanimity is not formally required. Some smaller Member States are also very influential, persuasive and good compromise generators, making them important in the negotiations as well as when it comes to a vote or seeking support for or opposition to an issue. Equally, their PR or DPR might be a particularly persuasive speaker and operator, working both behind the scenes and during the meeting to secure support for their issue.

Coreper is the key level of Council decision-making as it oversees all the Working Groups and prepares all the work for Council meetings, meaning that many of the final deals and decisions are made at this level. During the closing stages of a file's progression through Council, PRs and DPRs take the lead on the negotiations for the Member State, briefed by the attaché who in turn is acting on advice from the national government.

There is no limit to what Coreper can do with a file but, as noted above, once a file reaches the level of Coreper, the Presidency is focused on closing issues, not reopening them. The Presidency's aim is to secure a text that Coreper can agree on – e.g. as the basis for negotiation with the Parliament or as the final agreed text for Council to adopt (with or without discussion). If Coreper believes that an issue has not been sufficiently explored, it can request the Working Group to reconsider it and bring back a revised text following further technical deliberations.

The separate PR and DPR networks are a close-knit family as its members meet frequently and often have very good contacts. PRs and DPRs will communicate frequently with their opposite numbers in the time leading up to Coreper, and they will want to know from their attaché who they need to target on particular issues to maximise their influence. Furthermore, they cover a number of different sectoral Councils and therefore have much more of a helicopter view of all the decisions going through Council at a given time. They will be able to consider whether there are trade-offs to be made across files as well as pick up on wider trends in EU policy-making such as competency creep, inappropriate use of legal basis, or breach of key EU principles such as subsidiarity.

Outside of the Coreper meetings, PRs and DPRs will have time to engage with stakeholders but will clearly show a preference for those with a major national interest. They will almost always ask the relevant attaché(s) to prepare the note, overseen by the powerful Mertens or Antici.

The work of Coreper is prepared and facilitated by two preparatory groups, **the Antici and Mertens groups**. These are attachés based in the Permanent Representations who play an organisational and political filtering role: the Antici for the Permanent Representatives in Coreper II, and the Mertens for the Deputy Permanent Representatives in Coreper I. They will have detailed insight on files of a political, technical, procedural and timetabling nature and also of the evolving political climate in Coreper. They can become invaluable contacts, alongside the attaché, when your file is being negotiated by Coreper. They are in the thick of the negotiating action, so they will have up-to-date information.

It is important to establish and maintain contact with the Mertens and Antici: they can provide detailed and up-to-date information about the position of their own and other Member States with regard to all proposals before Coreper. They meet briefly prior to Coreper to agree the agenda and provide the Presidency with a signal on their Member States' approach in Coreper. During Coreper, they sit alongside or behind the PR/DPR and ensure that the relevant people from the Permanent Representation are ready and prepared for the discussion. They can also play a key role in helping to broker deals with their opposite numbers ahead of Coreper. Should you have a meeting with the PR/DPR, this can often be a good entry point for initiating contact. You should maintain this channel of communication throughout the negotiation. They will also have key information when it comes to the discussions taking place in the European Council. We will come back to this later.

11. Council meetings

Council meetings are very important due to their decision-taking power and the high-level political decisions being taken. Working with a Council vote is a very difficult task, much like trying to work with a College meeting in the Commission. It requires high-level political contacts in the national capitals and all the key players within the Permanent Representations. Good engagement at all the previous steps will greatly enhance the chances of success.

The Presidency will only want to bring to the Council issues where it was not possible to find a compromise at the Working Group or Coreper level. This usually involves highly politicised issues with national salience for several Member States. In essence, trying to work at this level represents the last resort.

The Presidency will be focused on listening to Ministers, in the build-up and during the Council and seeking to broker a deal based around new text or even previously seen text from the Working Group or Coreper. It is crucial for someone championing your cause to have a line into the Presidency and be already sharing possible alternative text – this could be the Minister, their adviser or a combination of the key players within the Permanent Representations.

Seeking to open a closed issue at this stage or starting to engage on a live issue for the first time are both extremely challenging and should only be attempted where the particular issue is of great significance for both you and them and where you have solid supporting evidence.

It is extremely useful to have a direct line of communication to a Minister or government leader, perhaps via their political advisers. If you can convince them of your issue, you can change the Member State's approach overnight – which can be essential ahead of a key decision in Coreper or at Council itself.

As politicians, they will have long established and deep political networks and alliances. They tend to have an inner circle of informal advisers they call on for advice. The inner advisers can be drawn from academia, think tanks, or their election campaign team and can all be useful access points to changing a Minister's stance. Equally, you will find in many government departments a senior official who has the ear of the Minister, whatever party is in power. Identifying and engaging with this person is also key. If the Minister and/or their advisers are resistant, then here the Head of Government's office or equivalent can be an effective route: each Head of Government has an office to make sure the machinery of government works and delivers on the government's agenda. Disagreement in government is not unusual and an agreed government line needs to be reached. This will differ from one Member State to another but understanding this is a key part of your advocacy strategy.

In an EU culture that depends on consensus, there is a natural propensity to want to 'get the deal done', sometimes whatever the cost and without wanting to 'rock the boat'. This is especially so if the Member State is saving their negotiating capital for another file being agreed in parallel. Bypassing the civil servants and officials and creating a back-channel to a politician will help overrule officials and impose an alternative position on them which they then must pursue in Council. This can make all the difference in the closing stages of a negotiation – while acknowledging, of course, that there are still many other players involved who may be pushing back against this.

If you succeed, you should expect that the officials will be cold on you for a while. They will know why the Minister has changed their position. Given the sensitivities in conducting such an approach, try to avoid casting aspersions on any individuals and feel your way into the discussion, being prepared to consider dropping the issue if they insist on directing you back to the lead official or the Permanent Representation.

At this point, it would be useful to recap, in the box below, what the previous sections have said are the main overarching engagement recommendations for working with Working Groups, Coreper and Council meetings.

1. The Working Group is where the majority of files find technical agreement. It is where you will already get a very clear idea of the chances of success of the file in Council as positions, coalitions and key issues become apparent.
2. Working with a Working Group means identifying the national experts who sit in the Working Group, the attachés in the Permanent Representation who deal with the file, the officials in the General Secretariat of the Council and the officials from the Commission who also attend.
3. Working with one, or several, Member State(s) to try and get issues into Council Conclusions can be very useful and is something that needs to be monitored.
4. Coreper typically deals with the most important issues of a file. It is an inherently political body and will require political input and arguments, mostly related to the Member State in question.
5. At the level of Coreper, you should be looking to ruthlessly prioritise your asks, ideally on one specific issue.
6. Working with Coreper and Council requires senior management activity and engagement.
7. Engagement with Ministers and key Council participants is very difficult and requires a combination of senior engagement via PR, DPR and national capitals.
8. Having a direct line to the key national politicians can make all the difference; finding the best route for this is key.
9. Always keep an eye on blocking minorities and coalitions formation in Coreper and Council; something that should have become apparent earlier in the Council decision-making (Working Group level).
10. The role of Antici and Mertens is to help the PR and DPR successfully achieve their country's goals in a negotiation. They play an integral role in Coreper and having their ear can be invaluable.
11. Trying to start work at the Council meeting stage should be a last resort given the difficulties of getting to the right people and the subsequent low chances of success.
12. Subjects for discussion at Council meeting level tend to be only the most sensitive files in which national positions are not aligned, making engagement on these issues difficult.
13. Council discussions are inherently national and political, so any material designed to work with the Council needs to take this into account.

> 14. If you want to find out the position of the Member States, you can make a request under Freedom of Information rules or equivalent to access the negotiating texts of recently adopted similar legislation.

12. Key people

Having looked at the different stages in the Council decision-making process, and what is needed to work with each level, it is useful to turn to the issue of people and how best to engage with them.

> **EU Whoiswho**
> http://europa.eu/whoiswho/public
>
> For the details of Member State officials working in Working Groups the best sources of information are:
>
> 1. The Permanent Representation (attaché in charge of the subject area).
> 2. The National Ministry in the Member State in question.
> 3. General Secretariat of the Council officials.
> 4. The Commission official who sits in the Working Group (the desk officer/HoU from the relevant Unit).

The first potentially difficult element of working with the Council is in finding the right contacts and their details. Some good sources are listed in the box below.

The limitation of the EU Whoiswho and the websites of the Permanent Representations is that they will only help you identify the Brussels-based Council actors. It will then be through these actors that you have to map the other key officials – the nationally-based power players and technical officials. It is for this reason that a mapping of key contacts in the Council can be much more elaborate and difficult to finalise.

The following are usually the best additional sources of information:

- Permanent Representations to the EU, based in Brussels.
- Trade associations and NGOs at the national level and their European counterparts.
- Any subsidiaries, local actors or partners you have (some advocacy training may be required for actors not involved in public affairs or government relations).
- Bilateral embassies/trade missions in EU capitals of the national country you are most affiliated with.

12.1 Officials and politicians in national capitals

As we have said before, officials and politicians back in the Member State capitals are important actors to work with if you are really trying to change the content and substance of a Member State position.

For this the following recommendations are useful:

1. **Know the politics on your issue at the national level**. You need to understand what is driving the national agenda, what the political structures and decision-making forums are, and who are the national actors in your field (usually associations and federations). Each country reaches agreed positions in different ways. In France, for example, the Élysée Palace plays a dominant role. You need to adapt your strategy for each country.
2. **Develop support at the national level for your issue**. The most powerful players are typically national trade associations but also individual companies, civil society, academics and other key opinion leaders and the media (both national and trade media). Working through/with national actors can be very useful in helping to overcome the inevitable cultural and linguistic challenges.
3. **Meet well in advance the national civil servants/experts leading on your issue**. Take a long-term perspective: make friends before you need them. Remember that national civil servants are likely to be experts on the file in question: be prepared for this and explain your position in a technical manner. The national policy lead plays a particularly key role on a file, because they must:
    a. Provide leadership (bringing together and leading the department team, including lawyers and economists; engaging with other government departments, regional bodies and stakeholders; and developing the Member State's negotiating position and strategy).
    b. Provide expertise (identifying key issues and balancing competing priorities; developing credibility with other Member State negotiators; providing negotiating instructions/drafting suggestions to the Permanent Representations).
    c. Have good communication skills (empathy and ability to explain the Member State's position effectively).
    d. Demonstrate political nous (identifying where the compromises lie and who to influence).
4. **Be prepared to escalate the issue** to senior management and Ministers and to raise the issue with different departments. Officials tend to act on instructions 'from above' and have limited room for negotiation, making identification of the decision-making structures in the Member State even more important. Equally, officials can 'go rogue' and pursue a position that is not in line with wider government policy or they simply may not brief the Minister on your issue for various reasons.
5. **Build a network across multiple Member States**. This is pivotal and can help create the support in Council for your issue.
6. Keep in mind that the **national officials will be responsible for the transposition into national law** of EU legislation as well as the **implementation and evaluation** of its effectiveness. This is useful to keep in mind throughout the negotiations since they have plenty at stake in the game and ought to have a strong interest in resolving as many issues as possible. Equally, there will

always be issues related to implementation and interpretation of the EU rules and as such, your national contacts could be very useful for this later stage. And finally, you need to keep this in mind if ever you look to work above their head – because invariably you will have to work with them again.
7. Pay attention to the voting behaviour in the European Parliament of **MEPs from the same governing party as the lead Minister**. Voting behaviour in the Parliament tends to be more about Political Group affiliations (as discussed in Chapter 7), rather than national ones. Consequently, potential divergences from the Political Group's line (or lack thereof) provide an idea of how sensitive an issue is for specific national parties. Journalists pay a lot of attention to MEPs' voting behaviour and will report inconsistencies in the parties' positions across the different institutions. If MEPs from a governing party contradict the position taken by their Ministers, this could either mean that the issue is not particularly sensitive, so MEPs feel free to take an independent line, or that there are significant divisions within their party on this matter.

12.2 The Presidency

The importance of the Presidency in driving the agenda and work of the Council for a six-month period makes it a key actor to work with. The Presidency acts as a shot of adrenalin to the Council's business, bringing a renewed sense of urgency every six months. Member States will be preparing for their Presidency at least one to two years, if not more, in advance. The most opportune moment to engage with them is well in advance so as to identify your interests and usefulness to them. During the Presidency itself, it will be extremely busy for all the officials involved and they will choose to limit their interactions with stakeholders to a minimum. The Presidency is especially useful to understand the timelines, the direction of discussions on a file and the compromises that are likely to result.

You should therefore aim to:

1. **Establish contact** with Member States holding forthcoming Presidencies **well in advance** so as to avoid the 'cold calling' effect that you will have by simply appearing during or just before the Presidency. You should consider presenting your priorities to an incoming Presidency for any particular upcoming legislative file or Council Conclusions.
2. **Understand the medium-term goals**. The Presidency will be concentrated on their priority files and on getting things done within their six months. They will also have an eye on what they have committed to do as part of the 18-month trio programme. Ministers will have their ambitions for the Presidency and it's important to understand what these are.
3. **Understand the role and limitations of what a Presidency can (and cannot) do**. The Presidency will hold the pen on redrafting the Commission's proposals during negotiations, and it will be their judgement on when to bring a file to Coreper and Council to reach a deal. The Presidency lead negotiations with the Commission and Parliament to facilitate co-decided agreements. You can help them achieve this by trying to offer solutions and compromises to find the middle ground. The Presidency will propose text for Council Conclusions and again will hold the pen

on any changes to those before Ministers sign them off in Council. The Presidency is impartial but not neutral and so it can also put forward its own position as a member of the Council. It is not, however, appropriate for a Presidency to be overtly pushing one option or another: the Presidency is always in the hands of the Council and must go with the majority view.
4. **Small countries will tend to rely on the Commission** for support behind the scenes in drafting text. Keeping contact with the lead official in the Commission will be important here. Equally, they may ask one or more Member States to help out with the chairing of some of the less high priority Working Groups such as those dealing with international issues where they may not have a particular expertise. Gaining an understanding of this in early conversations is key. Finally, they will also draw on the considerable expertise of the General Secretariat of the Council and the Council Legal Service in their re-drafts.

12.3 General Secretariat of the Council (GSC)

The GSC is an underestimated actor on the Brussels scene, contacted significantly less than its counterparts in the Parliament and Commission. The GSC has a goldmine of information at its disposal and can be a very influential actor in the internal decision-making of the Council. Like the Presidency, the GSC is more useful for sharing factual information (such as timings of meetings, processes and procedure) than it is for direct influencing work and substantive discussions, but the GSC will understand the issues in their technical and political dimensions and be able to analyse what this means for stakeholders better than almost any other actor around the Council. The GSC should form part of your comprehensive key actor mapping and be engaged with at all stages of the Council decision-making to establish positions, find information, contacts and further details. In addition:

1. Meet and **build a network in the GSC** as early as possible; don't just leave it until you have live issues on the table.
2. Bear in mind that the **GSC has a significant amount of information** at its disposal – Member State positions, procedural and timetable information, latest developments, Presidency information – as it is at the heart of all the action.
3. Be aware that although the GSC does not need technical information and positions to the same extent as its counterparts in the Commission, it does appreciate being **kept up-to-date with developments**.

12.4 Permanent Representations

A Permanent Representation's primary role is to represent the Member State in negotiations that take place at the EU level and promote the Member State's interests in dealing with other Member States, the Commission and MEPs. They do this by acting on instruction from their respective capitals and working towards agreed government policy positions.

Permanent Representations also have an influence on the development of their Member States' positions on EU issues that you should bear in mind. They do this through reporting back on meetings they attend (including external stakeholders), advising on the negotiating context in the EU institutions, or simply feeding in thoughts. Attachés ought to be an integral part of the capital's policy team.

This dual role is at the core of the Permanent Representation's work and why it has to strike the right balance. On the one hand, the national capital has to have full confidence that the Permanent Representation is 'working for us' in Brussels. On the other hand, the Permanent Representation has a role in challenging assumptions during its capital's policy development process – and this is often crucial in getting a balanced and deliverable position for EU negotiations. This balance may be different on different files, depending on the difficulty of the negotiation and the policy landscape back in the capital.

Some specific advice for dealing with Permanent Representations:

1. Clearly identify, and establish contact with, the person in charge of your file at all levels within a Permanent Representation (the attaché, any heads of section where this role exists, the Antici and/or Mertens and finally the PR and/or DPR). Having identified the key people **try to proactively meet with them to establish contact**. These contacts will help you understand the dynamics in Council meetings and where the information, compromises and positions are coming from. Remember that most attachés will be either preparing for or attending Working Groups or writing the notes of the meeting. Equally, in the run-up to Council, they will be extremely busy preparing the agenda and arranging any bilaterals. Remember too that, generally, Coreper I meets on a Wednesday (and Friday) and Coreper II on Thursdays so coordinate your meeting requests around this.
2. Permanent Representations will themselves be trying to influence the file in Brussels, so try to think how you could help them do this. Some Member States are more active (and open about) their influencing work in Brussels than others. You can often be of great assistance in **passing messages and making arguments on behalf of Permanent Representations** that they themselves would not be able to do or make: always think of what value you can bring to their interests.
3. Permanent Representations are informed about **the positions of all other Member States**, so it can be useful to ask for insights into how other Member States are lining up on an issue in Council.
4. Permanent Representations, like Cabinets in the Commission, are **more inclined to meet trade associations and federations** – in their case more likely national-level than European-level ones. While they have an obvious tendency to favour meeting national stakeholders, they can be open to meeting all stakeholders depending on the issue and their needs/objectives.
5. When working with **PRs or DPRs**, keep in mind that they are like Ministers and as such they **require engagement by senior management**. You should have a good overview of what else they will be working on to bring perspective to your issue and to help them make broader connections. Finally, they are both technical and political, with a focus on the latter, so political argument and communication is better suited.

13. Concluding guidance for engaging with the Council

Engagement with the Council is very different to that with the Commission and Parliament given the differing nature and needs of the institutions. It is clear that for effective engagement with the Council, the right balance of political, technical and national elements will need to come to the fore.

This means, for the Council:

1. **Always maintain double lines of communication with the Permanent Representations and national capitals**. As noted throughout this chapter, this is essential to make sure your messages are flowing between the two (national coordination issues). An attaché will usually act on instructions from the capital, so it is far more straightforward if you are able to convince the expert in the capital to take forward your issue and for them in turn to confirm this with the attaché. Maintaining contact with the Permanent Representations is in itself rewarding since they will know the latest state of affairs, have a broader political view and can provide you with insights on the negotiations and what can 'fly' in the Working Group. One obvious entry point for meeting national officials is by taking advantage of when the key national experts come to Brussels for meetings. Other options include working through those based in the capitals, such as country representatives of companies and national trade associations.
2. **Going to the top**: as noted in section 11 above, a useful method is to have a direct line of communication to the Head of Government and their office.
3. **National arguments and case studies will prevail** and when working with Member States on an issue it is advisable to tailor information and evidence to national interests.
4. **Communicating with Member States other than your own is essential**. As highlighted throughout this chapter, whilst you might wish to convert one Member State into being your champion you will need to engage much more widely to achieve success. The best approach is to build a network among those based in the capitals of Member States (the national experts, national politicians and key national stakeholders) as well as those in Brussels in the Permanent Representations. Big countries count most, of course, but small Member States can also be influential and may be more open to discussion and assistance. Furthermore, according to statistics for 2009–2019 provided by VoteWatch Europe, Germany is among the national governments that ends up in a minority the most often. This data further stresses the importance for stakeholders to establish links with more than a single national government, as even the Ministers from the biggest countries do not always get their way. Consider building coalitions with other nationalities via European associations and federations or on an ad hoc basis.
5. Building on point 4, **avoid the temptation to only work extensively with your 'own' Permanent Representation**. It is true that you are likely to have more support from your national representation, though this could of course depend very much on their position on your issue. Irrespective of this, however, you should always seek to establish good contacts in a number of other Permanent Representations as these can be useful for getting and verifying information, as well as their being actors you can try to influence and work with. If you have any links with other European countries these should be leveraged to build relations with other Permanent Representations.

6. **The best way to communicate with officials is face-to-face**, or as a fall-back via telephone or video-conferencing. You should consider carefully the information you share before, during and after any meeting. The aim should be to secure the meeting using an appropriate amount of targeted information and to follow up electronically all information used or referred to during the meeting. Relying solely on email advocacy will bring mixed results but can be deployed where the aim is solely to raise awareness.
7. It is also important for you to have a **good online presence** with, as a minimum, a clear website with organisational information and ideally on your issue. Increasingly, it is also important to have a presence on social media where you relay more up-to-date information and engage with key stakeholders. This is your window to the world and will be the first place the officials will turn to for more information on you.
8. **Understand how the media work and what to expect of them**. As discussed fully in Chapter 4, the media can play an important role on EU issues: publications such as the FT, Guardian, Politico, Euractiv and Le Monde are widely-read in the Brussels bubble, and national media may also be an important factor for your issue. You should know the trade media most read in your particular sector by national officials. An effective way to get Member States back into line can be to leak to the established political press back home. Ministers and their teams do not like reading in their national political press that they are backtracking on a public position. Friendly Member States will often provide you with a compromise text. If the Minister's team deny the compromise and the journalist has the compromise text, the story will run.
9. Engagement is always preferable where possible in the other person's mother-tongue but since English is the lingua franca in Brussels, as well as the language of the base text for most Council negotiations, **communication with the Permanent Representations is usually conducted in English**. Engagement with national officials will usually mean engaging with those for whom English is a second, third or even fourth language and so it's important to take account of linguistic considerations. You need to determine your ultimate audience if submitting position papers. If it is a national audience it should be translated into their language, particularly for French and German and to some extent Spanish speakers.

14. Engaging the European Council

Separate to the Council of the EU, the European Council (EUCO) is an institution in its own right. It comprises the Heads of State or Government of the 27 EU Member States, the European Council President and the President of the Commission. It is not one of the EU's legislating institutions, so it does not negotiate or adopt EU laws. Instead it defines the overall political direction and sets the EU's policy agenda, traditionally by adopting Conclusions during European Council meetings which identify issues of concern and actions to take. It tends to meet in March, June, October and December. The European Council has become better known, in recent years, however, for its series of emergency meetings on hot European political topics such as migration, Brexit and most recently COVID-19. It is the top direction-setting body for the whole of the EU and tends to focus only on major issues and crises.

Within the European Council, it is common to find the following Member States supporting and defending each other on major EU issues such as Eurozone matters, migration, foreign policy and defence:

- The 'Northern Lights' group comprising the EU's Nordic/Baltic members, Sweden, Denmark, Finland, Estonia, Latvia and Lithuania, plus Ireland and the Netherlands.
- The Visegrad group – Poland, Hungary, Czech Republic and Slovakia, often with Romania and Bulgaria.
- France, Italy and Spain along with other Mediterranean countries (Portugal, Greece, Malta, Cyprus, Croatia).

Such informal coalitions arise from natural affinities and shared interests, but they should not be taken as a given and they may in any case shift in the aftermath of both Brexit and COVID-19 as Member States realign with others depending on their new priorities both nationally and in the EU.

The output that you would be trying to influence from EUCO is the Conclusions referred to above. Getting your issues into these Conclusions can give a very powerful sense of direction that is difficult to change thereafter. For standing EUCO meetings (i.e. not the emergency ones) Conclusions start off in six-week cycles. The Council Secretariat will draft an annotated agenda for the EUCO, perhaps taking its cue from previous EUCO Conclusions. This agenda will then be approved at Coreper, amended as necessary. Following this, the Council Secretariat will draft a set of guidelines to inform and give direction to the Conclusions. The guidelines will also be approved by Coreper. Then, the Conclusions themselves are drafted by the Council Secretariat in consultation with the Presidency, approved by Coreper (via Anticis), and then the General Affairs Council (GAC) and finally adopted at EUCO.

During this period, Member States may also submit written comments, but crucially it is the role of the Council Secretariat to find the balance. They will often try to broker text among the big Member States before sharing more widely. If contentious, they can pass through the Member State sherpas ahead of GAC.

Despite the many layers involved to 'agree' the Conclusions, Heads of State and Government have the ultimate sign-off and there can still be a lot up for grabs during the EUCO itself. Key to influencing the Conclusions are good contacts within the political section of the Permanent Representation, the PRs and Anticis as well as senior officials advising the government leaders in capitals – all of whom will be part of the 10-strong delegation during a typical EUCO alongside, of course, the government leaders themselves and other members of the EUCO as mentioned above. Clearly, the Council Secretariat plays a key role in finding compromises as they deftly hold the pen. A good contact within the Council Secretariat is invaluable.

As in your high-level engagement with the Commission, you can try the long play or short play approach (see Chapter 6). Few, however, try to engage with EUCO, given the challenges and the high-level nature of the contacts required to be successful. At the same time, it should not be overlooked as part of a lobbying strategy given the importance of the decisions taken and the directions set at EUCO. If the EUCO gives a direction that is contrary to your interests you will spend years fighting against the tide (or accepting it) – whereas successful engagement at EUCO could have saved you this effort. So whilst difficult and hard to penetrate it should not be neglected if you have any good options for engagement.

9. How to Work with the Ordinary Legislative Procedure

By Roland Moore & Alan Hardacre

1. Introduction

The Ordinary Legislative Procedure (OLP) now applies to most EU legislative activity and entails **qualified majority voting in the Council and co-decision with the European Parliament (EP)**. A significant number of policy areas (for example, discrimination, citizenship, tax, the budget) nonetheless retain a special legislative procedure involving different institutions or with a lesser or no role for the Parliament.

The Treaty on the Functioning of the European Union (TFEU) sets out how the Ordinary Legislative Procedure works in theory, but it does not tell you what happens in practice. An understanding of how to engage on OLP will equip you to engage across a range of procedures – and this chapter is written and designed in such a way as to identify general and horizontal rules that can apply across the EU decision-making spectrum.

Having already outlined how to engage with the three main EU institutions, the bulk of the work is done – yet not all of it. You now need to know how to place all of that work into the context of the key decision-making procedure. Working with OLP involves not just working with the three key institutions and all of the key actors previously identified; it also means doing so over a likely timeframe of 18–24 months (if not more) and with a specific purpose. This will act as a door-opener in Brussels since files being negotiated are the talk of the Brussels bubble. You need to know what is required at each stage of the process and how to develop a best-in-class strategy to engage with OLP.

There are three key aspects of an OLP negotiation that matter the most from a lobbying perspective:

1. The process for the **Council reaching an agreement with the EP** as co-legislators.
2. The process for **reaching an agreement *within* the Council**.
3. The process for **reaching an agreement *within* the Parliament**.

2. Should you focus on the Council or the EP?

Given the prominence of the Council in OLP, it can be tempting to downplay the importance of the European Parliament. This would be a mistake, since at the heart of the OLP process is the fact that the EP may veto a legislative proposal and uses that threat to secure concessions from the Council to allow for an agreement.

The Commission is wise to this and in this area the EP matters as much to the Commission as the Council does, possibly more. Commissioners spend more time with MEPs than they do with national Ministers (especially during the monthly Plenary sessions in Strasbourg). MEPs on sectoral Committees spend most of their time thinking about the policy challenges that occupy the relevant Commissioner's mind, which inevitably creates a greater exchange and engagement between them.

Many national Ministers, by contrast, will spend only the minority of their time on EU policy and decision-making. This matters for legislative proposals. The EP may well have been influencing a legislative proposal before it appears, perhaps through an own-initiative report, through face-to-face discussions or by other means. Its role and influence should therefore not be underestimated, and any strategy to manage a negotiation needs to factor in the EP from the outset (and preferably from before legislative proposals are issued).

Accordingly, you should consider sounding out MEPs to become active in the upcoming file well in advance of its publication. You could even encourage them to become the rapporteur or shadow rapporteur for the file. If they are not on the lead Committee, you could ask them to consider joining the lead Committee at the mid-term point. And/or you could encourage the MEP to involve their own Committee as an associated or joint Committee, rather than leaving it just in the hands of the lead Committee.

The position of the Committee, in the form of the draft report as amended by MEPs, is normally more or less taken up by the full Parliament. Therefore influencing the EP begins with influencing a small sub-set of MEPs, whose political make-up is to some degree representative of the entire EP.

3. The dynamics of a qualified majority negotiation in the Council

The Ordinary Legislative Procedure forces compromise. An acceptable outcome depends on *influence* rather than *control*. And, most likely, influence on a small number of key issues given the complexities involved.

The Presidency can choose which files 'on the table' to progress and at what speed. They also hold the pen for drafting the compromise texts that are tabled in Working Groups, Coreper and Council. Any agreement on this, however, requires the support of a qualified majority of Member States. An able and determined Presidency will seek out and crystallise the compromises. While the preference is to agree by consensus, a Presidency may be prepared to marginalise one or more Member States, including the big Member States, to achieve its qualified majority and secure its deal. The big Member States are, nonetheless, highly skilled in securing many (if not all) of their objectives in negotiations.

The role of the Presidency is to know what the price of a Member State's support is. As the prospects of a deal get closer, the more organised Member States will ensure they communicate to the Presidency, usually in private, their one or two priorities – often framed in the context of a packaged approach so as not to gain one thing and lose another. This is extremely useful for the Presidency, enabling it to see how to secure a sufficient percentage of votes in exchange for a certain approach. Where a Member State comes with an entire shopping list of asks and no sense of prioritisation, the Presidency will decide it's too complicated to address this Member State's concerns and look to secure the necessary support from other Member States whose demands are fewer and clearer. As you look to engage in the process, knowing this and adapting to it is essential.

4. A word on the Commission

Once the European Commission has tabled its proposal, the chances of it reaching the EU statute books are extremely high. Since the inception of the Amsterdam Treaty in 1999, hundreds of proposals have passed through the co-decision procedure, while only a very small handful have failed and been withdrawn by the European Commission.

What this indicates is the **overwhelming likelihood that, when the Commission makes a legislative proposal, it will become law**. Furthermore, the eventual law will generally look very much like the Commission's proposal. These considerations run through the veins of the Brussels institutions and colour the whole approach to legislation.

At the second reading stage, the Commission can, and often does, exercise its veto powers on a particular European Parliament amendment. In cases where the Commission withdraws its support for a file, it effectively changes the Council voting from QMV to unanimity. This is a powerful weapon the Commission has up its sleeve late on when a deal is close and where the Commission is fundamentally opposed to an approach taken by Council.

In essence, the Commission stays close to the file after it tables it and tries to shepherd it through to its liking – exerting great influence along the way. The Commission is always a key driver and you always need to consider its view of what you are proposing in Council and Parliament. Always. Whatever you say or do with the two co-legislators will get back to the Commission – and as you will discover, there is no room to play games here.

5. Working successfully with OLP

Working successfully with OLP requires a dedicated and sustained campaign targeted towards the European Commission, the European Parliament and the Council over the course of the negotiations.

It is now extremely commonplace for files to be agreed at the first reading stage – 89% were in the 2014-2019 Parliament. As such, your campaign needs to be focused on **key early milestones**. This starts first with the Commission department drafting the proposal and the adoption by the College. Ideally, you will be ready to go even before this stage, through engagement on the Commission roadmap and Inception Impact Assessment (covered in Chapter 6).

Once the proposal is published, attention turns both to the European Parliament team (rapporteur, shadow rapporteur, advisers and other leading MEPs), and to the Presidency and Member States. At this point, you should be prepared to meet with the key actors with a well-reasoned case, backed up with a clear, concise and brief document that makes use of graphs and data. It is vital you present ready-made solutions. *Always think solutions.*

The Parliament for its part is more transparent, with the rapporteur's draft report and the MEPs' amendments to it normally published and debated publicly. Less transparent is how the rapporteur drafts the initial report and how they broker a series of compromise amendments among the shadow rapporteurs so as to secure their support to the final report, as amended. The rapporteur will need to secure the support of their own Political Group and a broad enough coalition of MEPs to get the report through the Committee and backed by the full Parliament.

This is why having a line into the rapporteur's office and/or a member of the shadow's team is critical. **You need to identify who is going to be doing the drafting**: the person holding the pen has influence. Sometimes it is one of the MEP's staffers, or the Committee Secretariat lead, or it is a Political Group adviser – or a combination of all three. Rarely is it the MEP. As a result, don't obsess about titles. Many MEPs delegate considerable responsibilities to their political staff or to the Group advisers. If offered a meeting with the political staff or Group adviser, take the meeting

On the Council side, the single document to influence is the text which Coreper or Council adopts to form the basis of the negotiation with the Parliament. Equally, there can often be **'unwritten' agreements** taken at Coreper which provide the Presidency with margin to manoeuvre throughout the course of negotiations in Council. These are rarely written down for fear of leaking and undermining the negotiation. Again, the work for influencing this begins as soon as the proposal is written and ahead of the first Working Group discussion, as discussed in the previous chapter.

Apart from the texts formally adopted by the Council, such as a **'General Approach'** or a first reading position, the **disclosure of documents containing draft positions of the Council or any of its delegations is prohibited**. The Council believes, rightly or wrongly, that disclosure would adversely affect the efficiency of the Council's decision-making process during negotiations by narrowing down delegations' room for compromise within the Council. This is because the Council believes delegations would cease to submit their views in writing, and instead would limit themselves to oral exchanges of views in the Council and its preparatory bodies. Future discussions on difficult and politically sensitive matters would then be held without having at delegations' disposal written material recording the different positions on the outstanding issues. Council believes there is a risk this would cause significant damage to the effectiveness of its work, which is based on continuous coordination among the delegations and where the precise knowledge of the different positions is essential to allow progress on complex issues. It asserts that this would also undermine the Council's internal decision-making process by impeding complex internal discussions on proposed acts and be seriously prejudicial to the overall transparency of the Council's decision-making process. In short, getting hold of documents is a challenge and one that has to be approached delicately. You will find more on how to manage this in the previous chapter.

Working with OLP requires a knowledge of the process by which each institution reaches its position and what each side is prepared to support in the spirit of compromise to secure a deal. Early engagement is critical to communicate your positions, understand the initial positions of others, and to develop relationships. The principle of **'the earlier the better'** is especially valid because you need to establish yourself as a key stakeholder at the very beginning of the first reading – and, should the dossier go any further, you will have established contacts to work with.

> **Following OLP**
>
> Phone: map your contacts and call them.
> Email: can be less invasive and used for less urgent/sensitive issues.
> Meetings: useful for passing on information.
> Trade association / federations
> Legislative trackers:
> - *Legislative Observatory*
> - *Pre-Lex RSS Feeds/Press/Alerts*
>
> Monitoring service
> Events/Networking/Contacts

Following OLP in detail will mean trying to follow all the formal and informal developments, especially the latter. The box on the left highlights the best ways to try and follow the OLP. The legislative trackers are good for background information and an overview of the file but they can be slightly out of date and they do not cover any informal aspects, such as trilogues for example. Likewise RSS Feeds, Google Alerts and the press are only likely to inform you of when something has happened – not when it is going to happen – and, obviously, if you want to influence the process you need to know things in advance. The single best way to do this is, having identified and mapped all the key actors on the dossier, to call around and try to find out the information you want from your established contacts around the file. Your work with OLP will ultimately depend on people giving you information and therefore on relationships.

The **European associations/federations** tend to be a very good source of information. They should be closely plugged into their key dossiers, and have extremely good contacts and networks that usually enable them to have the informal information at the right times. Officials have a clear preference to engage with trade associations, for two main reasons. First, officials are in extremely high demand and have to ruthlessly prioritise stakeholder requests. Associations can provide one central point of contact with an entire sector. Second, officials will expect trade associations to bring forward all the key issues for the sector they represent, thereby reassuring officials that they have 'listened to' the sector. And, even when in reality associations don't represent an entire sector, they will still speak for a significant proportion – so associations still represent an efficient way for officials to engage with stakeholders.

However you get hold of the information during OLP, it is imperative that you have a **few different sources across the institutions** because the information flow will be your lifeblood through the process. Banking on one good contact is risky and it is also unlikely that one person will have access to all the information required across all three institutions. As discussed elsewhere in this book, establishing contacts in advance of legislative developments enhances your chances of getting information as officials and staffers are only likely to pass on information where it is mutually beneficial.

Having the right information at the right time is, however, only useful if you are able to understand it, its context and implications, enabling you to then act on the information in the right way. You will need to be prepared for decisions to be taken extremely quickly at key junctures and without any public or stakeholder consultation. Your informal contacts and those of trade associations will be vital to track progress.

Equally important will be the ability to deliver information and expertise rapidly to **modify proposals** – as opposed to trying to kill them – in line with the underpinning EU idea of consensus that was detailed in previous chapters. An OLP file, through the negotiations that take place within the institutions and then between the institutions, is often an **accumulated compromise**. This is another reason why working from the earliest possible moment, and with all three and not just one institution, is essential. Once these compromises take shape, they get harder and harder to change as the process advances without unravelling prior agreements. This is also an important point with regard to why you can never stop working on an OLP file: because of the accumulated compromise nature of progress your interests are not guaranteed until the file has been passed. You need to secure your interests through successive rounds of negotiations.

As a final introductory note it is worth focusing, already, on possibly the most important moment in first reading: the **informal trilogue negotiations**. These are when the institutions try to negotiate a final agreement between themselves – and they are the crux of OLP negotiations. Like other aspects of OLP, as already mentioned, you will not find publicly available information on these (until perhaps 6-12 months after they happened). Therefore it is important to find out:

1. **When** they will take place
2. **Who** will be involved
3. **What** the issues in the negotiations are
4. **What** the outcome is

To do this you will need to have good contacts in the three institutions (people who will be in the trilogue meetings) because at this stage it is the only way you will get information. Finding out the information above three weeks after the meeting has taken place will be of no use to you. One way to see what is happening is to look for when Coreper agendas mention reports being made on trilogues – this can be a helpful guide if you are trying to follow from a distance. We will come back to this in more detail.

6. The three stages of working with OLP

In the following pages we will look at how to work with the **three different stages of the OLP: first, second and third readings**. All three phases require different approaches, information, communication and engagement. The most attention will obviously be devoted to the first reading stage given the fact that you should always engage with a file at the earliest possible moment and also because so many files are concluded in first reading. You should always treat your file as if it were going to be agreed in first reading – making sure you leave no stone unturned at this stage.

7. Working with OLP: first reading

In simple terms, if you want to succeed in engaging at OLP it all starts, and often ends, in first reading.

> **Key documents for First Reading**
>
> 1. Commission proposal – the basis for all discussions.
> 2. Commission Impact Assessment – the evidence base for discussions.
> 3. Parliament draft Committee report – usually the basis for trilogue negotiations.
> 4. Council Working Group texts – usually the basis for trilogue negotiations.

It can often come as a surprise that a text can be adopted without ever having been discussed substantively in Council. In practice much of the political negotiation happens in Coreper, or for CAP agriculture dossiers in the Special Committee for Agriculture (SCA). It is genuinely difficult for those not directly involved to get a feel for the pace and dynamics of co-decision negotiations, especially when a Presidency decides to push for a first reading deal.

If there is one headline message, it is that the meeting of Coreper, or SCA, that prepares a first mandate for discussion with the European Parliament (EP) is crucial. If your priorities are not registered and reflected in the text at that stage, the chances of securing your objectives vanish rapidly. Briefing and instructions for Member States for that meeting require clarity, prioritisation, and possibly leveraging contacts with Ministers in Member States.

Overall in the OLP procedure the first reading is the key opportunity to get your views across to MEPs, the Commission and the Member States. It is here where changes can be made and where points of principle need to be won. After first reading the debate narrows and closes down, and your room for action and influence also shrinks accordingly.

First reading is not your only chance to work with a dossier but it will always be your main chance. The institutions, through the OLP procedure, are aiming to conclude the best possible outcome at the earliest possible stage – this is always the starting logic on a dossier – so it makes sense to bring your arguments and evidence to the table as soon as possible.

7.1 Opening negotiations with the EP

The Presidency will need to decide whether the Council is ready to open negotiations with the EP. The Presidency might decide to ask Ministers to resolve outstanding agreements at a formal Council meeting by putting it on the agenda for a **General Approach**, but there is no obligation to do this. It is quite possible for a 'first reading agreement' to be reached without the Council itself having first discussed and agreed its formal position, instead basing its position on mandates for negotiation agreed at Coreper.

Just as the EP has been worried about political oversight of first reading deals, the same arguments hold true in the Council, where a General Approach allows Ministers to endorse a negotiating position. The General Approach is not mentioned in the TFEU, and as such its effect is purely political, rather than legal. But practice in seeking a General Approach is haphazard. In theory, the more contentious a file, the more useful a General Approach can be. But in practice the Presidency is likely to be influenced by the desire to chalk up a success. This is especially true where Councils meet only quarterly or bi-annually. If a first reading deal looks possible during the Presidency then they won't want to delay matters by waiting for a Council to secure a Council position. If a first reading deal looks difficult to achieve in the six-month Presidency period (perhaps because the EP is on a slower track), then a Presidency may choose to secure a General Approach at Council to demonstrate progress and have a tangible output of its Presidency.

Normally it will be obvious to a Presidency from Working Group discussions if a dossier is ripe for a negotiation with the EP. Occasionally a Presidency may decide that Working Group discussions have been unnecessarily bogged down in detailed discussions, and the prospect of opening negotiations with the EP is a good way to sharpen minds and expose the real red or bottom lines for Member States. Equally, the EP may have already reached its position and be applying pressure on the Council to negotiate via the Presidency, the Commission, the press and through national parties.

In any case, once a determined Presidency has set its sights on entering into negotiations with the EP (and usually agreed on the set of dates for this), it is hard to resist. In the vast majority of cases, once a negotiation has started it reaches an agreed outcome: this is because one or both parties usually conclude that they will get a better deal at that stage than by going forward to 2nd and/or 3rd reading.

7.2 Council's four-column document

As the Presidency prepares for the negotiation with the EP, once the EP has formally adopted its 'draft first reading' position the Presidency and Council Secretariat will prepare a document with four columns, showing:
1. The Commission's proposal.
2. The Council's position (from the latest Working Group discussion and subsequently the Coreper or General Approach text).

3. The Commission's text as the EP would like it amended as adopted in the Committee and Plenary.
4. What the Presidency proposes as a compromise between the two institutions, keeping in mind the Commission's original aims and intentions.

The Presidency will typically ask delegations whether they can support the intended compromise in the last column, as well as any other changes to the Council's text in Column 2. If there is not a blocking minority of Member States, the Presidency will consider that they have a mandate to go and negotiate with the EP. The Presidency will likely make a few changes to their proposal to reflect the conditional support entered by some Member States.

No formal vote is ever taken, but everyone will be doing the sums in their heads, above all the Council Secretariat. In cases where there is a blocking minority of Member States against the Presidency text (due to the phrasing of one or more articles), the Presidency may still decide to enter 'exploratory' discussions with the Parliament and may make a judgement that those objecting won't, in the end, withdraw their support. A Presidency may even use the opposition to put pressure on the EP to make more compromises as a means of 'selling' an overall improved package to Council. You will need to understand the strategy of a Presidency especially if your issue is one of those that is caught up in the tactics being employed by the Presidency.

7.3 The trilogue process

The way in which the formal Treaty provisions are put into practice is very different and involves a lot of informal contacts between the Council and the EP. These contacts happen in semi-formal meetings called **trilogues**. Trilogues are not mentioned in the Treaties but they are an essential part of the legislative machinery.

A trilogue is a conversation between the Council and EP, with the Commission also present to speak for its legislative proposal as well as to assist in brokering an agreement. There are two types: political and technical. Typically, the **technical trilogues** are attended by working level staff of the three institutions with the aim of resolving detailed issues which the political trilogue will then agree/finalise – depending on the issue, with or without a discussion. There is an increasing trend for these technical trilogues to support the work of the three institutions during negotiations.

At the **political trilogues**, the Presidency, normally in the person of the Ambassador or the Working Group chair, represents the Council and will be accompanied by the Council Secretariat and often the Council Legal Service. The EP will normally be represented by the rapporteur, shadow rapporteurs, their assistants and advisers and possibly the chair of the relevant EP Committee. The Commission will be represented at team leader, Head of Unit and Director level. In some cases, notably as part of the end game in conciliation, representation is elevated to political level, with a Minister or the Ambassador leading for the Presidency, and a DG or Commissioner and possibly an EP Vice-President leading the other delegations.

Essentially a first reading trilogue is about the Council and the Parliament exploring what text could be acceptable to both institutions. That text would then be formally adopted by the Parliament as its first reading position. Formal agreement to that text by the Council would constitute a **first reading agreement**. The purpose of this is to fast-track legislation and avoid the need for going through a second reading or conciliation in Parliament and Council. Essentially the conciliation process is applied but less formally. It avoids the binary question: *'can you agree to this, yes or no?'* Instead the question becomes: *'what text could we both agree?'*

To make this a meaningful negotiation each side needs to know they can deliver their institution. So the Presidency needs to be confident they can secure a qualified majority (QM) in Council for what they propose to the EP, and the EP delegation needs to be sure they can rally a majority at EP plenary.

Normally there will be a series of trilogues, each prepared in Coreper, with the Presidency seeking a mandate (usually, in Coreper I at least, based on the four-column document). A good Presidency will provide in advance a timetable that they have agreed with the EP. This needs to be taken seriously as trilogue timetables are generally respected. Timetables can be tight and a series of three trilogues can certainly be conducted within months.

In the trilogues, the Presidency will seek to defend the Council's position and press the EP to compromise. In Coreper they will try to explain where they think the EP's red lines are, and where compromise by the Council is needed if agreement is to be reached. Naturally the Parliament is doing the very same thing in reverse – trying to defend its own position and press the Council to compromise. It will be explaining back in Committee where it thinks the Council's red lines are and where compromise could be.

At the end of the trilogue process the Presidency will usually ask Coreper who cannot endorse the deal. A delegation may raise its flag and seek a last-minute change and should the Presidency need this to secure its qualified majority, then it would seek to resolve this bilaterally with the EP and then bring the file back to Coreper a few days later – or even later the same day if towards the end of a Presidency.

Equally, if the Presidency had completely misjudged Council and made too many concessions, delegations may consider they could get a better deal by holding out and therefore work together to reject what is on the table. If the Presidency has time, it will conduct a further trilogue to take forward or admit defeat and hand over to the next Presidency.

Alternatively, the Presidency may not see a way to secure a qualified majority on the basis of any deal with the EP. In that case, it may choose instead to propose to confirm its position formally at Council. Equally, the EP may also do likewise. In this scenario the file would move to a second reading.

7.4 Actors: first reading

When it comes to the key actors at first reading it is a question of combining the people analysis in the previous chapters on the individual institutions.

Figure 9.1 shows the key actors who will take part in the trilogues. Working with any OLP file, it will be essential to try and find at least one good contact within that inner circle of decision-making to be able to get the latest informal information. Figure 9.1 also nicely illustrates the need to engage simultaneously with these three institutional levels when your file is active. All three will be working on it at the same time with varying levels of influence on each other.

Figure 9.1: Ordinary Legislative Procedure first reading: Key actors

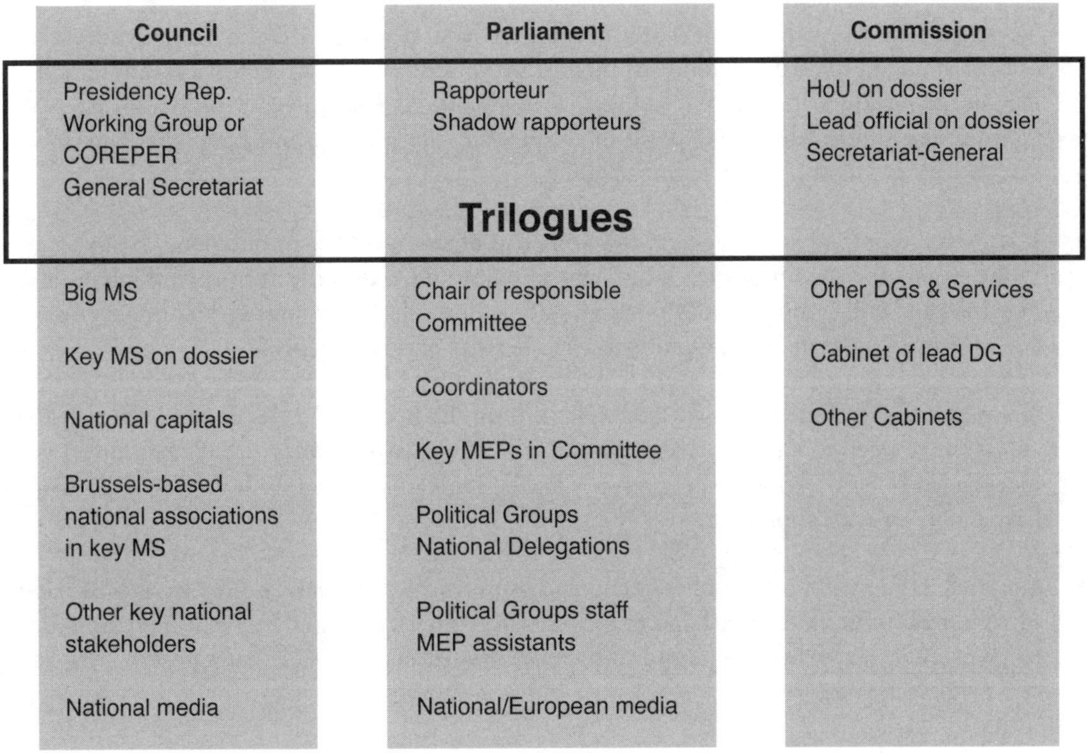

Council	Parliament	Commission
Presidency Rep. Working Group or COREPER General Secretariat	Rapporteur Shadow rapporteurs **Trilogues**	HoU on dossier Lead official on dossier Secretariat-General
Big MS Key MS on dossier National capitals Brussels-based national associations in key MS Other key national stakeholders National media	Chair of responsible Committee Coordinators Key MEPs in Committee Political Groups National Delegations Political Groups staff MEP assistants National/European media	Other DGs & Services Cabinet of lead DG Other Cabinets

Source: Alan Hardacre

Let us now give some guidance on how best to interact with this core group of stakeholders.

7.5 Engagement guidance: first reading

Define and understand your audience and know what interests them:
- A successful OLP file needs consensus and compromise within each institution and also between the institutions. This means that **coalition formation** is important between Member States, within the Parliament and by, and between, stakeholders. You will need to identify the coalitions and understand how this impacts your priorities. From there you can seek to engage.

- Member State positions will have emerged in Working Group; EP Committee level amendments will be in the public domain; and there will normally have been some Working Group consideration of the EP's draft amendments. Being aware of these and understanding them **will help you anticipate most of the changes** to an OLP file during its journey through the Council and EP.

- **Never neglect the role of the Commission in first reading.** OLP is formally about the co-legislators but the Commission sits in all trilogue meetings, in all Council meetings and all Parliament meetings. It is hugely influential in its role of mediator and facilitator. Keep the Commission informed of your position throughout the process, and remember that it will usually have the most up-to-date information.

- It is always important to understand **the objective of the OLP file** in question, usually set out in the recitals and the first article. This helps to frame and bound the purpose and intent of the new rules and will guide most of the stakeholders' approach. It is important to bring arguments and evidence that relate to the attainment or otherwise of this objective.

- Given that Council members will be implementing the new OLP rules in their country, they will be more open to arguments about impacts in **their own country**, ideally reinforced with independently verified facts and figures. For the Commission, in contrast, it will be important to have European-wide arguments.

- You need to know if the focus of your audience is **political (Coreper), policy (senior officials) or technical (national experts)** and adapt your messages accordingly. It's particularly important to try to understand what their agenda is (defending a national position, party position, the issue or a personal agenda).

- Whilst not explicitly discussed in this chapter, it is worth remembering that representatives from national parliaments, the Committee of the Regions (CoR), the European Economic and Social Committee (EESC) and the staff of the EU Agencies can all potentially play a meaningful role in the OLP, and should not simply be forgotten. There are many good contacts to be made amongst these people.

The process: who and what really matters

- For an average OLP file you will have to identify about **30-40 key people across the Parliament, Commission and Council**. In this sense working with first reading can be a very small world, and you soon discover that Brussels is a village. The key actors on the dossier will work very closely together across institutions. You need to be well-connected to a number of this core group if you are to succeed. You will need them for information, updates and ultimately influence.

- As an OLP dossier proceeds, you will discern a clear context and structure to the debate and negotiation and this is something you will have to take into account in your actions. Bearing in mind that you will not be able to influence everything in an OLP file, **you will need to prioritise and be ready to revisit these priorities** regularly as the context changes. (This aspect of public affairs work is stressed in Chapter 2 on the EU public affairs methodology.)

- Working with the EP is much easier than working with the Council. You need to engage with MEPs' assistants and advisers who will be drafting the rapporteur's report and amendments. You need to think not just about securing amendments that take forward your issue but also amendments that could neutralise changes being sought by opponents in Council. You need to be alert to this **strategic use of amendments** – and only by being aware of the bigger picture will you see this. If these favourable amendments are adopted by the EP Committee, this could later force your opponents to spend their negotiating capital defending their position, making it easier for you to defend yours.

- **Delegates, or MEPS, often have just a single intervention** to make all their points in Coreper, Council or in EP Committees. They must be clear and focus on top priority issues – both their red lines on hard-fought issues they want to retain and on text they want to resist from others in Council or the EP. This all requires careful consideration but it goes without saying that the more focused, clear and impactful support you can provide your stakeholders the more they are likely to use it.

- As Chapter 2 outlined, coalitions are important to understand, monitor and work with. This will also entail understanding the broader OLP environment and all the stakeholders that are engaged on the dossier on which you are working. You will also need to know **the positions of the key external stakeholders**, notably European associations and federations. This is particularly important given how much weight the EU institutions attach to the positions of trade associations versus individual companies.

Be clear in your messaging

- **You need to tailor your messages for each meeting, even within the institutions**. This does not necessarily mean having a new briefing paper/position paper or amendment, but it does mean having an appreciation of the different people you interact with and what they need/want in relation to the OLP file under discussion. Every context is different – you need to build on that.

- While you need to tailor your messages, you need to have a **consistent core message** and communication across, and between, the three institutions and all key stakeholders.

- **Prepare for all meetings thoroughly:** background, evidence, political messages, context, procedure, timelines, etc.

- Adapt your messages to the evolving public policy objectives and priorities. The debate will move and you need to move with it.

- **Always be concise and to the point.** Make sure you employ user-friendly language in your communication.

- Use reasonable arguments that strive towards consensus and compromise with each institution and also between the institutions – and **focus on solutions not problem**s. Everyone tends to be aware of the problems but few have solutions.

Some tactical considerations
- One or two close contacts on a dossier can be sufficient to keep you updated – but as noted earlier, the more the better. You should also **look for breadth in your contacts** as good contacts in one institution only will not likely have all the information you require.

- Use a multi-pronged approach as there are different people who can assist in OLP. You will need to **establish on a case-by-case basis who to work with and when to work with them**. For instance, you may need to establish two distinct networks: one network, or set of contacts, for information, and another for influencing (drawing on the information gathered).

- Always try to **canvass the key people** you are in contact with **for their opinions**. They know the dossier and the people involved in it better than anyone else, so they usually have very good ideas on how to proceed/approach things.

- The fact that the number of core people working on a dossier is so small means that **transparency, honesty and integrity are essential** – word of what you do or say will spread quickly. It is also why the Transparency Register is now fundamental to a stakeholder's activities in Brussels

- **Always keep the long-term in mind.** This small circle will likely follow these issues for some years to come, so you will need to work with them again.

- Be prepared for your position, your organisation, and even your senior management to be attacked during your engagements. Take the criticism and be ready to tell your story in an open and honest way (clearing lines within your organisation beforehand). **Avoid overly defending entrenched positions** as this will only harm your credibility and damage your long-term work.

- **Think and talk in terms of outcomes** and be ready and open to alternative ways to achieve the same goals. Equally, be ready to bring forward alternative ideas if your preferred approach is not gaining traction: i.e. if you see that plan A is not going to work, have a plan B.

Given the pivotal importance of first reading, it is worth us recapping the main engagement aspects of the previous section, as summarised in the box below.

Tips & Guidance for Working with OLP: First Reading

1. Act **as early as possible**. It is essential to be as early as possible in first reading to influence ideas before they hit paper. Create networks and become identified with the subject. When the Council and EP first discuss the file they often know little about the subject, so are in the market for knowledge. If you are ready to provide that knowledge from the outset, this gives you a valuable contact for when things get political later.
2. You should **work with the Commission first during the IA phase**, but be aware that the Parliament and Council can influence the Commission heavily in its thinking stages (Parliament own-initiative report or Council Conclusions for example).
3. Work with **all three institutions at once**: by keeping them all informed you keep in touch and find out more information, and they will always influence each other.
4. Remember that **first reading agreements involve a series of intra and inter-institutional** negotiations, so make sure your position does not get used as a negotiating chip. You need to ensure the support of both the legislators (and the Commission).
5. Follow **trilogues** very carefully. It is essential to understand the negotiations as they unfold. This means knowing the politics and having access to these key discussions.
6. **Know the procedure/timelines**: you need to know when things will happen in each institution as windows of opportunity can easily be missed.
7. **Know each institutional procedure**: you need to know all the possibilities and margin for manoeuvre as this will give you more opportunities.
8. **Know the political/institutional context**. You need to show an awareness of the context and situation of the dossier you are working on.
9. **Be involved**, even if your issue is addressed favourably, as things can change very quickly.
10. First reading is vital to set up your **engagement campaign and establish contacts**.
11. **Set your objectives and priorities** for the campaign; be realistic and clear about what you want.
12. **Create your supporting material** so it is ready for when you need to use (tailor) it.
13. **Map all the stakeholders** you could need; you never know when you will need them.

---

8. Working with OLP: second reading

If your file moves to second reading, then the way you work with OLP will have to change in light of the new procedural situation and the fact that negotiations in first reading broke down. While the key people will probably remain the same (only the Presidency is likely to change since it lasts just six months), the way these key people interact and the issues on which they interact will change significantly.

The fact that a file has come into second reading means that it was not possible to find agreement in first reading, so the very first thing to find out is what the reasons were – why did the Parliament and the Council not agree at the first reading stage? You need to know:

1. What were the **technical sticking points** from first reading?
2. What were the **political sticking points** from first reading?
3. What were the **interpersonal dynamics** in first reading?
4. Who were the **sources of resistance/support**?
5. What were the **compromises suggested that failed**?
6. What was the **last suggested compromise**?

The answers to these six questions will be essential to understanding the inter-institutional dynamics and the issues on the table in second reading. At second reading, larger majorities are required in the Parliament for support, and the debate becomes more inter-institutional and based on pre-existing principles and dynamics.

It is much harder to make large or important changes at this stage, but it can be very important to work with the institutions on their second reading – especially if your issue is particularly contentious or one that could still be traded to find a final compromise.

Working with second reading also, almost by definition, requires that you have already worked with first reading. Only in this way will you have access to the right people and will you know the exact context and dynamics of the issue and the negotiations. At second reading you should review your approach to the negotiation in the light of the position of the Council and the European Parliament at first reading. Consider how far the Council's common position and the EP's position are in line with your objectives. This will help to identify issues that you should still push.

The procedure is similar to the procedure at first reading but with the following differences:
- From this point on the text which the Parliament works from is **the Council's first reading position** (rather than the Commission's proposal).
- Only the **lead Committee will adopt a report** (the rapporteur will usually remain the same). Opinion-giving Committees at the first reading stage will not be consulted anew. The Committee adopts amendments by simple majority.
- **Amendments at this stage should be limited** to amendments adopted at first reading and not accepted by the Council; amendments to parts of the first reading text that did not appear in, or are substantially different from, the Commission's initial proposal; or compromise amendments designed to bridge the gap between the positions of the co-legislators.
- **The EP Plenary votes on amendments proposed by the lead Committee** and any other amendments tabled by Political Groups or by a minimum of 40 Members. The Commissioner will attend the Plenary meeting and indicate the Commission's views on the European Parliament's amendments. At this stage the plenary adopts amendments by **absolute majority** (i.e. a majority of the members who comprise Parliament: in its post-Brexit configuration, with 705 MEPs, the threshold for an absolute majority is 353 votes).

- Note that if elections to the European Parliament have taken place since the Parliament adopted its position at first reading, the rapporteur will usually be (re-)appointed and the first reading procedure will re-set (with the Commission referring its proposal again to the Parliament).

8.1 European Parliament second reading

A key difference between the two stages (first and second reading) is that the second reading stage is subject to strict time limits.

When the Council adopts its first reading position, it must be forwarded to the Parliament with a statement of reasons. The Parliament then has a three-month period from notification of the Council's position at first reading (extendable at the initiative of the European Parliament or the Council by one month) to take action. The time starts to run from the day following the day the President of the European Parliament announces receipt of the Council position to the Plenary. The statement of reasons is accompanied by any statements made by the Council and/or the Commission for the Council minutes, as well as unilateral statements by delegations.

If the European Parliament endorses the Council's first reading position or fails to adopt amendments within the three month time limit, the President of Parliament will declare that the Council's position at first reading is accepted.

8.2 Commission second reading

The Commission will adopt a Communication setting out its position. Where the Parliament proposes second reading amendments, the Treaty requires the Commission to deliver an opinion on those amendments. The Commission's position on the European Parliament's amendments will determine whether the Council can vote by qualified majority or whether unanimity is required (if the Commission has given a negative opinion on one or more amendments).

8.3 Council second reading

Where Parliament adopts a position at second reading, the Council itself has a period of three months (which may be extended by one month) to adopt its position at second reading. The procedure is similar to the procedure at first reading. The Council's second reading is prepared by the competent Working Group, submitted to Coreper or its equivalent and adopted by the Council.

If the Council agrees to accept all the amendments of the European Parliament, the legislative measure will be deemed to have been adopted in the form of the Council's first reading position as amended by the Parliament in its second reading.

8.4 Second reading agreement

If the Presidency and the rapporteur consider that an agreement at second reading may be possible, informal trilogues will (again) be set up to explore possibilities for an agreement, noting the three month deadline, or the file will move to third reading/conciliation.

Ahead of each trilogue, the Presidency will seek a mandate from Coreper and secure potential compromises from the Council on its first reading/General Approach position. As with first reading, it is vital to connect with those in the room such as the attachés and the Permanent Representatives.

As in first reading, the purpose of the trilogues is to get agreement on a package of amendments acceptable to the Council and the European Parliament. If the trilogues produce an agreement, then Parliament will adopt amendments in line with the new compromise agreement, on the understanding that the Council will approve them. These compromise amendments forming the new text are tabled either in EP Committee or, more frequently, just before the Plenary session. They are co-signed for their Political Groups by the rapporteur and the shadow rapporteurs. This should ensure that the compromise will achieve an adequate majority because MEPs in the Plenary will generally follow the voting recommendations of their Political Groups.

8.5 Actors: second reading

If you worked with first reading, second reading will be a question of continuing your working relationship with the contacts you have already established. MEPs, the Presidency, Member States and the Commission are very reluctant to work with anyone who was not active in the first reading. The key aspects in terms of people are:

1. Re-ignite first reading contacts.
2. Understand the new political context of your interactions.
3. Ask your contacts for their opinion on possible compromises and solutions and take all of these on board.
4. Keep a multi-pronged approach, but be aware that the room for manoeuvre is now limited.
5. Assess what new data/evidence or approach is required to get your message to land with the key people. What was missing? What is needed to change things?

8.6 Engagement guidance: second reading

Much like the issue of people, the majority of engagement will be based on what you did at first reading, and will build from there in second reading. There should, however, be a few changes:

1. You need to review your engagement materials for second reading in order to take account of the inter-institutional and political focus that has likely taken prominence.

2. You will need to be more political at second reading; you will need to show awareness of the wider context or your lack of understanding will dent your credibility.
3. The key is now inter-institutional compromise – based on a narrow playing field. Try to offer any constructive solutions you have to unblock the deadlock.

In essence it is unlikely that you will need to do the same level of convincing in second reading because the positions will already be defined, and likely entrenched, and will have been defended. Your job is more to stay tuned into the negotiations and continue to support those actors who you worked with in first reading – because it is almost certainly the politics that will bring things to a close now.

> **Tips and Guidance for Working with OLP: Second Reading**
>
> 1. The **debate closes down**, making it much harder to work at second reading.
> 2. **Strict time limits** are applicable: 3+1 months for each legislator. Your window of opportunity is very limited.
> 3. **Amendments are under strict conditions** and need absolute majority support to pass in the Parliament, making it more difficult to get positions supported.
> 4. **The negotiation is about first reading issues, not new issues**. Admissibility rules mean new issues are not allowed.
> 5. Because only previous amendments, and new ones relating to modifications by the Council, are admissible this makes your **engagement in first reading even more important**. If you did not make your point then, it is too late now.
> 6. The debate in Parliament tends to be less about content and more about **inter-institutional issues**. Therefore knowing the history and having been proactive at first reading will help.
> 7. **Re-establish links with all the key stakeholders** from first reading, and reiterate positions and arguments.
> 8. **Second reading agreements will need new elements of compromise** to find a consensus: follow the informal discussions very closely to see what possible compromises could be.
> 9. **Revise your objectives, strategy, communications and material from first reading**: the game has changed and you need to change with it.

The guidance in the box above makes it quite clear that working with second reading can be very limited and also very difficult, and even more so if you were not engaged with first reading. This highlights the importance of why you need to be engaged for the long-term with the EU institutions. Your work at second reading will largely depend on what you already did and worked on, for, against, with, etc. at first reading, and how you decided strategically to pursue this. Second reading is an entirely different procedure to first reading, so you need to adapt to the new situation as fast as possible. Clearly you are now limited in time and also in terms of room for manoeuvre, so your objectives might need to be modified along with your approach and communication. You need to be quick out of the door to meet and persuade people to take up your position. If your issue is still live going into second reading then it is also apparent that your argumentation was lacking something – you need to be creative in how you try to repackage and land your key messages.

9. Working with OLP: third reading

Third readings have become increasingly rare and indeed in the 2014–2019 legislature there were none at all. However we will cover this topic as third reading still remains a possibility.

If the Council does not approve all the amendments of the European Parliament within the time limit for second reading, then the Conciliation procedure will be initiated. The Presidency of the Council, in agreement with the President of the European Parliament, will formally convene a meeting of the Conciliation Committee. This must be done within six weeks (extendable by two weeks at the initiative of the European Parliament or the Council).

Informal trilogue meetings (with representatives of the Council, Commission and Parliament) will normally be arranged prior to the first meeting of the Conciliation Committee in order to prepare the ground. It is important to underline that **the timelines for third reading are incredibly compressed**: the usual Coreper mandate, trilogue meeting, Coreper debrief and mandate refresh take place rapidly, even within the same week.

If the file you are working on fails to find an agreement at second reading, the first thing is again to understand why this happened – something that will be much more transparent and obvious than in first reading. To start with, the divisive issues were already known at first reading and simply could not be resolved. As with second reading it is therefore essential to understand:

1. **Why** was a compromise not possible?
2. **Who** was blocking the compromise: where was the resistance/support?
3. **What** were the proposed compromise texts that failed?

These three questions will help you situate third reading. The very first thing to note about working with third reading is that only last ditch attempts for successful changes should be attempted, and any expectations should be watered down. If you have not won over support for your views before third reading, your chances of winning support now are very slim (if not non-existent). Third reading is all about inter-institutional dynamics and compromise – the arguments have been around since first reading and the positions are usually very clear. The key, as for second reading, is to find the inter-institutional compromise that has proved impossible to reach during the two previous readings.

As the Conciliation Committee is large, the majority of the work will be done, as noted above, in informal trilogues made up of a smaller number of representatives from each institution and in technical meetings, with those representatives then reporting back as necessary to the Council delegation and EP delegation respectively. The resultant compromise package will then be submitted to the Conciliation Committee for approval. Therefore, engagement must take place long before the Committee first convenes. Depending on the success of the trilogue and the nature of the file, there may or may not be a second Conciliation Committee. If there is, there will be a subsequent opportunity to engage as the institutions prepare for that meeting.

Negotiations will focus on the changes sought by the Parliament to the Council's second reading position. Each delegation to the Conciliation Committee must approve the joint text in accordance with its own rules, i.e. qualified majority for the Council's delegation (at this stage the Commission cannot prevent the Council acting by qualified majority) and simple majority for the European Parliament's delegation.

The Commission, which can attend the meetings of both the Parliament and the Council delegations, will play a mediating role and seek to propose compromises to facilitate an agreement. As we have seen before, in trilogues, each delegation needs to be sure that it can get any compromise agreed by its institution. There have been instances of texts agreed in conciliation that subsequently failed to get the required majority (in the European Parliament). Strict time limits apply for conciliation so a joint text must be agreed and approved by both institutions within six weeks (which may be extended by two weeks) from the first meeting of the Conciliation Committee.

As the **Council's delegation** is made up of representatives in Coreper or its equivalent, this is not normally a problem for the Council. However, the **Parliament's delegation** may not always be representative of the Parliament as a whole and therefore sometimes the joint text agreed in the Conciliation Committee may fail to get the support of the Parliament. If agreement is not found within the time limit then the act is not adopted; it is however open to the Commission to make a new proposal. As these deadlines are very tight, informal contacts often take place between the Presidency and the Parliament before the formal conclusion of the Council's second reading in order to maximise the time available for finding an agreement.

Once a file gets to third reading it will probably have been worked on for at least three years, with the majority of the same people still in the negotiating room. For this reason the contact networks, channels of influence, coalitions, positions, arguments, blocking positions, etc. are all known. The discussion is no longer a technical issue-based one: it is all about the legislators trying to find a (now political) compromise that means no one is seen to lose face and that is acceptable to all. It is for this reason that working with third reading can be very difficult – you can only really reiterate your previous positions.

If your key issue is still on the table you will obviously need to work with your key contacts again, but more from the perspective of getting information than from giving them anything new (if they supported you in first and second reading it is quite likely they will continue to support you). The key, for most stakeholders at this stage of the OLP procedure is to get information out of the informal procedures that make up third reading.

9.1 Actors: third reading

Much like with second reading, the key actors and the networks remain very much as they were and simply need to be reactivated. However, as the dossier is a political hot potato, a number of high-level political figures will enter into the discussions. When a proposal gets into third reading, the Presidency will have changed several times. If there have been elections for the European Parliament during the negotiations on the file, the main contact persons within this institution might also be different.

The only potential difference will be the need to engage at the political levels of the three institutions as you seek to try to influence proceedings – which may require extending your network for contacts. Clearly these contacts will be hard to activate (the higher up the political chain they are the more difficult they are to access) but as this is where decisions will be taken you need to find a way to access them. At the same time you should only seek to do this with the blessing of your existing stakeholders, i.e. do not be seen to be going above their heads.

9.2 Engagement guidance: third reading

When it comes to engagement at third reading, the options are very limited because, as highlighted before, the positions are well-known and the debate is inter-institutional. Engagement is now very much about personal contacts and getting information from the negotiations. If you are still actively involved on a live issue in third reading, then the key is to make sure you communicate with your contacts to increase the chances that they continue to support your issue – again while always trying to understand what possible compromises are on the table and how your issue could get linked.

The main elements of working with third reading are given in the box below.

> **Tips and Guidance for Working with OLP: Third Reading**
>
> 1. **It is not easy to influence or obtain information** at this stage of OLP; it is therefore very difficult to work with third reading.
> 2. **The debate has been reduced to inter-institutional negotiation.**
> 3. The issues and positions are usually common knowledge now; **the key is an inter-institutional agreement/compromise position.**
> 4. **At this stage it is unlikely that the Council or Parliament will need, or be interested in, external views** as the issues will be well known.
> 5. It is **essential to try and get information through the participants in the trilogues**, which reduces contact down to a small number of people.
> 6. **The solution at third reading will be driven almost 100% by politics.**

10. Working with Delegated & Implementing Acts

By Alan Hardacre & Aaron McLoughlin

1. Introduction

Part of the long-term nature of working with EU decision-making relates to the fact that once you have finished working with the Ordinary Legislative Procedure (OLP) it is quite likely that there will be tasks delegated to the Commission that will require Delegated and/or Implementing Acts (D&I) – so your work needs to start all over again (or continue). And given that the devil is often in the detail, and the impacts of D&I are much more localised, it is just as (if not more) important to work with D&I Acts.

Erik Akse's companion volume *How the EU Institutions Work* explains in detail the procedures of these two different types of acts along with those of the Regulatory Procedure with Scrutiny (RPS) – and this is an essential starting point. To get the most out of this chapter we assume that you understand the main actors and processes for D&I Acts. You need to understand these three different procedures so that you know who is involved, when and what they need to make decisions. This chapter will have sections on D&I Acts – but no dedicated section on RPS as guidance for how to work with that is covered in the section on Implementing Acts.

In reality most of the legislation the EU works on is technical which is why the institutions need so much stakeholder input. **Technical laws, such as D&I Acts, are an essential part of the system as they bring political intentions to life**. For this reason they can also be politically sensitive. Stories about bans on vacuum cleaners, toasters and church organs all stem from cases involving D&I Acts. In fact such was the political sensitivity of the last Commission to stories of EU bans on vacuum cleaners, that the Secretary-General and the Head of the President's Cabinet issued guidance to the Commission Services on the adoption of eco-design rules. There was then, and there is now, a growing recognition of this political aspect of D&I Acts from the Commission's leadership and they are looking at how to exert greater political scrutiny and control of technical lawmaking.

Former European Commission President Jean-Claude Juncker tried to change the rules relating to the approval process of pesticides and genetically modified organisms (GMOs). These substances, after receiving a scientific go-ahead, are put in front of committees of Member States' representatives but often they do not reach the qualified majority required to automatically allow them onto the market. From there, due to the procedural rules, the Commission is left with no other choice than to approve the substance – despite opposition from half of the Member States. President Juncker said *'It is not right that when EU countries cannot decide among themselves whether or not to ban the use of glyphosate in herbicides, the Commission is forced by Parliament and Council to take a decision.'* The case of glyphosate, and the intense lobbying around it, certainly highlights the importance that D&I Acts can have in Brussels.

Over the last five years the importance of D&A Acts has been recognised and there has been **an increase in political management within the Commission** of the process of bringing them into the Better Regulation mainstream. Correspondingly, there has been an increase in the exercise of political scrutiny by the Council and the European Parliament. All of these changes provide you with more opportunities to make your case and change outcomes.

As was noted in *How the EU Institutions Work*, most of the legislation passed in the EU comes in the form of D&I Acts. It is worth reminding ourselves, as seen in Table 10.1 below, of just how important D&I Acts are to the EU.

Table 10.1: Legislation adopted by the EU 2017-2018

Numbers	2017	2018
Implementing Acts	1687	1456
RPS Measures	113	90
Delegated Acts	132	119
Directives	14	18
Regulations	52	49

The world of D&I Acts is in some ways similar to working with OLP files given that it is likely an extension of the same subject and means working with the same set of stakeholders. At the same time it can be more challenging given that it requires additional procedural and technical knowledge, the timelines are shorter and much more happens behind closed doors. That said, it is vital for public affairs professionals in Brussels to know how to work with D&I Acts because small changes can have important impacts for your organisation. Despite the reputation of D&I Acts as being difficult to work with, on a general level one can say that:

1. **D&I Acts are increasingly known and understood in Brussels** making it easier to work with them. Key stakeholders understand the importance attached to them – in a way they perhaps didn't some 5-10 years ago. This makes engagement easier.
2. **The process is increasingly transparent and accessible**, notably for Delegated Acts. Finding information and following the process is becoming more straightforward.
3. Engaging offers more **opportunities for stakeholders** because of the shared powers of the legislators – notably because of the increased interest and activity in the Parliament.

4. **Engagement has a narrower, but usually manageable, window.** Working with D&I Acts is faster than OLP leading to faster outcomes and results – but usually allowing for engagement and opportunities to make your case.

To start the chapter it is useful to draw up some generic suggestions for how to approach and engage with D&I Acts which build on the conclusions of the previous chapter on OLP. Much of the guidance on how to engage with OLP, and the institutions, remains valid for D&I Acts and should be read again with D&I Acts in mind. The box below summarises the fundametals for dealing with D&I Acts.

Fundamentals for Working with Delegated & Implementing Acts

1. D&I Acts (and your work on them) do not start only in the implementation phase; they should be monitored and engaged with as of the legislative thinking phase (i.e. the very beginning).
2. Work with D&I Acts through OLP: small changes there can make an important difference later.
3. A good knowledge of the procedures for D&I Acts is essential, and more so than for OLP because they are generally less well understood (in the institutions as well).
4. You need to understand how D&I Acts work within the three main institutions and the exact roles that each can play – often so you can educate others on this.
5. Timing is essential for D&I Acts: the windows of opportunity are much smaller than those for OLP.
6. D&I Acts are inherently technical dossiers so you will need to have solid technical expertise to deliver, but packaged the right way for your different audiences.
7. D&I Acts (especially Delegated Acts) can also be political so do not neglect the importance of the politics that surround each dossier.
8. The circle of key actors is much reduced, so having longstanding contacts and networks can be invaluable.
9. Getting stakeholders engaged on D&I Acts can be challenging at times because D&I Acts are lower key and often much more specific and targeted. Unlike for OLP you often have to work out how to sell your subject – why should people be interested?
10. Much of the work on D&I Acts happens below the radar – in fact if you did not know what to follow or where to look you could be forgiven for missing them completely. You will need to know your way around this legislative underworld to succeed.

The basics of working with D&I Acts build on all that has been said in previous chapters, especially when it comes to the contacts and networks you have been able to establish. As we have noted it is, invariably, the same people within the institutions, especially the Commission, who will be working on D&I Acts after OLP. This is a clear illustration of how important engagement in OLP can be: if you have already established yourself as a transparent, honest and essential provider of information in OLP your task will be much easier with D&I Acts. Conversely, if you did not take the long-term view and made mistakes in OLP, working with D&I Acts can be very difficult. What you lost in OLP you can win back in D&I Acts if you play the long game.

One further horizontal element that is very useful in the context of working with D&I Acts is to understand the differences between the two types of acts. As a reminder, Table 10.2 sums up the differences described in *How the EU Institutions Work*, with a focus on the key elements we need to retain for working with D&I Acts.

Table 10.2: Essentials of engagement: Differences between Delegated and Implementing Acts

Implementing Acts (Article 291 TFEU)	Delegated Acts (Article 290 TFEU)
1. Routine implementation of EU legislation 2. Can only implement clearly defined tasks 3. Can be issues of general or individual scope	1. Sensitive implementation matters for the legislators 2. Can supplement, amend or delete non-essential elements of legislative act 3. Always issues of general scope
1. A binding framework - Implementing Acts Regulation 2. Horizontal framework - selection from two procedures (advisory and examination)	1. No binding framework - Common Understanding 2. No horizontal framework - objectives, content, scope and duration are decided on a case by case basis in each legislative act
1. Obligatory consultation of Comitology Committee 2. Committee = 1 representative of each MS (possible Observers like EU Agencies, EFTA Countries, etc.) 3. Chaired by Commission	1. No consultation of Comitology Committee 2. Probable use of Expert Groups, EU Agencies and other sources of information
Control by (Comitology Committee or Appeal Committee): 1. Advisory: Simple majority vote - non-binding opinion 2. Examination: Qualified majority vote (QMV*) to approve Commission proposal 3. Appeal Committee: referrals from Committee dealt with by representatives at 'appropriate level' * A QMV requires 55% of the Member States (this means in practice 15 out of 27), and 65% of the EU population	Control by (EP and/or Council): 1. Veto - object to an individual Delegated Act on any grounds within the deadline set by the legislative act (usually 2+2 months)* 2. Revocation - revoke the delegation of powers to the Commission altogether * Super qualified QMV to block = 72% of EU MS votes in favour and represents at least 65% of EU population
Observations: 1. Special cases for Common Commercial Policy 2. Flexibility for the Commission, which MAY adopt the draft measures where there is no qualified majority against 3. Right of Scrutiny for EP and Council - at any time	Observations: 1. Parliament and Council on perfect equal footing 2. Both legislatures define the modalities of Delegated Acts, but can revoke the delegation afterwards without the other's consent

Having outlined the key differences between, and the fundamentals for, working with D&I Acts, it is now possible to look at how we identify D&I Acts in legislative texts – an essential exercise before starting to work with them.

2. Identifying Delegated and Implementing Acts

The first place to start working with D&I Acts is in the final legislative text itself (or indeed in the Commission proposal), which you will have been working with in OLP. For this there are a series of steps that need to be followed. When you have a legislative act in front of you, you need to address the following:

1. **The recitals**
    The recitals come at the front of the legislative text. They define the scope of the legislative act and its respective articles, and therefore form a sort of guidance note to national administrators (and anyone else who is interested) who will have to work with the legislation at the national level. There will always be at least one recital concerning Delegated Acts and one concerning Implementing Acts if they are part of the legislation. This can sometimes be useful to help understand what has been delegated, and why. This short read can give you some useful context.

2. **The Delegated or Implementing Acts article(s)**
    The next things to look for are the articles that outline the procedures under which either a Delegated or Implementing Act can be decided – these are usually three or four articles from the end of the legislative text. There will usually be one Implementing Act article that will describe the procedures that are to be used (Examination or Advisory). There will usually be three Delegated Act articles describing, firstly, the exercise of the delegation (duration, scope, etc.), secondly, revocation and, finally, one on objections to Delegated Acts. For example Article 40 of a text could be entitled 'Implementing Act', 40.1 will name the Committee to be used, 40.2 will identify the Advisory procedure and 40.3 will identify the Examination procedure. After that, Article 41 could be entitled 'Exercise of the delegation', Article 42 'Revocation of the delegation' and Article 43 'Objections to Delegated Acts'.

3. **The tasks that have been delegated**
    Once you know the articles for Delegated and/or Implementing Acts you need to find references to these articles in the text because this is where the exact tasks delegated to the Commission are identified. For example you could find, in Article 5, a requirement for the Commission to draft a Delegated Act to modify some specific criteria (by amending or modifying) and this (in the example given above) will have an explicit reference to Article 41 – hence you know that it is a Delegated Act, and within Article 41 all the conditions will be explained. Unfortunately the only way to do this is to read through the text and spot the mentions (or 'search and find' on your computer).

If you follow these three steps you will have identified all the key elements of D&I Acts in the legislative text and be ready to work with them. To highlight the three stages above let's take the example of Regulation No. 995/2010: A Regulation laying down the obligations of operators who place timber and timber products on the market. Here we can see the three stages as follows:

Example recital

(28) The Commission should be empowered to adopt delegated acts in accordance with Article 290 of the Treaty on the Functioning of the European Union (TFEU) concerning the procedures for the recognition and withdrawal of recognition of monitoring organizations, concerning further relevant Risk Assessment criteria that may be necessary to supplement those already provided for in this Regulation and concerning the list of timber and timber products to which this Regulation applies. It is of particular importance that the Commission carry out appropriate consultations during its preparatory work, including at expert level.

Article 15
Exercise of the delegation

1. The power to adopt the delegated acts referred to in Articles 6(3), 8(7) and 14 shall be conferred on the Commission for a period of seven years from 2 December 2010. The Commission shall make a report in respect of the delegated powers not later than three months before the end of a three-year period after the date of application of this Regulation. The delegation of powers shall be automatically extended for periods of an identical duration, unless the European Parliament or the Council revokes it in accordance with Article 16.
2. As soon as it adopts a delegated act, the Commission shall notify it simultaneously to the European Parliament and to the Council.
3. The power to adopt delegated acts is conferred on the Commission subject to the conditions laid down in Articles 16 and 17.

Article 16
Revocation of the delegation

1. The delegation of powers referred to in Articles 6(3), 8(7) and 14 may be revoked at any time by the European Parliament or by the Council.
2. The institution which has commenced an internal procedure for deciding whether to revoke the delegation of powers shall endeavour to inform the other institution and the Commission within a reasonable time before the final decision is taken, indicating the delegated powers which could be subject to revocation and possible reasons for a revocation.
3. The decision of revocation shall put an end to the delegation of the powers specified in that decision. It shall take effect immediately or at a later date specified therein. It shall not affect the validity of the delegated acts already in force. It shall be published in the *Official Journal of the European Union*.

The recital clearly indicates the tasks that have been delegated to the Commission, and also how the Commission will go about preparing these, with the assistance of an Expert Group. We also find the articles dealing with the D&I Acts and the procedural information we need to know.

The four boxes for articles 15-18, three of them outlining Delegated Acts and one of them Implementing Acts, outline all the details of how the two types of acts can be formulated and what procedures apply. It is essential to know this information in advance – for example, to see if there is an Expert Group mentioned in the recital, or to find the name of the Committee that will be used: all information that will be needed later in the work with D&I Acts.

Article 17
Objections to delegated acts

1. The European Parliament or the Council may object to a delegated act within a period of two months from the date of notification. At the initiative of the European Parliament or the Council this period shall be extended by two months.
2. If, on expiry of that period, neither the European Parliament nor the Council has objected to the delegated act, it shall be published in the *Official Journal of the European Union* and shall enter into force on the date stated therein. The delegated act may be published in the *Official Journal of the European Union* and enter into force before the expiry of that period if the European Parliament and the Council have both informed the Commission of their intention not to raise objections.
3. If the European Parliament or the Council objects to a delegated act, the act shall not enter into force. The institution which objects shall state the reasons for objecting to the delegated act.

Article 18
Committee

1. The Commission shall be assisted by the Forest Law Enforcement Governance and Trade (FLEGT) Committee established under Article 11 of Regulation (EC) No. 2173/2005.
2. Where reference is made to this paragraph, Articles 5 and 7 of Decision 1999/468/EC shall apply, having regard to the provisions of Article 8 thereof. The period laid down in Article 5(6) of Decision 1999/468/EC shall be set at three months.

Instead of offering general guidance on both categories, this section will present guidance on how to work with D&I Acts separately, because it can be much more tailored and specific.

3. Working with Implementing Acts

Working with Implementing Acts is the first category we need to assess. It is also the category where there is the most accumulated experience, given that it is the realm of 'old Comitology' and the Committees that assist the Commission. The horizontal aspects of this section also apply to the old Regulatory Procedure with Scrutiny (RPS) measures which still exist in some legislation. Whilst Implementing Acts are acts of routine implementation of EU legislation, the devil can be in the detail so if you are following an issue into Implementing Acts the stakes can be very high.

> The European Commission's own *'Guidelines for the services of the Commission - Implementing Acts'* is a useful reference. If you work a lot on Implementing Acts, you will find it helpful.

The first thing to consider is the **operation of the Committees themselves, and the key actors** who are in them, as they will be the focal point of your work with Implementing Acts.

Implementing Acts: Committees

1. **Representatives of 27 Member States.**
2. MS representatives normally have mandates from their home Ministry.
3. Possible observers from third countries, EU Agencies, International Organisations, Industry, Non-governmental Organisations (or others depending on the needs of the Committee).
4. Committees can invite experts or concerned parties to address the meetings.
5. Committee decision-making is based on the 'reverse majority' principle, which allows the Commission in general to adopt the Implementing Act unless there is a qualified majority against the draft Implementing Act.
6. Chaired by Commission
7. Objective = consensus.
8. Very consensual and collaborative with good exchanges of information/views.
9. Member States can suggest and make changes to the Implementing Act under discussion – both in writing and in meetings.

A few points about the Committee need to be highlighted at this stage. The first is that although the key actors are always going to be the Commission and the Member State representatives, it is still worth trying to find out if any observers will be in the Committee meeting. The Commission will always be in the driving seat but any Member State can propose changes (and have them accepted), and if there is a majority opinion away from a Commission position it will usually prevail. Basically, Committee deliberations can be quite open and make substantive changes (in a short period of time).

From outlining the people in the Committee, it is useful next to look at how a Committee operates because these rules are procedurally very important. We will work with the standard rules of procedure for a Committee because they are an invaluable source of information. **Every Committee should** have its own **Rules of Procedure (RoP)** – so always ask (the Commission) to get the ones for the Committee you are working with. The main aspects of the standard RoP are as follows:

1. **Convening a meeting**: initiative of the chairman (Commission) or at the request of a simple majority of members.
2. **Agenda**: drawn up by the chairman (Commission) with two parts:
   * proposed Implementing Act(s) submitted to the vote;
   * other issues regarding information.
3. **Documentation to be sent to the members**: to be sent by the chairman to the Committee members no later than 14 days in advance (the chairman may shorten this period on his/her own initiative or at the request of a member).
4. **Informing the Parliament**: under OLP, transmission at the same time as to the Member States (see box later for more detail on what is transmitted).
5. **Opinion of the Committee**: Voting rules: simple majority in Advisory procedure (14 Member States) and qualified majority voting in the Examination procedure. The chairman may postpone the vote until the end of the meeting or a later meeting if a substantive change is made to the proposal during a meeting, the text for voting has been submitted during the meeting, a new point has been added to the agenda because of extreme urgency, or documents have not been sent within the deadline.
6. **Quorum**: Majority required for a successful vote (14 Member States).
7. **Representation**: One person per delegation is reimbursed (Member State experts can be present with the chairman's agreement).
8. **Working Groups**: the Committee may create Working Groups of experts. These can be standard Expert Groups, hence also chaired by the Commission.
9. **Admission of third parties**: participation of third countries or third organisations in accordance with a Council act. With the status of observer they do not vote and should leave the room when a vote takes place.
10. **Written procedure**: Response period for the Committee's opinion may not be less than 14 days. In cases of urgency the deadline may be shorter. If a member requests that the measure(s) be discussed at a meeting, the Written procedure will be terminated.
11. **Minutes and summary report**: Minutes are drafted by the chairman for the Committee members and a summary report which does not mention the individual position of Member States for the Parliament and the general public.
12. **Attendance list**: The Commission shall draw up an attendance list specifying the authorities or bodies to which the persons appointed by the Member States to represent them belong – but there should be no individual names.
13. **Correspondence**: always to be addressed to the Permanent Representations by e-mail and to the Commission (Service responsible).
14. **Transparency**: the Committee's discussions are confidential. Application of transparency rules through application of Regulation 1049/2001.

Source: Standard Rules of Procedure for Committee, OJ C.206/06/12.7. 2000

These RoP are very important to understand if you are working with Implementing Acts, and they also give a feel for how Committees work in practice. In general, the Commission circulates the documents in advance, including the draft Implementing Acts, so that experts in the Member States can evaluate their national positions. The Committee then meets with a clear agenda that separates items for vote (and under which procedure) and items for information and discussion.

The Commission uses these meetings to improve and finalise its draft Implementing Acts and tries to obtain a consensus in the Committee. The Commission will then call a vote once it has a consensus, or if positions are unlikely to change irrespective of any modification to the Implementing Act that the Commission could make. Almost exclusively, **deciding on Implementing Acts is a consensual practice with consistently few problems (the exception being GMOs)**, but knowing the rules of the Committees can be very useful when working on more problematic dossiers.

It is also worth noting that the **Ombudsman** takes a robust approach to backing greater transparency in the workings of committees. In Case 2142/2018 the Ombudsman considered a request for public access to documents containing the positions of EU Member States from the Standing Committee on Plants, Animals, Food and Feed. The Ombudsman ruled that the Commission's refusal to grant access amounted to maladministration.

The best way to understand many of the points listed above is to take a look at the Commission Comitology website and its register (still maintaining reference to the old world of Comitology). The **Commission Comitology Register** is home to a significant number of documents related to Implementing Acts, and all of the documents mentioned above can be found here. That said, some Committees do not update the information on the public register on time or often. This means that it is helpful to obtain documents through the Member States or the EP – especially if you are working on a live case.

The mnutes of the meetings are usually opaque and published late. It helps to speak to people who were at the meeting to get a read-out of the discussions and breakdown of where countries stood. This is important as you will find that countries may not take the line that they said they would take or, in some cases, vote the way they said they would.

The documents in the register also correspond to the documents that are sent to the Parliament to exercise its various powers under the Implementing Acts Regulation. This means that before the meeting of the Committee (and at the same time as the Member States) the Parliament gets:
1. Draft agenda of the meeting.
2. Draft initial Implementing Act(s) submitted to the Committee.

After the meeting the Parliament will then get:
1. List of participants (not individual names).
2. A summary record (not Member State positions).
3. Voting results (not individualised).
4. The draft final Implementing Act(s) following the Committee opinion.

It is worth noting that the summary minutes are often only validated at the next Committee meeting. The Commission makes an audio recording of the meeting for the preparation of an agreed set of minutes and once these are complete the audio recording is deleted.

If a measure relates to a **Special Legislative Procedure (SLP)** (as explained in *How the EU Institutions Work*), then the documents are the same except for the drafts of the Implementing Act itself, which are not transmitted to the Parliament.

The register is thus important for the work of Committees, with one obvious limitation: it is rarely updated in time for you to work on live issues. If you want to work effectively with (and not simply monitor post-fact) Implementing Acts you cannot rely on the register for your information: you will need to be in close cooperation with the key actors in the process. It is therefore essential to know exactly where else you can find the information. The most important source of information on Implementing Acts will always be the Unit responsible for drafting the Implementing Act in the Commission – which is why it is worth looking at the flow of an Implementing Act through the Commission, as shown in Figure 10.1.

Figure 10.1: The flow of an Implementing Act through the Commission

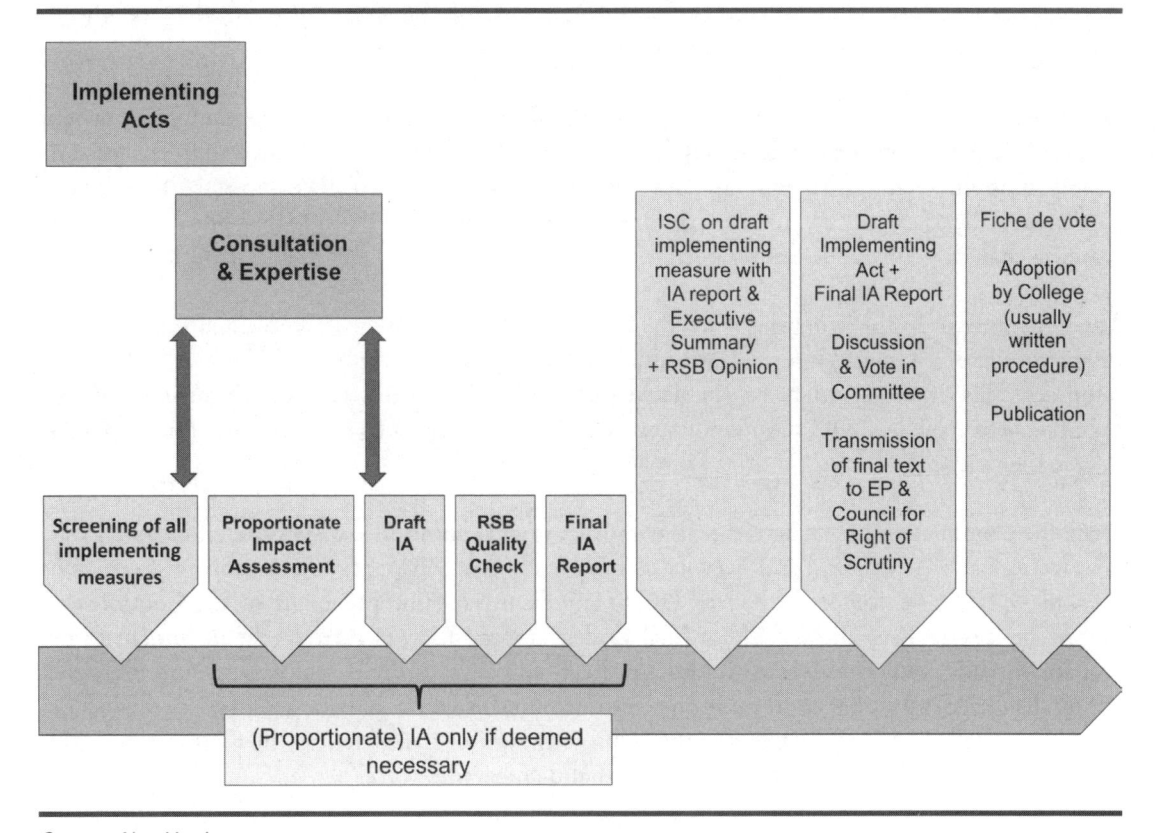

Source: Alan Hardacre

The key institution for Implementing Acts is without doubt the Commission because, through the powers conferred on it, it drafts the actual texts of the acts. The process in the Commission does not differ greatly from that of a legislative file. The Secretariat-General, in conjunction with the Directorates-General (DGs) and Services, screens all forthcoming Implementing Acts to see if they require an Impact Assessment (IA). IAs for Implementing Acts remain quite unusual (though not exceptional) and it is more likely that Delegated Acts will be subject to IA. However, it should not be ruled out that in the future more Implementing Acts will be subject to proportionate IAs.

It is vital that you flag to the Services and the Secretariat-General any draft Delegated and Implementing Acts being considered that are **politically sensitive or important**. You need to do this as early as possible. You cannot cry wolf and if you raise an issue you need a strong case to establish that it is politically sensitive or important. This threshold is not a monetary one alone, although a measure would likely need to have a financial impact in the € billion plus range to raise attention. Flagging clear second order impacts on Commission key political priorities is another. The threshold to invoke this check in the system is a moving one and is made by the Commission President and their close advisers.

The earlier you step in the better. The closer you get to adoption the harder it is to get the proposal blocked. If you have a good network, you can raise your case early on. If you step in late in the day, you will likely burn through all your political capital, and often needlessly so. And, as we will see later, the chances of blocking when you step in late in the day are low.

Delegated Acts, Implementing Acts, and Regulatory Procedure with Scrutiny measures can benefit from **public consultation**. This is usually for four weeks. The Commission's 'Have Your Say' website, has a section on 'technical rules or updates – draft delegated and implementing acts'. You need to participate. The feedback can give the Commission important feedback. In at least one case – mobile roaming charges – the public feedback led to the draft Implementing Acts being withdrawn.

The key moment in the process is when the Unit in the lead DG drafts its Implementing Act, using input from Expert Groups, informal consultations, EU Agencies, Committee members and its own resources. This draft text might be circulated formally, or informally, to the Committee to gather opinions before the lead DG submits the text into Inter-Service Consultation (ISC) for other DGs to give their views.

Once the Commission has an agreed text from ISC, it will submit it to discussion and a vote in the Committee itself. Assuming a positive vote (as happens in over 99% of cases), the **voting sheet** (*fiche de vote*) will then be needed by the lead DG to launch an adoption procedure by the Commission. Before the lead DG submits its file for final College approval it will forward the document to the Parliament and Council for them to exercise their right of scrutiny – which is seldom exercised. When the file goes for final approval in the Commission this will usually be a Written procedure, so all Cabinets will have a last look before the Implementing Act is adopted by the Commission, after which it is published in the Official Journal (OJ) and enters into force.

Several further points need to be made about the **vital role and influence of the Commission**:

1. First, if the Commission takes a strong stand, it is hard for the Member States to overturn its view. Getting a vote against the Commission in the Committee is a high threshold, one that is not easy to reach.

2. Second, whilst it is common for Member States not to support some aspects of the Commission's proposals, they will often fall into three rival camps. You end up with one group of countries supporting a tougher line, another supporting a weaker line, and another backing the Commission. Even if there is no majority for or against the Commission's proposal, the Commission will be able to adopt its preferred position.

3. Third, there is greater political scrutiny within the Commission of Delegated Acts and RPS measures. They need to be validated by the GRI. (Implementing Acts do not receive this degree of thorough political scrutiny.)

4. Fourth, your best hope of influencing the proposal the Commission issues is during Inter-service Consultation. They have the ability to edit the Services draft text. That said, it is difficult to get Cabinet officials interested in technical law-making.

5. Fifth, if the issue is especially important to you, you should get the Secretariat-General to attend the Committee/Expert Group to make sure that the Commission's chair follows the Commission's line.

6. Sixth, if you think a file is sensitive and important, you should flag it to the Secretariat-General. They are placed to raise questions with the Services. If you do this, you will need a strong and robust case. This needs to be summarised down into one page. It helps if you are able to identify how the Services are going against the Commission's political priorities, guidelines, or working methods. The intervention needs to be evidence-based. Too often people complain against the secondary act simply because it goes against their interests. They come unstuck when it becomes clear that the enabling legislation was designed to do just that. The Commission cannot rewrite the enabling legislation, it is bound by it.

7. Finally, a basic challenge of Implementing Acts is that the College of Commissioners are sometimes forced to back proposals they disagree with.

From the preceding sections it is possible to draw a series of conclusions about working with Implementing Acts, summarised in the box on the next page.

> **Working with Implementing Acts: General guidance**
>
> 1. Follow the legislative drafting of the Commission for the insertion of the Advisory and Examination procedures.
> 2. Work with the three institutions during the OLP phase on how Implementing Acts will work in the legislative act; the more clarity at this stage the better.
> 3. Read the final legislative act to understand exactly what has been delegated to the Commission.
> 4. Identify any Agency or experts assisting the Commission in drafting the Implementing Act and work with them, with technical evidence.
> 5. Work with the Commission Services drafting the Implementing Act.
> 6. Identify the Inter-Service Consultation on the Implementing Act.
> 7. Identify the relevant Comitology Committee and the members of the Committee and start to work with them. These will be key Member State technical experts.
> 8. Follow the work of the Comitology Committee and work with the Commission and Member States to suggest modifications in Committee.
> 9. Once the Implementing Act has been voted on in Committee the European Parliament and Council have a right of scrutiny, though it is very difficult to motivate them to use this.
> 10. If there has been a negative vote or 'no opinion' in the Examination procedure and the Implementing Act is referred to the Appeal Committee, work with members of the Committee to try and make modifications.

It is essential to emphasise that, in working with Implementing Acts, this should always start at the very earliest opportunity, i.e. working with the Commission when it is drafting the legislative proposal. It is important to ensure that the tasks delegated to the Commission are in accordance with your interests. Once you get to the actual drafting of Implementing Acts your room for manoeuvre is limited, because the Commission is working within a well-defined legislative context to implement the legislation. As we noted before though, the devil here can very much be in the detail and what can seem small things can make millions of euro of difference. Again, you will have to work with all three institutions, as per the guidance in the previous chapter on OLP, with the explicit objective of modifying or supporting aspects of the draft Implementing Act.

Once the text has been voted by the Committee, the Commission will move to adopt and bring into force the Implementing Act – leaving only one last avenue for work, the **Council and Parliament's right of scrutiny**. Here you need to bear in mind the limitations of this power and the difficulty of generating sufficient momentum to deliver a forceful enough opinion to get the Commission to change its mind.

Nonetheless, keep the Parliament and Council informed of your issues for future reference, as you never know what could come around again. The majority of this work will be of a technical nature and you will need to make sure you are well-versed in the technicalities of your file because your interlocutors will likely be experts in the field. Your communication should therefore be evidence, fact and case-study based.

4. Working with Delegated Acts: introductory remarks

Working with Delegated Acts matters because in Delegated Acts **the Commission is granted the power to amend, supplement and/or delete non-essential elements of the legislative act**. Here it is important to stress that this can mean very important and far-reaching changes with significant consequences. With Delegated Acts the impacts of changes are much more localised than in OLP and hence **much more important for specific sectors and stakeholders** than the impact of an OLP file.

> The European Commission's own *'Guidelines for the services of the Commission - Delegated Acts'* is a useful reference. If you work a lot on Delegated Acts, you will find it helpful.

What we say about Delegated Acts will be structured in much the same way as the previous section on Implementing Acts, but given the need to work more extensively with all three institutions, and to understand their internal decision-making procedures for Delegated Acts, there will be three separate sections to detail the nature of each of these processes institution by institution.

Before looking at the process for Delegated Acts within the three EU institutions, one aspect of interest concerns the **negotiation of Delegated Acts in the legislative phase**. There is a grey zone, in certain cases, as to whether a Delegated Act or an Implementing Act should or could be used – this will always play out in OLP negotiations. In general the Parliament will have more incentive to negotiate Delegated Acts into a text because it will benefit from significantly greater oversight. The Council, on the other hand, will have a preference for Implementing Acts, as this puts it firmly in the driving seat (and curtails the role of the Parliament). You need to be alert, and sensitive, to this dynamic and understand what it means for your issue.

5. Working with Delegated Acts: the Commission

The way the Commission prepares and adopts a Delegated Act is shown in Figure 10.2.

Figure 10.2 shows a very similar process to that for Implementing Acts, with the major difference that **there is no longer a Committee stage and the Commission adopts the Delegated Act before sending it to the legislators**. The phase of screening for an Impact Assessment is more important for Delegated Acts and a number of Delegated Acts have already been given proportionate IAs – a trend that is likely to continue in the future. If this is the case, it is important to work with the Commission as it drafts the Impact Assessment.

An Impact Assessment can potentially benefit your case. It may reveal important issues and consequences arising from what otherwise looks like a technical measure. But this is not easy to get. Asking for an Impact Assessment is often seen as a device to play for time – and as the data in the box on the next page shows, only a small minority of either Implementing or Delegated Acts get one.

Figure 10.2: The Commission and Delegated Acts

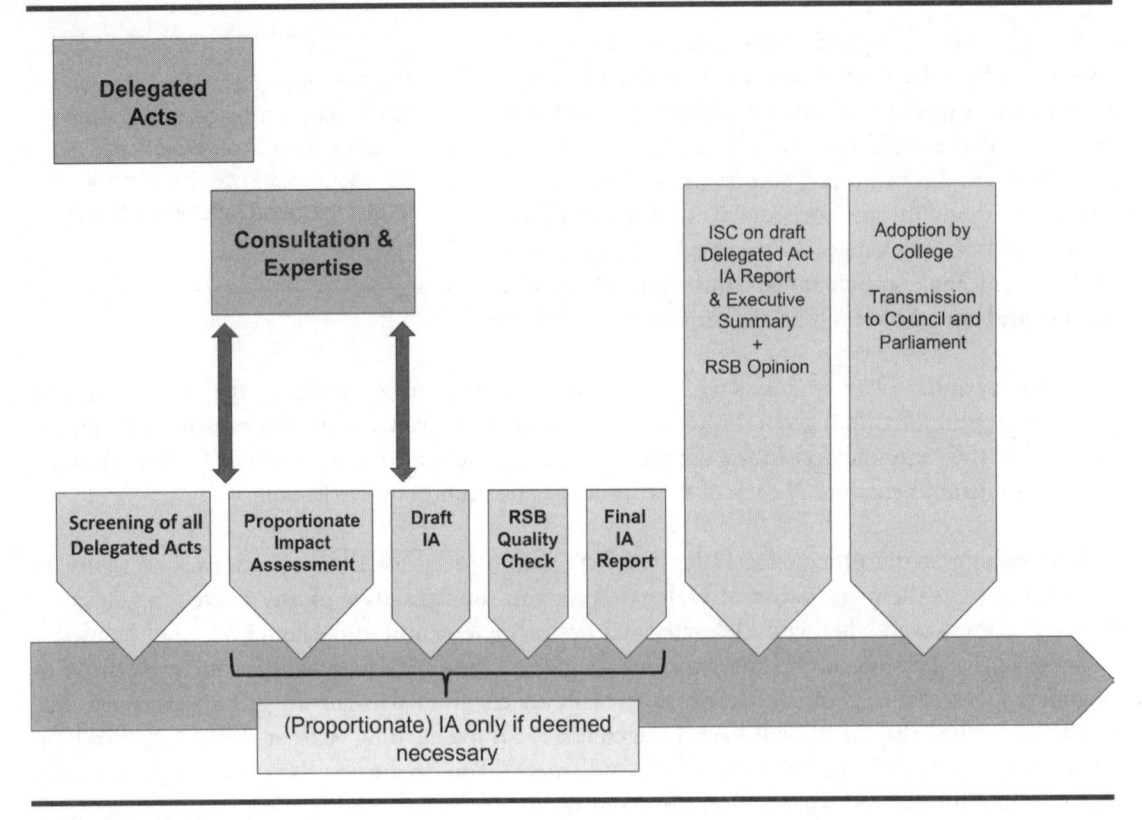

[Flowchart showing: Delegated Acts → Consultation & Expertise, with stages: Screening of all Delegated Acts, Proportionate Impact Assessment, Draft IA, RSB Quality Check, Final IA Report, ISC on draft Delegated Act IA Report & Executive Summary + RSB Opinion, Adoption by College / Transmission to Council and Parliament. Bracket notes: "(Proportionate) IA only if deemed necessary"]

Source: Alan Hardacre

Running an Impact Assessment for a Delegated Act is therefore **an exception, and is granted at the discretion of the Commission**. You can increase your chances of getting the Commission to launch an IA by presenting a shadow impact assessment of your own. A shadow impact assessment should mirror the Commission's own guidelines, and present a clear and compelling case that otherwise seemingly innocuous provisions will have significant consequences.

Delegated and Implementing Acts: Number of Impact Assessments

Implementing Acts January 2018-December 2019:
1,779 Implementing Acts, 12 got an IA

Delegated Acts January to May 2019:
71 Delegated Acts, 3 got a full IA and 5 were undertaken by Agencies

You will need to draw on two core Commission rule books, the Working Methods of the European Commission (1.2.2019) and the Better Regulation Toolbox No.9. An Impact Assessment is required for Commission initiatives that are likely to have significant economic, environmental or social impacts. The Working Methods notes that *'All initiatives likely to have significant direct economic, social or environmental impacts should be accompanied by an impact assessment and a positive opinion from the Regulatory Scrutiny Board. These principles also apply to ... delegated and implementing acts expected to have significant impacts.'* (p.10 Working Methods).

A second key difference from Implementing Acts relates to the consultation phase in the drafting of a Delegated Act, as **the Commission now uses Expert Groups, EU Agencies and other sources of expertise to improve its Delegated Acts**. From this perspective the Commission is likely to be more open to working with engaged stakeholders on Delegated Acts.

Like an Implementing Act, a Delegated Act will also go through ISC and then Cabinet approval. There is only one potential difference in this process, which is that the Cabinet has more room for manoeuvre for making changes with Delegated Acts (because when a Cabinet sees an Implementing Act it has already been adopted by the Committee). Once the Commission has adopted the Delegated Act (again usually by Written procedure) it will be forwarded to the Parliament and Council for them to exercise their control.

The Commission will remain very active through this period as it tries to steer its proposal through the two legislators without any problems – so the Commission will still be very engaged. Experience shows that when either legislator is considering opposing or changing something, the Commission mounts serious campaigns of its own to keep its measures as they were. This is something that needs to be understood if you are working with the legislators against a Delegated Act: you will be working against the Commission and this can be very delicate for you (and your longer-term engagement).

6. Working with Delegated Acts: Parliament

Once the Delegated Act is forwarded to the European Parliament it follows the same route as a legislative proposal, as detailed in *How the EU Institutions Work*. Hence the Committee responsible will be sent the Delegated Act and it will have to decide whether to object to the individual act or revoke the delegation – or do nothing during its period of control.

When it comes to **how the Parliament deals with the volume of Delegated Acts and their technical nature** it is a rather complicated, and evolving, picture. The Parliament outlines its internal procedures in Rule 111 of its Rules of Procedure. There are a number of issues with how the Parliament deals with Delegated Acts which need to be understood. Firstly, it is clear from both a capacity and a technical perspective, that further efforts are needed by the Parliament to deal with the influx of Delegated Acts. Nearly all parliamentary Committees are still striving to find their own best practice for dealing with them, and some Committees, due to the increased number of Delegated Acts they have to deal with, are more advanced than others. There are important horizontal efforts to streamline best practice and deal with Delegated Acts in a more uniform way.

The real key in this regard is that it is vital to make sure that MEPs are fully briefed on the developments in the importance and use of Delegated Acts, so that they understand what they are and how they can use their powers. This is especially important just after elections when many MEPs will be new to the world of Delegated Acts and their implications. From a procedural perspective we are likely to see a continuation of the trend of a few key MEPs driving the scrutiny of Delegated Acts within Committees: the coordinators, OLP rapporteurs, Committee chairs, and Secretariat and Political Group staff.

From this it is clear that Delegated Acts offer an opportunity for stakeholders to work with MEPs. To do this you need:

1. To **bring the Delegated Act to their attention**: it is unlikely to be top of their priority list so you might need to alert them to it. You will need to 'sell' your case and why they should invest precious time in this.
2. To **explain what it is and why it is important**: this is why you have to understand Delegated Acts and the procedures so well.
3. To **outline your position clearly** – this is not easy if you have a 300-page technical Delegated Act, so you need to make it user-friendly and understandable.
4. To **explain how the MEP can support you**: which means you need to know the procedure and timelines. You also need to carefully package information for them to use.

A big hurdle to get over in engaging with MEPs is their level of understanding and interest in engaging with Delegated Acts. The Parliament is first and foremost a legislative body and MEPs are mainly concerned with this aspect of their work. Whilst it is not difficult for an MEP to get to grips with the procedure of Delegated Acts, it is a different story for them to grasp all the implications of the substance of individual acts, especially within such short deadlines.

In addition, there is the problem of the low level of interest MEPs usually have in investing political capital in detailed Delegated Acts. This is understandable given that an MEP has limited time and resources and this underworld of legislation is hardly a guaranteed ticket to publicity and re-election. Quite simply, in many cases you will need to 'sell' this to MEPs and to do this you will need a compelling package offer. You should have a clear grasp of what working on this will mean/do for them, their profile and visibility and also reputation – you really need to put yourself in their shoes.

The procedure in the Parliament is illustrated in the next three figures.

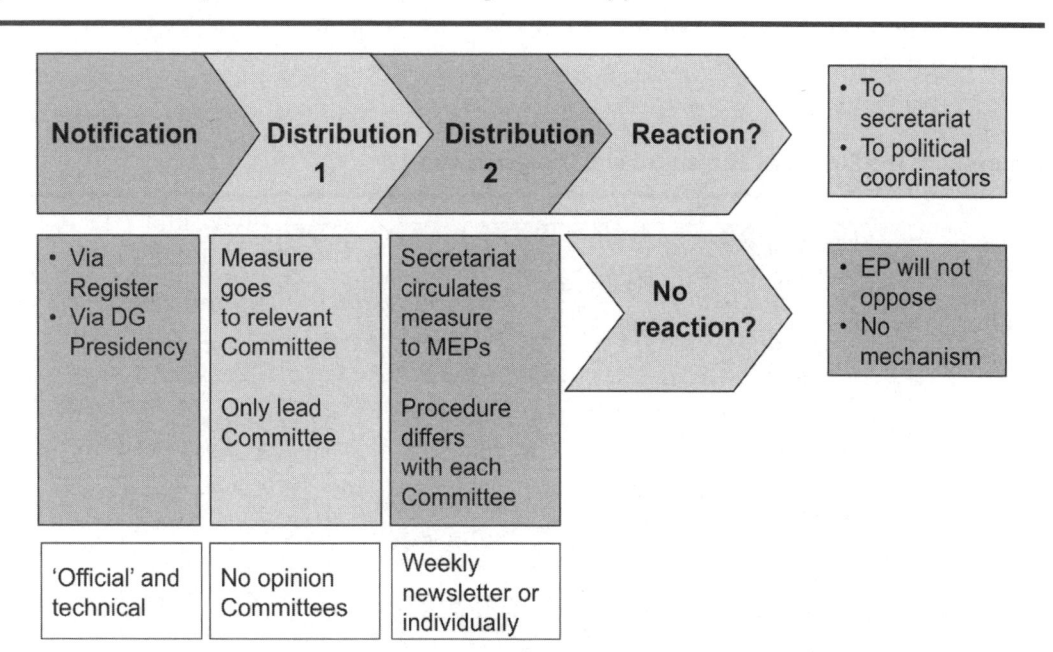

Figure 10.3: The European Parliament and Delegated Acts (1)

Notification	Distribution 1	Distribution 2	Reaction?	
• Via Register • Via DG Presidency	Measure goes to relevant Committee Only lead Committee	Secretariat circulates measure to MEPs Procedure differs with each Committee	No reaction?	• To secretariat • To political coordinators • EP will not oppose • No mechanism
'Official' and technical	No opinion Committees	Weekly newsletter or individually		

Source: Alan Hardacre

Figure 10.3 shows the beginning of the Delegated Acts process in the Parliament. A Delegated Act is received via DG Presidency in the Parliament and is attributed to the appropriate Committee. Like in OLP second reading, the Delegated Act only goes to the **Committee responsible**, as there is limited time to incorporate opinion-giving Committees.

The next stage is a vital one in the Parliament – how does a Committee notify its members of the Delegated Acts that have come in, and with what level of analysis and comment? Some Committees circulate every act individually as they come in, and others combine them into periodic newsletters. This is important because it is through this distribution that an MEP in the Committee, at this stage, needs to assess whether or not to proceed with an objection to the Delegated Act, or to revoke the delegation.

There are three likely sources of information as to whether or not to proceed with an objection or revocation: an individual MEP with a close interest in the issue, such as the rapporteur of the basic act; Secretariat or Political Group staff with technical expertise or whose job it is to look at Delegated Acts; or from an outside stakeholder. In the majority of cases the Parliament does not attempt to object, simply because there is nothing to object to – perhaps its concerns were filtered to the Commission earlier and have been taken into account. It is worth noting that when the European Parliament is in recess, it cannot actively perform its scrutiny role. So, twice a year, the Commission does not transmit Delegated Acts: from 22 December to 6 January and from 15 July to 20 August each year.

It is rare that files arouse Parliament's interest – taking things to the next stage in the process. If the Parliament does decide to proceed with an objection or a revocation, then it follows the process outlined in Figure 10.4.

Figure 10.4: The European Parliament and Delegated Acts (2)

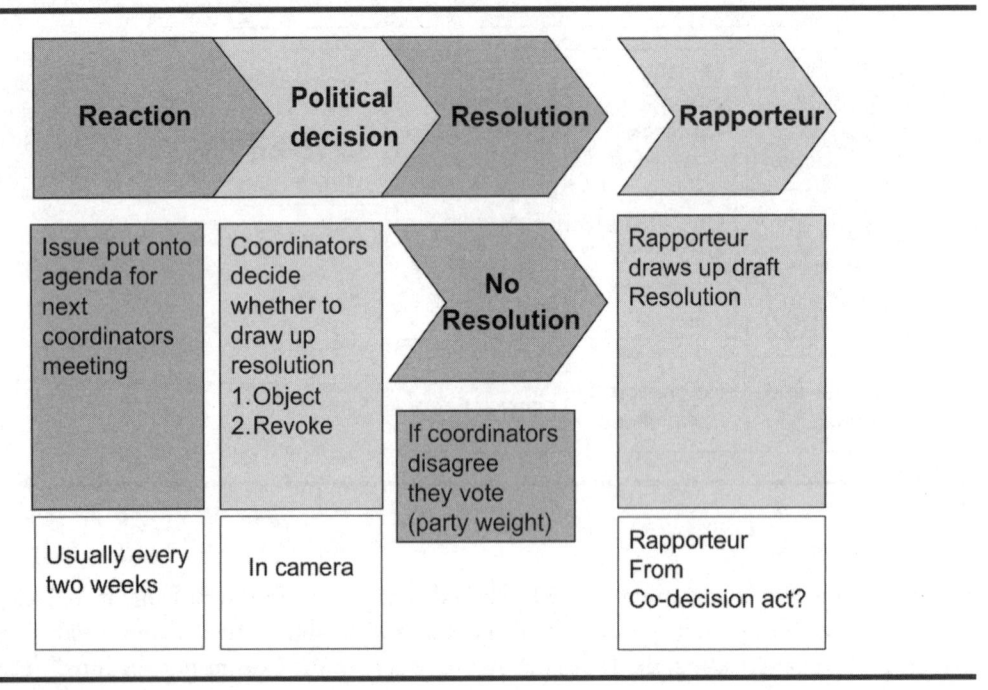

```
[Reaction] → [Political decision] → [Resolution] → [Rapporteur]
```

Reaction	Political decision	Resolution / No Resolution	Rapporteur
Issue put onto agenda for next coordinators meeting	Coordinators decide whether to draw up resolution 1. Object 2. Revoke	If coordinators disagree they vote (party weight)	Rapporteur draws up draft Resolution
Usually every two weeks	In camera		Rapporteur From Co-decision act?

Source: Alan Hardacre

Figure 10.4 shows the stage in the Parliament where the decision to draft a **Resolution to object, or revoke**, is taken. If an MEP, or a number of MEPs, have indicated problems with the Delegated Act it will be placed on the next coordinators' agenda, and the decision to take an objection or revocation further is taken by the coordinators at their 'in camera' meeting. If they decide to continue with opposition, or revocation, the next step is to appoint a rapporteur. This is usually the same MEP who drafted the legislative text, if they are still in the Parliament and in the same Committee.

The rapporteur is tasked with drawing up a Resolution for opposition to the Delegated Act, or for revocation of the delegation, which only needs to outline what the Parliament objects to. Remember that the Parliament cannot modify the Delegated Act – it can only object – but that if its objection is successful then the Commission will most likely incorporate its modification in a new Delegated Act, so modification is possible (albeit difficult) through this form of **'soft amendment'**.

It must be noted just how serious the issue needs to be to get this far. Given the time, resource and energy required on behalf of the Parliament to advance with an objection, this is not a small undertaking. A well drafted challenge takes about a week of work to prepare and secure support from across the Political Groups. It is not taken lightly. If it does get to a Resolution, this will be a short document specifying the exact objections of the Parliament, which will then need to be voted through the Committee and Plenary, as shown in Figure 10.5.

Figure 10.5: The European Parliament and Delegated Acts (3)

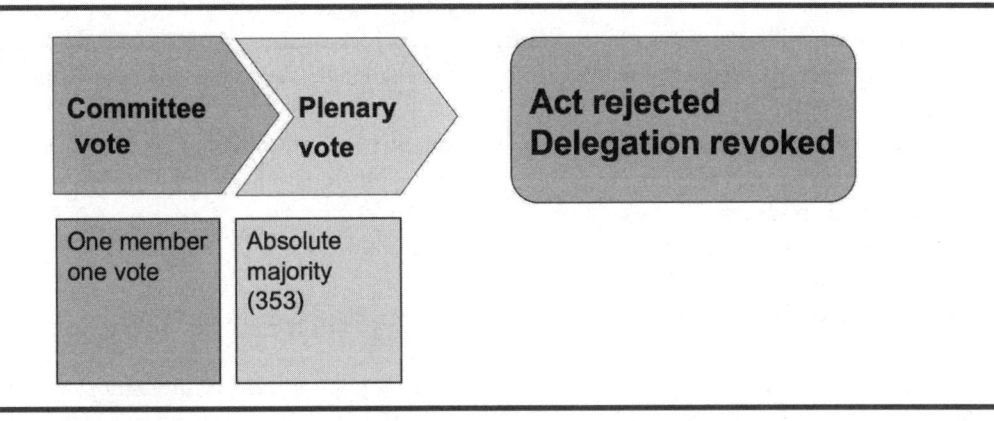

```
Committee  >  Plenary   >   Act rejected
vote          vote          Delegation revoked

One member    Absolute
one vote      majority
              (353)
```

Source: Alan Hardacre

Figure 10.5 shows the final stages of a Resolution in the Parliament for objection to, or revocation of, a Delegated Act. The Parliament has to work very quickly to draft a Resolution and vote it through both Committee and Plenary within the allotted timeframes (usually two to three months).

The vote in Committee is the first part of the process that needs attention because, as noted earlier in this chapter, it will usually involve heavy work from the Commission to support its Delegated Act. A simple majority in a Committee is not that difficult to attain, but the discussions will take place in a very short period of time. Often the challenge goes to the next Plenary in two weeks' time. A good indicator of success in the Plenary is to look at the winning margin in the Committee. The closer the vote in the Committee, the less chance for adoption in the Plenary. The absolute majority in Plenary, now 353 MEPs, if a Resolution to object or revoke gets this far, is very difficult to obtain.

If you look at successful challenges the following conditions are present:

1. Objections tabled by just one Political Group do not succeed. Challenges backed by **three Political Groups or more** stand the greatest chance of success.
2. **A broad coalition of Political Groups is best**. Acting only with your preferred political allies will not be enough.

3. Successful challenges are brought forward with a **balanced mix of reasons**: political, legal, and procedural.
4. **Common factors behind successful challenges** include (1) a substantive error of law, (2) procedural errors, and (3) the proposal ignored something obvious that should have been taken into account.
5. **A challenge is not brought lightly**. A considerable amount of work in a short period of time needs to be done. The clock is ticking. It is not easy to achieve.
6. **The Commission will go to great efforts to stop a challenge**. It will attend the Committee exchange of views on the challenge and answer questions. Sometimes, it will send Committee members a detailed question and answer on the challenge. This is a useful document to obtain. The Commission will also reach out to Political Group coordinators, who often help set their Group's voting lists, to persuade them not to back the challenge. Successful challenges find their way on to the College's agenda for discussion.
7. **If you want to challenge a Delegated Act, you do not have months** to build a cross-party majority to back your case. You have weeks. This is a major undertaking, which statistically has very little chance of success.
8. Your **best chance of success** is working with trusted Political Group advisers and respected MEPs with cross-party appeal.
9. **You need a champion** in the Committee to raise the issue and table the challenge.

It is worth noting that a challenge at the Committee can be enough for the Commission to withdraw a proposal. This is a soft power of amendment and has happened in three cases: in the Committee for the environment (animal testing, pesticide residue) and in the Committee for transport and tourism (on the use of seatbelts for children in airplanes).

If a challenge fails at the Committee stage, it can be re-tabled at the Plenary by a Political Group. Failure to reach a majority at the Committee is, however, a good indication that it is unlikely that it will reach the majority needed at the Plenary. This has happened just twice: the first on diet replacement foods (6 September 2017) and the second on titanium dioxide (30 January 2020). There has been one case where a challenge was tabled direct to the full Plenary – a challenge to grant an exemption for the use of cadmium (13 May 2015). This was adopted.

6.1 Parliamentary scrutiny during an election year

While elections to the European Parliament happen only once every five years, they have impacts that merit attention. Special arrangements exist during the run-up to the European elections and for this it is useful to look at what happened for the May 2019 European elections. Based on the 2019 Inter-institutional Agreement on the European Election Recess ('the Recess Agreement'), the Commission would not formally transmit any Delegated Acts or final draft RPS measures to the European Parliament and the Council from Friday 15 March 2019, except if certain special cases required this. Otherwise it was agreed that transmission could re-start:
- for final draft RPS measures, from Wednesday 10 July 2019
- for Delegated Acts, from Thursday 18 July 2019

Practically-speaking, this meant that if you had a proposal you wanted to challenge you needed three things:
1. Firstly, you needed to alert the Political Group adviser(s) of the issue and the grounds to challenge. Turnover of Group advisers is less extensive than for sitting MEPs.
2. Secondly, as soon as MEPs were elected, the clock was ticking. Ideally, you needed to have primed returning or newly elected MEPs on the issue, so that they were ready to take action.
3. Thirdly, you needed to have prepared a well-reasoned case and the supporting text of a draft challenge.

The recess period does not apply to Implementing Acts. The Commission continues to send to the Parliament all draft and final Implementing Acts.

Around November in the year before the election recess, the Committee coordinators meet. They mandate the Committee chair to write to the Commission and request information on Delegated Acts, Implementing Acts and RPS measures in preparation or planned for adoption during the election process. This allows the Committee to scrutinise upcoming measures and, if necessary, take preemptive action by challenging the file.

7. Working with Delegated Acts: Council

The final institutional process is that of the Council, which is somewhat more straightforward.

Figure 10.6: The Council and Delegated Acts

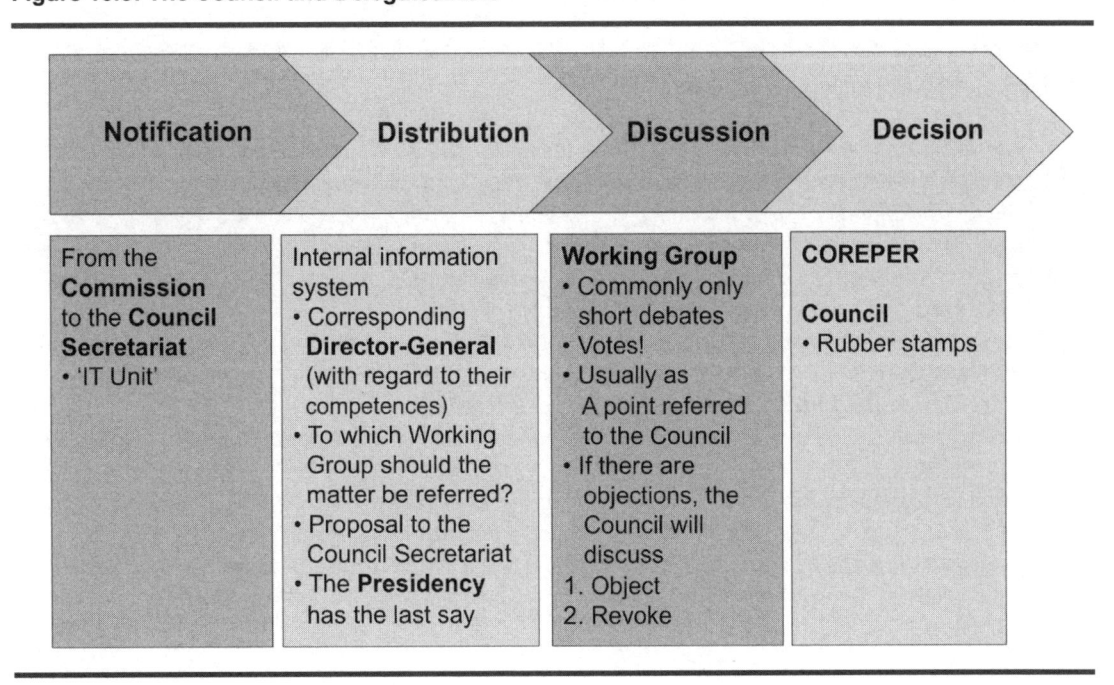

Notification	Distribution	Discussion	Decision
From the **Commission** to the **Council Secretariat** • 'IT Unit'	Internal information system • Corresponding **Director-General** (with regard to their competences) • To which Working Group should the matter be referred? • Proposal to the Council Secretariat • The **Presidency** has the last say	**Working Group** • Commonly only short debates • Votes! • Usually as A point referred to the Council • If there are objections, the Council will discuss 1. Object 2. Revoke	**COREPER** **Council** • Rubber stamps

Source: Alan Hardacre

Figure 10.6 illustrates the process of dealing with Delegated Acts in the Council. In essence if there is strong national coordination, then the Member States in Council should already be aware of the acts because their experts will have assisted the Commission via an Expert Group.

For Delegated Acts, each act is sent to the relevant Working Group in the Council where there are short debates. If there are problems identified in the Working Group, or if nothing comes of the discussion, the acts are then sent up the hierarchy to Coreper. At this level there will be a final, more political, check of the Delegated Act to see whether the Council will object or revoke. In the past Working Groups rarely had any problems with Delegated Acts, but Coreper has picked up a number of issues that have led to several Council objections.

Some of these objections arose from the Commission having included correlation tables (obligations on Member States to report to the Commission demonstrating how EU legislation has been transposed into national law). The Member States do not enjoy having to fill in correlation tables. This was something that experts in Working Groups did not see a problem with but that Coreper took exception to. Coreper is thus an important actor when it comes to the scrutiny of Delegated Acts in the Council architecture. The decision of Coreper to object, to revoke or to do nothing will then be forwarded for final sign-off by the next available Council meeting – a mechanism that sees the Council effectively agree to D&I Acts, which it is not formally required to do.

From these three institutional sections on how to work with Delegated Acts, it is now possible to draw together some conclusions on working with Delegated Acts, as summarised in the box below. These conclusions reinforce the point that working with Delegated Acts is very much focused in time, in context and in terms of the small group of interested actors.

Working with Delegated Acts: General guidance

1. Follow the legislative drafting of the Commission for the objectives, scope, duration and the conditions to which the delegation is subject. This could also involve an Expert Group.
2. Work with the three institutions during the OLP phase on how Delegated Acts will work in the legislative act to get as much clarity as possible.
3. Read the final legislative act: understand exactly what has been delegated and to what conditions it is subject and remember they could be different in each case.
4. Identify the Expert Group, or Agency, assisting the Commission in drafting the Delegated Act and work with them.
5. Work with the Commission Service drafting the Delegated Act.
6. Identify the Inter-Service Consultation on the Delegated Act: it is the last real chance to modify the text.
7. Once the Delegated Act has been transmitted to the Council and Parliament you have to identify what your objectives are: support or reject the act, or revoke the delegation.
8. It will usually be easier to work with the Parliament to support or reject a Delegated Act, so identify the competent Committee, the coordinators, the Secretariat staff, the interested MEPs, the OLP rapporteur.

9. Working to reject a Delegated Act will require an absolute majority so political work as well as technical arguments are needed.
10. Remember that working against a Delegated Act means working against the Commission, so consider the long-term consequences that this could have.
11. Also work with Council experts and Coreper: they too will be working with the Commission and Parliament.

8. Some legal considerations

Even if you are not actively considering taking a fully blown legal case it is important to know the legal options with regard to D&I Acts. There are at least five pathways you need to consider:

1. Firstly, **a well-placed intervention from the Legal Service of either the European Parliament or the Council** can be key. MEPs or Member States can request an opinion from their respective institutions' Legal Services. You can alert MEPs and Member State officials to legal issues in the hope that they will seek a more formal opinion from the Legal Service of the Parliament or Council. If they give their opinion in favour of your line, this will sway decisions. The request is never undertaken lightly, but the opinion can be pivotal. Politicians and Member States are not keen to ignore the law.

2. Secondly, when you have run out of political avenues to win your case, you can go to law. So, even if a Delegated Act, Implementing Act or RPS measure is adopted and published in the Official Journal, there are chances to **go to the European Court**. This is an option for Member States, the European Parliament, Council and individuals. For an individual, it is not something to be taken lightly. It is an expensive option, with an intervention costing in the range of €150,000 to €200,000. Aside from the cost, the more important consideration is that if the case is not strong, and the judgment is against you, it will set a negative precedent. For the Council or European Parliament to head to Court the internal hurdles are high.

3. Thirdly, it is important to realise that the **Commission's flexibility and discretion is tightly constrained when using secondary legislation**. The Commission must act within the carefully defined conditions laid down by EU law (see Case C-14/06, Denmark v. Commission). Any measures adopted outside those tightly confined conditions are invalid. Even if the Commission wants to support you, it can only do so if the enabling legislation allows it to. If the original legislation is against you, you cannot fix it through a Delegated or Implementing Act. The only way to fix a problem is by re-opening the legislation. That, however, comes with political risks that many do not want to face. It also (again) highlights the importance of getting your D&I Acts right in OLP. Miss this chance and it will take you years to set things straight.

4. Fourthly, **Member States and the European Parliament** have gone to the European Court of Justice both **to preserve their privileges and enforce the law**. Raising these two pressure points will often drive otherwise agnostic Parliamentarians and Member States to support you. In Case T-521/14, Sweden v. Commission, Sweden challenged the European Commission for its failure to adopt a Delegated Act by the deadline set out in the legislation. The Court gave judgment *'that the Commission has failed to fulfill its obligations ... by abstaining from adopting delegated act'*. The case was brought to bring pressure on the Commission to act. It succeeded. The progress of the file was looked at the by the Secretary-General weekly.

5. Finally, it is settled case law that a **delegation of legislative powers may not touch upon essential elements of the legislative act**, as those are clearly reserved for the Union legislature and may not be delegated. The concept of 'essential' elements has, for a long time, been defined in the Court's case law as referring to *'rules which (...) are essential to the subject-matter envisaged and which are intended to give concrete shape to the fundamental guidelines of Community policy.'*

In more recent times, the Court has further specified that this concept covers *'provisions which, in order to be adopted, require political choices falling within the responsibilities of the European Union legislature'*. In the Court's words, such are the choices that require *'the conflicting interests at issue to be weighed up on the basis of a number of assessments'*. The Court has made it clear that *'ascertaining which elements of a matter must be categorised as essential is not ... for the assessment of the European Union legislature alone, but must be based on objective factors amenable to judicial review'*, and for that purpose, *'it is necessary to take account of the characteristics and particularities of the domain concerned'*.

Fundamental political choices are responsibilities of the Union legislative branch and may not be delegated. There are some important choices that MEPs and Ministers might prefer to avoid, but these cannot be decided by Agencies, the Commission or Committees. So, even if a proposal is tabled by the Commission, is adopted by a Committee, and passes scrutiny by the Council and the European Parliament, you can still go to the European Court. That will, however, take you several years of time, investment, and patience.

9. Summary

If there is one most critical thing to retain from this chapter, then it is to build the best possible relationship with the European Commission officials in charge of your files. You can get essential information from them and in turn give them essential information. They are the key stakeholders to work with in the pivotal phase of both types of Act – namely, that of drafting them. You can extend your work to Member State officials and known experts and agencies – if you have the reach. But the key is the drafting phase and how you get your views across to a relatively small number of people within a short timeframe. And the timeframe is also a vital consideration: the timelines are very short so things can change on a day-to-day basis, making close monitoring and contacts important.

If at this initial stage you miss this opportunity, or if you do not land your points, then you will be working uphill in an increasingly political environment – one with few chances of success given the nature of what you are requesting, namely that one legislator will vote to reject a piece of Commission work. If it gets to that point, you will need a champion in one of the legislators making your case for you – you cannot succeed on your own.

All of this goes to emphasise that the best work on D&I Acts happens in the drafting phase and is based on solid relationships built up during OLP. The game of trying to organise objections to a Delegated Act to get a change introduced is really only a last-ditch strategy with limited chances of success and guaranteed blowback for your relations with the European Commission.

Part 3

Summary

11. Recommendations for Best Practice in EU Public Affairs

By Alan Hardacre

Working with the European Union institutions is a real challenge for any professional or team of professionals. It involves several institutions, a multitude of stakeholders, a variety of nationalities and languages and often lengthy processes. Added to that it is always changing – the people, issues, prevailing political winds and the stakeholders change with time.

Ultimately there is no single recipe for success so you need to build experience over time. You need to change too. The public affairs profession is evolving – it is constantly offering new tools to harvest information, share information or support your engagement. So you should always be adapting how you work in the EU in order not just to stay afloat but to be constantly striving to be best-in-class in what you do and how you do it – according to your resources.

The EU public affairs methodology chapter, Chapter 2, is the foundation in respect of building out a final set of horizontal recommendations.

> **Recommendations**
>
> Working with the EU institutions & decision-making is a complex undertaking as the chapters in this book have shown. Each chapter outlined recommendations and guidance for how to do this better. Here, in the final chapter, we will pull out the most important horizontal recommendations for you to retain.
>
> There is no secret formula, or silver bullet, for success in EU engagement. Rather there needs to be lots of hard work on understanding, working with and leveraging a set of fundamental recommendations. Successful lobbying is about how you manage a number of different processes over time – adapting, keeping your discipline and abiding by the best practice rules. And also understanding what not to do.

Before we move into these recommendations it is worth being reminded of the value of looking at our public affairs work in the EU through the lens of the following figure:

Figure 11.1: Public affairs strategy: Three methodological phases & seven key areas

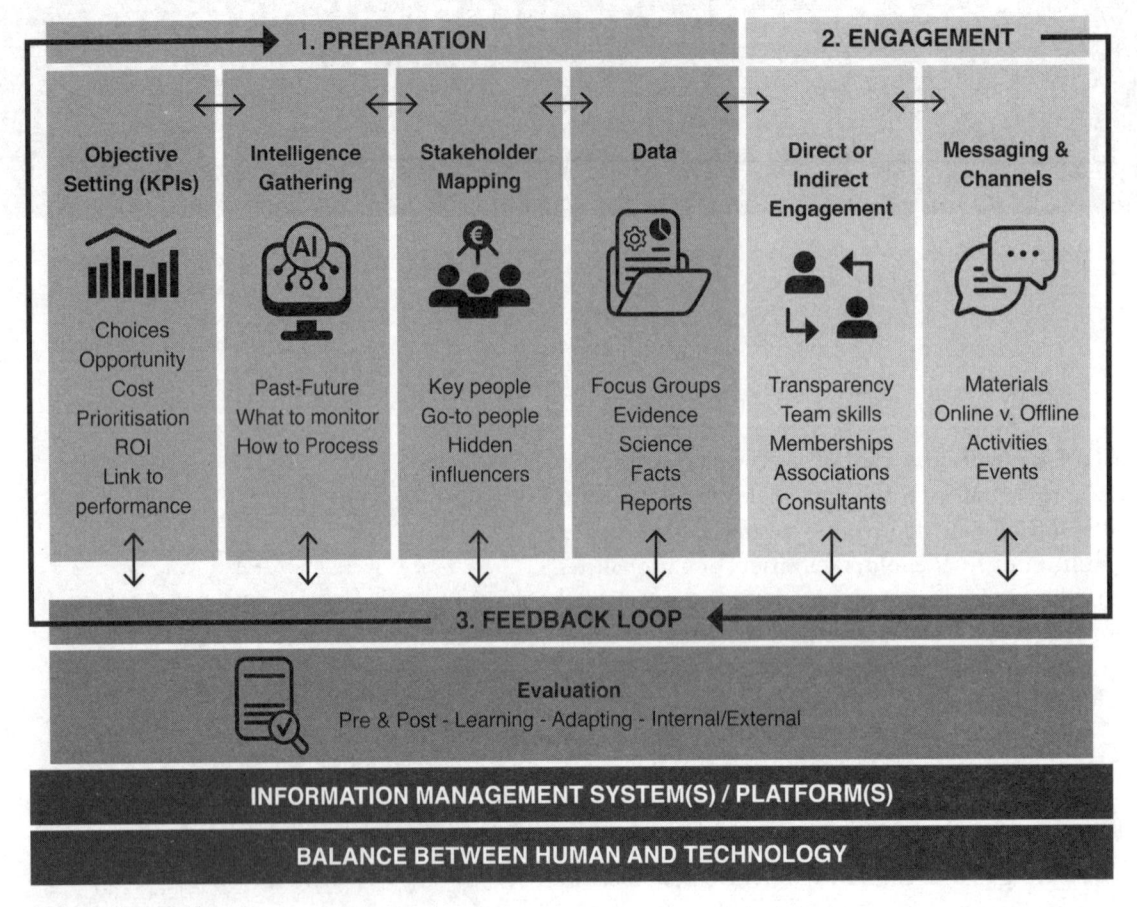

1. PREPARATION				2. ENGAGEMENT	
Objective Setting (KPIs)	**Intelligence Gathering**	**Stakeholder Mapping**	**Data**	**Direct or Indirect Engagement**	**Messaging & Channels**
Choices Opportunity Cost Prioritisation ROI Link to performance	Past-Future What to monitor How to Process	Key people Go-to people Hidden influencers	Focus Groups Evidence Science Facts Reports	Transparency Team skills Memberships Associations Consultants	Materials Online v. Offline Activities Events

3. FEEDBACK LOOP

Evaluation
Pre & Post - Learning - Adapting - Internal/External

INFORMATION MANAGEMENT SYSTEM(S) / PLATFORM(S)

BALANCE BETWEEN HUMAN AND TECHNOLOGY

Source: Alan Hardacre

As you think about the fundamentals you need to get right to succeed in EU public affairs this is a good starting place:
- Do you have a clear view of the three phases and the seven key areas and what you are doing (or not doing) in each?
- Are they all linked together seamlessly?
- Do they all build to the same objective and delivery?
- Are you constantly reviewing and revising this to make sure what you are doing is always supporting your objectives?

You could profitably spend some time reviewing this – you will be surprised at what you find and how a few tweaks and adaptations can make your work more effective and efficient.

Moving beyond the methodology, it is possible to make some key recommendations that public affairs professionals should look to as a priority list for their successful engagement in the EU. As you will see the list is built on two distinct areas of recommendations:
1. Firstly, the key horizontal recommendations for things you absolutely **should do** that have come out of the previous chapters.
2. Secondly, the key recommendations of things you **should NOT do**.

Table 11.1 captures the top 20 horizontal recommendations. This chapter will take each of them in turn to briefly outline what the recommendation is and how you can make the most of it to build solid public affairs strategies.

Table 11.1: The Top 20 recommendations for successful EU public affairs

Recommendations for Best Practice EU Public Affairs: Must DO
1. Use the EU public affairs methodology (Chapter 2) – Structure your thinking & work
2. Understand influence & how to better achieve it – Build your capability
3. Understand the legislative process and its technicalities – Know the processes
4. Start early, get in early – Invest from the start
5. Know what you want/be realistic – Be focused and have solid objectives
6. Gather and manage intelligence efficiently – Get your human-digital balance right
7. Be transparent and honest – Never compromise on your integrity
8. Tailor information, arguments, evidence and data – Focus on your audience
9. Understand your audience, put yourself in their shoes – Land your messages
10. Mobilise people to act, work with allies – Invest the time to build relationships
11. Recognise Europe's diversity and integration objectives – Bring EU solutions
12. Present yourself creatively and professionally to differentiate yourself in a crowded space – Engagement is relative, i.e. benchmarked against others
13. Influence is reciprocal – Understand the nature of give and take
14. Adapt, change, evolve – Constantly evaluate and be ready to change

Recommendations for Best Practice EU Public Affairs: Must NOT DO
15. Don't be negative, focus only on problems/be anti-European – Think solutions
16. Don't be aggressive or make threats – Always remain constructive
17. Never jeopardise your credibility – Work within your constraints
18. Don't keep going when the cause is lost – Know when to leave something
19. Don't talk more than you listen – Stay open to information
20. Don't stop learning, evaluating, challenging and trying – Always challenge yourself

☑ Recommendations for best practice in EU public affairs: MUST DO

1. **Use the EU public affairs methodology**
   Use the EU public affairs methodology in Chapter 2 to review your public affairs strategy, or to build a new one. Make sure you have a public affairs strategy with clear objectives and KPIs from day one. All your actions need to flow from your strategy. Once you have your seven key areas plan, get it reviewed and take feedback. Once operational you should constantly be evaluating and also putting in key moments when you want to do structured evaluation and learning sessions. Using a clear methodological structure in this way gives you the possibility to better understand every aspect of your work (and convey that to others), and make improvements. Use the methodology to structure your thinking. Adapt the methodology to suit your needs.

2. **Understand influence and how better to achieve it**
   Make sure you fully grasp the essence and nature of influence before you design your strategy. This will ensure you can do so in such a way as to build on your strengths, address any gaps and ultimately make sure you are being effective in your use of time and resources. You should always be thinking about how to influence, and how you can get better at achieving it, building this into your cycle of evaluations.

3. **Understand the legislative process and its technicalities**
   EU decision-making is a long series of negotiated compromises. This makes it essential for you to understand the ins and outs of every aspect of the process. To be able to focus your efforts at influencing you need to know who, where and when.

4. **Start early – get in early**
   Every chapter has highlighted the importance of this recommendation – it is simply essential to start working on an issue and/or building your network as soon as possible. If you can follow the issue through all stages of policy development that is even better. Joining the debate after it is already well underway is considered by many policy-makers to be poor practice, and the later you join, the less likely it is that you will succeed or influence. The earlier you intervene in the legislative process, the more effective you will be.

   A crucial aspect of this recommendation is to build your relationships before you actually need something. Schedule introductory meetings with officials and other contact persons to get to know each other and exchange views. This will also help you to adopt the right approach with every official when the time comes. Get your contacts embedded as an absolute priority before you need them. Build over time. Never stop.

5. **Know what you want – be realistic**
   Your EU public affairs work can be like a house of cards – it needs to be built on solid foundations. The key foundation is to have realistic and clear objectives that take account of both your own organisation's needs AND the external reality of EU decision-making. Invest the time in creating the right objectives that you can then fully get behind. You should then look to review these quarterly, or ad hoc on the back of major developments, to make sure they remain attuned to the external reality you are working in.

6. **Gather and manage intelligence efficiently**
   Obtaining timely and actionable information is a major challenge in the EU and you also run the risk of being swamped by information. You need to look for the sweet spot between human and digital intelligence to make sure you have what you need to be effective in influencing. Digital platforms today represent the state of the art in intelligence gathering and (more importantly) in how that information can be effectively managed. You need to investigate what digital tools you can benefit from to make you more efficient.

7. **Be transparent and honest**
   Policy-makers see a lack of transparency as poor practice, and for many decision-makers in Brussels this is a determining factor in deciding whether to speak to a lobbyist let alone believe them. Brussels is a village when it comes to the core circle of people you will work with over time and reputation and credibility is something you build up slowly and painfully – and something you can lose in an instant. Policy-makers are increasingly reporting to their colleagues and the public on who they meet and on what issue – so act transparently.

   Signing up to the Transparency Register is a must. Signing voluntary/industry codes of conduct is good. Having an organisation code of conduct (recognised and in line with Transparency International) is also good practice.

8. **Tailor information, arguments, evidence and data**
   Policy-makers can, at times, find themselves drowning in information and (often conflicting) evidence. You need to work hard to understand what they need and how best you can deliver it. Information and evidence on its own is not necessarily going to help you – how you use it, focus it and present it can be equally as important. What matters is to make your data concise, directly relevant and actionable – then you will maximise your chances of success.

9. **Understand your audience – put yourself in their shoes**
   Several chapters, from the very first one on influence, have identified the need to put yourself in the shoes of your key stakeholders. You should always be looking at their situation, their needs and how to help them. That last part is important to reiterate – you should be thinking about how you can help your key stakeholders. That might be finding a solution, giving them ammunition for a debate or meeting, or providing sound-bites in a timely manner. It will differ according to stakeholders and over time – so stay attuned to what people need.

A further aspect of this recommendation is to know your audience before you meet them. Do your homework. The chapter on working with a digital platform that can give you live information shows the importance of fine margins – knowing what an MEP tweeted two minutes before you meet them, for example. Before approaching a government department, understand that particular department's agenda and interests. In the European Commission, for example, DG Environment may have different interests from DG GROW. Adapting your message to their interests will help you gain their attention and influence their decision-making.

Finally, for your key stakeholders always follow up. One secret to successful lobbying is to follow up every lead, every letter you write, every contact you make, and every initiative you take. Write a thank-you letter to an official you have met. It will give you the opportunity to restate your arguments and repeat what you expect from him or her.

10. Mobilise people to act – work with allies
As you will have understood from the institutional and decision-making chapters, the lobbying environment can be complex and competitive. Searching for allies and working within coalitions whenever possible can help make a real difference. Resources pooled together can open doors, access information, and deliver more than you perhaps could on your own. The best example of this in Brussels is the trade associations because most policy-makers value the input of aggregated interests (saving them time and work). Working together in partnerships and even temporary coalitions can bear fruit.

It is very rare that a single interest group can make a strong enough case. Building alliances with related groups (e.g. European counterpart associations) is indispensable to your lobbying campaign. Creating an ad hoc, umbrella organisation to represent an alliance of interests on a focused issue is an option.

A final point about working with others is that the minimum you should look to do is align with others working on the same issue. Alignment can help drive coherent lobbying. An example of incoherent lobbying, from recent years, is the draft directive on internet copyright when numerous trade and industry bodies (and other pressure groups) lobbied separately. Many of them would have been better off, and carried more weight, if they had been able to work together. Officials, parliamentarians and Members of the Economic and Social Committee and Committee of the Regions, get very frustrated when more than one pressure group says more or less the same thing but in different words.

11. Recognise Europe's diversity and integration objectives

Often you, or your organisation, might not like or agree with aspects of a policy. This is absolutely natural and to be expected. The key is what happens next in how you choose to respond and frame your concerns. The best way is to embrace a constructive and pro-integration approach to frame your concerns – and present solutions. Your case should always be presented as being able to contribute to the aims of European integration, which is based on a number of principles, such as free movement of goods and persons, social cohesion, the fight against unemployment, and competitiveness. Highlighting these principles, on which all European legislation and initiatives are based, will enhance your profile.

As you look to engage across the variety of stakeholders in EU files, keep in mind the local, national and European dimensions of every issue you are working on. This will present you with opportunities to leverage the differences in attitudes between policy-makers in different countries.

12. Present yourself creatively and professionally to differentiate yourself in a crowded space

Engagement is a relative exercise in that you will never be doing it alone. Policy-makers have to make choices about who to meet and what information to take onboard. Ask yourself this question: 'what differentiates me from the others?' It is of course easy to say that you need to be creative, memorable and professional from start to finish but it is less easy to know how to do this. Being professional does not need more explanation (as this has been covered elsewhere) but when it comes to being creative, perhaps a few words will help put this recommendation in context. In every aspect of your interaction with policy-makers you should never forget that you are competing for their time, energy and ultimately influence. Briefing materials, events and other activities that draw attention to your messages help lead to success. There is no definitive solution here – but a recommendation to always keep this in mind.

13. Influence is reciprocal

Never take without giving. There is a chronic and apparent need on the part of EU decision-makers for market data, industry information, and expertise. The best way to capture an EU official's interest and also indirectly influence decision-makers is to provide this data. You may even find your information being used by the European legislator. Always offer an acceptable alternative when you are trying to prevent or change a regulation. Provide useful information, or support the Commission. You need to always be aware of what you are asking for, and what you are giving.

14. Adapt – change – evolve

The EU public affairs methodology and information management chapters were both explicit on the need to always be evaluating and evolving your strategy and ideas. The external environment and politics are always changing, as is the public affairs industry itself. Revisit your ideas, strategy, approach and communication on a constant basis: things change and you need to change with them. Working with EU decision-making is in fact a series of back-to-back mini-campaigns – and these can take time (sometimes years). You need to keep learning, adapting and evolving to remain successful.

☒ Recommendations for best practice in EU public affairs: MUST NOT DO

15. Don't be negative
This recommendation is not a direct opposite of number 11 – although it covers some of the same ground. No matter what circumstances you find yourself in or how difficult a meeting is, you should always try to retain a positive and constructive outlook. Like in many situations, negativity does not do you too many favours. Whilst hard at times you should always, in your external engagement, remain constructive. This does not mean you can't express contrary views, challenge or voice opinions. It is all in how you do it.

16. Don't be aggressive or make threats
When engagement is not going your way lobbyists, or organisations, have a tendency to want to increase the pressure for their case to make it heard. One of the ways they often consider is to be more aggressive in their approach – for example, stressing (or threatening) job losses or relocations. This is almost always a losing game to play and for several reasons. Firstly, if you threaten these things, in order to retain credibility you would need to actually do them if things turn out as you don't want – which rarely ever happens. Secondly, from a relationship perspective, you need to always think about the potential aftermath of your lobbying: remember, decision-making is also for the long-term. If you move from OLP to D&I Acts you don't want the specter of your threats hanging over you as it will only damage your credibility and ability to influence.

17. Never jeopardise your credibility
Linked to recommendation 16, and based on the guidance of several chapters (most importantly the first chapter on the art of influence), is the need to protect your credibility. Brussels is a village in many senses and once you lose credibility (personally or as an organisation) you will struggle to get it back. This means acting with integrity at all times and making sure you act towards others as you want them to act towards you. It can also mean you might need to stand up to your own organisation on what they want to do (or more likely how they want to do it). You (and they) always need to consider you (and their) credibility in Brussels and what might jeopardise it.

18. Don't keep going when the cause is lost
It is difficult to let go of something you have worked on for many years or into which you have invested so much. But sometimes it can be the right thing to do. This in part harks back to the recommendation to set clear and realistic objectives (recommendation 5) – but sometimes even with clear and realistic objectives you might find yourself in a situation that is impossible to influence as you would wish. It is all about having the insight and judgement to know when to then move on and invest your resources elsewhere. You have to build experience to know when this is – but you can also ask the key stakeholders you meet with what they think the chances of success are.

19. Don't talk more than you listen

This may seem a rather odd recommendation to find its way into the list but it is important to understand that in the lobbying environment in Brussels there will be many occasions when you need to listen and not talk. Don't fight to get time with key decision-makers only to then spend it doing all the talking because you feel you have to. Your de facto mode should always be asking questions (listening and getting answers) and probing the positions and thoughts of others.

20. Don't stop learning, evaluating, challenging and trying

This is very much the same thing as recommendation 14, but it is so important to also stress it from the negative perspective as well as from the positive. Rarely are two situations the same in the EU public affairs context, meaning that you should not be approaching them as such. For every situation you find yourself in, something will have changed – which means that your approach, message or indeed strategy should have evolved. This is all about staying open to learning and developing as you build your experience in EU public affairs. It can be one of the most exciting professions to work in – precisely because of the constant change – as long as you make it a fundamental part of your approach to embrace the challenge of constantly adapting.

Further Reading

For this book we asked seasoned public affairs professionals to tell us their essential reads for understanding and working in public affairs in Brussels. You can find the full list of their recommendations at the Public Affairs Council website: https://pac.org/eur/lockdown-reading-list. For the book we have selected some key reading highlights below:

Classics
The Prince, Niccolo Machiavelli
Meditations, Marcus Aurelius
Politics and the English Language, George Orwell
The Art of War, Sun Tzu

Culture for Lobbying
The Culture Map, Erin Meyer
Capital, Robert Menasse
In Europe, Geert Mak
Don't Mention the Wars: A Journey through European Stereotypes, Tony Connelly
Monsignore Quixote, Graham Greene

Campaigns
Pre-suasion, Robert Cialdini
How to Win Campaigns, Chris Rose

EU Institutions
Understanding the European Union, John McCormick
Alarums & Excursions, Luuk van Middelaar

Policy
Factfulness, Hans Rosling

Communication
Made to Stick, Chip and Dan Heath
Don't Think of an Elephant, George Lakoff

Persuasiveness/Psychology
Persuasion, Robert Cialdini
The Influential Mind, Tali Sharot
How to Win Friends and Influence People, Dale Carnegie

Strategy
The Art of Lobbying: Building Trust and Selling Policy, Bertram J Levine